Middlebrow Modernism

SYDNEY STUDIES IN AUSTRALIAN LITERATURE

Meg Brayshaw, Series Editor

The Sydney Studies in Australian Literature series publishes original, peer-reviewed research in the field of Australian literary studies. It offers engagingly written evaluations of the nature and importance of Australian literature, and aims to reinvigorate its study both locally and internationally.
SUP thanks Professor Robert Dixon, Founding Editor

Alex Miller: The Ruin of Time
Robert Dixon

Australian Books and Authors in the American Marketplace 1840s–1940s
David Carter and Roger Osborne

Christina Stead and the Matter of America
Fiona Morrison

Colonial Australian Fiction: Character Types, Social Formations and the Colonial Economy
Ken Gelder and Rachael Weaver

Contemporary Australian Literature: A World Not Yet Dead
Nicholas Birns

Eliza Hamilton Dunlop: Writing from the Colonial Frontier
Ed. Anna Johnston and Elizabeth Webby

Elizabeth Harrower: Critical Essays
Ed. Elizabeth McMahon and Brigitta Olubas

Fallen Among Reformers: Miles Franklin, Modernity, and the New Woman
Janet Lee

The Fiction of Tim Winton: Earthed and Sacred
Lyn McCredden

Gail Jones: Word, Image, Ethics
Tanya Dalziell

Gerald Murnane: Another World in This One
Ed. Anthony Uhlmann

Inner and Outer Worlds: Gail Jones' Fiction
Ed. Anthony Uhlmann

The Life of Such is Life: A Cultural History of an Australian Classic
Roger Osborne

Middlebrow Modernism: Eleanor Dark's Interwar Fiction
Melinda J. Cooper

Patrick White's Theatre: Australian Modernism on Stage, 1960–2018
Denise Varney

Richard Flanagan: Critical Essays
Ed. Robert Dixon

Shirley Hazzard: New Critical Essays
Ed. Brigitta Olubas

Middlebrow Modernism

Eleanor Dark's Interwar Fiction

Melinda J. Cooper

SYDNEY UNIVERSITY PRESS

First published by Sydney University Press 2022
© Melinda J. Cooper 2022
© Sydney University Press 2022

Sydney University Press
Fisher Library F03
University of Sydney NSW 2006
Australia
sup.info@sydney.edu.au
sydneyuniversitypress.com.au

A catalogue record for this book is available from the National Library of Australia.

NATIONAL
LIBRARY
OF AUSTRALIA

ISBN 9781743328569 paperback
ISBN 9781743328576 epub
ISBN 9781743328668 pdf

Cover image: *Eleanor Dark* c. 1935 (printed 1940) by Max Dupain. National Portrait Gallery of Australia. Purchased with funds provided by Timothy Fairfax AC 2003. Cover design: Miguel Yamin

Figure 3.1 on p. 109: Max Dupain (Australia 1911–1992), "Advertisement for Hoover", 1937. Gelatin silver photograph, 34.7 (H) x 25.2 (W) cm. National Gallery of Australia, Canberra; purchased 1982. 1982.1152

Figure 3.2 on p. 111: Olive Cotton (Australia 1911–2003), *Glasses*, circa 1937. Gelatin silver photograph, 21.2 x 15.6 cm. Art Gallery of New South Wales, gift of the artist 1982. Image © Art Gallery of New South Wales 141.1982

Some chapters use material from Copyright © 2021 Melinda J. Cooper, "News from Australia: Global Modernism Studies and the Case of Australian Modernism" in *The Routledge Companion to Australian Literature*, edited by Jessica Gildersleeve, 181–92. New York: Routledge, 2021. Reproduced by permission of Taylor & Francis Group, LLC, a division of Informa plc.

We acknowledge the traditional owners of the lands on which Sydney University Press is located, the Gadigal people of the Eora Nation, and we pay our respects to the knowledge embedded forever within the Aboriginal Custodianship of Country.

Some quotations from scholarly sources may contain terms or views that were considered acceptable within mainstream Australian society when they were written, but may no longer be considered appropriate. The wording in these quotes does not necessarily reflect the views of Sydney University Press or the author.

Acknowledgements

My sincere thanks go to Emeritus Professor Robert Dixon, General Editor of the Sydney University Press Studies in Australian Literature series, whose careful editing and insightful feedback have strengthened this project. Part of the research for this study was completed during two residencies at Varuna, the National Writers' House: the former home of Eleanor and Eric Dark. It was a delight to explore archival material in the home that Eleanor helped to design and in which she lived for most of her life. I would like to thank the staff at Varuna for their support of my project. I particularly thank Barbara Palmer, who generously shared her knowledge of the Darks with me. I thank Jill Dark for sharing her family memories. I am grateful for Jill's permission to use photographs and quotations from archival material in this book. I also thank the staff at the Mitchell Library, State Library of New South Wales, and the National Library of Australia, who made the Eleanor Dark Papers available to me. The archival research that informs this study was made possible by research and travel grants awarded by the Modernist Studies Association and the University of Sydney. I thank those mentors and colleagues who provided feedback on work in progress, including Associate Professor Brigid Rooney, Professor Brigitta Olubas, Emeritus Professor David Carter, Professor Nicole Moore, Dr Meg Brayshaw, Dr Caitlin Maling and Stephen Cooper. Ideas and earlier versions of chapters from this book have hitherto been published in the journals *Modernist Cultures*, *Australian Literary Studies* and *JASAL: Journal of the Association for the Study of Australian Literature*, and in the chapter "News from Australia: Global Modernism Studies and the Case of Australian Modernism", in *The Routledge Companion to Australian Literature* (2021), edited by Jessica Gildersleeve. Special thanks go to my husband, Vinny Do, who has lived with this book as I have, and whose support, patience and encouragement have helped me to see the project through to completion. This book is dedicated to Vinny and Harriet.

I acknowledge and pay respect to the Gadigal and Wangal peoples of the Eora Nation, on whose unceded territory this book was written.

Contents

Introduction
Middlebrow Modernism: Negotiating Settler-colonial Modernity, Regional Cosmopolitanism and Liberal Humanism

> But what, you may ask, is a middlebrow? And that, to tell the truth, is no easy question to answer. They are neither one thing nor the other. They are not highbrows, whose brows are high; nor lowbrows, whose brows are low. Their brows are betwixt and between.
> Virginia Woolf, "Middlebrow", 1932.[1]

> We are something betwixt and between a colony and a nation, something vaguely called a "Dominion".
> P.R. Stephensen, *The Foundations of Culture in Australia*, 1936.[2]

In Eleanor Dark's novel *Waterway* (1938), the artist Lois Denning surveys her painting in an exhibition in the Art Gallery of New South Wales and observes, "They've put me among the moderns this year, but I'm afraid I'll look just as funny there as I did among the conservatives last year. They find me rather a trial, I'm afraid – I just don't seem to fit."[3] Lois' claim is one of several moments in Dark's fiction when she points to the inadequacy of aesthetic or ideological oppositions (in this case, the categorisation of "modern" versus "conservative" art). It is the contention of this book that the active questioning and negotiation of such dualisms was a vital and productive component of Dark's work. It was a key part of her distinctive aesthetic style, which blended attributes of literary modernism with popular fiction – a calibration which I refer to as middlebrow modernism.[4] It also captures the balance of cosmopolitan commitments with more

---

1   Virginia Woolf in a letter to the *New Statesman* written in 1932, published as "Middlebrow" in Virginia Woolf, *Collected Essays*, vol. 2 (London: Hogarth Press, 1942), 115.
2   P.R. Stephensen, *The Foundations of Culture in Australia: An Essay Towards National Self Respect* (Gordon, NSW: W.J. Miles, 1936), 18. The first instalment of this essay was first published in the *Australian Mercury* in 1935.
3   Eleanor Dark, *Waterway* (North Ryde, NSW: Angus & Robertson, [1938] 1990), 244–45. All subsequent references are to this edition and appear in parentheses in the text.

place-based attachments to nation and local community in Dark's writing – an accommodation of "regional cosmopolitanism", involving both "rootedness and detachment".[5] More broadly, it evokes the ambivalent situation of a mid-century woman writer mediating international modernity from a position within a settler-colonial nation.

The "middle" quality of Dark's writing – her affiliation with middle-class culture, her liberal humanist commitments and use of genres associated with the middlebrow – has generated some of the strongest criticisms of her work. Yet a middle space is often a meeting place or contact zone, involving active negotiation with the positions on either side, rather than a stable location between two different entities. Due to this relational quality, a position betwixt and between two other categories is often able to disrupt and defamiliarise dualistic ways of thinking by pointing to the interstitial space between and the constitutive relations of such apparent opposites. Dark was suspicious of dualisms: in *Waterway*, one character laments "[t]he pernicious doctrine of dualism, always trying to divide the indivisible!" (106). Instead of a dualistic approach, Dark's work offers a relational one, formed by both a modernist emphasis on complexity and experimentation, and tactics frequently associated with the middlebrow of mediating, calibrating and balancing.

In the chapters that follow, we will consider how Dark's middlebrow modernism reveals important and often obscured elements of modernism and modernity, including the dialogic relationships between modernism and commercial culture, modernity and settler colonialism, cosmopolitanism and regionalism, and liberal humanism and experimental aesthetics. Her work seems to anticipate and speak to recent scholarly findings that propose a relational or dialogic approach in favour of a dualistic one, underpinned by the conviction that "[i]ncessant movement *within* people, things, peoples, cultures and systems, and constant trafficking *between* them, is the work of the world".[6] The fact that Dark's relational approach emerged from within a settler-colonial context is also significant. *Middlebrow Modernism: Eleanor Dark's Interwar Fiction* invites us to consider how the writings produced in such societies might contribute to and expand the understandings imported from more metropolitan disciplinary contexts. Settler-colonial societies are structured by an ongoing and triangular

---

4   The term middlebrow modernism has also been used by Daniel Tracy in relation to Anita Loos' serial novel *Gentlemen Prefer Blondes* (1925), and by Christopher Chowrimootoo to describe the operas of British composer Benjamin Britten. See Daniel Tracy, "From Vernacular Humor to Middlebrow Modernism: *Gentlemen Prefer Blondes* and the Creation of Literary Value", *Arizona Quarterly: A Journal of American Literature, Culture, and Theory* 66, no. 1 (2010): 115–43; Christopher Chowrimootoo, *Middlebrow Modernism: Britten's Operas and the Great Divide* (Berkeley, CA: University of California Press, 2018).

5   Jason Arthur, *Violet America: Regional Cosmopolitanism in U.S. Fiction Since the Great Depression* (Iowa City: University of Iowa Press, 2003), xxii.

6   Terry Smith, "Modernism, Modernity and Otherness", *Australian Journal of Art* 13, no. 1 (1996): 146.

system of relationships involving settler, metropolitan (in this case British) and Indigenous agencies.[7] A middlebrow aesthetic was perhaps well suited to a writer operating from what Stephen Slemon calls "colonialism's middle ground" of settler culture.[8] The same connotations associated with the often feminised middlebrow – of cultural mediocrity and a lack of innovation – were also linked with Australia in the interwar period. As the epigraphs to this introduction demonstrate, both the middlebrow and the recently federated Australian nation occupied ambivalent positions betwixt and between more authentic (or at least more clearly delineated) forms of culture: between the lowbrow and the highbrow, a dependent colony and an independent nation, or the imperial and the Indigenous. While this ambivalent status suggests the "unfinished business" of a settler culture's struggles for cultural legitimacy,[9] it also means that settler writers were often attuned to the complex and relational dynamics that belie the binaries of centre/periphery, modernity/colony, nation/world and high/low culture. Dark's work is not only capable of disrupting the ways in which we often think about interwar Australian culture, but also points to the fact that the categories imported from elsewhere often do not map on to the Australian situation.

In exploring the ways in which Dark navigated between and disrupted dichotomous ways of thinking and representing, this study aims to demonstrate larger realities about the porous, dialogic and relational dynamics of culture and aesthetics in the twentieth century. Drawing on a transnational paradigm, it asks how Dark's writing participated in the transmission and circulation of experimental aesthetics, modern ideas and material print cultures around the world, contributing to recent accounts of Australian cultural history that suggest that interwar Australia was contemporary and internationally engaged rather than only preoccupied with cultural nationalism. At the same time, we will ponder what role the nation continued to have in Dark's work, both in terms of her anti-imperial nationalism and claims for settler belonging. Even a cosmopolitan stance is articulated from a position "*within* a national identity", and national borders matter to those who are attempting to assert cultural legitimacy on contested land.[10]

While Dark's fiction participated in multi-directional forms of travel, these routes of exchange were often highly asymmetrical, reflecting Australia's unequal

---

7   See Patrick Wolfe, *Settler Colonialism and the Transformation of Anthropology: The Politics and Poetics of an Ethnographic Event* (London; New York: Cassell, 1999); Lorenzo Veracini, *Settler Colonialism: A Theoretical Overview* (Basingstoke: Palgrave Macmillan, 2010), 21; *The Settler Colonial Present* (London: Palgrave Macmillan, 2015).

8   Stephen Slemon, "Unsettling the Empire: Resistance Theory for the Second World", *World Literature Written in English* 30, no. 2 (1990): 34. Victoria Kuttainen makes this point in "Trafficking Literature: Travel, Modernity, and the Middle Ground of Canadian and Australian Middlebrow Print Cultures", *International Journal of Canadian Studies* 48 (2014): 85–103.

9   Bob Hodge and Vijay Mishra, *Dark Side of the Dream: Australian Literature and the Postcolonial Mind* (Sydney: Allen & Unwin, 1992), 23.

10   Jon Hegglund, *World Views: Metageographics of Modernist Fiction* (New York: Oxford University Press, 2012), 15.

position within world culture in the interwar period. Dark also contributed to some of the uneven structures of mid-century modernity, as her writing reinforces elements of class and racial privilege, even as it tries to draw attention to these issues. As we embark on this study, we need to exercise caution in thinking that any writing produced within modernity – and particularly in a settler-colonial expression of it – has the ability to completely undo the binaries that modernity seeks to produce. Fredric Jameson cautions that "[r]adical alternatives, systemic transformations, cannot be theorized or even imagined within the conceptual field governed by the word 'modern'".[11] While mid-century settler writers were sometimes able to question binary ways of thinking, they were just as likely to reinforce such ideas by producing their own Others.

The complexities of Dark's aesthetic and ideological position demand a similarly agile methodological approach to her work. This study will seek to balance, on the one hand, the circulation model of world literature studies, which emphasises the conditions of transnational contact and exchange, with, on the other, paradigms which attend to local differences and uneven power structures. Dark's writing at times offers glimpses of an accommodation between diverse theoretical approaches, as she balances enthusiasm for international modernity with a leftist scepticism about its promises, and attempts to reconcile a cosmopolitan humanist ethic with a strategic commitment to the semi-peripheral nation. Like the middlebrow, which represents a "constant, nervous juggling of [high culture and the mass market] … rather than the formation of a stable in-between category of literary value",[12] Dark's writing anxiously moves between these paradigms, and sometimes struggles to reconcile them. This study aims to apply a similarly dexterous approach in order to illuminate both the liberating and limiting qualities of Dark's middlebrow modernism and to explore her nuanced engagement with mid-century modernity.

Eleanor Dark and Interwar Australia

Dark's body of work is extensive, encompassing ten novels published between 1932 and 1959, a wide range of poems and short stories that appeared in Australian periodicals in the 1920s and 1930s, non-fiction essays produced between the 1930s and 1950s and several unpublished manuscripts of novels and plays. This study focuses predominantly on the fiction that Dark wrote and published during the interwar period, while reading these texts in light of her larger oeuvre.

The interwar period was extremely formative to Dark's writing career. The 1920s and 1930s saw her progress from a relatively unknown writer of poetry,

---

11 Fredric Jameson, *A Singular Modernity: Essay on the Ontology of the Present* (London: Verso, 2002), 215.
12 Lorraine York, *Literary Celebrity in Canada* (Toronto: University of Toronto Press, 2016), 176.

magazine fiction and popular romance novels, to one who was accepted – albeit with some reservations – by the loosely affiliated group of intellectuals and writers who formed Australia's literary culture. By the end of the 1930s, Dark had twice received the Australian Literary Society Gold Medal for best Australian novel and had a growing international reputation: a number of her novels had been published in London and New York, and were reviewed in such publications as the *New York Times*. With the publication of *The Timeless Land* (1941), she achieved a level of international visibility and commercial success that was highly unusual for a mid-century Australian writer.

Dark's 1930s novels have been acknowledged as "the most recognisably modernist of Australia's predominantly realist canon of women's writing from this period".[13] From the time *Prelude to Christopher* was published in Australia in 1934, and *Return to Coolami* in London and New York in 1936, critics noted Dark's use of characteristically modernist devices, including compressed time frames, multi-perspectival narration and an emphasis on interior states. The one-day time frame, which she used in *Sun Across the Sky* (1937) and *Waterway*, is a device that appeared in key interwar modernist novels such as James Joyce's *Ulysses* (1922) and Virginia Woolf's *Mrs Dalloway* (1925). Like these writers, Dark employed a form of interior monologue and free indirect discourse which reviewers frequently described as stream of consciousness – a technique that became synonymous with international modernism after the term was first coined in relation to Dorothy Richardson's novel *Pointed Roofs* (1915). Dark also used flashbacks and other experimental approaches to narrative time, seeking to provide, as one character describes in *The Little Company* (1945), "the technical intricacy of recording a man's existence as an endless present moment, moving snailwise in time, carrying the past and future on its back".[14] Dark also engaged with distinctively modern concerns related to speed, technology, psychology, time, gender, sexuality and visual perception.

Literary modernism had an ambivalent status for Australian intellectuals and writers in the interwar period. During the 1930s, Dark began corresponding with a number of significant literary and cultural figures, including Marjorie Barnard, Flora Eldershaw, Kylie Tennant, Jean Devanny, Katharine Susannah Prichard, Miles Franklin, Vance and Nettie Palmer and Percy Reginald ("Inky") Stephensen. While these writers and critics represent a broad and shifting range of political positions, from the communism of Devanny and Prichard, to the left-leaning liberalism of Barnard and Dark, to what would develop into Stephensen's pro-fascism in the late 1930s, they all shared a commitment to developing an "indigenous" (by which they meant settler) Australian literature. In general, they embraced realism over experimental modernism, often associating modernism with a declining imperial

---

13   Nicole Moore, "The Rational Natural: Conflicts of the Modern in Eleanor Dark", *Hecate* 27, no.1 (2001): 20.
14   Eleanor Dark, *The Little Company* (Sydney: Collins, 1945), 185.

British culture. Stephensen, for example, described modernism as a sign "of England going downhill" that went "against the grain of our potentially-expansionist Australian culture".[15]

These commentators and writers quickly noted Dark's use of modernist devices. In the first extended study of her work in 1938, M. Barnard Eldershaw (the pseudonym for the literary partnership between Barnard and Eldershaw) pointed to Dark's "stream-of-consciousness method" and a "difficult and involved technique, especially in respect to the handling of time".[16] Barnard Eldershaw were somewhat critical of Dark's modernist style, arguing that her prose lacked "the plasticity and variation … of the true stream-of-consciousness as recognized by the psychologist or practised by James Joyce".[17] These criticisms reflect the difficulty of navigating the politics of prose style in interwar Australia, when the work of a writer using experimental techniques could be labelled as too modern, or dismissed as imitative and belated. Despite these reservations, the response of most of Dark's contemporaries to her work was surprisingly positive, especially when considered alongside their reactions to other expressions of literary modernism. Stephensen, who published Dark's most experimental novel, *Prelude to Christopher*, described her as "a novelist undoubtedly of world calibre", and Nettie Palmer told Dark that her writing would "go a long way towards arousing expectations of sensitive writing here".[18] Franklin, who was scathing about the modernism of expatriate Australian writers such as Christina Stead, was extremely supportive of Dark's writing.[19]

Perhaps Dark appealed to such figures as Stephensen, Franklin and the Palmers because she demonstrated a strong commitment to local culture. Dark spent her childhood in Sydney and most of her married life in Katoomba in the Blue Mountains, with periods of time living in Montville in the South East Queensland hinterland in the 1950s. As the daughter of a well-known Australian writer and Labor politician, Dowell Philip O'Reilly, she represented what cultural nationalists most longed for, a homegrown Australian literary tradition. Dark set her novels in Australia, with most featuring identifiable locations in Sydney, Katoomba and Montville, and expressed anti-imperialist views that resonated with those of Stephensen and the Palmers. By living in Australia, she was able to show that she was not one of the émigré artists whom Stephensen described as dazzled by "the

---

15 Stephensen, *Foundations*, 56.

16 M. Barnard Eldershaw, *Essays in Australian Fiction* (Freeport, NY: Books for Libraries Press, [1938] 1970), 195–96.

17 Barnard Eldershaw, *Essays*, 197. Barnard Eldershaw also employed techniques associated with literary modernism in their novels, such as the one-day time frame and stream of consciousness used in *Tomorrow and Tomorrow and Tomorrow* (1947; 1983).

18 Stephensen, *Foundations*, 110–11; Nettie Palmer to Eleanor Dark, 9 May 1934, Eleanor Dark Papers, National Library of Australia, MS 4998, Binder 1.

19 See, for example, Miles Franklin's comments on Christina Stead's *Seven Poor Men of Sydney* (1934) in *Laughter, Not for a Cage: Notes on Australian Writing, with Biographical Emphasis on the Struggles, Function, and Achievements of the Novel in Three Half-Centuries* (Sydney: Angus & Robertson, 1956), 172–79.

fantasies of European glamour and European antiquity" – writers who had "funked their job" of building a national culture – but one who was invested in the formation of an indigenous Australian literary tradition.[20]

Regional Cosmopolitanism

Is Dark best described, then, as a writer engaged primarily with national or international forms of culture? And what does the answer to such a question reveal about the interactions between local, national and international scales? The writers and cultural figures discussed above are often referred to in accounts of interwar Australia as cultural nationalists. As we will see in this study, Dark's inclusion in this category is complicated by her openness to literary modernism and suspicion of particular kinds of nationalism which, in the late interwar period, she increasingly associated with fascism. Her 1930s fiction staged a debate between cultural nationalism and cosmopolitan humanism, as she searched for a more capacious, world-minded ethic that would support her view that "one's loyalties must be human loyalties rather than national".[21] At the same time, Dark's novels share many of the settler-colonial desires that also underpinned Australian cultural nationalism: they express a desire for settler indigenisation, wherein settler culture frames itself as a form of native culture, and for a national autonomy that would differentiate Australia from British imperial interests.

Dark's politics also separated her from some of her Australian contemporaries in the increasingly politicised environment of the 1930s. While some of her friends such as Jean Devanny and Katharine Susannah Prichard turned to communism, Dark strengthened her beliefs in liberal humanism. Throughout her life she consistently described herself as a kind of socialist: she recounted how, as a teenager, she heard about a coal strike and reacted against the idea of private ownership of natural resources, feeling that "the things the earth produced belonged to everyone in common".[22] As a number of critics have observed, however, Dark's socialism tended to be based on intuitive ideas rather than a coherent theory, and it lacked an institutional basis. She and her husband, Eric Payten Dark, supported some of the causes of the Australian Communist Party, and in the 1930s Eric became active in the left wing of the Labor Party; however, Eleanor refused to join any political party, even though she was denounced as an underground Communist Party sympathiser in Australian Parliament in 1947.[23]

---

20   Stephensen, *Foundations*, 123.
21   Eleanor Dark to W.A.R. Collins, 29 July 1940, Eleanor Dark Papers, Mitchell Library, State Library of New South Wales, MLMSS 4545, Box 25.
22   Eleanor Dark, "Political Parties", quoted in Marivic Wyndham, *"A World-Proof Life": Eleanor Dark, A Writer in Her Times 1901–1985* (Sydney: UTS ePress, 2007), 141.
23   Susan Carson, "Surveillance and Slander: Eleanor Dark in the 1940s and 1950s", *Hecate* 27, no. 1 (2001): 37.

We will see in the chapters that follow that the negotiations in Dark's writing – between regional attachments to the settler nation and more international commitments to modernism, liberal humanism and socialism – mean that her work has the potential to trouble rigid distinctions between provincial nationalism and expatriate, cosmopolitan modernism. Such a distinction has often structured accounts of twentieth-century Australian literature, so that the so-called provincial commitments of writers such as the Jindyworobak poets or Vance Palmer are pitted against the more cosmopolitan perspectives and experimental aesthetics of expatriate writers such as Patrick White or Christina Stead.[24] Yet this binary obscures some of the ways in which cultural nationalists engaged with modern forms of culture, and the contemporaneity and internationalism of their nationalisms. Recent accounts of interwar Australia emphasise the connections between Australian cultural nationalism and what Pascale Casanova calls "world literary space".[25] Peter Kirkpatrick examines the poetry of the Jindyworobaks as part of the modernist avant-garde, and Ellen Smith suggests they were "provincial modernists" whose attachment to local place represents "a response to modern social conditions".[26] Deborah Jordan similarly argues that the writings of Vance and Nettie Palmer, which were both internationalist and cultural-nationalist, can be reframed as demonstrating a "modernist critique of modernity".[27] Even Australian commentators' arguments *against* modernity and internationalism were "part of an international collective response" wherein critics drew on similar ideas to express resistance to elements of popular culture, thereby linking Australian cultural nationalism to contemporaneous debates by British figures such as F.R. Leavis.[28] Rather than reactive and provincial, the nationalism of a number of Australian cultural figures can be described as that of a "modernising nationalism": it was strategic, internationalist and embedded in modern culture.[29]

This recent scholarship helps to collapse some of the distinctions between cosmopolitan modernism and nationalism in accounts of Australian literature. Dark's

---

24 For a discussion of how this binary has functioned in Australian literary studies, see Ellen Smith, "Local Moderns: The Jindyworobak Movement and Australian Modernism", *Australian Literary Studies* 27, no. 1 (2012): 1–17.

25 Pascale Casanova, *The World Republic of Letters*, trans. M.B. DeBevoise (Cambridge, MA; London: Harvard University Press, 2004), 109.

26 Peter Kirkpatrick, "Jindy Modernist: The Jindyworobaks as Avant Garde", in *Republics of Letters: Literary Communities in Australia*, eds. Peter Kirkpatrick and Robert Dixon (Sydney: Sydney University Press, 2012), 99–112; Smith, "Local Moderns", 4.

27 Deborah Jordan, "'Written to Tickle the Ears of the Groundings in Garden Cities': The Aesthetic of Modernity—Vance and Nettie Palmer and the *New Age*", in *Impact of the Modern: Vernacular Modernities in Australia 1870s–1960s*, eds. Robert Dixon and Veronica Kelly (Sydney: Sydney University Press, 2008), 92.

28 Jill Julius Matthews, *Dance Hall and Picture Palace: Sydney's Romance with Modernity* (Sydney: Currency Press, 2005), 9, 11–12; Robert Dixon and Veronica Kelly, "Australian Vernacular Modernities: People, Sites and Practices", in *Impact of the Modern*, xviii.

29 David Carter, "Modernising Anglocentrism: *Desiderata* and Literary Time", in *Republics of Letters*, 90.

interwar fiction provides a further, important case study that works to defamiliarise these categories. Her work suggests that a writer could be invested in both nationalist *and* cosmopolitan styles and commitments, and in this way it contributes to recent investigations about the relationships between cosmopolitanism, regionalism and modernism. Traditionally, modernism has been defined as both metropolitan and internationalist – a narrative that, as Neal Alexander and James Moran point out, is underpinned by the assumption that a writer who is truly cosmopolitan will express detachment from local and national place.[30] Even modernists from colonial locations, such as Katherine Mansfield or Christina Stead, are usually associated with extended periods of living in more metropolitan locations, so that cosmopolitanism is conflated with travel and expatriation. Recent scholarship has sought to modify the meaning of cosmopolitanism, however, from a sense of detached universalism wherein local or national commitments are subsumed by the global, to what Rebecca Walkowitz describes as "multiple or flexible *attachments*".[31] Whether called "rooted cosmopolitanism", "partial cosmopolitanism", "critical cosmopolitanism", "regional modernism" or "regional cosmopolitanism", these more flexible and dialectical forms of cosmopolitanism all challenge the idea that writers who are invested in local place and express national commitments must, by necessity, reject the global.[32] Dark's work similarly suggests that one could balance local, national and global commitments, although this study will also point to some of the tensions that existed between these scales for interwar Australian writers.

In demonstrating that modernist aesthetics, cosmopolitan commitments and regional attachments could coexist and even enable one another, Dark's writing contributes to the alternative articulations of modernism provided by the "new modernist" studies of the past two decades. Proponents of new modernist studies call for temporally, geographically and aesthetically expanded understandings of modernism and modernity, in light of critical developments in the fields of postcolonialism, postmodernism studies and world literature.[33] Scholars such as Susan Stanford Friedman, Laura Doyle and Laura Winkiel challenge traditional definitions of modernism as an elite cultural practice of émigré intellectuals in Europe, England and America in the late nineteenth and early twentieth centuries,

---

30   Neal Alexander and James Moran, "Introduction: Regional Modernisms", in *Regional Modernisms*, eds. Neal Alexander and James Moran (Edinburgh: Edinburgh University Press, 2013), 1.

31   Rebecca L. Walkowitz, *Cosmopolitan Style: Modernism Beyond the Nation* (New York: Columbia University Press, 2006), 9.

32   See Kwame Anthony Appiah, "Cosmopolitan Patriots", *Critical Inquiry* 23, no. 3 (1997): 617–39; *Cosmopolitanism: Ethics in a World of Strangers* (New York: W.W. Norton, 2006), xvi–xvii; Jessica Berman, "Toward a Regional Cosmopolitanism: The Case of Mulk Raj Anand", *MFS: Modern Fiction Studies* 55, no. 1 (2009): 142–62; James Clifford, "Mixed Feelings", in *Cosmopolitics: Thinking and Feeling Beyond the Nation*, eds. Pheng Cheah and Bruce Robbins (Minneapolis: University of Minnesota Press, 1998): 362–70; Scott Herring, "Regional Modernism: A Reintroduction", *MFS: Modern Fiction Studies* 55, no. 1 (2009): 1–10.

33   Douglas Mao and Rebecca L. Walkowitz, "The New Modernist Studies", *PMLA* 123, no. 3 (2008): 737.

showing that this spatialisation and temporalisation excludes the emerging modernities of postcolonial nations, whose modernisms often look different, and occur at different times, to those produced at the centre.[34] Friedman conceives of modernity as "the temporal rupture of before/after wherever and whenever such ruptures might occur in time and space" – a definition which opens the term up to a more diverse range of temporalities and non-Western locations.[35] Modernism is similarly reframed as a relational term that constitutes "the *expressive dimension of modernity*, one that encompasses a range of styles among creative forms that share family resemblances based on an engagement with the historical conditions of modernity in a particular location".[36] The phrase "in a particular location" suggests that the conditions of modernity will vary in differing contexts, and will be expressed by a wide range of styles and forms.

One of the results of these expanded definitions of modernism is a greater recognition of the regional commitments of many modernist writers, so that scholars are increasingly recognising the "variety of affiliations within and across national spaces" that constitute modernist textual practices.[37] This is a crucial development for the study of Dark's work, and, more generally, of Australian modernism. Jed Esty, David James and Alexandra Harris have shown that British modernist writers of the interwar and postwar periods frequently focused on local landscapes and customs.[38] This is even truer of writers and artists in interwar Australia, who were experimenting with modernist styles and ideas at precisely the same point when the desire for a national, post-Federation settler culture came to the fore. The result was that, in the Australian situation, aesthetic modernism and Australian nationalism were not "opposite traditions" but rather "mutually enabled" each other, fusing together in complex and interesting ways.[39]

While employing the concept of regional cosmopolitanism, this study will also raise questions about the usefulness of the term, asking to what extent it reflects a move away from the category of the nation in world literature studies, whether its proponents are too quick to assume a connection between the aesthetic and

---

34 See, for example, Laura Doyle and Laura Winkiel, "Introduction: The Global Horizons of Modernism", in *Geomodernisms: Race, Modernism, Modernity*, eds. Laura Doyle and Laura Winkiel (Bloomington: Indiana University Press, 2005), 1–14; Susan Stanford Friedman, "Periodizing Modernism: Postcolonial Modernities and the Space/Time Borders of Modernist Studies", *Modernism/modernity* 13, no. 3 (2006): 425–43; "World Modernisms, World Literature, and Comparativity", in *The Oxford Handbook of Global Modernisms*, eds. Mark Wollaeger with Matt Eatough (New York: Oxford University Press, 2012), 499–525.

35 Friedman, "Periodizing Modernism", 433.

36 Friedman, "Periodizing Modernism", 432.

37 Mao and Walkowitz, "New Modernist Studies", 739.

38 See Jed Esty, *A Shrinking Island: Modernism and National Culture in England* (Princeton, NJ: Princeton University Press, 2004); Alexandra Harris, *Romantic Moderns: English Writers, Artists and the Imagination from Virginia Woolf to John Piper* (New York: Thames & Hudson, 2010); David James, "Localising Late Modernism: Interwar Regionalism and the Genesis of the 'Micro Novel'", *Journal of Modern Literature* 32, no. 4 (2009): 43–64.

39 Smith, "Local Moderns", 8–9.

political realms and to what extent this concept can accommodate the complex dynamics of a settler-colonial context.

Settler-colonial Modernity

What kinds of paradigms are best employed to investigate the multiple and flexible commitments of a writer such as Dark? In addressing this question, I have drawn on Robert Dixon's concept of "colonial modernity", a term that captures the often uneven "flows of people and ideas across and between national borders" that shaped twentieth-century Australian modernity.[40] Dark was similarly aware of both Australia's connection to international currents *and* its fundamentally unequal position in a world system. To fully grasp her work, we may need to employ a paradigm somewhere between the circulation model offered by the transnational turn, as articulated by world literature and the new modernist studies, and the emphasis on the uneven economic conditions that shaped modernity provided by postcolonial studies, settler-colonial studies and world-systems theory.

Dark's work speaks quite powerfully to a transnational paradigm that suggests that culture involves processes of contact, mobility and exchange, rather than quarantine and stasis. In the 1990s and early 2000s, proponents of world literature such as David Damrosch, Wai Chee Dimock and Susan Stanford Friedman advocated a transnational approach to literary studies based on the idea of circulation, pushing against the metaphors provided by postcolonial studies of core and periphery.[41] Within the new modernist studies, theorists called for a "polycentric model of global modernities and modernisms" rather than one based on the idea of a diffusionist, one-directional movement of culture from centre to periphery.[42] Instead of core and periphery, these scholars advocate spatial imaginaries of interconnected webs, networks and circles. Dixon's concept of colonial modernity speaks to these new spatial metaphors, suggesting that Australia was part of a "network of relations" rather than the recipient of a "one-way transfer of culture and authority".[43] This means that settler Australia always operated as

---

40   Robert Dixon, *Photography, Early Cinema and Colonial Modernity: Frank Hurley's Synchronized Lecture Entertainments* (London: Anthem Press, 2013), xxvi.

41   Robert Dixon and Brigid Rooney, "Introduction: Australian Literature, Globalisation and the Literary Province", in *Scenes of Reading: Is Australian Literature a World Literature?*, eds. Robert Dixon and Brigid Rooney (North Melbourne: Australian Scholarly, 2013), xii–xiii. See also David Damrosch, *What is World Literature?* (Princeton, NJ: Princeton University Press, 2003); Wai Chee Dimock, *Through Other Continents: American Literature Across Deep Time* (Princeton, NJ: Princeton University Press, 2006); Susan Stanford Friedman, *Planetary Modernisms: Provocations on Modernity Across Time* (New York: Columbia University Press, 2015).

42   Friedman, "World Modernisms", 511. See also Laura Doyle, "Modernist Studies and Inter-imperiality in the *Longue Durée*", in *Oxford Handbook*, 681; Susan Stanford Friedman, "Planetarity: Musing Modernist Studies", *Modernism/modernity* 17, no. 3 (2010): 493.

43   Dixon, *Photography*, xxiv.

part of "an ever-widening series of networks and flows", first through its imperial connections to Britain and then through its transnational ones.[44] Drawing on the distinction made within settler-colonial studies between colonial and settler-colonial contexts,[45] in this study I use the term "settler-colonial modernity" to further refine Dixon's term.

As a writer who lived exclusively in Australia, and who only travelled overseas once, on a trip to the United States and Canada in 1937, Dark may appear an unusual candidate for demonstrating what anthropologist James Clifford describes as "travelling cultures".[46] Yet if "[i]ntercultural connection is, and has long been, the norm" of all identities and cultures, then one does not need literally to travel to participate in the circulation of ideas and aesthetics.[47] Dark's mid-century writing participated in the international traffic of modern ideas and styles, and literally crossed national borders as her manuscripts were sent to London, and from there to New York and exported back to Australia, travelling along what David Carter and Roger Osborne describe as "the two-sided triangle" of Australia's imperial connection with London, and the transatlantic connection between Britain and America.[48] There are also some instances when Dark's books moved beyond this triangle, and even beyond the English-speaking world: *Prelude to Christopher* was published by a German press in 1937, *Sun Across the Sky* was translated into Italian and French in 1948 and *The Timeless Land* had Japanese, Swedish and German editions and was issued to Australian troops on active duty in the Pacific during the Second World War. This study of Dark's writing will reveal the increased importance of America and the Pacific to interwar Australia, and as such it contributes to new work which challenges the idea that Australia was primarily engaged with its imperial connection to England in this period.[49]

In demonstrating some of the circuitous routes of travel that constituted settler-colonial modernity, Dark's writing fits with the work of historians who, influenced by the transnational turn, have challenged the image of interwar Australia as culturally isolated from international influences. For a long time, a sense of geographical and cultural isolation structured accounts of

44 Dixon, *Photography*, xxix–xxx.
45 See Wolfe, *Settler Colonialism*, 163; Lorenzo Veracini, "Introducing: Settler Colonial Studies", *Settler Colonial Studies* 1, no. 1 (2011): 1–5.
46 See James Clifford, *Routes: Travel and Translation in the Late Twentieth Century* (Cambridge, MA: Harvard University Press, 1997).
47 Clifford, *Routes*, 3–5.
48 David Carter and Roger Osborne, *Australian Books and Authors in the American Marketplace 1840s–1940s* (Sydney: Sydney University Press, 2018), 2.
49 See, for example, Carter and Osborne, *American Marketplace*; Dixon, *Photography*; Paul Giles, *Antipodean America: Australasia and the Constitution of U.S. Literature* (New York: Oxford University Press, 2014), 37; Anna Johnston, "Becoming 'Pacific-Minded': Australian Middlebrow Writers in the 1940s and the Mobility of Texts", *Transfers: Interdisciplinary Journal of Mobility Studies* 7, no. 1 (2017): 88–107; Victoria Kuttainen, Susann Liebich and Sarah Galletly, *Transported Imagination: Australian Interwar Magazines and the Geographical Imaginaries of Colonial Modernity* (Amherst, NY: Cambria Press, 2018), 32.

twentieth-century Australian cultural history. One influential articulation of this idea is John F. Williams' *The Quarantined Culture: Australian Reactions to Modernism* (1995), which argues that, in the interwar years, "an improvised, unstated but de facto cultural quarantine existed in Australia".[50] Challenging this and shifting attention to Australia's embrace of mass modernity, historians such as Jill Julius Matthews argue that interwar Australia was "a cosmopolitan centre of modern pleasure", as its "cities were all coastal ports open to the ships of the world conveying goods, ideas and people".[51] In contesting the view that interwar Australia was insular and provincial, these versions of cultural history present a challenge to the fixed conceptions of space that underpin accounts of the nation as a static and culturally quarantined entity.

The field of Australian literary studies has similarly responded to the transnational turn by investigating the ways in which Australian literature is embedded in wider international space. Robert Dixon and Veronica Kelly's collection, *Impact of the Modern: Vernacular Modernities in Australia 1870s–1960s* (2008), offers an image of Australia as "a vital generating centre of international cultural innovation".[52] Dixon and Brigid Rooney's volume of essays, *Scenes of Reading: Is Australian Literature a World Literature?* (2013), investigates how a national literature "can be read productively in the wider context of world literature", challenging ideas of Australian literary studies as a "nationally bounded field of inquiry".[53] These projects illuminate the ways in which Australian writers engaged with broadly modernising processes rather than a narrowly defined experimental modernism, allowing us to "read the 'modernity' of texts that are partly or even wholly resistant to modernism but engaged, nonetheless with their own contemporaneity".[54] In doing so, critics such as David Carter, Dixon and Rooney challenge the "diffusionist" accounts of cultural history that suggest that "modernity is first invented in the metropolitan centre and then exported to the colonial peripheries, which are always, by definition, belated", instead revealing interwar Australia as "engaged, productive, and itself 'modernising'".[55] As such, they often go further than the new modernist studies in stressing the active nature of peripheral modernities in responding to international culture and aesthetic modernism. In explicating the transnational nature of modernisms, Peter Brooker and Andrew Thacker suggest that "modernist practices travel and migrate across nations and are, in turn, transformed by encounters with indigenous national

---

50 John F. Williams, *The Quarantined Culture: Australian Reactions to Modernism, 1913–1939* (New York: Cambridge University Press, 1995), 5.

51 Matthews, *Dance Hall*, 8, 12. See also Anne Rees, "Reading Australian Modernity: Unsettled Settlers and Cultures of Mobility", *History Compass* 15, no. 11 (2017): 1–13.

52 Dixon and Kelly, "Australian Vernacular Modernities", xvii.

53 Dixon and Rooney, "Introduction", xiii–xiv, xxix–xxx.

54 David Carter, *Always Almost Modern: Australian Print Cultures and Modernity* (North Melbourne: Australian Scholarly, 2013), x.

55 Dixon, *Photography*, xxiii; Carter, *Always Almost*, xii.

cultures".[56] Friedman refers to this process as "indigenization": "a form of making native or indigenous something from elsewhere", by which "the practices that take hold in their new location are changed".[57] Yet terms such as indigenisation, as well as being problematic when applied to settler contexts, remain reactive: in giving priority to the imported agent, modernism remains something that arrives from elsewhere, even though it is eventually projected back to the centre in an altered form. A more multi-directional and decentred account would suggest that Australia produced its own distinct modernisms contemporaneously and in dialogue with the modernisms produced elsewhere. Dark's interwar writing developed through her relationship to both international and local forms of culture, so that it was different from and connected to the modernisms that emerged in other locations.

Eleanor Dark and the Transnational Turn

The ideas produced by the paradigmatic shifts of transnationalism and the new modernist studies afford useful ways of addressing Dark's writing. In particular, they help to overcome a key difficulty that has confronted critics of Dark's work: that of trying to make her quite diverse body of work cohere. Scholars have struggled to unite her more psychologically focused and recognisably modernist 1930s novels with the nationally oriented historical fiction that followed. By the 1950s and 1960s, critical accounts of Dark's writing were dominated by the *Timeless Land* historical trilogy (1941–53), which was viewed as both the crowning achievement of her oeuvre and a departure from her earlier work. In his 1951 essay "The Progress of Eleanor Dark", G.A. Wilkes viewed the first two historical novels as a significant "progression" from Dark's earlier stage of writing.[58] H.M. Green's account of Dark in *A History of Australian Literature* (1961) and A.K. Thomson's in *Understanding the Novel: The Timeless Land* (1966) similarly emphasise her as a writer of historical fiction.

In the 1970s and 1980s, Humphrey McQueen and Drusilla Modjeska shifted attention back to Dark's 1930s novels by investigating her engagement with modernism. Writing about the emergence of Australian modernism in visual art in *The Black Swan of Trespass* (1979), McQueen noted that both *Sun Across the Sky* and *Waterway* "fitted the Joycean model of summing up an entire life in the activities of a single day".[59] McQueen's account, which explored the interrelationships between Australian painting, writing, interior design, fabric and architecture, represents

---

56   Peter Brooker and Andrew Thacker, "Introduction: Locating the Modern", in *Geographies of Modernism: Literatures, Cultures, Spaces*, eds. Peter Brooker and Andrew Thacker (London; New York: Routledge, 2005), 4.
57   Friedman, "Periodizing Modernism", 430–31.
58   G.A. Wilkes, "The Progress of Eleanor Dark", *Southerly* 12, no. 3 (1951): 140.
59   Humphrey McQueen, *The Black Swan of Trespass: The Emergence of Modernist Painting in Australia to 1944* (Sydney: Alternative Publishing, 1979), 100.

a broadening of understandings of Australian modernism to include both high and commercial forms. In her important study *Exiles at Home: Australian Women Writers 1925–1945* (1981), aimed at recovering the details of mid-century women writers, Drusilla Modjeska similarly drew attention to Dark's modernism, arguing that she "experimented with techniques and devices that were being taken up in Europe between the wars".[60] Modjeska's preference for Dark's earlier, feminist and modernist works over her historical fiction nonetheless produced a similarly segmented approach to that of earlier accounts of Dark's writing. In her interpretation of modernism as an elite and largely European mode, Modjeska's account also signifies a return to a narrower conception of modernist aesthetics than that of McQueen's study.

Modjeska's analysis also reflects the largely national framework within which studies of Dark's work – and Australian literary studies more generally – operated until the 1980s. While very significant in drawing attention to formerly neglected Australian women writers, *Exiles at Home* relies upon the limiting spatial tropes of nation and home, often producing a binary between nationally focused writers such as Dark, Marjorie Barnard and Miles Franklin, and those associated with expatriatism and cosmopolitanism, such as Christina Stead. Modjeska's view that Australia in the early part of the twentieth century was insulated from the broader world is exemplified in the statement that "the only novelists who can really be said to have made the shift into an idiom and aesthetic of modernism were those who left the country".[61]

It was not until the 1990s that critics explored fully the strong links between Dark's historical and modernist novels. In 1999, Susan Carson examined all of Dark's writing as a distinctive synthesis between international modernism and Australian nationalism, anticipating the broadened definitions of modernism developed by the new modernist studies.[62] Brenton Doecke similarly called for more flexible ways of understanding the historical novel in order to relate *The Timeless Land* to literary modernism.[63] In 2001, there was a special issue of the journal *Hecate* dedicated to Dark's writing, with accounts by Australian feminist scholars such as Carole Ferrier, Barbara Brooks, Nicole Moore and Susan Carson. These re-evaluations of Dark's work were strengthened by the release of her private papers, and by publications which have made these archival materials more widely available, including the two biographies of Dark, *Eleanor Dark: A Writer's Life* (1998), written by Barbara Brooks with Judith Clark, and *"A World-Proof Life":*

---

60 Drusilla Modjeska, *Exiles at Home: Australian Women Writers 1925–1945* (Sydney: Sirius Books, 1981), 218.
61 Modjeska, *Exiles at Home*, 40.
62 Susan Carson, "Making the Modern: The Writing of Eleanor Dark" (PhD thesis, University of Queensland, 1999). Carson has gone on to publish extensively on Dark's work in a number of important articles.
63 Brenton Doecke, "Challenging History Making: Realism, Revolution and Utopia in *The Timeless Land*", *Australian Literary Studies* 17, no. 1 (1995): 49–50.

Eleanor Dark, A Writer in Her Times 1901–1985 (2007), by Marivic Wyndham, and biographical readings of her fiction by Dark's relative, Helen O'Reilly.[64]

There have been further expansions of readings of Dark's work in the wake of the transnational turn, which have sought to liberate her writing from a solely national framework. Bonnie Kime Scott's essay on Dark in the 2009 special issue of *Hecate* based on transnational modernisms explores *The Timeless Land* in relation to novels written by Virginia Woolf, Jessie Redmon Fauset and Rebecca West, finding connections in terms of their critiques of gender systems, colonialism and capitalism.[65] In her chapter in *Transnational Ties: Australian Lives in the World* (2008), Susan Carson explores Dark's work in terms of "the transmission of new cultural, political and social convictions that swirled around the world in the 1930s".[66] Carson goes some way towards bridging the opposition between Dark and Stead, arguing that the "development of a gap between those who write 'at home' and 'away' … tends to gloss over the ways in which the writers meet imaginatively, and travel through literature, in turn representing and influencing how Australians think about their world".[67] Similarly, Brigid Rooney explores the "travelling modernisms, trafficking … in multiple directions" in *Waterway*.[68] In his recent study *Backgazing: Reverse Time in Modernist Culture* (2019), Paul Giles emphasises the internationalism and experimentalism of Dark's work. He compares Dark's oeuvre to that of mid-century American writer James T. Farrell, arguing that both authors foreground "a heterodox version of temporality in which the recursive passage from present to past carries as much weight as the existential charge from present to future".[69] Importantly, Giles accords a significant place to *The Timeless Land* trilogy in demonstrating that Dark was "always engaged not just with national states of affairs but with world culture".[70]

Relational and Uneven

As these analyses of Dark's work show, both a transnational paradigm and the new modernist studies have been particularly generative for studies of Dark's writing

64   Barbara Brooks with Judith Clark, *Eleanor Dark: A Writer's Life* (Sydney: Pan Macmillan, 1998); Wyndham, *"A World-Proof Life"*; Helen O'Reilly, "Time and Memory in the Novels of Eleanor Dark" (PhD thesis, University of New South Wales, 2009).

65   Bonnie Kime Scott, "First Drafts for Transnational Women's Writing: A Revisiting of the Modernisms of Woolf, West, Fauset and Dark", *Hecate* 35 (2009): 10–28.

66   Susan Carson, "Paris and Beyond: The Transnational/National in the Writing of Christina Stead and Eleanor Dark", in *Transnational Ties: Australian Lives in the World*, eds. Desley Deacon, Penny Russell and Angela Woollacott (Acton, ACT: ANU Press, 2008), 229.

67   Carson, "Paris and Beyond", 232.

68   Brigid Rooney, "Time's Abyss: Australian Literary Modernism and the Scene of the Ferry Wreck", in *Scenes of Reading*, 101.

69   Paul Giles, *Backgazing: Reverse Time in Modernist Culture* (Oxford: Oxford University Press, 2019), 199.

70   Giles, *Backgazing*, 202.

over the past few decades. Yet as Australian literary studies responds to such paradigms, it is important that it remains cognisant of the uneven conditions that prompted writers such as Dark to maintain strong local and national attachments.

While a circulation model aptly conveys the multi-directional forms of cultural and material travel in which Dark's interwar fiction participated, it does not always capture the constraints that she faced as a woman writer operating from a relatively peripheral location in which literary engagements with modernism and other forms of international culture were often strictly policed and censored. Over time, Dark came to appreciate that despite its claims to bring about "universal peace, progress and plenty", capitalist modernity in fact "functions in a way that structures rather than diminishes uneven development and discriminatory power relations".[71] As she expressed it in the final novel that she published, *Lantana Lane* (1959), "the little businesses [are] being swallowed by the big businesses, the suburbs being swallowed by the cities, the little nations crouching beneath the wings of the big nations from whose benevolent shelter they never will emerge".[72] This description of the "little nations" struggling to "emerge" from the cultural imperialism of larger ones resonates with Dark's own experience of trying to get her work published in a market that was largely determined by overseas publishers and critics. In the interwar fiction examined in this book, we will see Dark's fears about modernity grow, shifting from a confidence that it will bring about equal work and marriage conditions for women (albeit, only for middle-class, professional white women), to an increasing recognition of the asymmetrical class and racial relationships that constituted the modern world.

These tensions in Dark's work, between the allure of international modernity and an awareness of its uneven structures, suggest that utopian conceptions of modernity and modernism as unrestrained forms of movement, circulation and exchange may not always hold true for Dark's experience. Conceptual geographies of cultural exchange as a web or a network can be too decentred, "as if cultural authority and opportunity were evenly disseminated throughout the Anglosphere".[73] Proponents of world literature and global modernism do try to acknowledge this: Susan Stanford Friedman, for instance, suggests the need to prevent "discourses of modernity's fluidity, multi-directionality, and reciprocal exchange from sliding into a utopian rhetoric of happy hybridity", arguing that we can counter this utopian impulse by remembering that modernities and their modernisms often involved periods of significant social crisis and rupture.[74]

It is heartening to see that some of the critiques of Dark's work produced in the wake of the transnational turn also point to the ongoing importance of

---

71 Paul Young, "Peripheralizing Modernity: Global Modernism and Uneven Development", *Literature Compass* 9, no. 9 (2012): 611, 613.
72 Eleanor Dark, *Lantana Lane* (London: Collins, 1959), 81.
73 Dixon, *Photography*, 214.
74 Friedman, "Planetarity", 482.

the national scale and settler-colonial context in her writing, and in Australian literary studies more broadly. Brigid Rooney, for instance, argues that Dark was interested in a "predominantly national – albeit culturally progressive national" community, and Susan Carson similarly suggests that Dark's novels were ultimately focused on "what it meant to be an Australian in that period of modernity".[75] In her recent study of interwar Australian writing, *Sydney and its Waterway in Australian Literary Modernism* (2021), Meg Brayshaw examines Dark's *Waterway* as a novel that "champions a modern Australia rebuilt upon values of community and conservation".[76] Importantly, Brayshaw cautions against "a purely transnational or 'world' approach [which] risks minimising the impact of these systems on settler texts, which are often imbricated with racialised logics in complex ways".[77] Some critics have opted for regional rather than transnational approaches to Dark's writing. Sarah Ailwood, for example, compares Dark's engagement with modernism and the settler nation to the writing of Katherine Mansfield, and Jessica Gildersleeve explores *The Little Company* as an example of the "traumatic cosmopolitanism" experienced by British and Australian women in a regional articulation of modernity.[78] David Carter and Roger Osborne have recently investigated Dark's engagement with the American book market in *Australian Books and Authors in the American Marketplace 1840s–1940s* (2018) – a particularly important account for this study, as it recognises the significance of middlebrow taste and cultural institutions to the publication of Dark's work in the United States, particularly in relation to *The Timeless Land*.[79] By avoiding the tendency of more extreme formulations of transnational or world literature to absorb local differences, these accounts move towards providing a "scale-sensitive" mode of reading that is attentive to the particular conditions of mid-century Australia,[80] just as *Middlebrow Modernism: Eleanor Dark's Interwar Fiction* strives to do.

Although this study favours a decentred and multi-directional model of culture, it will at times draw on other paradigms to capture the ways in which Dark's writing was shaped by her position as a woman writer in a semi-peripheral location implicated in a wider capitalist world-system. I will sometimes make use of contested terms such as core, centre and periphery because, as Mark Wollaeger argues, they continue to have resonance in mapping "the unequal distribution

---

75 Rooney, "Time's Abyss", 108; Carson, "Paris and Beyond", 235, 239.
76 Meg Brayshaw, *Sydney and Its Waterway in Australian Literary Modernism* (Sydney: Palgrave Macmillan, 2021), 109.
77 Brayshaw, *Sydney and Its Waterway*, 14–15.
78 Sarah Ailwood, "Anxious Beginnings: Mental Illness, Reproduction and Nation Building in 'Prelude' and *Prelude to Christopher*", *Katherine Mansfield Studies* 2 (2010): 20–38; Jessica Gildersleeve, "Traumatic Cosmopolitanism: Eleanor Dark and the World at War", *Hecate* 41, no. 1–2 (2016): 7–17.
79 See Carter and Osborne, *American Marketplace*, 262–70.
80 Robert Dixon, "Australian Literature, Scale, and the Problem of the World" in *Text, Translation, Transnationalism: World Literature in Twenty-First Century Australia*, ed. Peter Morgan (Melbourne: Australian Scholarly, 2016), 22.

of economic power across the globe".[81] Equally, the idea of a singular modernity organised around capitalism, offered by Marxist critics such as Fredric Jameson and in Immanuel Wallerstein's world-systems theory, has value for capturing the ways in which settler-colonial modernity was linked in to and shaped by more powerful locations. Drawing on the Marxist understanding of modernity as "simply capitalism itself", Jameson understands it as a singular phenomenon constituted by structural unevenness.[82] Wallerstein proposes that the world can be divided into three zones of core, periphery and semi-periphery, and that one can "understand the structural differences between the zones only if you look … at the logic that held the whole world together: that is, the world-system".[83] Drawing on these ideas, Pascale Casanova and Franco Moretti link literature with global capitalism. Moretti, for example, suggests that there is "one literary system (of inter-related literatures)" and that this system is "profoundly unequal".[84]

Dark's cultural output, and the way it was shaped by the expectations of publishers in the more powerful locations of London and New York, similarly speaks to the unequal position of settler-colonial modernity within a world-system, demonstrating how opportunity and access were not evenly distributed across the globe. Opportunities to publish locally were scarce, and interwar Australian writers relied significantly on the London and New York book markets for publication.[85] All except one of Dark's interwar novels were published first in London or New York and then shipped back to Australia. In navigating the complex expectations of publishers and reviewers across three continents, Dark had to make a number of pragmatic choices in her writing. She struggled to achieve overseas publication for her more experimental novel, *Prelude to Christopher*, due to resistance from her agents and publishers in England and America, and this forced her to make some stylistic and thematic compromises in her subsequent work, *Return to Coolami*.

---

81   Mark Wollaeger, "Introduction", in *Oxford Handbook*, 6.
82   Jameson, *Singular Modernity*, 80.
83   David Palumbo-Liu, Bruce Robbins and Nirvana Tanoukhi, "Introduction: The Most Important Thing Happening", in *Immanuel Wallerstein and the Problem of the World: System, Scale, Culture*, eds. David Palumbo-Liu, Bruce Robbins and Nirvana Tanoukhi (Durham, NC: Duke University Press, 2011), 2. See Immanuel Wallerstein, *The Modern World-System* (New York: Academic Press, 1974).
84   Franco Moretti, "Conjectures on World Literature", *New Left Review* 1, no. 1 (2000): 55–56. See also Casanova, *World Republic*; Franco Moretti, *Modern Epic: The World-System from Goethe to García Márquez* (London; New York: Verso, 1996); "World-Systems Analysis, Evolutionary Theory, *Weltliteratur*", *Review* 28, no. 3 (2005): 217–28.
85   Robert Dixon, "Australian Fiction and the World Republic of Letters, 1890–1950", in *The Cambridge History of Australian Literature*, ed. Peter Pierce (Cambridge: Cambridge University Press, 2009), 225; Richard Nile and David Walker, "The 'Paternoster Row Machine' and the Australian Book Trade, 1890–1945", in *History of the Book in Australia, 1891–1945: A National Culture in a Colonised Market*, eds. John Arnold and Martyn Lyons (St. Lucia: University of Queensland Press, 2001), 5, 7–8. See also Richard Nile, *The Making of the Australian Literary Imagination* (St. Lucia: University of Queensland Press, 2002).

The concept of structural unevenness is also important in revealing that Dark not only recognised some of the unequal power relationships that shaped modernity, but also unconsciously participated in them. Dark based her ethics on a form of liberal humanism that made her sensitive to the ways in which the state encroached on certain elements of human liberty; however, she remained somewhat blind to the whiteness and middle-class nature of this ideological position. As such, her writing participated in the ongoing displacement of Aboriginal peoples, even as it tried to engage with historical injustices against them. Dark's work goes further than that of many other settler writers of the period in recognising colonisation as an ongoing act of invasion; however, her politics were limited by "available discourses" that associated Aboriginal people with primitivism and timelessness.[86] Like other examples of modernist primitivism, such as D.H. Lawrence's *The Plumed Serpent* (1925) or Katharine Susannah Prichard's *Coonardoo* (1928), Dark frequently approached Indigenous cultures as sources of renewal, providing a "fundamental critique of bourgeois civilization and its ideology of progress" that rested upon a binary between the primitive and the modern.[87] For example, her idea of the mythic timelessness of the Australian landscape and its peoples, which appears first in her interwar writing and is expressed most fully in *The Timeless Land*, allowed her to invest Aboriginal peoples with a vitalist significance; however, it also relied upon what Johannes Fabian calls the "denial of coevalness", wherein Indigenous cultures are relegated to "a Time other than the present of the producer of anthropological discourse".[88]

Dark's novels also perpetuated the "dying race" trope at a time when it was becoming increasingly untenable. *Waterway* was published in 1938, the year of the Sesquicentenary, during which the Aborigines Progressive Association (APA) and the Australian Aborigines League (AAL) staged the Day of Mourning, a protest timed to coincide with the official Australia Day celebrations that marked 150 years since the arrival of the First Fleet on 26 January 1788. APA members William Ferguson and Jack Patten called for Aboriginal people to be "accorded full citizen rights, and to be accepted into the Australian community on a basis of equal opportunity".[89] Dark was in contact with some of the non-Indigenous supporters who helped to organise the protest, including P.R. Stephensen and Xavier Herbert,

---

86   Susan Carson, "Conversations with the Land: Environmental Questions and Eleanor Dark", in *Land and Identity: Proceedings of the 1997 Conference University of New England Armidale New South Wales 27–30 September 1997*, eds. Michael Deves and Jennifer A. McDonnell (Association for the Study of Australian Literature, 1998), 193. See also Stephen Muecke, *Textual Spaces: Aboriginality and Cultural Studies* (Sydney: UNSW Press, 1992), 19–35.

87   Andreas Huyssen, "Geographies of Modernism in a Globalizing World", in *Geographies of Modernism*, 7. See also Marianna Torgovnik, *Gone Primitive: Savage Intellects, Modern Lives* (Chicago, IL: University of Chicago Press, 1990).

88   Johannes Fabian, *Time and the Other: How Anthropology Makes its Object* (New York: Columbia University Press, 2014), 31.

89   Aborigines Progressive Association, J.T. Patten and W. Ferguson, "Aborigines Claim Citizen Rights!: A Statement of the Case for the Aborigines Progressive Association", *Publicist*, 1938.

and this event would surely have called attention to problems with the dying race theory.[90] Yet although she begins *Waterway* with the central character, Oliver Denning, imagining the arrival of the First Fleet from the point of view of an Eora man 150 years before, Dark also describes Aboriginal people as "a brave and ancient race fading slowly to extinction, its language scantily recorded, its virtues unremembered, its miseries ignored" (11, 12). The fact that she resigned Indigenous peoples to the past drastically limited her ability to engage with the material demands for equal access to citizenship, education and employment expressed by Aboriginal activists, or to challenge the policies designed to eliminate racial minorities in 1930s "White Australia". There are no contemporary Indigenous characters in Dark's novels, and her most in-depth study of the effects of colonisation on First Nations peoples (in *The Timeless Land*) relegates the issue to the past. Dark's settler position was in some ways powerful in its sense of distance from the metropolitan centre, and in other ways limited in its failure to recognise the forms of injustice, avoidance and displacement in which it was complicit.

Middlebrow Modernism

One of the ways in which *Middlebrow Modernism: Eleanor Dark's Interwar Fiction* differs from recent studies of Dark's work is in its emphasis on her engagement with mid-century middlebrow culture. While the modernist qualities of Dark's 1930s writing were readily observed at the time of publication, and have recently been the subject of renewed critical interest, what has been less apparent in studies of her work is the relationship between these styles and the middlebrow. Critics have frequently pointed to the ways in which Dark's novels combine elements of popular fiction such as romance with modernist narrative techniques; however, few have identified this as a middlebrow strategy. As Faye Hammill and Michelle Smith observe in their analysis of mid-century Canadian travel magazines, middlebrow print cultures offer "a space where high and popular culture meet, and where art encounters consumerism", so that the combination of mass and high cultural elements is characteristic of the middlebrow.[91] This gap in the literature on Dark seems to be the product of what David Carter calls the "missing middlebrow" in Australian literary and cultural studies – the exclusion of the mid-range from a field which has been more interested in high and low expressions of culture – than of any lack of relevance of the term.[92]

---

90 For an account of Stephensen and Herbert's involvement in the Day of Mourning staged by Aboriginal protest groups, see Craig Munro, *Inky Stephensen: Wild Man of Letters* (St. Lucia: University of Queensland Press, 1992), 180–85; Ellen Smith, "White Aborigines: Xavier Herbert, P.R. Stephensen and the *Publicist*", *Interventions* 16, no. 1 (2014): 97–116.

91 Faye Hammill and Michelle Smith, *Magazines, Travel, and Middlebrow Culture: Canadian Periodicals in English and French, 1925–1960* (Liverpool: Liverpool University Press, 2015), 10.

The fact that Dark's writing can be considered both modernist *and* middlebrow is unusual, given that these are often viewed as antithetical modes. In historical terms, the word middlebrow emerged out of a modern cultural scene in which it was defined against high modernism.[93] When it was first coined in the 1920s, the term was wielded by cultural elites against products that appeared to lack the status and experimentalism of high culture and the legitimacy of low culture.[94] The earliest use of the term in print has been traced to an article that appeared in London's *Daily Chronicle* in 1923, which was quoted in an Australian newspaper in the same year.[95] The more oft-cited early example is a comment in *Punch* in 1925 that "[t]he BBC claim to have discovered a new type, the 'middlebrow'. It consists of people who are hoping that some day they will get used to the stuff they ought to like."[96] In key publications, including F.R. Leavis' *Mass Civilisation and Minority Culture* (1930), Q.D. Leavis' *Fiction and the Reading Public* (1932) and Virginia Woolf's satirical essay "Middlebrow" (published posthumously in 1942), British cultural elites outlined their oppositions to mass culture and the new cultural category it had produced, the aspirational middlebrow.

Because the terms highbrow, middlebrow and lowbrow are unstable categories and have complex meanings depending on who is invoking them, they are extremely difficult to define. One of the main characteristics associated with the middlebrow is accessibility and broad appeal, whereas modernism is usually associated with aesthetic difficulty.[97] Those who defended the middlebrow associated this accessibility with a democratic quality, as in J.B. Priestley's exploration of the "broadbrow"; however, others such as F.R. Leavis linked it with mass consumer culture and a "process of levelling-down".[98] Scholars who have investigated the historical middlebrow in the British context, including Rosa Marie Bracco and Nicola Humble, focus on the ways in which it encoded and negotiated middle-class values, particularly those relating to gender and class, as in Humble's conception of the "feminine middlebrow".[99] Studies of the American middlebrow

---

92 David Carter, "The Mystery of the Missing Middlebrow or The C(o)urse of Good Taste", in *Imagining Australia: Literature and Culture in the New New World*, eds. Judith Ryan and Chris Wallace-Crabbe (Cambridge, MA; London: Harvard University Press, 2004), 174.

93 Phyllis Lassner, Ann Rea and Genevieve Brassard, "Reading Sideways: Middlebrow into Modernism", *The Space Between* 9, no. 1 (2013): 7.

94 Lisa Botshon and Meredith Goldsmith, "Introduction", in *Middlebrow Moderns: Popular American Women Writers of the 1920s*, eds. Lisa Botshon and Meredith Goldsmith (Boston, MA: Northeastern University Press, 2003), 3.

95 *The Queenslander*, 12 May 1923, quoted in Kate Macdonald, "Introduction: Identifying the Middlebrow, the Masculine and Mr Miniver", in *The Masculine Middlebrow, 1880–1950: What Mr. Miniver Read*, ed. Kate Macdonald (New York: Palgrave Macmillan, 2011), 6, 23.

96 *Punch*, 23 December 1925, quoted in Macdonald, "Introduction", 7.

97 Jaime Harker, *America the Middlebrow: Women's Novels, Progressivism, and Middlebrow Authorship Between the Wars* (Amherst: University of Massachusetts Press, 2007), 19.

98 J.B. Priestley, *The Balconinny and Other Essays* (London: Methuen, 1929), 166–67; F.R. Leavis, *For Continuity*, Essay Index Reprint Series (Freeport, NY: Books for Libraries Press, [1933] 1968), 18.

by scholars such as Janice Radway and Joan Shelley Rubin examine the institutions of subscriber book clubs and endorsed book collections, showing how these produced middlebrow, aspirational taste.[100] In Australia, researchers investigating mid-century middlebrow culture, including David Carter, Victoria Kuttainen, Susann Liebich, Sarah Galletly, Robyn Greaves, Anna Johnston, Mitchell Rolls and Robert Dixon, have focused particularly on the modernising and internationalising qualities of middlebrow reading, so that their work helps to shift images of interwar Australia as closed and provincial.[101]

In what ways can the fiction discussed in this book be associated with the middlebrow? The short stories that Dark wrote in the 1920s were produced for a variety of Australian commercial magazines which have been linked with national middlebrow culture, including the *Triad* (1915–27), *Art in Australia* (1916–42) and *The Home* (1920–42). Dark later used the skills she developed in her 1920s magazine writing to produce novels that combined modernist narrative techniques with elements of popular romance. By repackaging experimental devices and progressive ideas in accessible and entertaining stories, the middlebrow modernism of her 1930s novels provided readers with a winning combination of both quality and entertainment.[102]

Dark's work suffered many of the same criticisms that were frequently levelled at the feminine middlebrow. The middlebrow is an inherently gendered concept, often linked with women, whereas the highbrow has traditionally been gendered as masculine.[103] Although there has been some expansion of middlebrow studies to investigate the "masculine middlebrow" – for example, in the essay collection *The Masculine Middlebrow, 1880–1950: What Mr. Miniver Read* (2011) – the terms

---

99 See Rosa Maria Brocco, *Merchants of Hope: British Middlebrow Writers and the First World War, 1919–1939* (Providence, RI: Berg, 1993); Nicola Humble, *The Feminine Middlebrow Novel, 1920s to 1950s: Class, Domesticity, and Bohemianism* (Oxford: Oxford University Press, 2001); "Sitting Forward Or Sitting Back: Highbrow v. Middlebrow Reading", *Modernist Cultures* 6, no. 1 (2011): 41–59.

100 See Janice Radway, *A Feeling for Books: The Book-of-the-Month Club, Literary Taste, and Middle-Class Desire* (Chapel Hill: University of North Carolina Press, 1997); Joan Shelley Rubin, *The Making of Middlebrow Culture* (Chapel Hill: University of North Carolina Press, 1992).

101 See Carter, "Mystery", 173–201; Sarah Galletly, "The Spectacular Traveling Woman: Australian and Canadian Visions of Women, Modernity, and Mobility between the Wars", *Transfers: Interdisciplinary Journal of Mobility Studies* 7, no. 1 (2017): 70–87; Robyn Greaves, "A 'Grim and Fascinating' Land of Opportunity: The *Walkabout* Women and Australia", *JASAL: Journal of the Association for the Study of Australian Literature* 14, no. 5 (2014): 1–12; Anna Johnston and Mitchell Rolls, *Travelling Home, Walkabout Magazine and Mid-Twentieth-Century Australia* (London; New York: Anthem Press, 2016); Victoria Kuttainen, "Illustrating Mobility: Networks of Visual Print Culture and the Periodical Contexts of Modern Australian Writing", *JASAL: Journal of the Association for the Study of Australian Literature* 17, no. 2 (2017): 1–16; Victoria Kuttainen and Susann Liebich, "Worldly Tastes: Mobility and the Geographical Imaginaries of Interwar Australian Magazines", *Transfers: Interdisciplinary Journal of Mobility Studies* 7, no. 1 (2017): 52–69; Kuttainen, Liebich and Galletly, *Transported Imagination*.

102 David Carter suggests that this combination was essential to the middlebrow, in "'Some Means of Learning of the Best New Books': All About Books and the Modern Reader", *Australian Literary Studies* 22, no. 3 (2006): 333.

that were usually levelled at middlebrow writers, including romantic, earnest, conservative and sentimental, are also ones commonly gendered as feminine. Dark's contemporaries did not use the term middlebrow to describe her work but it was nonetheless implied in their critiques. M. Barnard Eldershaw suggested that an "unwilling or thinly disguised romanticism" made Dark's plots "conventional", and that her novels were filled with "the stuff of melodrama".[104] Nettie Palmer seems to have implied the middlebrow when she wrote in her journal that *Return to Coolami* was written to "*high* magazine standard".[105] G.A. Wilkes used the term "slick" to describe Dark's 1930s novels when reviewing them in 1951, as did A. Grove Day when writing about Dark's short stories in his full-length study, *Eleanor Dark* (1976).[106] These critiques, which link Dark's work with both mass consumer culture and the sentimentality associated with the feminine middlebrow, go some way towards explaining why she took such pains to assert and defend the seriousness of her work when she came into contact with important cultural figures such as the Palmers in the 1930s.

We will see in this study that Dark's middle-class values and liberal humanist beliefs fit well with a middlebrow emphasis on feeling, emotional identification, education and ethical behaviour. Her interwar writing focuses mostly on characters from the social class with which she was most familiar, that of the middle-class professional. Dark was uniquely positioned to represent members of this newly emerging professional-managerial class: her husband, Eric Dark, was a general medical practitioner who was involved in developing a new treatment for tuberculosis, and published books such as *Diathermy in General Practice* (1930) and *Medicine and the Social Order* (1942). Her aunt, Marion Louisa Piddington, was a radical advocate for family planning and a founder of the New South Wales Racial Hygiene Association. Both were part of the new class of professionals who, in the first decades of the twentieth century, participated in the scientific management of social reform.[107] The works discussed in the chapters that follow provide fascinating insight into, and at times question, these changing social roles.

In all of her novels, Dark presents her modern ideas through characters that make quintessentially middlebrow appeals to readers' emotions and empathy. Her writing draws on what Janice Radway calls middlebrow "personalism": "an

---

103 See Christoph Ehland and Cornelia Wächter, "Introduction: '… All Granite, Fog and Female Fiction", in *Middlebrow and Gender, 1890-1945*, eds. Christoph Ehland and Cornelia Wächter (Leiden; Boston: Brill Rodopi, 2016), 1–17.

104 Barnard Eldershaw, *Essays*, 189, 197.

105 Nettie Palmer diary, 15 May 1936, quoted in Brooks with Clark, *Eleanor Dark*, 143.

106 Wilkes, "The Progress of Eleanor Dark", 142; A. Grove Day, *Eleanor Dark* (Boston: Twayne, 1976), 28.

107 Kerreen M. Reiger, *The Disenchantment of the Home: Modernizing the Australian Family, 1880-1940* (Melbourne: Oxford University Press, 1985), 1–2. For discussions of the role of science and medicine in Dark's work, see Susan Carson, "Finding Hy-Brazil: Eugenics and Modernism in the Pacific", *Hecate* 35, no. 1–2 (2009): 124–33; Anne Maxwell, "Biopolitics and Eleanor Dark's *Prelude to Christopher*", *Australian Literary Studies* 26, no. 2 (2011): 76–90.

individualism of both affect and empathy" which recognised that "[p]eople felt – and they felt for others".[108] As Radway shows in her study of the American Book-of-the-Month Club, middlebrow novels invite readers to "inhabit the parallel self provided by a book, to feel the way it vibrated both physically and emotionally in response to its own context, and to participate in a difference that was thereby rendered comprehensible".[109] This focus on feeling meant that Dark could emphasise what Emmanuel Levinas describes as the ethical realm of the "face-to-face": moments that offer individuals the opportunity for "ethical awareness between the self and the face of the other", and which open the reader up to an Other that is "startling in its otherness, compelling in its demands upon the self".[110]

Dark's interwar fiction can be read alongside the work of writers in other international contexts who similarly navigated the realm of the "high middlebrow".[111] Significantly, these are the writers who Dark also read. In 1928, she was interviewed by Zora Cross for a profile piece in *The Australian Woman's Mirror* (1924–61). Although Dark had yet to publish any novels, Cross (writing under the pseudonym of Bernice May) described her as "one of the sincerest and most gifted of our women writers", referencing the short stories and poems Dark had published in the *Bulletin* under the pseudonym of Patricia O'Rane.[112] Cross recalls speaking to Dark at her home in Katoomba:

> After luncheon we talked books in the enchanted garden. Patricia O'Rane is fond of the moderns. Galsworthy is a god – but so is Dickens, and she has a passion for the feminine writers, Rebecca West, Tennyson Jesse, Storm Jameson and G.B. Stern.[113]

Dark rarely spoke publicly about her literary influences, and so this list provides an intriguing insight into her reading tastes (or at the least the tastes that Cross chose to share with readers of the *Mirror*). Most of the writers listed here as "moderns" are contemporary without necessarily being modern*ist* in the more traditional sense of the term. Rather, they are writers of the feminine middlebrow, and also members of the English political middlebrow: male writers associated with the Edwardian period whose works were popular in the 1920s and 1930s, such as John Galsworthy.[114] To this list, we can add H.G. Wells, George Bernard Shaw and

---

108 Radway, *Feeling*, 283.
109 Radway, *Feeling*, 284.
110 Jessica Berman summarising Levinas, in "Ethical Folds: Ethics, Aesthetics, Woolf", *MFS: Modern Fiction Studies* 50, no. 1 (2004): 152.
111 Nicola Humble in Elke D'hoker and Nicola Humble, "Theorizing the Middlebrow: An Interview with Nicola Humble", *Interférences littéraires/Literaire interferenties* 7 (2011): 260.
112 "Bernice May" [Zora Cross], "Patricia O'Rane", *The Australian Woman's Mirror* 4, no. 44 (25 September 1928), 54.
113 May, "Patricia O'Rane", 8, 54.

Aldous Huxley – writers whom Eleanor and Eric Dark both enjoyed. The fact that Dark was reading these authors suggests that she was engaged with work that spoke to a space between highbrow and lowbrow culture where, as Carter observes of the magazine the *Triad*, "wide appeal, literary quality, entertainment, and intellectual interest could still be imagined together".[115]

Middlebrow Modernism in Interwar Australia

The middlebrow quality of Dark's modernist engagements was to some extent a product of the material conditions faced by Australian writers in the interwar period. Australian readers, whose tastes were "largely international and middlebrow", often used English and American reviews and prizes to determine their reading choices.[116] If, as Beth Driscoll argues, one of the characteristics of the middlebrow is that it is overtly mediated through distribution mechanisms and cultural institutions, then, in an era when "responses of overseas reviewers were eagerly awaited at home and had a powerful effect on a writer's domestic sales and reputation", all interwar Australian writers seeking to gain any success needed to rely on middlebrow institutions, including reviews, awards and subscriber book clubs.[117] Furthermore, the relative lack of elite cultural institutions such as university presses (at least compared to the English and American contexts) meant that Australian writers and critics – many of whom expressed resistance to the influence of both low- and middlebrow American culture – needed to publish in the middlebrow sphere.[118] Vance Palmer, Miles Franklin, Marjorie Barnard and Katharine Susannah Prichard all published extensively in commercial publications such as newspapers and magazines, rather than in high culture journals like the English *Scrutiny*, so that their work was "located institutionally on the cusp of highbrow and middlebrow".[119]

Dark similarly had to cater for the middlebrow tastes of local readers and overseas publishers, agents and critics. Yet despite the fact that the middlebrow quality of her writing was in some ways a forced choice, we will see that Dark navigated the middlebrow market in ways that were particularly skilful. The accommodations that Australian writers had to make in order to achieve overseas publication and local visibility were not *only* negative: as David Carter and Roger

---

114 Anna Vaninskaya, "The Political Middlebrow from Chesterton to Orwell", in *Masculine Middlebrow*, 164.

115 David Carter, "Literary, but Not Too Literary; Joyous, but Not Jazzy: *Triad* Magazine, Antipodean Modernity and the Middlebrow", *Modernism/modernity* 25, no. 2 (2018): 263.

116 Dixon, "Australian Fiction", 226–27.

117 Beth Driscoll, *The New Literary Middlebrow: Tastemakers and Reading in the Twenty-First Century* (Sydney: Palgrave Macmillan, 2014), 25–32; Dixon, "Australian Fiction", 224.

118 Dixon and Rooney, "Introduction", xiii; David Carter, "Modernity and the Gendering of Middlebrow Book Culture in Australia", in *Masculine Middlebrow*, 143.

119 Carter, "Modernity", 143.

Osborne have argued, the fact that Australian writers were compelled to navigate international book markets could act as a vector of modernisation and internationalism, "giving books the power to travel further, and what we might call the power to be modern".[120] The skilful ways in which Dark combined modernism with popular romance to meet the tastes of her publishers and readers speaks to recent middlebrow studies which reformulate the middlebrow not as an inferior mode of reading and writing but as "a sophisticated integration of a range of cultural practices in order to provide an entertaining and intellectual understanding of modernity".[121] Faye Hammill, for instance, argues that the middlebrow was a "productive, affirmative standpoint for writers who were not wholly aligned with either high modernism or popular culture".[122]

In *Middlebrow Modernism: Eleanor Dark's Interwar Fiction*, I read the middlebrow quality of Dark's work not as an inherently constraining factor but as one which demonstrates her successful and intelligent negotiation of a complex range of cultural and market trends. Rather than lament the middlebrow qualities in her writing, and regret the ways in which she increasingly moved away from more recognisably modernist styles to experiment with other genres such as historical fiction in the 1940s, it is the cross-generic, hybrid nature of her fiction and the ways in which it represents an engagement with both settler-colonial modernity and mid-century international culture that most interests me. Her work represents one of the more successful ways in which a settler Australian writer navigated new transnational opportunities and contributed to the transmission of modern ideas and aesthetic styles in the mid-century period, as shown by the selection of *The Timeless Land* for the Book-of-the-Month Club – an institution which Joan Shelley Rubin and Janice Radway suggest was profoundly middlebrow.[123] In Dark's work, modernism was mediated by middlebrow tastes, making her modernist engagements more accessible, more subject to affect and attachment and more aligned with middle-class rather than elite forms of culture. Her fiction may have opened up mid-century Australian writing to more experimental and non-realist modes, as her novels offered more nuanced ideas and modernist narrative techniques than the "middlebrow nationalism" of Ernestine Hill, Henrietta Drake-Brockman, Ion L. Idriess and Frank Clune, but were also more accessible than the works of Christina Stead and Patrick White.[124] Dark's middlebrow modernism was not a lesser, weaker form of modernism than the

120 Carter and Osborne, *American Marketplace*, 3; Carter, "Modernity", 138.
121 Melissa Sullivan and Sophie Blanch, "Introduction: The Middlebrow – Within or Without Modernism", *Modernist Cultures* 6, no. 1 (2011): 5.
122 Faye Hammill, *Women, Celebrity and Literary Culture Between the Wars* (Austin: University of Texas Press, 2007), 6.
123 Dixon, "Australian Fiction", 244. See Rubin, *Middlebrow Culture*; Radway, *Feeling*.
124 Carter, "Mystery", 184. See also Greaves, "'Grim and Fascinating'", 1–12; Anna Johnston, "1943: Ernestine Hill's *The Great Australian Loneliness* is packed into U.S. Armed Service Kitbags", in *Telling Stories: Australian Literary Cultures 1935–2010*, eds. Tanya Dalziell and Paul Genoni (Melbourne, Monash University Press, 2013), 84–90.

high modernism that emerged in other contexts at the same time; rather, it was a different kind of modernism: "a modernism askew", as Daniel Tracy suggests of the middlebrow modernism he identifies in Anita Loos' serial novel *Gentlemen Prefer Blondes* (1925).[125] While some British and American writers also combined modernism and the middlebrow in productive ways, the Australian case was unusual in that modernism often emerged in middlebrow publications rather than in high culture institutions; in this sense, middlebrow modernism was one of the key ways in which literary modernism first developed in Australia in the interwar years.[126]

The fact that Dark's modernism emerged in relation to and through commercial forms of culture illuminates some of the parallels between the Australian literary and visual arts scenes. As Ann Stephen, Andrew McNamara and Philip Goad observe in *Modernism & Australia: Documents on Art, Design and Architecture 1917–1967* (2006), in the Australian context modernist artistic practices often emerged through such interdisciplinary fields as design and architecture, rather than through more conventional sources of high culture.[127] While in the realm of high art there was some resistance to modernist abstraction, in the commercial sphere it was retailers, department stores, advertisers and middlebrow periodicals such as *The Home* and *Art in Australia* that were "among the earliest to turn modern", so that artistic modernism had a particularly commercial flavour.[128] While the late interwar period saw the emergence of Australian institutions designed to support modern art, such as the Contemporary Art Society established in Victoria in 1938, the Australian public was still much more likely to encounter artistic modernism through advertisements and illustrations than in gallery exhibitions and art schools.[129] In the same way, Dark's middlebrow modernism, which includes an engagement with mass forms of consumer culture such as magazine fiction, romance and popular cinema, suggests that commercial culture may have acted as a conduit for literary modernism in the Australian context.

Mapping Eleanor Dark's Middlebrow Modernism

This study provides the first full-length, single-author account of Dark's writing to be published since American literary scholar A. Grove Day produced the first one in 1976. The lack of sustained critical attention to Dark's work is quite remarkable

---

125 Tracy, "Vernacular Humor", 138.
126 See Carter, "Mystery", 173–201.
127 Ann Stephen, Andrew McNamara and Philip Goad, "Introduction", in *Modernism & Australia: Documents on Art, Design and Architecture 1917–1967*, eds. Ann Stephen, Andrew McNamara and Philip Goad (Carlton, Vic: Miegunyah Press, 2006), 4.
128 Stephen, McNamara and Goad, "Introduction", 4.
129 Helen Ennis, *Photography and Australia* (London: Reaktion Books, 2007), 82.

given that she is one of the most important and well-known Australian writers of the mid-century period. As discussed earlier in this introduction, there have certainly been important essays on Dark's writing produced over the last few decades, including in recent years by both emerging Australian scholars and international critics.[130] *Middlebrow Modernism: Eleanor Dark's Interwar Fiction* seeks to build upon and stimulate this developing critical interest by providing a much-needed, in-depth study of a crucial stage of Dark's writing. In drawing attention to her engagements with not only literary modernism but also a wide range of commitments – settler nationalist, cosmopolitan, regional, liberal humanist, commercial and middlebrow – I aim to ensure that the varied ways in which Dark mediated modernity are not obscured in her recovery as an important modernist.

This book seeks to make space for an element of Dark's fiction that has been particularly under-examined in studies of her work: her liberal humanism. Dark's liberalism was problematic for many of her contemporaries in the politically polarised atmosphere of the 1930s. A number of her friends who joined the Communist Party were uncomfortable with the middle-class nature of Dark's status as a doctor's wife and her large house in Katoomba: Jean Devanny remarked in 1945, in response to reading *The Little Company*, "Fancy wasting her lovely talent on such stuff as the mental and moral gropings of a pettybourgeois [sic] writer in days like these! It's being stuck in that beautiful home on top of a mountain. She is in the clouds."[131] More recently, in the context of the rigorous critiques of the racial, class and gendered blind spots of liberal humanism that have taken place over the last few decades in literary studies, Dark's liberal humanism has again been treated as a conservative element of her writing.[132] It will not be the aim of this

---

130 Examples of new work on Dark by Australian scholars include: Meg Brayshaw, "Trans-Scalar Sydney, Narrative Form and Ethics in Eleanor Dark's *Waterway*", *JASAL: Journal of the Association for the Study of Australian Literature* 17, no. 1 (2017): 1–10; *Sydney and Its Waterway*, 105–34; Melinda J. Cooper, "'A Masterpiece of Camouflage': Modernism and Interwar Australia", *Modernist Cultures* 15, no. 3 (2020): 316–40; "'Adjusted' Vision: Interwar Settler Modernism in Eleanor Dark's *Return to Coolami*", *Australian Literary Studies* 33, no. 2 (2018): 1–28; Kathleen Davidson, "Landscapes and Mindscapes: The Confluence of Modernism and Ecopoetics in Eleanor Dark's *Return to Coolami*", *Philament: A Journal of Literature, Arts, and Culture* 24, no. 2 (2018): 1–31; Gildersleeve, "Traumatic Cosmopolitanism", 7–17. A collected volume of essays on Dark's writing, edited by Fiona Morrison and Brigid Rooney, is in progress and due to be published by Sydney University Press in 2023. A conference on Dark, "Beyond Time: Reading Eleanor Dark in 2020", was scheduled to be held in Sydney in May 2020 but was postponed due to restrictions attending the COVID-19 pandemic. For evidence of increasing international engagement with Dark's work, see David Trotter's discussion of *Waterway* in *The Literature of Connection: Signal, Medium, Interface, 1850–1950* (Oxford: Oxford University Press, 2020), 155–59; and Emma Garman's exploration of *Prelude to Christopher* in "Feminize Your Canon: Eleanor Dark", *Paris Review*, 9 January 2019.

131 Jean Devanny to Frank Ryland, 15 August 1945, in *As Good as a Yarn with You: Letters between Miles Franklin, Katharine Susannah Prichard, Jean Devanny, Marjorie Barnard, Flora Eldershaw and Eleanor Dark*, ed. Carole Ferrier (Cambridge, UK; Oakleigh, Vic: Cambridge University Press, 1992), 131.

study completely to recuperate her liberal humanist commitments, but rather to try to understand them from the point of view of the interwar period, rather than only in terms of the exclusions which post-1980s theory has revealed.

Each of the six chapters that follows engages with a particular novel that Dark worked on or published during the interwar years, while also making links between these and her other writings. I will read these works of fiction in terms of their engagement with the key critical concepts that have been introduced here: middlebrow modernism, regional cosmopolitanism, settler-colonial modernity and liberal humanism. The first chapter explores how Dark mediated images and ideas circulated through the mass marketplace in both the short stories she produced for Australian periodicals in the 1920s and her early novel, *Slow Dawning* (1932). In tracing how Dark capitalised on the growing demand for women's romance and light fiction that took place as a transnational phenomenon in the interwar period, this chapter will show how she used these market opportunities to explore a number of progressive concerns related to issues such as travel, technology, sexuality, censorship and the Modern Woman. This early, 1920s stage of Dark's writing has generally been minimised in studies of her work, yet it is important in illuminating how an Australian writer contributed with confidence to the transmission of modern ideas and new types of popular and middlebrow fiction in the interwar period.

Chapter 1 will also investigate Dark's early expression of liberal humanism, showing how in her 1920s fiction she drew on an intellectual heritage of New Liberalism to extend modern rights and freedoms to particular social groups who were often regarded as outside of its scope, including new kinds of middle-class, professional white women. *Slow Dawning* provides a narrative about a Modern Woman whose individual struggles are entangled with collective women's emancipation, and in this sense, it demonstrates the political potential of post-suffragist, progressive middlebrow women's fiction in a period when New Liberal intellectuals sought to reconcile the individual and the state.

Chapter 2 focuses on Dark's experimental novel *Prelude to Christopher* (1934), using it to explore the relationship between literary modernism and cultural nationalism in interwar Australia. Drawing on the metaphors of disease and contagion that Dark foregrounds in the novel, this chapter reads *Prelude to Christopher* as a commentary about interwar Australia's openness to international cultural influences. It also explores some of the developments that occurred in Dark's liberal humanist thinking in the 1930s. In contrast to *Slow Dawning*, *Prelude to Christopher* signifies a retreat from some of the state-based solutions of Dark's

---

132 One scholar who has examined some of the emancipatory potential of Dark's liberal humanism, particularly in relation to *Prelude to Christopher*, is Anne Maxwell. See Anne Maxwell, "Education, Literature and the Emotions: A Salute to Eleanor Dark's *Prelude to Christopher*", *JASAL: Journal of the Association for the Study of Australian Literature* 12, no. 1 (2012): 1–11; "Biopolitics", 76–90.

father's generation of liberal reformism to offer a more traditional emphasis on the ideas of classical liberalism, including the primacy of the individual human subject, freedom of expression and the importance of culture and art.

The third chapter explores the role of mass consumer culture in Dark's modernism. While modernism has typically been associated with high culture, there is a growing body of research that explores its close relationship with the commercial marketplace.[133] Dark's writing aptly demonstrates this interconnection, frequently crossing over what Andreas Huyssen famously called the "great divide" between mass and high expressions of culture.[134] We can observe this in the close connection between Dark's modernist narrative style and the cinematic conventions she observed in Hollywood cinema. Through an examination of *Return to Coolami* (1936), I show how Dark embraced some of the new technologies of mass culture, including the changing forms of visual perception, speed and mobility produced by motor travel, cinema and photography. Although the entanglement between modernism and commercial culture is not unique to Dark's work, she gave elements of popular culture great prominence in her writing, making her short stories and novels strong examples of what Miriam Hansen refers to as "vernacular modernism".[135] Chapter 3 also explores how Dark's vernacular modernism was connected to her settler nationalism, as she used both modernist and popular ways of representing visual perception, time, memory and psychology to articulate claims for cultural legitimacy.

The second half of this study, which focuses on *Sun Across the Sky* (1937), *Waterway* (1938) and *The Timeless Land* (1941), examines Dark's fiction in terms of its response to the pressures of the late interwar period. As the 1930s progressed, Dark increasingly engaged with large-scale social issues and questions of class and race, so that her writing shifted from the feminine middlebrow towards the political middlebrow. Like the British authors Storm Jameson and Winifred Holtby (both of whom she read), Dark used the middlebrow novel form to express leftist political commitments and provide social critique, exploring such issues as the Depression, the spread of fascism and the likely advent of a second global conflict. In *Sun Across the Sky*, which is the subject of Chapter 4, Dark emphasises the

---

133 See, for example, Ann L. Ardis and Patrick Collier, *Transatlantic Print Culture, 1880–1940: Emerging Media, Emerging Modernisms* (New York; Basingstoke: Palgrave Macmillan, 2008); Dixon and Kelly, eds., *Impact of the Modern*; Celia Marshik, *At the Mercy of their Clothes: Modernism, the Middlebrow, and British Garment Culture* (New York: Columbia University Press, 2016); Lawrence Rainey, *Institutions of Modernism: Literary Elites and Public Culture* (New Haven, CT; London: Yale University Press, 1999).

134 See Andreas Huyssen, *After the Great Divide: Modernism, Mass Culture, Postmodernism* (Bloomington: Indiana University Press, 1986), 44–62. Christopher Chowrimootoo makes a similar claim of the middlebrow modernism of British composer Benjamin Britten, arguing for the usefulness of the middlebrow category in destabilising hierarchies of high and low culture. See Chowrimootoo, *Middlebrow Modernism*, 1–29.

135 Miriam Bratu Hansen, "The Mass Production of the Senses: Classical Cinema as Vernacular Modernism", *Modernism/modernity* 6, no. 2 (1999): 59–77.

social role performed by culture – a stance that David Carter refers to as "aesthetic utopianism" – and offers visual art and poetry as means of achieving cultural continuity in a period of significant rupture and crisis.[136]

Both Chapters 4 and 5 will demonstrate some of the difficulties faced by writers of Dark's generation in adapting the novel form to meet the challenges of the late interwar period. In *Waterway*, which is the subject of Chapter 5, Dark registers some of these tensions by depicting Sydney Harbour as a contested site associated with both the romance of international travel, and significant friction between the local and the global. Chapter 5 also provides some discussion of Dark's wartime novel *The Little Company* (1945), which extends the aesthetic utopianism of both *Sun Across the Sky* and *Waterway*.

While some of Dark's earlier works show great enthusiasm for elements of commercial culture, her late 1930s fiction increasingly frames mass modernity as a threat to the organic community. In these novels, a different form of vernacular culture emerges: that of the organic national community, which Dark locates in the precolonial Aboriginal past and in settler Australians such as the fisher-folk in *Sun Across the Sky*, whom she depicts as Aboriginal cultures' natural successors. In yearning for more authentic forms of culture, Dark's work connects with the views of contemporary British critics such as F.R. Leavis, and their Australian cultural-nationalist counterparts such as Vance Palmer.[137] These critics argued that the organic society of the pre-industrial era was under significant threat because of mass consumer culture.[138] Dark similarly pits an organic, settler Australian culture against mass modernity, although while Leavis mourned for a pre-existing British folk tradition, the one envisaged by Dark does not fully exist yet but will take its bearings from Aboriginal culture. As we will see, Dark shared the tendency of many mid-century settler artists and writers to express their hopes for white Australian culture through a fascination with and appropriation of "the Aboriginal figure and her unquestioned claim to be born of the land".[139]

The final chapter examines Dark's most radical investment in the tactic of middlebrow personalism and her most extended treatment of settler and Indigenous race relations, in the first instalment of her historical trilogy, *The Timeless Land* (1941). Written during the late interwar period and published in the early years of the Second World War, this novel was remarkable in its time for depicting Australian colonial history through the imagined perspectives of a number of Aboriginal characters. Chapter 6 reads *The Timeless Land* as an example of mid-century "middlebrow orientalism" (or what I refer to as middlebrow *Aboriginalism*): the invocation of non-Western cultures to provide a reading

---

136 Carter, *Always Almost*, 197.
137 Matthews, *Dance Hall*, 19–20.
138 See, for example, F.R. Leavis and Denys Thompson, *Culture and Environment* (London: Chatto & Windus, 1933).
139 Smith, "White Aborigines", 104. See also Belinda McKay, "The Art of Living: Vance Palmer and Eleanor Dark on the Sunshine Coast", *Queensland Review* 24, no. 2 (2017): 202–14.

experience based on alterity, empathy and imagination.[140] While middlebrow studies today often frames such strategies as productive (albeit limited) engagements with cultural difference in the mid-century context, this chapter asks how Dark's middlebrow Aboriginalism was implicated in the broader desires and projects of settler nationalism and modernist primitivism.

Taken together, the chapters in this study aim to paint a picture of Dark's middlebrow modernism as a complex, often skilful and sometimes conflicted negotiation of a number of aspects of interwar culture that have often been excluded from accounts of modernism/modernity. In the conclusion of the book, I will draw together the various strands that emerge in this study and briefly consider the fiction that Dark produced after the interwar period, to reinforce how her whole body of work has the potential to defamiliarise our understandings of modernism and expand our conceptions of how modernity was experienced, translated and mediated in and across various locations in the mid-century period.

---

140 The term "middlebrow orientalism" is drawn from Christina Klein's study, *Cold War Orientalism: Asia in the Middlebrow Imagination, 1945–1961* (Berkeley: University of California Press, 2003).

1

"Whether You Deal in Books or Peanut Brittle": Writing for the Popular Market in Eleanor Dark's 1920s Magazine Fiction and *Slow Dawning* (1932)

[T]here are now two distinct worlds of literature – that is to say, there is literature and there is the Ladies' Circulating Library.
Dowell O'Reilly, "The 'Ta Ta!' Woman", 1915.[1]

"Whether you deal in books or peanut brittle I guess the principle's the same. Keep your goods pure, my lad, that's the secret – the public likes purity."
Patricia O'Rane, "The Book, the Bishop and the Ban", 1925.[2]

Eleanor Dark's first forays into fiction were in the form of short stories written for a variety of Australian periodicals. As a young, emerging writer, she was well placed to take advantage of the growing demand for women's romance and light fiction that took place in Australia as it did in England and America during the interwar period.[3] Publishers of Australian periodicals embraced this burgeoning market. In 1924, the *Bulletin* started *The Australian Woman's Mirror* in order to "make use of that large amount of purely feminine writing which ha[d] been offered".[4] Writing to Dark, the editor of the *Bulletin* asked her for stories "with a strongly sentimental note – you know the sort of thing".[5] Between 1923 and 1937, Dark published at least twenty-two stories in commercial Australian magazines,

---

1   Dowell O'Reilly, "The 'Ta Ta!' Woman", *Bulletin*, 18 November 1915, 52.
2   Patricia O'Rane, "The Book, the Bishop and the Ban", *Bulletin*, 2 July 1925, 48. (Patricia O'Rane is the pseudonym under which Eleanor Dark most commonly published her poetry and short stories in the 1920s.) All subsequent references to this story appear in parentheses in the text.
3   David Carter and Roger Osborne, *Australian Books and Authors in the American Marketplace 1840s–1940s* (Sydney: Sydney University Press, 2018), 161, 192; Sharyn Pearce, *Shameless Scribblers: Australian Women's Journalism 1880–1995* (Rockhampton: Central Queensland University Press, 1998), 70.
4   "A Talk about Ourselves", *The Australian Woman's Mirror*, 25 November 1924, quoted in Sarah Galletly, "The Spectacular Traveling Woman: Australian and Canadian Visions of Women, Modernity, and Mobility between the Wars", *Transfers: Interdisciplinary Journal of Mobility Studies* 7, no. 1 (2017): 73.

including the *Bulletin*, *The Australian Woman's Mirror*, the *Triad*, *Art in Australia* and *The Home*. Most of her stories were domestic dramas, usually involving a romantic element, although she also drew on other genres such as the detective story and science fiction.

In 1925, Dark published a story entitled "The Book, the Bishop and the Ban" in the *Bulletin* under the name of Patricia O'Rane – a pseudonym that she often used for her stories and poems, as it shared the same initials as her childhood nickname, Pixie O'Reilly. The plot focuses on Esmerelda, daughter of the "Peanut Brittle King", whose lover, Eustace, wants to publish a novel (47). Eustace has high cultural aspirations: his clothes are described in "a state of picturesque disrepair", and he twirls a cane "with an air of artistic boredom" (47). His manuscript, "The Gates of Paradise", is hopelessly Victorian, and according to Esmerelda, it "wouldn't make five pounds" (47). In order to win Eustace his fortune and thus enable the pair to marry, Esmerelda transforms the manuscript into a salacious tale of pulp romance:

> First she went right through, eliminating the "sweetheart" and "betrothed" and substituting "mistress" and "lovers". Then, where practicable, she refurnished the drawing-rooms as bedrooms or boudoirs. Wherever the hero had "gazed reverently" at the heroine he now "devoured her passionately with burning eyes" … Then she rescued the heroine from the sticky suicide to which Eustace had condemned her and married her in the last chapter, with a clergyman and a ring and everything complete.
>
> While it was in the first stages of publication she commissioned an artist to design a cover while she stood at his shoulder directing. There was a luminous cross and a devil and a man in evening clothes and a woman in none at all. It was most satisfactory. (47)

Esmerelda's scheme is successful. The novel, retitled "Desire and Damnation", is censured by the Bishop as an example of "the pernicious literature of the day" and banned in libraries, and thus becomes a bestseller (47). Esmerelda's father congratulates Eustace, saying, "Whether you deal in books or peanut brittle I guess the principle's the same. Keep your goods pure, my lad, that's the secret – the public likes purity" (48).

Although her magazine fiction was not as sensationalist as the pulp romance of "Desire and Damnation", Dark shared with Esmerelda a capacity for understanding the tastes of the popular market and producing the kind of women's romance fiction that became a "distinct market segment" in the interwar years.[6] There is a playful element to many of Dark's 1920s stories which suggests that writing

---

5   S.H. Prior to Eleanor Dark, 11 September 1924, Eleanor Dark Papers, Mitchell Library, State Library of New South Wales, MLMSS 4545, Box 15.

6   Carter and Osborne, *American Marketplace*, 161–62.

women's magazine fiction was something she could do with ease, enjoyment and some irony. She was able to exploit this new market trend to achieve publication and remuneration, and to participate in the transmission of images about what Liz Conor calls "the New Woman of modernity".[7] The women characters in Dark's magazine fiction are sophisticated and clever, dress fashionably and balance a professional life with romantic fulfilment: they are Australian iterations of the new phenomenon of the Modern Girl, "the first cultural figure to travel along the multi-directional, intersecting flows of transnational capital".[8]

One of Dark's 1920s *Bulletin* tales provided a condensed version of a novel she had been writing, which would eventually be published as *Slow Dawning* in London in 1932. Focusing on a woman doctor in a rural Australian town in the 1920s, *Slow Dawning* draws attention to the social prejudices that restricted white, professional, middle-class women's full participation in the workplace, making a case for such women to be accepted as equal citizens. In presenting Australian examples of the Modern Woman, Dark's magazine stories and first novel participated in an international, post-suffragist discourse about women's shifting social roles. The distinguishing feature of 1920s feminism was the claim of an "essential sameness" between men and women and the argument for women's equal participation in the public sphere.[9] As Maureen Honey observes of American periodicals in the 1920s, writers of women's romance were able to address the issue of women's autonomy much more directly than high culture artists.[10] In Sydney, freelance journalists such as Dulcie Deamer produced stories, poetry and articles for a variety of Australian magazines and newspapers, including *The Australian Woman's Mirror* and the *Bulletin*, commentating on and mediating the image of the Modern Woman for popular and middlebrow readers.[11] Susan Sheridan and Sharyn Pearce show that, although women's magazines such as *The Australian Woman's Mirror* mostly conveyed a sense of "cosy middle-class respectability" and emphasised the importance of marriage and motherhood, they also contributed to shifting ideas about women's social roles and provided "a meeting ground for women writers and their readers".[12] The transmission of new ideas about gender relations was one of

---

7   Liz Conor, *The Spectacular Modern Woman: Feminine Visibility in the 1920s* (Bloomington: Indiana University Press, 2004), 2.

8   Conor, *Spectacular Modern Woman*, 7, 10. See also Alys Eve Weinbaum and Modern Girl Around the World Research Group, *The Modern Girl Around the World: Consumption, Modernity, and Globalization* (Durham, NC: Duke University Press, 2008).

9   Maureen Honey, "Feminist New Woman Fiction in Periodicals of the 1920s", in *Middlebrow Moderns: Popular American Women Writers of the 1920s*, eds. Lisa Botshon and Meredith Goldsmith (Boston, MA: Northeastern University Press, 2003), 89.

10   Honey, "Feminist", 87.

11   See Pearce's chapter on Dulcie Deamer in *Shameless Scribblers*, 68–97.

12   Pearce, *Shameless Scribblers*, 70, 76; Susan Sheridan, "'Opposing All the Things They Stand For': Women Writers and the Women's Magazine", in *Republics of Letters: Literary Communities in Australia*, eds. Peter Kirkpatrick and Robert Dixon (Sydney: Sydney University Press, 2012), 195.

the ways in which mainstream magazines mediated international modernity for their readers.

In this chapter I suggest that Dark was highly successful in navigating the new market trends and cultural types that emerged in the 1920s, and that writing for the popular market provided a strong foundation for her 1930s novels. In the novels that followed *Slow Dawning*, she continued to draw on elements of popular romance, blending these with modernist narrative techniques and cultural-nationalist ideas to produce what I have called middlebrow modernism. The mass cultural forms of women's magazine fiction and popular romance were therefore essential components of her modernism – a finding that contributes to recent scholarship seeking to challenge "the myth of modernism's isolation from mass print culture".[13] Even more than this, however, Dark's 1920s fiction is interesting in its own right, and not simply as a pathway to her modernism. An examination of her light fiction shifts the narrative from a writer focused only on literary modernism or cultural nationalism, to one who engaged confidently with the transmission of new, international ideas about gender, romance, psychology, sexuality, technology and social reform. It involves trying to read interwar Australian literature apart from the structuring narratives of metropolitan forms of modernism: as David Carter puts it, "trying to avoid the critical habit of 'barracking' for modernism, as if we always already knew the historical outcomes".[14]

In the 1930s, Dark came to express anxiety about commercialised forms of publishing. In positioning herself as a serious writer, she revised her earlier playful attitude about books that were marketed "like peanut brittle", and came to disown *Slow Dawning*, instead preferring to list the more experimental *Prelude to Christopher* (1934) as her first novel. Yet *Slow Dawning* deserves further examination within Dark's oeuvre, as it provides the first extended treatment of her liberal humanism, and suggests the close connection between her early writing and New Liberal reformism. It was in her popular fiction that Dark made some of the most direct links between middlebrow personalism and the political realm.

Reframing Eleanor Dark's 1920s Fiction

Dark's writing from the 1920s is usually under-examined in studies of her work. Her 1920s fiction is scattered and often difficult to locate. Dark's magazine stories were published under a variety of pseudonyms, and most have never been republished. *Slow Dawning* received very little recognition at the time of its

---

13   Alice Wood, "Modernism and the Middlebrow in British Women's Magazines", in *Middlebrow and Gender, 1890–1945*, eds. Christoph Ehland and Cornelia Wächter (Leiden; Boston: Brill Rodopi, 2016), 58.

14   David Carter, *Always Almost Modern: Australian Print Cultures and Modernity* (North Melbourne: Australian Scholarly, 2013), 54.

publication and remains difficult to obtain, and the other novel that Dark wrote in the 1920s, "Pilgrimage", has never been published. Where her magazine stories have been considered, it is usually as an apprenticeship to her novels, reflecting a devaluing of popular forms in Australian literary studies. A. Grove Day, for instance, observes that Dark's stories "[a]ll show a certain smooth popular appeal, verging on slickness".[15] Day concludes that short story writing was not Dark's proper medium and that "[h]er greatest art required the broad canvas of the novel".[16] In her biography of Dark, Marivic Wyndham similarly approaches magazine writing as "the playground of the apprentice, the laboratory of the future writer, the seedbed of her serious literature", although she acknowledges that Dark's stories had "a free uncontrived quality that disappeared with the 1930s and her embrace of serious writing".[17]

There are a number of important paradigmatic shifts that enable this chapter's examination of Dark's 1920s fiction. One is the challenge from 1980s and 1990s Australian feminist scholars to reconsider romance fiction as a serious literary form that was capable not only of replicating the conventions of the genre, but also of manipulating, negotiating and subverting these norms. Susan Sheridan, for example, along with other Australian feminist scholars, challenges traditional and gendered understandings of late nineteenth and early twentieth-century romance forms as formulaic, non-experimental and politically conservative, and shows that, far from being homogenous, Australian romance fiction reflects the same diversity found in other forms of Australian writing. Key Australian women writers of the 1890s such as Rosa Praed, Ada Cambridge and Catherine Martin, and their successors Barbara Baynton and Miles Franklin, were able to work both within and against the conventions of the romance fiction genre to challenge and satisfy the expectations of their readers.[18]

Dark's interwar writing was part of a subsequent period of romance fiction – that of the 1920s and 1930s. Early critics of her work considered the influence of the romance form on her writing to be a problem. M. Barnard Eldershaw, writing

---

15   A. Grove Day, *Eleanor Dark* (Boston: Twayne, 1976), 28.
16   Grove Day, *Eleanor Dark*, 33.
17   Marivic Wyndham, *"A World-Proof Life": Eleanor Dark, A Writer in Her Times 1901–1985* (Sydney: UTS ePress, 2007), 65, 66.
18   For key work on this topic, see Susan Sheridan, *Along the Faultlines: Sex, Race and Nation in Australian Women's Writing, 1880s–1930s* (St. Leonards, NSW: Allen & Unwin, 1995); "'Temper Romantic; Bias Offensively Feminine': Australian Women Writers and Literary Nationalism", *Kunapipi* 7, no. 2–3 (1985): 49–58; Fiona Giles, "Romance: An Embarrassing Subject", in *The Penguin New Literary History of Australia*, ed. Laurie Hergenhan (Ringwood, Vic.: Penguin Books, 1988), 223–37; Juliet Flesch, *From Australia with Love: A History of Modern Australian Popular Romance Novels* (Fremantle, WA: Fremantle Arts Centre, 2004); Robert Dixon, *Writing the Colonial Adventure: Race, Gender, and Nation in Anglo-Australian Popular Fiction, 1875–1914* (Cambridge: Cambridge University Press, 1995); Susan Lever, *Real Relations: The Feminist Politics of Form in Australian Fiction* (Rushcutters Bay, NSW: Halstead Press, 2000); Tanya Dalziell, *Settler Romances and the Australian Girl* (Crawley, WA: University of Western Australia Press, 2004).

about Dark's first three novels in *Essays in Australian Fiction* (1938), noted her reliance on "the romantic tradition", arguing that an "unwilling or thinly disguised romanticism" underpinned *Slow Dawning*, *Prelude to Christopher* and *Return to Coolami* (1936), and that each novel contained melodramatic plots that depended on "[c]oincidence and accident".[19] The terms "romantic" and "sentimental" would continue to feature in postwar studies of Dark's fiction, used interchangeably to describe the prevalence of marriage plotlines and happy endings, and her attitude towards various social issues. H.M. Green called Dark "an intellectual romantic", writing, "[h]er subject is always love, as complicated and thwarted by unhappy marriage, and since she finds it difficult to leave any of her men and women permanently unhappy, there is always a risk of an inartistic if sentimentally satisfactory ending".[20] Like Barnard Eldershaw, Green drew attention to the formulaic and constructed nature of Dark's plots, which frequently involved a love triangle and "a final release of stresses by the convenient removal of the undesired partner or partners".[21] We can see in these critiques the inherently gendered nature of understandings of popular culture, with the romance form linked to much that "woman" stands for in Western culture: emotion, sentiment and consumer culture.[22]

This chapter draws on late twentieth-century feminist scholarship but also extends it in some important ways. Contributing to the transnational turn in literary and cultural studies, it illuminates how an Australian writer engaged with international market trends and new cultural types, and adds to a growing focus on Australian periodicals in recent assessments of Australian interwar modernity.[23] It also gives greater attention to Dark's liberal humanist engagement, seeking to move beyond the post-1980s dismissal of liberal humanism as an intrinsically conservative and homogenous ideology.[24] Drusilla Modjeska was one of the first to recognise the significance of Dark's early writing, praising *Slow Dawning* as Dark's "most explicit feminist statement" in *Exiles at Home: Australian Women Writers 1925–1945* (1981).[25] Yet while Modjeska celebrated the feminism of *Slow Dawning*, she also felt that Dark's dependence on romantic and humanist ideas such as "Love

---

19 M. Barnard Eldershaw, *Essays in Australian Fiction* (Freeport, NY: Books for Libraries Press, [1938] 1970), 184, 188–90.

20 H.M. Green, *A History of Australian Literature, Pure and Applied: A Critical Review of all Forms of Literature Produced in Australia from the First Books Published After the Arrival of the First Fleet Until 1950, with Short Accounts of Later Publications Up to 1960* (Sydney: Angus & Robertson, 1961), 1078.

21 Green, *History*, 1078.

22 Andreas Huyssen, *After the Great Divide: Modernism, Mass Culture, Postmodernism* (Bloomington: Indiana University Press, 1986), 46–47. Susan Sheridan makes this point in relation to Australian women's romance writing of the 1890s in her essay "Temper Romantic".

23 See, for example, Victoria Kuttainen, Susann Liebich and Sarah Galletly, *Transported Imagination: Australian Interwar Magazines and the Geographical Imaginaries of Colonial Modernity* (Amherst, NY: Cambria Press, 2018).

24 Andy Mousley, *Re-humanising Shakespeare* (Edinburgh: Edinburgh University Press, 2007), 13–14. See also Emily Apter, "Saidian Humanism", *Boundary 2* 31, no. 2 (2004): 35–53.

will find a way" made the novel "conventional" and reflective of "the feminism of a middle-class, educated woman".[26] According to Modjeska's feminist-Marxist methodology, Dark's liberal humanism was implicated in significant gender, class and racial disenfranchisements: it was "incapable of a political analysis that could deal successfully with both fascism and women's oppression".[27] Marivic Wyndham's biography offers a similar sense of humanism as an intrinsically conservative and homogenous ideology.[28] This chapter acknowledges some of these limitations but also explores the potential of Dark's progressive liberal humanism, examining her early fiction as a creative engagement with a particular moment in the history of international liberal thinking. I have included *Slow Dawning* in this discussion because, although the novel was not published until 1932, Dark wrote it in the early 1920s, and as such it belongs to an earlier period of her writing. In particular, *Slow Dawning* differs from Dark's subsequent novels in the extent to which it expresses confidence in the new social role of the professional, middle-class technical expert, and shows a greater readiness to link individual self-development to larger forms of social progress. This engagement with New Liberalism is another and yet significantly under-examined way in which Dark contributed to the transmission of international ideas.

Technological Modernity

A detailed examination of all of Dark's magazine fiction is beyond the scope of this chapter; however, I will discuss selected stories to show how Dark represented some of the key indexes of the Australian modern. One of these is travel: Australian magazines frequently promoted both domestic and international forms of travel as a means by which readers could appear modern and cosmopolitan.[29] Only a few of Dark's magazine tales deal directly with international travel. "How Uncle Aubrey Went to London", published in the *Bulletin* in 1928, is recounted from a point in the future when international transportation is conducted via wireless wavelengths. The narrator recalls a time "before the traveller by wireless was received in London by the present smooth and gradual process and re-created in his entirety" to when he was "reassembled in bits".[30] In these early days, sometime

---

25   Drusilla Modjeska, *Exiles at Home: Australian Women Writers 1925–1945* (Sydney: Sirius Books, 1981), 215.

26   Modjeska, *Exiles at Home*, 215–17.

27   Modjeska, *Exiles at Home*, 13.

28   Wyndham, *"A World-Proof Life"*, 5.

29   Kuttainen, Liebich and Galletly, *Transported Imagination*, 3–4. See also Victoria Kuttainen and Sarah Galletly, "Making Friends of the Nations: Australian Interwar Magazines and Middlebrow Orientalism in the Pacific", *Journeys: The International Journal of Travel and Travel Writing* 17, no. 2 (2016): 23–48.

30   Patricia O'Rane, "How Uncle Aubrey Went to London", *Bulletin*, 30 May 1928, 57. All subsequent references to this story appear in parentheses in the text.

after "the Smith brothers flew from England to Australia in the weird thing that is now in the Museum", wireless travel was liable to involve accidents (57). This is the case for Uncle Aubrey, who attempts to travel via wireless despite fears that it was "wrong … to transmute one's human flesh and blood into wavelengths" (57). His fears are confirmed when he is transported from Australia to London in four hours but reassembled with another man's leg.

"How Uncle Aubrey Went to London" is comical in nature, and interesting in the way that it presents technology as a means of overcoming the geographical distance and time lag between Australia and England. It is written for readers who might find the idea of travelling via wireless waves amusing, but who would nonetheless identify with the desire to get from Australia to London as quickly and conveniently as possible. It also shows how, even as she embraced the new market opportunities that came with modernity, Dark often expressed ambivalence about the rapid forms of change that came with it. The story concludes with Aubrey vowing to return to Australia by the slower but safer route of aeroplane travel. Dark's story highlights how anti-modern attitudes could operate as one feature of the modern.

This combination of fascination with and resistance to the modern is something that we will see throughout Dark's interwar writing. She associated the rapid forms of change in the 1920s and 1930s with both opportunity and loss. Dark wrote in an unpublished note about the shrinking of time and space produced through air travel: "When I was seventeen and saw Kingsford Smith arriving in Sydney after the first flight from England to Australia I felt that nations could never again be separate as they had been before, and this feeling became a conviction as the years passed."[31] In this recollection, Dark appears to have confused Charles Kingsford Smith (who in 1928 made the first transpacific flight from the United States to Australia) with the Smith brothers, who landed in Sydney in February 1920 after winning the competition sponsored by the Australian government to inspire the first flight from Britain to Australia within the temporal limit of thirty days (Ross and Keith Smith accomplished it in twenty-eight days). Nonetheless, in connecting aviation to speed and the eradication of distance, Dark's comment draws attention to the radical shifts in understandings of time and space that occurred in the early twentieth century.[32] Dark was somewhat cautious about the compression of time and conquering of space brought about by international travel. While she was interested in cosmopolitan ways of thinking, she also warned against the potential of technological development to disconnect humans from their local environment and from one another. Her ambivalence about so-called progress grew

31   Eleanor Dark, unpublished note, quoted in Susan Carson, "Paris and Beyond: The Transnational/National in the Writing of Christina Stead and Eleanor Dark", in *Transnational Ties: Australian Lives in the World*, eds. Desley Deacon, Penny Russell and Angela Woollacott (Acton, ACT: ANU Press, 2008), 236.

32   See Stephen Kern, *The Culture of Time and Space 1880–1918* (Cambridge, MA: Harvard University Press, 1983).

over time, so that in 1959 she wrote in the voice of small-scale farmers poised precariously on the brink of change, "We are not entirely convinced that speed and convenience add up to civilisation … to become civilised, one must, first of all, remain human. And being human … has at least something to do with treading on earth, getting sweaty, seeing the sun rise, making things grow, having animals around, … taking one's time, getting on with one's neighbours."[33] If the 1920s marked the height of Dark's embrace of cosmopolitan modernity, in contrast to what often appears to be a retreat from it in the postwar climate of the 1950s, even these early works contain elements of scepticism about modernity's promises.

Dark conveys a similar sense of ambivalence about mass forms of technological change in her unpublished novel "Pilgrimage". She began writing this semi-autobiographical novel in January 1921, a year before her marriage to Eric Dark, and finished it in the late 1920s.[34] The events that occur to the central character, Anne Heritage, closely parallel those of Dark's early life. After attending a private school named "Clarendon", which is similar to Dark's Sydney college, Redlands, Anne (like Dark) finds that she is unable to attend university. Instead, she goes to Business College where she trains to be a secretary, as did Dark. There is a sense of class distinction in Anne's response to her classmates: she describes them as "frowsy-haired, under-washed, over-powdered" and "the scrapings of the city".[35] Dark links these women with technological modernity through the act of typing. In an arresting passage, Anne imagines her fellow typists transformed into "automata" through repetitive typing, their hands moving "exactly like the movement of a well-oiled bit of machinery" (155). As she learns to type, Anne sees herself "being made into a machine, like all the other machines – sitting there blank and stupid, while her fingers worked and her brain atrophied" (155–56). "Pilgrimage" thus registers a negative response to technological modernity at a specific moment in time, when women were first entering the metropolitan, industrial scene and creating new female types of the Office Girl and the Business Girl – types which Dark describes negatively as a mixture of "high heels, imitation silk stockings, lip-stick, powder, superciliousness" (152).[36] Intriguingly, Dark provides a relatively early Australian example of what Jon Cockburn calls the "mechanical woman".[37] A number of international films and advertisements in the 1920s and 1930s linked women to technological modernity through "the analogy of the female body as machine".[38] As in her magazine stories, in "Pilgrimage" Dark is fascinated with the

---

33   Eleanor Dark, *Lantana Lane* (London: Collins, 1959), 252.
34   Helen O'Reilly, "Time and Memory in the Novels of Eleanor Dark" (PhD thesis, University of New South Wales, 2009), 51.
35   Eleanor Dark, "Pilgrimage", Eleanor Dark Collection, Varuna, the National Writers' House, 153. All subsequent references are to this edition and appear in parentheses in the text.
36   Conor, *Spectacular Modern Woman*, 47–76. I discuss this passage from "Pilgrimage" in further detail in Melinda J. Cooper, "'Being Made into a Machine': An Extract from Eleanor Dark's Unpublished Novel 'Pilgrimage'", *Hecate* 43, no. 1–2 (2017): 95–104.
37   See Jon Cockburn, "Olivetti and the Missing Third: Fashion, Working Women and Images of the Mechanical-flâneuse in the 1920s and 1930s", *Fashion Theory* 19, no. 5 (2015): 637–86.

process of mechanisation and yet also presents it as one of dehumanisation and alienation.

The Modern Woman

Dark's magazine fiction often engaged with the international image of the clever and sophisticated Modern Woman, presenting her in a positive light to Australian readers and at times moderating what she perceived as the excesses of this type. As Jill Julius Matthews shows, in the interwar period "the modern girl … the flapper, was both the subject and the metaphor at the heart of the international discourse of modernity": she was "simultaneously the sign of all that was wrong with the direction society was taking and the promise of a brave new world".[39] Esmerelda is presented as a positive embodiment of the Modern Woman in "The Book, the Bishop and the Ban". The story recognises the role of religious institutions in censorship debates, and makes clear the link between explicit descriptions of sexuality and the types of cultural products that were often banned in Australia;[40] yet Esmerelda adeptly manages and even manipulates her lover, her father, the Bishop and the reading public to bring about the desired result of both fortune and marriage. She possesses the benefits of a "costly education" but also the business acumen of her father (47). Esmerelda is one of a series of capable Modern Girls that appeared across the world in mass forms of modern culture: in advertisements, on the screen and radio, and in magazine stories and novels. White Australian women achieved suffrage in 1902, only a year after Dark was born, and her stories assume the contemporaneity of white Australian women with their sisters across the English-speaking world.

In a story entitled "Benevolence: The Story of a Hypocrite", published in the *Triad* in 1926, Dark offers another portrait of an empowered and subversive female character.[41] Jean McNeil, a "modern, efficient secretary" at the "Benevolent Home for Fallen Women", forms an impassioned liaison with her boss, Mr Massingham (the "hypocrite" of the story's subtitle), and subsequently falls pregnant.[42] Rather than succumb to the fate of being labelled a "fallen woman", Jean procures an illegal abortion through the help of Mr Massingham's wife, and is reinstated to her

---

38   Cockburn, "Olivetti", 558, 663; Conor, *Spectacular Modern Woman*, 68.
39   Jill Julius Matthews, *Dance Hall and Picture Palace: Sydney's Romance with Modernity* (Sydney: Currency Press, 2005), 19.
40   See Nicole Moore, *The Censor's Library: Uncovering the Lost History of Australia's Banned Books* (St. Lucia: University of Queensland Press, 2012).
41   "Benevolence" is one of the few of Dark's stories to receive critical attention in recent decades, in Nicole Moore, "The Rational Natural: Conflicts of the Modern in Eleanor Dark", *Hecate* 27, no. 1 (2001): 19–31.
42   Patricia O'Rane, "Benevolence: The Story of a Hypocrite", *Triad*, 1 July 1926, 4. All subsequent references to this story appear in parentheses in the text.

position as secretary. There, she colludes with the cleaning girl, Jessie, also a "fallen woman", to turn Mr Massingham's life into a living "Hell":

> It was strange but undeniable, that his disgrace lay not in the fact that he had seduced an ignorant girl, but in that she had vanquished him by refusing to "fall". By all the laws of the game she should have been nursing an illegitimate child in an unfriendly world. But she had tricked him – she sat at her flower-scented desk in the sunlit office, she earned a larger salary, and the dim, cynical smile with which she watched the world was armour for her – of his forging. (6)

In contrast to "Pilgrimage", in this story the female typist is associated with rational management, control and a subversive form of female sexual power. In the final scene, Jean employs her shorthand skills to take minutes for a meeting of the Home's directors, and taunts Mr Massingham by looking at him directly when he says the word "benevolence" (6). The Modern Woman triumphs in this scene, wielding her shorthand as a symbol of the rational management Jean employed in organising a successful abortion. Nicole Moore relates this story to "an Australian feminine modernism" which involved "defending women's investment and involvement in society at that instant when the new woman becomes the object of concern for science".[43] As Moore points out, "Benevolence" was published in the same issue of the *Triad* in which appeared the beginning of a debate between male medical correspondents about birth control, so that Dark's depiction of a woman's competent management of an unwanted pregnancy represents a form of intervention in this debate.[44]

The women who featured in Dark's magazine fiction offered readers a source of entertainment but also "a covert education" in modern culture and behaviour: a combination of enjoyment and education that was often associated with the middlebrow.[45] Dark often published her stories in the quality culture and leisure magazines which appealed to the desires of middle-class readers for social mobility, such as *Art in Australia* and *The Home*. In "The Desire of the Moth", published in *Art in Australia* in 1924 under the pseudonym of "Henry Head", Dark provides a central female character, Mrs Brand, who reads Russian and French novels, expresses interest in psychology, Theosophy and sexology, has a copy of *The Psychology of Sex* on open display in her living room and hosts elegant dinner parties. As a quality magazine, *Art in Australia* was pitched at a modern audience who "wanted contemporary art in their homes – and modern advertising in their magazines".[46] Dark's story seems designed to appeal to the aspirational tastes of these readers: it emphasises the sophisticated décor of Mrs Brand's house,

---

43   Moore, "Rational Natural", 26.
44   Moore, "Rational Natural", 24.
45   Faye Hammill and Michelle Smith, *Magazines, Travel, and Middlebrow Culture: Canadian Periodicals in English and French, 1925–1960* (Liverpool: Liverpool University Press, 2015), 11.
46   Carter, *Always Almost*, 62.

describing a dining table artistically decorated with "reflections of silver and glass in its polished wood", "three shallow, vivid finger-bowls", and "dark burning-red roses in the centre".[47] The fact that Mrs Brand is Australian and that the narrative takes place in Australia seems to be of little matter to Dark's story; it is assumed that the central character shares with readers an interest in international literature and modern decorating tastes.

A number of Dark's contemporaries also wrote for similar magazines and provided other Australian examples of the Modern Woman, contributing to what Sarah Galletly describes as the international fascination with this cultural type in the transnational print marketplace of the interwar years.[48] The short stories that Marjorie Barnard wrote for *The Home* and the *Bulletin* frequently drew attention to the details of women's clothing and leisure activities, depicting women in such modern undertakings as buying a hat, getting a permanent wave at a hairdresser or reading a copy of *Vogue* magazine.[49] The Modern Woman also occurred in Katharine Susannah Prichard's pastoral romance novel *Coonardoo* (1929), which first appeared in serialised form in the *Bulletin* in 1928 and was subsequently published in London and New York. Hugh Watt's daughter Phyllis arrives at the remote station of Wytaliba in the north west of Western Australia displaying all the cultural symbols of the flapper: she is driving a car, reveals "naked-looking silken-clad legs", wears a "short frock", has hair "cut like a boy's", smokes a cigarette, and speaks in animated slang, calling her father a "parent bird".[50] Prichard's internationally published novel shows how Australian iterations of the cultural type of the Modern Girl travelled beyond national borders but also how such representations were inflected through the desires and complexities of settler culture. Prichard contrasts Phyllis' modern forms of speech and behaviour with those of the central Aboriginal character, Coonardoo, who is mostly portrayed as silent and obedient to Phyllis' instructions. Compared to Phyllis, Coonardoo is represented as "[s]omething primitive, fundamental, nearer … to the source of things".[51] As in Dark's stories, in Prichard's novel the cultural type of the Modern Girl is reserved for white and mostly middle-class women.[52]

---

47 "Henry Head", "The Desire of the Moth", *Art in Australia*, no. 10, December 1924, n.p.
48 Galletly, "Spectacular Traveling Woman", 73. For a recent discussion of the figure of the Modern Girl in Dymphna Cusack's interwar novel, *Jungfrau* (1936), see Jilly Lippmann and Victoria Kuttainen, "The Troublesome Modern Girl: *Jungfrau*, National Literature, and the Vexations of Transnational Modernity", *The Space Between* 15 (2019): 1.
49 See, for example, "Beauty is Strength" and "The Hat" in Marjorie Barnard, *The Persimmon Tree and Other Stories* (Sydney: Clarendon Publishing Co., 1943), 26–36, 63–65.
50 Katharine Susannah Prichard, *Coonardoo* (Sydney: HarperCollins, [1929] 2013), 184.
51 Prichard, *Coonardoo*, 109.
52 Susan Lever suggests that Phyllis' stylised behaviour and speech could also highlight a broader point in Prichard's novel about the "failure of everyday speech to express the emotional lives and understandings of the characters". Prichard conveys this idea most explicitly through the characterisation of Coonardoo, whose subjectivity involves language and experiences that are disconcerting to and unknown by non-Indigenous readers. In proposing this, Lever suggests that Prichard's novel "declares its awareness that its literary forms are inadequate to the

Through her magazine fiction, Dark also contributed to regulating and curtailing the freedoms of the Modern Woman. In another story featuring the same character of Mrs Brand, published in the *Bulletin* in 1925, the reader is led to question the morality of the central character's tactics of psychologically manipulating her acquaintances through â€œmental vivisection".[53] The tale raises the question as to whether Mrs Brand is somewhat *too* modern in her grasp of psychology. She receives her comeuppance when she meets Miss Wyndham, an unmarried science teacher. Miss Wyndham suggests that children are more important than a career, commenting, "It's a dreadful thing for an intelligent and emancipated woman of the twentieth century to say, but does a woman really want freedom?" (44). It is a question calculated to draw attention to Mrs Brand's childlessness. Despite all her accomplishments – a "beautiful home … husband … all these wonderful books and pictures" – Mrs Brand feels "shame that anyone should recognise the triumphant womanhood which shone from her as incomplete" (44). The story concludes with Miss Wyndham revealing herself as the former lover of Mrs Brand's husband and mother of his love-child – a revelation that reinforces the importance of motherhood as women's highest achievement. The reader is positioned to feel glad that Mrs Brand is left humbled by her inability to produce children. Such conservative attitudes about women's roles also appeared in the articles produced by Dulcie Deamer for *The Australian Woman's Mirror*, which frequently suggested that women's liberation had progressed too far.[54] Narratives involving the Modern Woman could be used for a wide variety of purposes, then: to normalise shifting social expectations about women's roles; to facilitate the social aspirations of white, middle-class readers; or to voice resistance to and control the rate of modern change.

"The Ladies' Circulating Library": Eleanor Dark and Her Father

Dark participated in 1920s mass culture not only through her magazine fiction, but also because she herself was marketed as an Australian example of the Modern Woman. In 1928, Zora Cross published a profile piece on "Patricia O'Rane" in *The Australian Woman's Mirror*, in which she presents Dark as a prototype of the "true writing woman", capable of balancing the demands of being a doctor's wife with a freelance writing career (Fig. 1.1):

---

experience of its subject". Perhaps settler writers could use images of the Modern Woman in ways that challenged aspects of settler-colonial modernity, albeit in limited ways. See Lever, *Real Relations*, 61–62.

53   Patricia O'Rane, "Wheels", *Bulletin*, 12 December 1925, 44. All subsequent references to this story appear in parentheses in the text.

54   Pearce, *Shameless Scribblers*, 77.

Figure 1.1 Bernice May [Zora Cross]. "Patricia O'Rane". *The Australian Woman's Mirror* 4, no. 44 (25 September 1928), 8.

I naturally asked her why she did not use the name of O'Reilly when writing, and she replied, woman-like, that she wanted to arrive, if she ever did arrive, off her own bat, so to speak, and not because she was a well-known writer's daughter. This spirit is very marked among women writers, I find. Innate honesty and a desire to do her own work are born in the true writing woman.[55]

---

55 Bernice May [Zora Cross], "Patricia O'Rane", *The Australian Woman's Mirror* 4, no. 44 (25 September 1928), 8.

As Sharyn Pearce notes of *The Australian Woman's Mirror*, while this magazine mostly emphasised women's traditional social roles, it did show "some interest in the changing image of Australian women" in the interwar period.[56] The magazine often featured articles about significant professional women in fields such as law, aviation, tourism and mechanics. In line with this, Dark is presented here as a model for aspiring women writers, with Cross drawing attention to her independent spirit and "[i]nnate honesty". In this sense, it was not only Dark's fiction that capitalised on readers' enthusiasm for the Modern Woman, but she herself was also offered as a real-life example. It is a point that could be interpreted negatively, as evidence of the over-determined roles available to women in the 1920s, or positively. Like Dulcie Deamer, who styled herself as the "Queen of Bohemia", or Irene Castle, the American ballroom dancer who became a cinema sensation and capitalised on her celebrity by endorsing a range of dance-related, mass-produced products such as records and dancing shoes, Dark was involved in selling "the desire and the possibility of being modern".[57]

Cross' profile piece also shows how, in these early representations of Dark as an author, she was often compared to and contrasted with her father, Dowell O'Reilly. O'Reilly died in 1923, one year after Eleanor and Eric married, and the same year in which Dark published her first short story in the *Bulletin*. Cross suggests that Dark was following in the footsteps of her father, who, as a poet and short story writer, "shall be forever remembered while Australian women live … for his divine understanding of our sex" in *Tears and Triumph* (1913), which Cross believes "gets under the skin of women as do few other studies of the sex".[58] The relationship between Dark's work and that of her father has been the focus of some debate, and is important here in light of Dark's representation of the Modern Woman.

Dowell O'Reilly had strong links to the women's suffrage movement: he was a friend of Rose Scott and Mary Gilmore, and introduced the first bill for the extension of the franchise to (non-Indigenous) women in September 1894 as a member of the New South Wales Legislative Assembly. Yet, like other middle-class intellectuals of his generation, including Bernard O'Dowd, O'Reilly became disenchanted with the women's movement after women's suffrage had been achieved, and went on to express many ideas that appear contrary to it.[59] In his writings, O'Reilly elevated motherhood to a high status, and suggested that women were incapable of reconciling intellectual work with their essential purpose as mothers. In a piece called "The 'Ta Ta!' Woman" published in the *Bulletin* in 1915, he wrote:

---

56   Pearce, *Shameless Scribblers*, 70.
57   Matthews, *Dance Hall*, 95–99.
58   May [Cross], "Patricia O'Rane", 8.
59   Frank Bongiorno, "'Every Woman a Mother': Radical Intellectuals, Sex Reform and the 'Woman Question' in Australia, 1890–1918", *Hecate* 27, no. 1 (2001): 45.

Are man and woman equal? Equal in sex? – in intellect? … their intellects differ as widely as their sexes … Immutable law has set aside woman for childbirth and man for thought-birth, and while woman loves children there can never be any "great woman question". While woman loves children, she may be trusted to deal with the "militant feminist" – that vile abortionist who secretly murders the dream-child that stirs in every virgin's heart.[60]

As this passage shows, O'Reilly was particularly vitriolic when writing about the suffragette or "Intellectual Woman" – "those women, who still retain, in a more or less atrophied form, the power to procreate ideas, as well as to receive them".[61] Although he was friends with many politically and intellectually engaged women, he argued that motherhood had given Intellectual Woman "notice to quit".[62] O'Reilly described the militancy of the suffragette as "the frenzy of the wounded insect that stings itself to death", asking:

[W]hat are they? A vanishing eddy of froth. Life ranks them with its picture-shows and other minor amusements. They don't matter. Woman will get her vote, of course, in England as elsewhere. Her vote! All this pother for a Vote! Do you seriously think that is the goal of these refined, brutal, educated, criminal, intellectual, insane women?[63]

Given O'Reilly's idiosyncratic, conflicting views, it is easy to see why Dark's work has been read, on the one hand, as a product of "an old internalized debate with her father" about the ability of women "to reconcile love and work, motherhood and creative work", and, on the other, as an extension of some of the ideas that preoccupied O'Reilly and his generation of social progressives.[64] Both are true. Certainly, the idea that women were capable of balancing a professional life with marriage and children is a strong theme across Dark's fiction, suggesting that she disagreed with her father on this important point.

The genre of women's romance provided Dark with the ready-made cultural type of the Modern Woman, through whom she could challenge some of O'Reilly's views. Light romantic fiction of the interwar period often invited the reader to identify with an unconventional heroine while still providing a romantic resolution that would satisfy popular tastes.[65] Much of Dark's magazine fiction drew on the

---

60   O'Reilly, "'Ta Ta!'", 52.
61   Dowell O'Reilly to Bernard O'Dowd, 5 October 1912, quoted in Bongiorno, "'Every Woman a Mother'", 53.
62   Dowell O'Reilly to Bernard O'Dowd, 5 October 1912, quoted in Bongiorno, "'Every Woman a Mother'", 53.
63   Dowell O'Reilly to Lou Miles, 30 November 1913, in *Dowell O'Reilly: From His Letters*, ed. Marie O'Reilly (London: Simpkin, Marshall, Hamilton, Kent and Co., 1927), 5.
64   Barbara Brooks, "Rereading *Prelude to Christopher*", in Eleanor Dark, *Prelude to Christopher* (Rushcutters Bay, NSW: Halstead Press, [1934] 1999), 187; Bongiorno, "'Every Woman a Mother'", 52.

common trope of a New Woman seeking to reconcile her career aspirations with her emotional life. In 1926, she published a short story called "Wind" in the *Bulletin*, based on a condensed version of *Slow Dawning*. "Wind" focuses on a woman doctor, Valerie Spencer, who displays the characteristics of the Modern Woman: she dresses beautifully, drives a car, has a university education and a profession, reads "portly medical books" and "slender French novels", has a "scientific brain" and displays "a very feminine mixture of logic and heart".[66] Valerie's capable nature forces her former lover, Norman, to grapple with the idea of equality between the sexes: "He had heard much of the 'equality' of men and women, but until now he had never felt it. This girl was not afraid of what she saw in his face; she was not shocked; she was not even shy" (48). When Valerie is driven out of her hometown by a malicious rumour, Dark concludes the story by contrasting Valerie's modern views about women with the outdated ones of her colleague, Dr McNab:

> "I'm going to be a practical demonstration of my own pet theory," she said. "A woman can't start off scratch with the men. Her sex hangs around her neck like a mill-stone. But it's my idea that even with such a handicap we can make a dead-heat of it."
>
> As she walked down the path to the gate the eternal masculine soliloquised, shaking its white head. "She should marry, an' hae bairns," it said. (48)

Although this ending leaves the issue unresolved, the way in which the story aligns the reader with Valerie's perspective suggests that Dark was encouraging her Bulletin readers similarly to reject Dr McNab's perspective as unmodern. Was she thinking of her father when she wrote of the tendency of the "eternal masculine" to dismiss women's place in the professional world?

It is difficult to reconcile Dark's positive comments about her father with the clear disparity that must have occurred between some of their views. Dark said that O'Reilly encouraged her writing, yet he was scathing about the development of women's fiction as a distinct market category. In 1915 he wrote:

> Yesterday – in the history of mankind – she [Woman] learned to read, and was greatly annoyed to find that man had written nothing worth reading … she instantly brought forth her own literature-while-you-wait. As she had neither time for thought, nor thought for time, she wrote it by "intuition".
>
> So there are now two distinct worlds of literature – that is to say, there is literature and there is the Ladies' Circulating Library. The former reeks of tobacco

---

65   Carter and Osborne, *American Marketplace*, 162; Janice Radway, "The Utopian Impulse in Popular Literature: Gothic Romances and 'Feminist' Protest," *American Quarterly* 33, no. 2 (1981): 143.

66   Patricia O'Rane, "Wind", *Bulletin*, 21 January 1926, 47, 48. All other references to this story appear in parentheses in the text.

and thought; the latter exhales a subtle perfume of bad grammar and putrid construction … Ten to one the shopgirl who takes your seat in the morning tram without saying "Thank you" will instantly open a book. You think she is reading? Not at all. Romance – which is her pretty word for sex – has swallowed her up.[67]

In this passage, popular fiction is clearly gendered as feminine, and modern romance linked with frivolity and sex, whereas literature is associated with serious, masculine qualities (tobacco and thought). In Britain, male cultural elites similarly expressed misogynistic attitudes towards the popular woman writer and her female readers in the early part of the twentieth century.[68] O'Reilly also conveys a sense of class prejudice in focusing his critique on a "shopgirl" who is reading romance narratives on the tram. If Dark showed a similar sense of elitism in her satirical treatment of popular romance as a commodified product likened to "peanut brittle", then she differed from her father in giving comic treatment to masculine high culture as well. In "The Book, the Bishop and the Ban", she holds herself apart from *both* lowbrow romance *and* highbrow literature (by which she means sentimental and Victorian rather than modernist), while also showing a willingness to exploit the conventions of the former to achieve publication. There is some irony that, ten years after O'Reilly wrote the above critique, his daughter would publish a subversive tale about women exploiting a sexualised form of pulp fiction in the same magazine in which he denigrated such writing and reading formations.

The question of Dark's relationship with her father has arisen in recent years because of revelations of a feud that divided her extended family and which centred on O'Reilly's treatment of Dark's mother, Eleanor Grace O'Reilly (nee McCulloch), who died in Callan Park Hospital for the Insane in 1914.[69] When O'Reilly sought to remarry three years after his first wife's death, his sister Marion Piddington wrote to the prospective bride, Marie ("Mollie") Miles, warning her about his real character. In the heated correspondence that followed, Piddington claimed that her brother had sexually abused his first wife, and that this abuse, as well as his many extra-marital affairs, had contributed to Dark's mother's psychological breakdown and death. Piddington described O'Reilly as "vile to a woman's body" and pointed out the disparity between his views about and his actual treatment of women, writing to him, "[y]ou transmute the violence of private lust into the energy of public inculcation to mankind to worship the woman and mother".[70] O'Reilly rejected his sister's allegations, saying that her "broodings on sex had confounded her mind" – a reference to her interest in eugenics and work on sex education and birth control.[71] He threatened to send the correspondence to the

---

67   O'Reilly, "'Ta Ta!'", 52.
68   Paul Delaney, *Literature, Money and the Market: From Trollope to Amis* (Basingstoke: Palgrave, 2002), 150.
69   The details of this feud are outlined in O'Reilly, "Time and Memory", 9–19.
70   Marion Piddington to Dowell O'Reilly, 2 June 1917, quoted in O'Reilly, "Time and Memory", 17.
71   Dowell O'Reilly to Marion Piddington, 4 June 1917, quoted in O'Reilly, "Time and Memory", 13.

federal government, in a move that would have threatened the distinguished legal and political career of Marion's husband, Albert Bathurst ("Bert") Piddington, who had served on the High Court of Australia. Mollie also rejected the allegations, and she and O'Reilly were married that year.[72]

This dispute caused a permanent rift between O'Reilly's and Piddington's respective families; however, Dark never spoke publicly about it, even though the letters that contained the charges were in her possession at one point. She appears to have wanted to protect her father's pro-woman legacy. Dark's silence about her family history has prompted scholars to consider the ways in which her novels engaged with aspects of her private life. In particular, the fate of her mother has been linked to *Prelude to Christopher*, which focuses on the issue of hereditary insanity. Dark was close to her stepmother, and corresponded with her regularly until Mollie's suicide in 1948. Dark said little about her parents' marriage, although in "Pilgrimage", which she was working on at the time of her father's death, she wrote compassionately about the experience of a young child living with parents who create "an atmosphere of discord, of strain, of tortured and incomprehensible emotionalism" (25).

Whether it was something that she acknowledged or not, Dark's 1920s short stories present images of women that frequently contest the ideas articulated by her father. Women's fiction – which O'Reilly described disparagingly as the "Ladies' Circulating Library" – provided a rich means of subverting and challenging her father's romanticised and often sexist depictions of women.

"My Unspeakable Slow Dawning"

In early 1926, Dark wrote to Angus & Robertson for information about publishing her novel *Slow Dawning*, and they advised her to send it to England.[73] Later that year, Mollie O'Reilly took it with her on a trip to London and left it with the literary agent John Farquharson. The English publisher John Long, who released *Slow Dawning* in 1932, presumably felt that the novel filled a market demand for romantic fiction. In contrast, when Dark attempted to find a publisher for "Pilgrimage" in 1931, she was told that it was "not lowbrow enough, on the one hand, nor, on the other, highbrow enough to succeed".[74] It was one of many instances when Dark was told by overseas publishers and agents that she should produce straightforward romantic narratives if she wanted to achieve publication.

---

72   After Dowell's death in 1923, Mollie O'Reilly remained staunchly loyal to his legacy, and published *Dowell O'Reilly: From His Letters* in 1927.

73   Barbara Brooks with Judith Clark, *Eleanor Dark: A Writer's Life* (Sydney: Pan Macmillan, 1998), 119. Angus & Robertson refused a number of major Australian authors, including Vance Palmer, Christina Stead and Katharine Susannah Prichard.

74   Hurst and Blackett to John Farquharson, 11 June 1931, quoted in Brooks with Clark, *Eleanor Dark*, 122.

Even though *Slow Dawning* seemed to conform to the lowbrow market, it did not sell well, appears to have received minimal attention when it was published and has never been reprinted.

Slow Dawning provides an extended treatment of the career and romantic development of the central character featured in Dark's *Bulletin* tale "Wind", Valerie Spencer. At nine years old, Valerie decides she will one day become a doctor. When she is eighteen, she leaves her hometown of Kawarra – "three hours from Sydney by car" – and a budding romance with her childhood sweetheart, Jim Hunter, to begin her medical degree at the University of Sydney.[75] Seven years later, in 1924, Valerie emerges as a fully qualified doctor. She returns to Kawarra to establish her own medical practice, hoping to reconnect with Jim. Once there, Valerie soon discovers that Jim has become engaged to someone else – Kitty Ray, a girl several years younger than Valerie. Valerie must face the emotional disappointment of Jim's marriage to Kitty while attempting to establish a medical practice in a town that is prejudiced against women doctors. The situation is complicated by the arrival of another doctor in town, Dr Heriot, and by the unscrupulous actions of the neighbouring Dr Hughes. Valerie's business suffers from the increased competition. When Kitty dies tragically, the incident is unfairly blamed on the woman doctor, and Valerie's practice seems in danger of collapsing altogether. The solution comes when Heriot, who has fallen in love with Valerie, offers a marriage that will provide both affection and a means of saving her business. Heriot, and the romantic solution he provides, is one of the key ways in which the novel's plot differs from that of "Wind".

The significant time lapse between the writing and publication of *Slow Dawning* meant that Dark came to regret its release. It appeared under her real name rather than a pseudonym, at a time when she was trying to establish herself as a serious writer amongst Australian cultural figures who generally expressed resistance to commercially driven writing. These included Vance and Nettie Palmer who, in their aim to create an indigenous Australian literature, pitted what they deemed as serious writing against the kind of commercial fiction published by Angus & Robertson.[76] Dark was embarrassed to show *Slow Dawning* to Nettie[77] and later told Jean Devanny, "it was the only time in my life when I wrote dishonestly, deliberately wrote down with the object of making money".[78] She referred to the novel as "my unspeakable *Slow Dawning*" and did not keep a copy of it on her

---

75 Eleanor Dark, *Slow Dawning* (London: John Long, 1932), 24. All subsequent references are to this edition and appear in parentheses in the text.

76 Richard Nile, "Literary Democracy and the Politics of Reputation", in *The Oxford Literary History of Australia*, eds. Bruce Bennett, Jennifer Strauss and Chris Wallace-Crabbe (Melbourne: Oxford University Press, 1998), 131–32.

77 For her part, Nettie Palmer congratulated Dark on being able to tell the difference between a book written "for food" and "for its own sake". Nettie Palmer to Eleanor Dark, 21 May 1932, Eleanor Dark Papers, National Library of Australia, MS 4998, Binder 1.

78 Eleanor Dark, quoted in Jean Devanny, *Bird of Paradise* (Sydney: Frank Johnson, 1945), 248.

bookshelves; reports suggest she even went so far as to buy copies from bookshops and burn them.[79]

In the novels that Dark went on to write in the 1930s, she sometimes expressed the view that popular forms of culture such as magazine fiction and radio were less worthy than expressions of high art such as literary fiction, poetry or landscape painting. One of the characters in *Sun Across the Sky* (1937), Kit Marshall, is a formulaic writer who lacks a sincere commitment to his art. With a "chameleon-like flair for assuming the colour of the periodical he was 'after'", Kit "knew his market" and modelled his style on what would "delight … the palate of the reading public".[80] The fact that Kit is killed off in an accident with a vacuum cleaner aptly conveys Dark's 1930s judgement on the commercially driven writer. In *Waterway* (1938), another of her characters, Lesley Channon, also writes for "the weekly and monthly journals", although Dark is more sympathetic towards the fact that she is driven to freelance journalism by "financial stress".[81] Lesley writes "stories … brief articles, household hints, and earnest advice to wives upon how to retain their husbands' waning love" – cultural products at which "she scowled or giggled according to her mood" (189). Lesley also writes "innocuous verse of that convenient two-inch length which so comfortably fills the odd corners of a women's paper, and which, at sixpence a line, paid her quite well for the ten minutes spent in its composition" (189). As Dark's biographers note, this satirical description bears a strong resemblance to Dark's own writing experience in the 1920s.[82]

Despite the fact that Dark came to distance herself from *Slow Dawning* in the 1930s, the novel is worthy of critical attention. It is not modernist in form; rather, it follows a chronological narrative structure and has an omniscient narrator. It is a novel fascinated with new cultural types, including the New Woman, the war-affected man and the scientific technical expert, and contributes to the shifting conventions of middle-class marriage and romance in the interwar period.

A New Kind of Citizen: The Middle-class, Professional Woman

Slow Dawning is a hybrid novel. It features many aspects of popular romance, including a love triangle between Jim, Valerie and Kitty, coincidences and a happy ending involving marriage. It also follows the narrative trajectory of what Susan Sheridan calls "romances of experience": novels which combine romance with the *Bildungsroman* form to provide a story based on women's experience.[83] Sheridan identifies a number of these novels in the first three decades of twentieth-century

---

79 Brooks with Clark, *Eleanor Dark*, 95–96; Modjeska, *Exiles at Home*, 84.
80 Eleanor Dark, *Sun Across the Sky* (London: Collins, [1937] 1946), 73, 75.
81 Eleanor Dark, *Waterway* (North Ryde, NSW: Angus & Robertson, [1938] 1990), 189. All subsequent references are to this edition and appear in parentheses in the text.
82 Brooks with Clark, *Eleanor Dark*, 81–82.
83 Sheridan, *Faultlines*, 52.

Australian literature, including Miles Franklin's *My Brilliant Career* (1901), *Painted Clay* (1917) by Capel Boake (Doris Boake Kerr), Mabel Forrest's *The Wild Moth* (1924) and Jane Laker's *Among the Reeds* (1933). In their focus on women's participation in the workplace, romances of experience reflect the new social possibilities available to women at this time, and are Australian examples of what Esther Kleinbord Labovitz calls the "female *Bildungsroman*".[84] Traditional examples of the *Bildungsroman* presuppose a man's access to particular types of education and experience, and so it was only in the twentieth century, when "cultural and social structures appeared to support women's struggle for independence, to go out into the world, engage in careers, in self-discovery and fulfilment", that the female version of the form fully emerged.[85]

As with all *Bildungsromane*, *Slow Dawning* focuses on the development of a central character from childhood to maturity. Valerie, like many heroic protagonists, is orphaned by the death of her parents, rejects the provincial attitudes of her small-town upbringing and receives her real apprenticeship to life once she has left her formal education.[86] Whereas many *Bildungsromane* take place predominantly in the urban environment of the city, in *Slow Dawning* Valerie returns to her hometown for the majority of the novel. This is an interesting generic difference, and contrasts not only with the usual plotline of the *Bildungsroman*, but also with the dominant narrative trajectory of international magazine romance fiction of the 1920s. Most romantic heroines in American magazine fiction abandoned their small-town communities and embraced the opportunities of the urban centre.[87] In these stories, the small town is represented as "on the periphery of life", whereas the city embodies the public sphere and is "alive with possibility".[88] *Slow Dawning*'s unusual plot progression raises the question as to whether it was as easy for the modern Australian woman to escape the provinces as her American counterpart. When Valerie considers ending her social isolation by having a child with "any decent and healthy man", she plans that once the baby is born, she will "go away – right away, perhaps, to another country" where her "work and her child would fill her whole life" (241–42). In this fantasy, Valerie must go overseas and not merely to an Australian city to achieve anonymity and social freedom.

Dark brings into the romance of experience a confident and independent heroine who reflects the changing class identities of the interwar period. It was not unusual for the heroines of this genre to participate in paid work; however,

---

84 Esther Kleinbord Labovitz, *The Myth of the Heroine: The Female Bildungsroman in the Twentieth Century: Dorothy Richardson, Simone de Beauvoir, Doris Lessing, Christa Wolf* (New York: P. Lang, 1986).

85 Labovitz, *The Myth of the Heroine*, 2, 3, 7. Labovitz identifies some nineteenth-century precursors (such as *Jane Eyre* and *Middlemarch*) to the more fully developed twentieth-century female *Bildungsroman*.

86 Jerome Hamilton Buckley, *Season of Youth: The Bildungsroman from Dickens to Golding* (Cambridge, MA: Harvard University Press, 1974), 17–20; Sheridan, *Faultlines*, 53.

87 Honey, "Feminist", 88.

88 Honey, "Feminist", 89.

they usually come from lower middle-class or working-class backgrounds, and undertake roles such as shopgirl or office clerk.[89] In contrast, *Slow Dawning* features an emphatically middle-class heroine with a university education and a medical qualification. In fact, in its attentiveness to the shifting roles of middle-class women in interwar Australia, *Slow Dawning* shares similarities with the feminine middlebrow novel, a field which Nicola Humble associates with the works of British authors from the 1920s to the 1950s, such as Margery Allingham, Elizabeth Bowen, Ivy Compton-Burnett and Angela Thirkell.[90] The feminine middlebrow novel was ideologically and generically flexible and operated as "a powerful force in establishing and consolidating, but also in resisting, new class and gender identities".[91] It spanned a number of genres, including romance, detective fiction and the *Bildungsroman*, and often combined them. The flexible generic conventions of this field allowed it quickly to respond to the significant shifts in gender roles in the interwar years, while its commitment to respectability meant that writers could "explore new gender and sexual identities which were otherwise perceived as dangerously disruptive to social values".[92]

In using the *Bildungsroman* – a form which calls on modernity to deliver on its "still unfilled promise" of universal rights – Dark presents an argument for the professional white woman to be "capacitated as a citizen-subject" and afforded the same rights and respect given to professional white men.[93] The difficulties faced by Valerie stem from the disparity between her professional, modern role as doctor, and residual Victorian conceptions of femininity in an Australian country town. Although she is able to access the same education and career as a man, she is not judged by the same social expectations as a male doctor, showing the difficulties that women faced in entering the public sphere as equal citizens. Dark prefaces *Slow Dawning* with an extract from the Hippocratic Oath, inferring that, as a doctor, Valerie should inherit all the rights and obligations of the profession. The Oath's promise that Valerie be permitted "to enjoy life and the practise of my art, respected always by all men", provided that she live in "purity and holiness" and "abstain from every voluntary act of mischief and corruption", becomes ironic in the context of Kawarra's prejudice against women doctors. The town gossips believe that "the practise of medicine must be death to the natural bashfulness and modesty of womanhood" and that "women doctors have no modesty and no morals" (113, 120). Valerie is viewed by some as an "unwomanly woman" and "a very monster

---

89   Clare in Mary Fullerton's *Two Women (Clare: Margaret)* (1923) is a rare exception of a heroine with access to a university education. She studies law but is unable to practise. See Sheridan, *Faultlines*, 55–56.

90   Nicola Humble, *The Feminine Middlebrow Novel, 1920s to 1950s: Class, Domesticity, and Bohemianism* (Oxford: Oxford University Press, 2001). The English novelist Angela Thirkell lived in Australia between 1920 and 1929.

91   Humble, *Feminine Middlebrow*, 3.

92   Humble, *Feminine Middlebrow*, 5.

93   Joseph R. Slaughter, "Enabling Fictions and Novel Subjects: The 'Bildungsroman' and International Human Rights Law", *PMLA* 121, no. 5 (October 2006): 1411, 1419.

of iniquity and depravity" (124), so that Dark points to the paradox of Australia extending voting rights to white women yet not allowing them full and equal participation in the public sphere. In a startling passage, Valerie questions why, given that she has the same "mental and physical needs, and desires" as men, she can't "satisfy the physical ones with casual unions, as men do?":

> I have money and I have knowledge; I could protect myself from disease, and see that I didn't bear illegitimate children. But there are no – facilities – for me, as there are for any drunken labourer who likes to carry syphilis from a prostitute to infect his wife and unborn children … (90–91)

The comparison between Valerie's own situation and the sexual freedoms available to men draws attention to the unequal social conditions – "the intolerable and unnatural restraints which convention thrust upon her merely because she was not a man" (209).[94] At the same time, Dark frames female sexual desire as one of the hallmarks of the Modern Woman.

As in "Wind", in *Slow Dawning* Dark adopts the metaphor of a physical "handicap" to describe the unjust social expectations that constrain white middle-class women's involvement in the workforce. This handicap is the result of social prejudice rather than any intrinsic lack of skill on the part of women, as revealed by a conversation between Dr McNab and Heriot:

> "She's as sound a doctor as I know … but she carries a handicap."
> "What handicap?"
> "Her sex."
> Heriot laughed softly.
> "The moral is, surely, that she should have kept to some walk of life where her sex would not be a handicap."
> Mrs McNab spoke caustically:
> "Ye're old-fashioned, Doctor Heriot." (142–43)

Heriot's belief that women should remain in a feminine "walk of life" is positioned as "old-fashioned" through the intervention of Mrs McNab. Dark extends the metaphor of professional women operating under a social handicap by creating a parallel between Heriot's physical disability – a war wound which at times prevents him from working – and Valerie's gender. The image of the war-maimed, disabled male body was a commonplace one in fiction written during and after the Great War, and modified images of masculine identity.[95] In one conversation Valerie

---

94   It was these unorthodox claims about the rights of women to free sexual liaisons that made Humphrey McQueen argue that Dark was a radical. See Humphrey McQueen, "Eleanor Dark – Disturbing the Status Quo", Talk given at the Katoomba Section of the Sydney Writers' Festival, 17 May 2011 (Canberra: Australian Society for the Study of Labour History) https://bit.ly/3qUbqZf.

remarks that she and Heriot "start fairly scratch … I with this handicap of scandal, and you with your wound", to which Heriot admits, "Your handicap is far heavier than mine. Mine will win me a certain amount of sympathy. Yours will only estrange people from you" (198). Conforming to the narrative progression of New Woman fiction of the 1920s, Heriot's initial suspicions of Valerie's ambitions progress to acceptance and collaboration.[96] He eventually recognises the injustice of Valerie's gender handicap making her "a mark for all the poisonous gossip of a country town", and acts towards her with friendship and collegiality rather than competition (182–83).

The Changing Nature of Marriage and Romance

If *Slow Dawning* is an attempt to incorporate a new kind of citizen into society – the professional, modern white woman – then the entrance of such a figure into women's romance also alters the generic conventions of this form. The new discourses about masculinity and femininity in the first decades of the twentieth century brought about a "radical reassessment of romance" in both the British feminine middlebrow novel and the Australian romance of experience.[97] The heroines of these novels display confidence, emotional restraint and professional competence. Miles Franklin's *My Brilliant Career* provides the most famous, early Australian example of this radical questioning of romance; however, even in the many novels in which marriage is presented as the ultimate outcome, there was a significant shift in romantic conventions. In *Slow Dawning*, Valerie is portrayed as modern through her ability to contain and control her strong emotions and desires. Dark frequently provides scenes where Valerie successfully conquers her emotions, such as when she encounters the newly married Jim:

> At the sight of him such a tumult, such a wild hurricane of physical and emotional longing swept over Valerie that she stood still as death … Her will forsook her utterly. If he had demanded of her then: "Do you love me?" she would have replied nakedly: "Yes." If he had taken her in his arms she would have submitted with trance-like ecstasy …
>
> "I've hardly seen you since you came back, Valerie."
>
> She answered lightly: "You've been far too busy getting married – and I've been far too busy settling down to work." …

---

95   Joanna Burke, *Dismembering the Male: Men's Bodies, Britain and the Great War* (Chicago: University of Chicago Press, 1996), 15–16; Kate Macdonald, "Gender, Disability, Wartime: The Woman's Body and the Disabled Ex-Serviceman in the First World War", in *Middlebrow and Gender*, 60–62.

96   Honey, "Feminist", 96.

97   Humble, *Feminine Middlebrow*, 198; Sheridan, *Faultlines*, 53.

He felt oddly nettled by her calm, her easy pronunciation of his name. No woman who had just been in the grip of an emotion strong enough to transform her face as Valerie's had been transformed should be able to master herself so quickly. (110–11)

The description of Valerie standing "still as death" in "a wild hurricane of … longing" reflects the hyperbolic emotional register of the romance genre. Yet Dark disrupts this register through the constrained conversation between Jim and Valerie. Such restraint characterised the "new language of romance" in interwar women's novels, as the interaction between the competent Modern Woman and the war-wounded man meant that "evasion rather than declaration becomes the new textual currency of love".[98] Thus the descriptions of Valerie submitting to Jim's declarations of love "utterly … nakedly … with trance-like ecstasy" are restricted to the conditional tense (*'If* he had demanded of her …' , "*If* he had taken her in his arms …'), reinforcing Jim's passivity and his lack of comprehension of a woman who can "master herself so quickly".

Slow Dawning also reflects new generic conventions of the interwar romance novel in its ironic treatment of the very concept of romance. This is an aspect of Dark's novel that has been missed by critics who have viewed it as a straight-forward romance.[99] Valerie is aware of romantic traditions, associating the river in Kawarra with Tennyson and describing it as "exactly what we think of as a perfect setting for Romance" (77). She also subverts romantic expectations: in one scene, she considers throwing Hughes' flowers into the wastepaper basket in a fit of "rage", but decides that this behaviour is too "[t]heatrical" (179). Valerie's rational and anti-romantic approach characterises her as modern, linking her to the New Woman characters that frequently featured in interwar middlebrow women's novels such as Stella Gibbons' *Cold Comfort Farm* (1932) or Margery Allingham's *Sweet Danger* (1933). When Jim calls Valerie "an angel", using the established lexicon of the romance genre, Valerie finds the choice of name "so unimaginative and so commonplace" that she reflects "[t]here was something unformed about him – something lost and uncertain: a primitive man let loose in civilization without the subtlety of wit to understand his own racking emotions" (267). If Jim's reliance on romantic tropes is "primitive", then Valerie is represented as thoroughly evolved. She easily performs practical tasks, including driving and fixing her Buick, mowing the lawn and answering the telephone, as well as delivering babies and performing operations. She ultimately concludes that romance belongs to a prewar era when there was "beauty everywhere" and "[a]ll soldiers were romance" (288). Whilst she feels love and affection for Heriot, she does not experience romance, implying that the modern, postwar age is one that has moved beyond the illusions of the past.

---

98 Humble, *Feminine Middlebrow*, 198, 209.
99 See, for example, Olga Asal Connolly, "The Early Work of Eleanor Dark" (PhD thesis, Florida State University, 1995), 129.

Although Valerie's marriage to Heriot provides the happy ending necessitated by the romance form, even this conclusion registers some significant shifts in middle-class expectations of marriage. By the 1920s, New Woman narratives and women's advice manuals such as Marie Stopes' *Married Love* (1918) had challenged the traditional, hierarchical model of marriage, replacing it with companionate marriage in which romantic unions afforded women opportunities for financial success, professional work, supportive relationships and sexual satisfaction.[100] Reflecting these new social expectations, Heriot provides Valerie with a necessary shield from scandal, a colleague with whom to combine her medical practice, love and affection, the opportunity to have children and the freedom to "go off alone for a while if the stress of married life became too great" (279). It is an arrangement reminiscent of Eleanor and Eric's own marriage in 1922 (Fig. 1.2). Valerie and Heriot are twelve years apart in age; Eleanor and Eric had a gap of eleven years. Heriot and Valerie undertake a secret trial marriage before Valerie decides to accept his offer; Eleanor suggested a similar secret affair in 1921.[101] Valerie's marriage allows her to continue her vocation; Eleanor and Eric's union was undertaken with the understanding that she would be given domestic help so that she could pursue her writing career. In this sense, *Slow Dawning* pursues a question with which a number of other Australian romances of experience also engaged: "Is there life after marriage?"[102] While Drusilla Modjeska's criticism may be true, that *Slow Dawning*'s conclusion relies on "a bourgeois conception of the family and bourgeois expectations of work",[103] then it is also true that bourgeois marriage was changing in this period, and that Dark's novel contributes to the normalisation and negotiation of such shifts for middle-class white women.

Valerie and the "Army of Women": The Individual and the Collective

Slow Dawning provides a fascinating insight into an early period of Dark's liberal humanism. As the child of a Labor politician, and a student of Redlands, a school that advocated Christian socialism, Dark grew up with a progressive form of liberalism that expressed confidence in the ability of the state to enact meaningful social reform. The arguments Dowell O'Reilly presented in favour of women's franchise were based on liberal philosophical grounds that were similar to those of John Stuart Mill.[104] O'Reilly's sister Marion, and her husband Bert Piddington, were similarly influenced by the liberal reformism which came to the rise in the

---

100 Honey, "Feminist", 88, 97; Ann Rea, "'Ordinary' Sexuality, the 'Dirty Little Secret' and the Indecent Highbrow Modernist: Sexuality in *Married Love* and *Lady Chatterley's Lover*", in *Middlebrow and Gender*, 253–57.
101 Brooks with Clark, *Eleanor Dark*, 56.
102 Sheridan, *Faultlines*, 52.
103 Modjeska, *Exiles at Home*, 217.
104 Bongiorno, "'Every Woman a Mother'", 45, 60.

English-speaking world in the late nineteenth and early twentieth centuries, and which challenged the emphasis of older forms of nineteenth-century liberalism on protecting the individual from the state, instead underlining the role of the state in facilitating individual development.[105] New Liberals sought to move beyond the dualism of the individual and the state by providing a neo-Hegelian synthesis of the two; Francis Anderson, the Challis Professor of Philosophy at the University of Sydney and an influential New Liberal thinker, claimed in 1922, "[w]e may … dismiss as a false antithesis the opposition between individual and social interest which has been in the past … the source of so much futile political controversy".[106] Fusing liberalism and socialism, New Liberals argued that the goal of the state was individual self-development, so that liberals should invest in "forms of social and political organisation [that] will help and not hinder the free self-development of the members of the community".[107] The result was a significant convergence between New Liberalism and state socialism in the early twentieth-century period.[108]

The New Liberalism of Dark's father's generation was an international phenomenon. In their attempts to reconcile individualism and collectivism, Australian political figures such as Alfred Deakin drew upon the philosophical idealism of English thinkers T.H. Green, D.G. Ritchie and Henry Jones.[109] Jones visited Australia in 1908, where he argued that the state should play an important role in the moral development of individual citizens.[110] Anderson had studied under Green, and he taught his ideas to new generations of Australian students, including the New South Wales politician and judge Herbert Vere ("Bert") Evatt, who went on to marry one of Dark's school friends. In the prize-winning essay he wrote for the University of Sydney in 1918, *Liberalism in Australia*, Evatt argued that the "newer political philosophy" which overcame earlier dualisms between the state and the individual subject had found its expression in "the legislation of our young Commonwealth" – a claim that shows how, in the Australian context, state intervention was framed more positively and given greater impetus due to the nationalism of the post-Federation decades.[111]

---

105 Michael Roe, *Nine Australian Progressives: Vitalism in Bourgeois Social Thought, 1890–1960* (St. Lucia: University of Queensland Press, 1984), 15; Peter Beilharz, "The Young Evatt – Labor's New Liberal", *Australian Journal of Politics and History* 39, no. 2 (1993): 161.

106 Francis Anderson, "Liberalism and Socialism", address as president of section G of the Australian Association for the Advancement of Science, 1922, 4.

107 Anderson, "Liberalism and Socialism", 4.

108 Tim Rowse, *Australian Liberalism and National Character* (Melbourne: Kibble Books, 1978), 125; Ian Tregenza, "Are We 'All Socialists Now'? New Liberalism, State Socialism and the Australian Settlement", *Labour History* 102 (2012): 88, 95.

109 Tregenza, "'All Socialists'", 90; Tod Moore, "Saving Private Hegel: Australian Liberalism and the 1914–1918 War", *Australian Journal of Politics & History* 61, no. 4 (2015): 502.

110 Tregenza, "'All Socialists'", 91.

111 H.V. Evatt, *Liberalism in Australia: An Historical Sketch of Australian Politics Down to the Year 1915* (The Law Book Co. of Australasia: Sydney, 1918), 77; Tregenza, "'All Socialists'", 89.

Figure 1.2 Unknown photographer. Eleanor and Eric Dark's wedding, 1 February 1922, Sydney. Eleanor Dark Collection, Varuna, the National Writers' House. © Jill Dark.

Of all of Dark's interwar novels, *Slow Dawning* is most comfortable with connecting individual behaviour to broader political struggles, suggesting its connection to New Liberal reformism. Valerie espouses a Christian-inflected humanism: although she is "agnostic", she tries to maintain a belief in the values of "Faith", "Knowledge", "Love", "Honesty" and "Courage" (151). Dark frames Valerie's personal struggles as a constituent part of women's collective emancipation:

> It was in this way that she had seen her fellow-women. They would climb at last, she dreamed, to a height where they would perform not only the artistic or intellectual work to which their natures inclined, but the normal functions of wifehood and motherhood as well – carrying a double burden as only they were privileged to carry it. A terrible fight, and a slow one, but epic in its magnificence. Generations it would take … (90)

In this post-suffragist narrative of progress, women will eventually achieve both "artistic or intellectual work" *and* "wifehood and motherhood", without having to sacrifice either "the brain or the sex" (278). The fulfilment of both needs will create in women "a nobler work of God than an honest man" (278). It was Dark's vision of the "army of women" that excited Drusilla Modjeska and, according to her Marxist methodology, provided "a hint of collective political action by women", although she argued that this was ultimately "overridden" by the novel's "reliance on individual solutions".[112] Yet Modjeska's binary between individualism and collectivism overlooks the fact that, within the neo-Hegelian synthesis for which New Liberals strived, these were not viewed as dialectical opposites but as interdependent.[113] Valerie's achievement of marriage and a profession contributes to the triumph of all women; at the same time, the "army of women" gives sustenance to her individual ethical behaviour. Faced with the exhaustion of coping alone, she considers what it would mean to "let go" of her personal creed and thus "let the army of women go on without her":

> She seemed to see the army – the huge marching shadow – passing her without a backward look … She would aim, now, for success – personal success. She would no longer regard herself as one of the units which made the army, governing herself always with the good repute of that army in her mind. (151–52)

Valerie's belief that she is "one of the units" of an international army of emancipated women ensures that she acts in a manner consistent with "the good repute" of all women in mind. To abandon that struggle and think individualistically would mean pursuing "personal success" rather than authentic behaviour. She eventually overcomes this spiritual crisis and rejects the values of self-interested ambition. At

---

112 Modjeska, *Exiles at Home*, 217.
113 Tregenza, "'All Socialists'", 271.

this point of Dark's liberal thinking, the individual was inextricably caught up with the collective.

The Technical Expert

Slow Dawning reflects a particular moment in Australian liberal thinking when the concepts of efficiency and scientific management came to replace the idealism of the earlier Deakinite years. Scientific management became increasingly important to Australian liberal intellectuals during the second half of the Great War. As Tod Moore shows, the United States' entry into the war in 1917 meant that American ideas of Progressivism, which involved an emphasis on the role of the scientific expert, paralleled the rise of such ideas in Australian intellectual institutions such as the Workers' Educational Association (WEA).[114] An example of this increased focus on practical science amongst Australian liberal intellectuals was the conference held in November 1916 by the WEA on "The Teaching of Sex Hygiene" at the University of Sydney, organised by Meredith Atkinson.[115]

This emphasis on scientific managerialism and efficiency brought about a new social class of technical experts who were responsible for overseeing educational and medical reforms, including the management of sexually transmitted diseases, and women's reproduction and sexuality.[116] Dark was connected to a number of these scientific and medical reformers. She wrote *Slow Dawning* during Eric's first years as a general medical practitioner in Katoomba, where he was involved in pioneering a new treatment for tuberculosis and had one of the earliest long-range diathermy machines in Australia.[117] Dark's aunt, Marion Piddington, was another example of the scientific reformer: she was a radical advocate for family planning, and drew her ideas from international authorities such as Sigmund Freud, Havelock Ellis, Marie Stopes and Margaret Sanger.[118] Piddington agreed with Stopes' idea, popularised in *Married Love*, that women should be educated about the sexual act so that they could experience sexual pleasure in the context of a loving marriage, and she put these ideas into practice by giving lectures to groups of parents about how to provide sex education to their children. In 1926, the year that Dark completed *Slow Dawning*, Piddington published a book called *Tell Them, or, the*

---

114 Moore, "Saving Private Hegel", 511.

115 *The Teaching of Sex Hygiene: Report of a Conference Organised by the Workers' Education Association of New South Wales*, Union Hall, Sydney University, 23–25 November 1916 (Sydney: Burrows & Co., 1918).

116 Kerreen M. Reiger, *The Disenchantment of the Home: Modernizing the Australian Family, 1880–1940* (Melbourne: Oxford University Press, 1985), 2.

117 Susan Carson, "Finding Hy-Brazil: Eugenics and Modernism in the Pacific", *Hecate* 35, no. 1–2 (2009): 128. See Eric Payten Dark, *Diathermy in General Practice* (Sydney: Angus & Robertson, 1930).

118 Ellen Warne, "Sex Education Debates and the Modest Mother in Australia, 1890s to the 1930s", *Women's History Review* 8, no. 2 (1999): 318–19.

Second Stage of Mothercraft: A Hand-book of Suggestions for the Sex-Training of the Child. Anne Rees summarises the main argument of Piddington's treatise as:

> children had a natural curiosity about sex which, if not satisfied within the family, would lead them to seek information from other, less wholesome, sources. This would, almost inevitably, precipitate a slide into sexual depravity and infection with venereal disease. Not only did venereal disease cause physical and mental disability among the infected, but it also produced hereditary defects, such as blindness, deafness and retardation. Transmitted en masse, these disabilities would imperil the fitness of the race. The only way to halt this alarming prospect was to ensure that children were comprehensively educated on matters of sexual health and morality. Sex education was therefore, according to Piddington, an urgent imperative directly linked to eugenic principles.[119]

As in *Married Love*, Piddington's book attempted to combine a rational, scientific description of sex with poetic Edwardian language.[120]

Writers of the feminine middlebrow novel similarly participated in the international attempt of women reformers to articulate sexual matters in socially acceptable ways.[121] Ann Rea connects middlebrow women's fiction with advice manuals such as those written by Stopes, arguing that the two worked in tandem to normalise ideas of modern companionate marriage, birth control and female sexual desire in the interwar period.[122] This connection is demonstrated in *Slow Dawning*, which seems to reflect Piddington's ideas about the importance of parents providing sex education to children. Kitty's mother, Mrs Ray, tries to keep her daughter "ignorant" about sexual matters, so that for Kitty sex evokes thoughts of "slugs and slimy toads and hairy-legged spiders" (47, 50). There is a strong sense of censure from Dark's narrator about this lack of parental sex education. Dark writes that, "inconceivable as it may seem, Kitty, in the year 1924, and at the age of nineteen, was almost as ignorant of everything pertaining to sex as a child of three" (48). Valerie steps into the role of professional expert when Kitty visits her on the eve of her wedding day seeking information about the sexual act, explaining it as "beautiful" and "an expression of love" (67, 69), using the "vocabularies of sentimental love" offered by Piddington and Stopes.[123] Valerie also uses technical terms, teaching Kitty the phrase "sexual union", which Kitty's mother later describes as an "*awful* expression" not fit to appear in newspapers (123). Through these scenes, Dark points to the difficulty of locating an adequate language for female

---

119 Anne Rees, "'The Quality and Not Only the Quantity of Australia's People': Ruby Rich and the Racial Hygiene Association of NSW", *Australian Feminist Studies* 27, no. 71 (2012): 77.
120 Paul Peppis, "Rewriting Sex: Mina Loy, Marie Stopes, and Sexology", *Modernism/modernity* 9, no. 4 (2002): 568.
121 Humble, *Feminine Middlebrow*, 231.
122 Rea, "'Ordinary' Sexuality", 257.
123 Peppis, "Rewriting Sex", 566.

sexual experience. Valerie finds that "one had to choose, for the most part, between scientific words and the words of the gutter" (67). Dark's narrator describes the process wherein Valerie strives to make the topic clear, rational and respectable:

> Quietly, at last, neither raising nor lowering her voice, she began to explain. Her eyes held Kitty's from time to time, daring her, by their calm, impersonal tranquility, to smirch the deliberate words with any hint of shame. She chose them carefully, explaining the technical ones with a little string of others less technical. Where there was a popular and kindly-sounding word she used it. Her pencil, a couple of times, made little clear diagrams. (67)

The description of combining "technical" terms with "popular and kindly-sounding" ones, echoes the strategy used in Piddington's and Stopes' sex manuals, as does the reference to Valerie making "little clear diagrams". Like real-life Australian examples of women doctors, including Constance Ellis and Isabella Younger-Ross, Valerie is a member of the emerging professional middle class that was at the forefront of reforms aimed "to extend the principles of rational, orderly conduct to sexual behaviour, particularly in the interests of production of a healthy, efficient race", and *Slow Dawning* contributes towards normalising these ideas.[124]

Similarly in Dark's story "Benevolence", it is the medical professional who provides sex education when the parent fails to do so. Jean's "rigid little Presbyterian mother had conveyed to her, with all the subtle indirectness of prudery, that the sex relationship was a dreadfully unfortunate mistake of the Creator's, and that His people must tactfully ignore it" (4). When Jean's lack of information about sexuality and contraception leads to an unwanted pregnancy, Doctor Sterne speaks to her with "kindly sounding words that did not hurt, or technical ones that were gratefully impersonal" (4). He protects Jean's secret when she decides to obtain an illicit abortion against his advice, caring only for her health. In this story, Dark again foregrounds the new social role of technical expert, providing covert forms of education to women readers by encouraging mothers to express openness about sexual matters and extending the principles of rational scientific management to her women characters.

Race and Class

Although *Slow Dawning* engages with new types of managerial, liberal reform, and examines the issue of gender discrimination, it does not interrogate the ways in which these issues intersected with race or class. Dark takes for granted middle-class white women's intellectual equality with men; however, she does not

---

124 Reiger, *Disenchantment*, 131, 190.

in any way engage with the fact that, at the time the novel was written and published, First Nations peoples were not counted as citizens or given the right to vote in federal elections. The novel also frames working-class women as obstacles to, rather than participants in, women's collective emancipation. Valerie's housekeeper Mrs Gillogley is used mostly as a source of comedy in the novel, and exhibits the supposed superstitions and prejudices of working-class women. When Mrs Gillogley expresses suspicions about modern medicine, Valerie looks at her with "a kind of horror", imagining her blocking the path of the marching army of women: "What battle, what misery before she was finally overthrown and the army went on!" (93–94). Dark's failure to engage with the experiences of working-class women or to broaden the scope of her rights-based discourse to include women of colour reflects some of the blind spots of 1920s middle-class feminism and the managerial approach of liberal reformers[125] – a blind spot that extends into much later examples of mid-century Australian writing such as Patrick White's Sarsaparilla drama and novels.

As in much of Dark's magazine fiction, *Slow Dawning* makes little of its Australian setting. Although Kawarra is clearly an Australian town, questions about Australia are not explicitly addressed, and are far less important than in Dark's subsequent novels, reinforcing the idea that popular fiction of the kind that *Slow Dawning* grew out of promoted an "outward-looking, international, and cosmopolitan atmosphere" rather than a nationally focused one.[126] Nonetheless, Dark's novel unconsciously reinforces some of settler culture's racialised and class-based fears about national population, including the fear that the working classes were reproducing too quickly and producing children of inferior quality. Valerie recognises that "men and women produced unwanted children and more unwanted children, in poverty and filth, through prudish ignorance or sheer callous indifference" (35). She compares the children that she has delivered to working-class parents to the ones that she would produce as an educated, middle-class woman:

> She could not help making a mental procession of all the tragic babies she had introduced into the world – stillborn, deformed, syphilitic, idiot, and, almost as bad, unwanted ... here was a solution to her loneliness, and an antidote to the poison of those many warped and stunted little lives. Why should she not have a baby – a beautiful, well-cared for and much desired child? Its father – any decent and healthy man would do – it would be *her* baby. It was not good for a child to be fatherless, but one good parent was better than two bad ones – so many babies had two bad ones. (241)

---

125 See Moore, "Saving Private Hegel", 504.
126 Kuttainen, Galletly and Liebich, *Transported Imagination*, 11.

Here Dark implicitly seems to endorse the views of the racial hygiene movement, which suggested that a wanted baby from a white middle-class background would be the best kind to enhance the racial fitness of the nation. As Anne Rees and Ann Curthoys point out, the eugenics movement had close links to interwar Australian feminism, with reformers such as Marion Piddington and Ruby Rich advocating a utopian eugenic vision based on female freedom, wherein "[w]omen would be spared the burden of raising unhealthy children, whilst every child born would be both healthy and wanted".[127] In *Slow Dawning*, Dark frequently emphasises Valerie's physical fitness and suitability as a potential mother. Like the modern "Australian Girl" and Dark herself, Valerie enjoys walking outdoors and plays tennis.[128] She is also financially independent, university educated, and owns her own house and car. Angela Woollacott notes that the "health and vigour" of Australian women meant that their bodies "came to represent the modern".[129] Valerie's childlessness is presented as a tragedy and a waste. Kitty says to her, "I'd be so glad if you got married. I often think how lonely you must be, and how … how wasted you are … you'd love so beautifully …" (167). Similarly, Heriot reflects, "If ever there was a woman with brains and humour and vitality – the very stuff of life – it was she; unthinkable that her essential usefulness should be wasted in struggling and solitude" (263). The terms that Dark employs here of "waste" and "usefulness" evoke the efficiency and instrumentalism of the eugenics movement – values which she went on to problematise in *Prelude to Christopher*. The conclusion of *Slow Dawning* promises readers that Valerie will find intellectual, emotional and maternal fulfilment in a marriage with a similarly educated mate, reflecting the emphasis of the racial hygiene movement on the choice of marriage partner. This ending not only reinforces the popular romance novel's ideal of companionate marriage based on love, but is also unconsciously entangled with the hopes of a settler-colonial nation to strengthen the perceived quality of its population.

Conclusion

The image of Dark that emerges from this chapter is of one who, like her fictional character Esmerelda, navigated with confidence the new market trends, cultural types and material constraints of the interwar period. The skill of discerning and writing for a market may not be the kind of serious cultural work for which Dark or her cultural-nationalist contemporaries wanted to be known, but it was nonetheless a kind of "sideways feminism" that allowed Dark to achieve publication, visibility and remuneration for her writing.[130] Although not modernist in form, the works

---

127   Rees, "Quality", 84. See also Ann Curthoys, "Eugenics, Feminism, and Birth Control: The Case of Marion Piddington", *Hecate* 15, no. 1 (1989): 73–89.
128   Angela Woollacott, *To Try Her Fortune in London: Australian Women, Colonialism, and Modernity* (New York: Oxford University Press, 2001), 189.
129   Woollacott, *Try Her Fortune*, 182, 188.

she published in the 1920s were certainly engaged with a number of distinctively modern concerns related to gender, sexuality, science, technology and travel. In *Slow Dawning*, Dark asked readers to recognise women's growing participation in the middle-class, professional workforce. The solutions that she envisaged as to how women could overcome the conflict identified by her father, between intellectual work and motherhood, were based on middle-class opportunities and overlooked the issue of race; however, they did reflect significant changes to white middle-class expectations of marriage, romance and work in the interwar period. The popular romance form and the middlebrow women's novel therefore did not only register but also actively negotiated and contributed to the evolution of class and gender-based expectations.

Dark's work in the 1920s would put her in good stead for the subsequent stage of her writing, in which she combined the romance form that she had developed in her magazine fiction with modernist narrative techniques and both cultural-nationalist and cosmopolitan ideas. Despite her own claims to the contrary, the early period of Dark's writing is therefore important – both to studies of her work, and to investigations of Australian cultural history more generally. Through examining an earlier stage of Dark's writing than is usually considered, this chapter shifts the narrative from a writer engaged primarily with cultural nationalism or literary modernism, to one who was keenly interested in international modernity and the shifting roles of women in the interwar period. It also contributes to the broadening of Australian literary studies, from considering texts invested in high culture, to a more diverse range of cultural products, including magazine fiction, and popular and middlebrow expressions of romance.

Slow Dawning also reveals Dark's early confidence in the relationship between the work of the medical expert and the broader health of the settler nation. As will be discussed in the next chapter, it is a relationship that she would call into question in a radical way in her subsequent novel, *Prelude to Christopher*. From this point on, Dark's novels show an uneasy tension between the individual and the social collective, reflecting 1930s fears about the dangers of authoritarianism and state control. *Slow Dawning* is important, therefore, in illuminating an earlier stage of Dark's liberalism, and in revealing that, at this point of her writing, Dark was unconscious of both the whiteness and middle-class nature of her supposedly universal subject.

---

130 Margaret D. Stetz associates "sideways feminism" with British writer Rebecca West, who pioneered "subversive feminist middlebrow fiction" by taking advantage of American publishing opportunities in the 1920s, in "Sideways Feminism: Rebecca West and the *Saturday Evening Post*, 1928", *The Space Between* 9, no. 1 (2013): 61–62.

2

"A Masterpiece of Camouflage": Australian Modernism and *Prelude to Christopher* (1934)

> I refer to certain tendencies which characterize the so-called modernist school of literature, which during the last two decades has spread like a creeping paralysis over England and America, and already threatens to spread its stultifying example to this country.
>
> A.E. Pearse, "Modernist Poetry: The Case Contra", 1935.[1]

> Infection – disease – rottenness – creeping and invading …
> A brain slowly and surely decomposing …
>
> Eleanor Dark, *Prelude to Christopher*, 1934.[2]

In 1935, Eleanor Dark published a short story entitled "Curtain" in the *Australian Mercury*, a literary periodical newly created by the Australian writer and publisher P.R. ("Inky") Stephensen to foster an "indigenous" (that is, settler) Australian culture. Recently returned from England, where he had published *The Paintings of D.H. Lawrence* (1929) and collaborated with fellow Australian Jack Lindsay to produce the periodical the *London Aphrodite* (1928–29), Stephensen hoped that the *Australian Mercury* would reflect "the standards set by the *London Mercury*, the *American Mercury*, and the *Mercure de France*".[3] The inclusion of one of Dark's stories in the *Australian Mercury* suggests her transition from popular writer to one who was navigating what Australian cultural nationalists thought of as serious literature. Also published in the same issue was an essay billed on the front cover as "The Case Against Modernist Poetry" (Fig. 2.1). In this essay, the Oxford-trained

---

1   A.E. Pearse, "Modernist Poetry: The Case Contra", *Australian Mercury* 1 (1935): 76.
2   Eleanor Dark, *Prelude to Christopher* (Rushcutters Bay, NSW: Halstead Press, [1934] 1999), 183. All subsequent references are to this edition and appear in parentheses in the text.
3   P.R. Stephensen to F.W. Robinson, 22 May 1935, quoted in Craig Munro, *Inky Stephensen: Wild Man of Letters* (St. Lucia: University of Queensland Press, 1992), 154. Despite Stephensen's hopes, only the first issue of the *Australian Mercury* ever made it to print. Although a second issue was planned, the magazine was discontinued due to Stephensen's financial difficulties.

Australian poet A.E. Pearse described "the so-called modernist school of literature" as a disease which had "spread like a creeping paralysis over England and America", and which "already threatens to extend its stultifying example to this country".[4] Using the poetry of T.S. Eliot as an example, Pearse diagnosed modernism as "obscure", "unbalanced" and "morbid": it was written by "yahoos and degenerates", and had "infested" English literature.[5] His polemic demonstrates how cultural conservatives frequently used the language of disease and racial hygiene to describe the dangerous influence of modern styles such as modernism.[6]

Pearse's essay is just one of many instances of anti-modernism in Australian cultural history. Other frequently cited examples include the denunciations of the 1939 *Herald* Exhibition of French and British Contemporary Art (the exhibition, which showcased paintings by Vincent van Gogh and Pablo Picasso, was described by the director of the National Gallery of Victoria as "the work of degenerates and perverts"), and the Ern Malley hoax of 1944, in which the poets James McAuley and Harold Stewart undertook a literary experiment designed to expose the absurdity of modernist poetic trends.[7] Although such anti-modernist critiques were not unique to Australia, they have helped to construct a narrative that the nation largely resisted the arrival of literary and artistic modernism. Australia's perceived distance from metropolitan centres of power, its historical position as a colonial outpost, and its unique geographical status as an island continent appear to reinforce these tropes of isolation and insularity. Until recently, the dominant view has been that international modernism arrived in Australia in a piecemeal or abortive fashion, with a truly Australian version of it developing only belatedly in such postwar examples as Patrick White's and Dorothy Hewett's experimental novels and plays.

Parts of this narrative are true: 1930s Australian cultural figures such as Stephensen and Vance and Nettie Palmer did channel their energies into developing a distinctive national literary culture, and frequently expressed ambivalence about British literary modernism. Meanwhile, the Australian government legislated against literary engagements with modernism by employing

---

4   Pearse, "Modernist Poetry", 76. Archibald Ernest Edgar Pearse was born in London, studied Latin and Greek at the University of Queensland, and went on to study English literature at Oxford. His poems focused on his experience as a soldier in the Great War.
5   Pearse, "Modernist Poetry", 76.
6   Nicole Moore, *The Censor's Library: Uncovering the Lost History of Australia's Banned Books* (St. Lucia: University of Queensland Press, 2012), 105; Meaghan Morris, "Import Rhetoric: Semiotics in/and Australia", in *The Foreign Bodies Papers*, Local Consumption Series, eds. Peter Botsman, Chris Burns and Peter Hutchings (Sydney: Local Consumption Publications, 1981), 125–26.
7   On these events and their legacies, see David Brooks, *The Sons of Clovis: Ern Malley, Adoré Floupette and a Secret History of Australian Poetry* (St. Lucia: University of Queensland Press, 2011); Eileen Chanin, Judith Pugh and Steven Miller, *Degenerates and Perverts: The 1939 Herald Exhibition of French and British Contemporary Art* (Carlton, Vic: Miegunyah Press, 2005); Michael Heyward, *The Ern Malley Affair* (St. Lucia: University of Queensland Press, 1993); Philip Mead, *Networked Language: Culture & History in Australian Poetry* (North Melbourne: Australian Scholarly, 2008), 87–185.

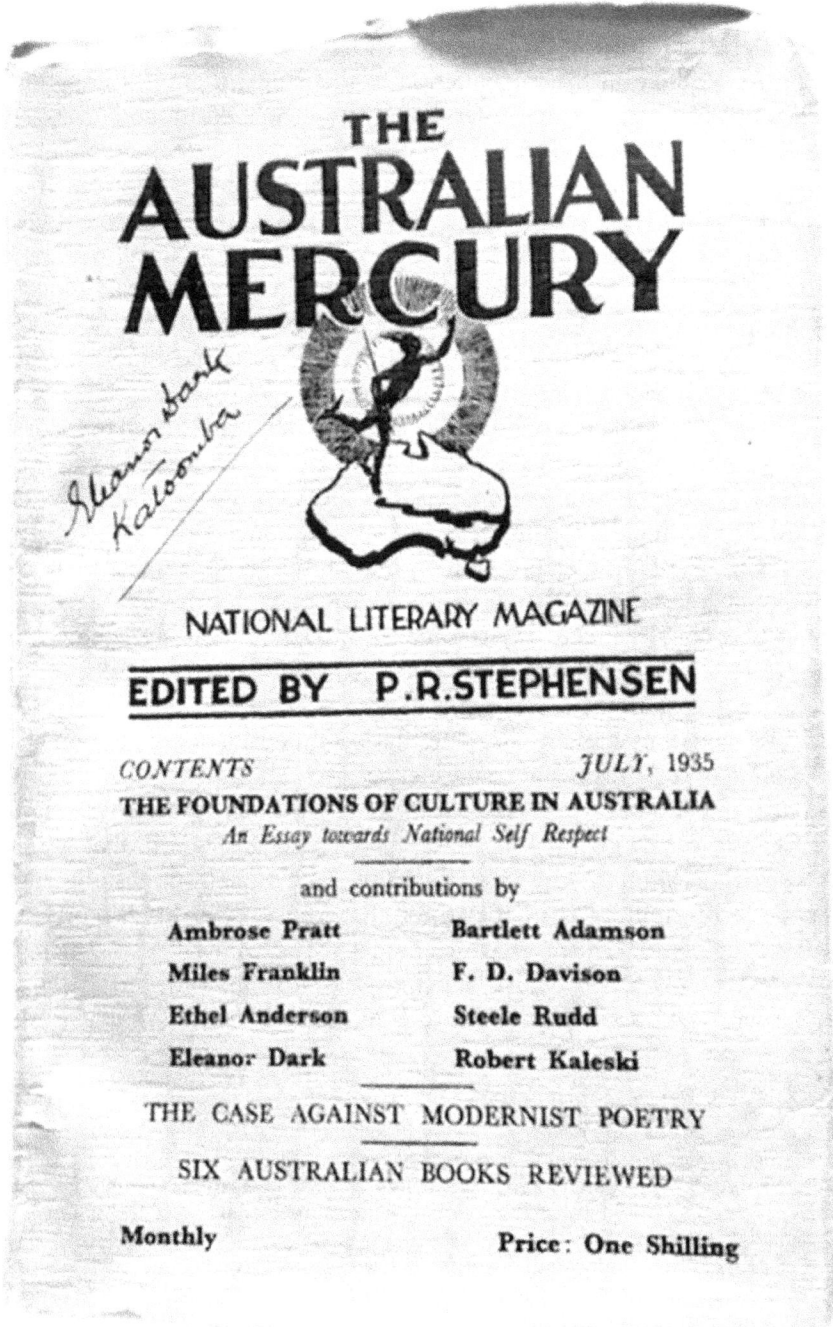

Figure 2.1 Eleanor Dark's personal copy of the *Australian Mercury* 1 (1935). Eleanor Dark Collection, Varuna, the National Writers' House.

strict forms of censorship and quarantine.[8] Yet the idea that this produced an insular nation that was both anti-modern and anti-modernist is ultimately unhelpful. As outlined in the Introduction to this study, there is a growing body of scholarship that suggests that interwar Australia was cosmopolitan, open and outward-looking rather than culturally quarantined, and that the relationship between cultural nationalism and modernism was far more complex than has hitherto been recognised. Vance Palmer worked with A.R. Orage, the editor of the *New Age* – a periodical in which a number of important modernist manifestoes were first published. Nettie Palmer, who advocated the importance of a local book publishing industry in *Modern Australian Literature 1900–1923* (1924), also showed a broad knowledge of world literature, and reviewed the works of D.H. Lawrence, Virginia Woolf, Katherine Mansfield, Marcel Proust and Rebecca West.[9] The Jindyworobaks – a school of poetry in which settler writers tried to incorporate elements of Aboriginal language and culture into their work – can be read productively as both cultural nationalists *and* local expressions of the modernist avant-garde.[10] Although Stephensen often lampooned elements of literary modernism, he shared friendships with prominent modern authors such as Aldous Huxley and Lawrence. Even Pearse's anti-modernist polemic had a position "*within* modernity" – a point that David Carter makes in relation to the anti-modernism of Australian art magazine *Vision* (1923–24), whose editors "knew their modernism better than anyone else in the country".[11] The same might be said of McAuley and Stewart, whose attempts to discredit literary modernism relied upon a strong understanding of surrealism and Dadaist experimentation.

Stephensen placed Pearse's essay directly after Dark's story, thereby bringing the two writers into conversation. This editorial choice resonates with that of the *New Age*, whose editors similarly cultivated diversity and dissent by publishing opposing arguments by contributors – a phenomenon that Ann Ardis treats as representative of "the dialogics of modernism", in which modernism has "the ability to incorporate its opposites".[12] Only a year before launching the *Australian Mercury*, Stephensen had published Dark's second novel, *Prelude to Christopher* (1934), and was elated

---

8   See Moore, *Censor's Library*, 99–129.
9   Robert Dixon, "Australian Fiction and the World Republic of Letters, 1890–1950", in *The Cambridge History of Australian Literature*, ed. Peter Pierce (Cambridge: Cambridge University Press, 2009), 236–37; Deborah Jordan, "'Written to Tickle the Ears of the Groundings in Garden Cities': The Aesthetic of Modernity: Vance and Nettie Palmer and the *New Age*", in *Impact of the Modern*, 92.
10 See Peter Kirkpatrick, "Jindy Modernist: The Jindyworobaks as Avant Garde", in *Republics of Letters: Literary Communities in Australia*, eds. Peter Kirkpatrick and Robert Dixon (Sydney: Sydney University Press, 2012), 99–112; Ellen Smith, "Local Moderns: The Jindyworobak Movement and Australian Modernism", *Australian Literary Studies* 27, no. 1 (2012): 1–17.
11 David Carter, *Always Almost Modern: Australian Print Cultures and Modernity* (North Melbourne: Australian Scholarly, 2013), x, 6.
12 Ann L. Ardis, *Modernism and Cultural Conflict, 1880–1922* (Cambridge, UK; New York: Cambridge University Press, 2002), 145; "The Dialogics of Modernism(s) in the *New Age*", *Modernism/modernity* 14, no. 3 (2007), 407–34.

when it won the Australian Literary Society Gold Medal, describing the work as "an absolute epoch in Australia's development".[13] *Prelude to Christopher* was the first of Dark's novels to feature recognisably modernist techniques, including a compressed time frame, flashbacks, a form of stream of consciousness and multifocal narration. Dark's novel also aligns the reader with a subversive female character who is linked to madness and degeneracy. Linda Hendon supposedly carries a "hereditary taint" of madness and represents the threat of "[i]nfection – disease – rottenness – creeping and invading": the very terms used by such commentators as Pearse to describe modernism (41, 183). Although "Curtain" was not as overtly modernist in style and theme as *Prelude to Christopher*, it nonetheless demonstrates Dark's ongoing interest in psychology, and employs the same free indirect discourse which came to characterise her 1930s novels.

The presence of Pearse's essay alongside Dark's story in the *Australian Mercury* suggests that modernist and anti-modernist positions were able to coexist in the same cultural field in interwar Australia. Dark makes a similar point in *Prelude to Christopher*: any attempt to quarantine culture is bound to fail because of the presence of not only outside influences but also inside ones. In this chapter I will use Dark's novel to argue a similar point about interwar Australia: that it already contained its own latent modernisms and modernities, which were often hidden amongst and inside of seemingly anti-modernist and anti-modern discourses.

Reading Modernism and Modernity into Cultural Nationalism

Dark started writing *Prelude to Christopher* in April 1930, just over a year after the birth of her son, Michael (Mick) Dark. The novel focuses on the complicated relationship between Nigel Hendon – a eugenicist who once founded a utopian colony on a Pacific island, "Hy-Brazil" – and his wife, Linda. The reader learns through flashbacks that, after discovering Linda's genetic predisposition to insanity on their wedding night, Nigel refuses her children. The novel is set many years after the failure of Nigel's social experiment in the Pacific. Nigel and Linda are now living in a small New South Wales country town called Moondoona, where Nigel works as a local doctor and Linda is viewed by her neighbours as a witch and a madwoman. As Nigel lies in hospital recovering from a motor accident, Linda is left alone with her disturbing thoughts and memories. The novel ends with Linda taking her own life, clearing the way for a future relationship between Nigel and the young nurse Kay – a relationship which will presumably lead to the birth of Kay's hoped-for child, Christopher.

In its four-day narrative structure, *Prelude to Christopher* evokes other modernist novels which similarly utilise a compressed time frame, such as James Joyce's *Ulysses*

---

13   P.R. Stephensen to Eleanor Dark, 24 October 1935, Eleanor Dark Papers, Mitchell Library, State Library of New South Wales, MLMSS 4545, Box 24.

(1922) and Virginia Woolf's *Mrs Dalloway* (1925). Like these authors, Dark employs a polyphonic form of narration, focalising the story through a small cast of characters: Nigel, Linda, Nigel's mother Mrs Hendon, Kay and Nigel's colleague Doctor Marlow (a name that Dark drew from Joseph Conrad's *Heart of Darkness*). The thoughts of each character are conveyed through a form of free indirect discourse that is similar to the stream of consciousness of other modernist writers such as Dorothy Richardson and Joyce. Australian commentators recognised these modernist devices in *Prelude to Christopher*: Nettie Palmer noted in her journal that Dark's method was "directed, in the modern way, at squeezing all the inwardness out of the subject", and Barnard Eldershaw employed the term "stream of consciousness" in relation to the novel.[14]

The reception of *Prelude to Christopher* is important as it challenges the idea that the gatekeepers of Australian literary culture were wholly resistant to modernism in the interwar period. Somewhat surprisingly, the very commentators who expressed considerable ambivalence about modernist style largely embraced Dark's novel. In Stephensen's influential essay *The Foundations of Culture in Australia: An Essay Towards National Self Respect* (1936) – the opening instalment of which was published in the *Australian Mercury* – he was particularly critical of the tendency of British modernists to explore depressing themes, treating Eliot as indicative of the "pessimism, dismay, and sickness of spirit" which had "afflicted all mankind" since the war.[15] In contrast, Australian writers were able to represent "a resurgence of the Spirit of Life" because the nation was "young enough, in mind and nerve, to remain uncynical under terrific shocks of fate". Stephensen cited *Lady Chatterley's Lover* (1928) and *Brave New World* (1932) as works of "decadence" and "ultra-sophistication" that represented Britain's "culture of decline" – criticisms that appear somewhat contradictory given that Stephensen was responsible for publishing an uncensored, secret edition of Lawrence's novel in London in 1930, and had featured works by Huxley in the *London Aphrodite*.[16] Perhaps the fact that both *Lady Chatterley's Lover* and *Brave New World* were banned in Australia at the time made them easy targets.

Expressing ambivalence about the decadence of English literature was also a means by which Australian writers could delineate their national interests from those of Britain. Miles Franklin was even more virulent than Stephensen in her rejection of writing that she associated with modernism. She was particularly critical of expatriate Australian writer Christina Stead's *Seven Poor Men of Sydney* (1934), which was published in the same year as *Prelude to Christopher*, writing that the former novel arrived "like a very big toad into our backyard puddle".[17] Franklin objected to the internationalism of Stead's novel, as well as its focus on

---

14 Nettie Palmer journal, 4 May 1934, quoted in Barbara Brooks with Judith Clark, *Eleanor Dark: A Writer's Life* (Sydney: Pan Macmillan, 1998), 129; M. Barnard Eldershaw, *Essays in Australian Fiction* (Freeport, NY: Books for Libraries Press, [1938] 1970), 197.

15 P.R. Stephensen, *The Foundations of Culture in Australia: An Essay Towards National Self Respect* (Gordon, NSW: W.J. Miles, 1936), 92–93.

16 Stephensen, *Foundations*, 55. See Moore, *Censor's Library*, 99, 109–10.

psychological introspection, referring to it as "Seven Poor Men of Bloomsbury … because of Sydney being presented in terms of the Bloomsbury coteries", and arguing that the characters were "touched with the brush of the coteries of the Latin Quarter, or Greenwich Village, or Bloomsbury".[18]

Why were these same criticisms not levelled at Dark's novel? If *Seven Poor Men of Sydney* involved psychological introspection, then so too did *Prelude to Christopher*. The same pessimistic tone that Stephensen traced in British literature was also evident in Dark's novel, and yet Stephensen celebrated the "tragic genre" of *Prelude to Christopher*, likening it to Shakespeare's *Hamlet*.[19] Nettie Palmer reviewed Dark's novel positively in her column in *All About Books*; Vance Palmer also liked it, writing to Dark to express "what a good book" he thought it was.[20] Franklin referred to it as "your splendidly terrible study with its brilliant technique", and wrote a review which Dark thought was the most perceptive she had read.[21] There were some who were more critical of the novel: Marjorie Barnard described it in a letter to Nettie as "a pretentious, over-written and unconvincing story", and more than one reviewer found it "somewhat hard to read".[22] These more negative reactions notwithstanding, the response of Australia's literary establishment towards such a recognisably modernist novel as *Prelude to Christopher* was surprisingly positive.

Dark's choice to publish her novel with a local press may have contributed to this positive Australian reception. In a courageous move given the importance of London publishers to Australian writers in this period, she wrote to her English literary agent John Farquharson that she was "anxious that it be published first in my own country, if possible".[23] She published the novel with Stephensen's Sydney press, despite being warned by Farquharson that this might preclude her from publishing the novel overseas. Choosing P.R. Stephensen & Co. was a financial risk for Dark: she had to fund the publication herself and lost money when Stephensen

---

17 Miles Franklin, *Laughter, Not for a Cage: Notes on Australian Writing, with Biographical Emphasis on the Struggles, Function, and Achievements of the Novel in Three Half-Centuries* (Sydney: Angus & Robertson, 1956), 172.
18 Franklin, *Laughter*, 172, 179.
19 P.R. Stephensen to Eleanor Dark, 28 June 1933, Dark Papers, MLMSS 4545, Box 24.
20 Vance Palmer to Eleanor Dark, 10 June 1934 [misdated 1933], Eleanor Dark Papers, National Library of Australia, MS 4998, Binder 1.
21 Miles Franklin to Eleanor Dark, 21 May 1934, Dark Papers, NLA MS 4998, Binder 1; Barbara Brooks, "Rereading *Prelude to Christopher*", in Eleanor Dark, *Prelude to Christopher* (Rushcutters Bay, NSW: Halstead Press, [1934] 1999), 185. Franklin's review of *Prelude to Christopher* was scheduled to appear in the second edition of the *Australian Mercury*, which never made it to print.
22 Marjorie Barnard to Nettie Palmer, 25 November 1935, quoted in Brooks with Clark, *Eleanor Dark*, 138; "A Satchel of Books", *Bulletin*, 30 May 1934, 5, from Eleanor Dark's album of newspaper clippings, Dark Papers, MLMSS 4545, Box 24. Other reviews mentioned in this chapter are also from this source, unless otherwise stated.
23 Eleanor Dark to John Farquharson, 19 December 1933, Dark Papers, MLMSS 4545, Box 24.

went bankrupt the following year. Nonetheless, *Prelude to Christopher* won her the Gold Medal, and she believed it was the best book she had written.[24]

The positive reception of *Prelude to Christopher* by key Australian cultural figures also demonstrates the modernity and internationalism of their form of nationalism. As Robert Dixon describes, these commentators hoped to "bring into being a national literature strong enough to survive internationally as both an import and an export culture".[25] In praising *Prelude to Christopher*, these critics referred to the impact it would have not only on local culture, but also on Australia's international reputation. Experimental modernism was therefore used as a benchmark by which to measure Australia's literary progress, even by commentators who expressed ambivalence about this style. Clearly, there was room within Australian cultural nationalism for pro-modernist positions, if only at particular and strategic moments.

In contrast to the generally positive reception of *Prelude to Christopher* by Australian critics, Dark struggled to get the novel published in London. It was viewed as too experimental by Collins, who only agreed to publish it after the more conventional novel that followed, *Return to Coolami* (1936).[26] Macmillan rejected *Prelude to Christopher* for publication in America, relaying to Dark through her agent at Curtis Brown that they found it too "melodramatic in conception".[27] The international agents and publishers with whom Dark corresponded and whom she relied upon for publication expressed fairly rigid ideas about the appropriate subject matter and style for an Australian woman writer, urging her to produce more formulaic romances that provided "a strong human theme" approached with "sincerity and sympathy, and preferably also with humour".[28] Drusilla Modjeska suggests that these expectations had a permanent effect on Dark's style and on the fate of Australian modernism more generally.[29] Although Dark continued to employ modernist techniques in her subsequent novels, she did so in more covert and less challenging ways. The point remains, however, that one of Australia's earliest and most important modernist novels was promoted and published by an Australian commentator who generally expressed resistance to modernism, while at the same time it was rejected by American publishers and accepted only with reluctance in England.

---

24   Brooks, "Rereading", 186.
25   Dixon, "Australian Fiction", 240.
26   See Helen Gildfind, "The Difficult Business of Writing: The Story of *Return to Coolami*'s Publication", *Antipodes* 27, no. 2 (2013), 157–60.
27   Alan C. Collins [Manager of Curtis Brown, New York Office] to Eleanor Dark, 7 December 1936, Dark Papers, MLMSS 4545, Box 24.
28   John Farquharson to Eleanor Dark, 23 June 1932, Dark Papers, MLMSS 4545, Box 24.
29   Drusilla Modjeska, "'A Hoodoo on That Book': The Publishing Misfortunes of an Eleanor Dark Novel", *Southerly* 57, no. 2 (1997): 79.

2 "A Masterpiece of Camouflage"

Eugenics, Modernism and the Modern Woman

The promotion of *Prelude to Christopher* by key cultural-nationalist figures suggests the same point that Dark makes on a thematic level in her novel: that culture cannot be quarantined from outside, dangerous influences, because these potential disruptions are already within. Dark suggests this by foregrounding the perspective of Linda, a middle-class white woman whose apparent genetic predisposition to insanity poses a threat to notions of white racial fitness.

As we saw in the preceding chapter, Dark was closely connected to a number of medical reformers whose work intersected with social medicine and eugenics, including her husband, Eric, and aunt Marion Piddington. Piddington was a founding member of the Racial Hygiene Association of New South Wales, intially called the Race Improvement Society. In her study of the Australian eugenics movement, historian Diana Wyndham describes Marion as "Australia's most energetic eugenist".[30] At the time that Dark was writing *Prelude to Christopher*, Marion was establishing the "Institute for Family Relations" at her flat in Sydney, where she provided classes and lectures on birth control, sex education and sterilisation. In the 1930s there was widespread anxiety in Australia that the nation's vast geography and relatively low population growth rate would make it vulnerable to foreign invasion, particularly from Asia.[31] Writing in *The World's Population Problems and a White Australia* (1930), H.L. Wilkinson noted the "very considerable nervousness amongst all classes of people in Australia in regard to Asiatic migration and the policy of restricting it".[32] Stephenson drew upon this anxiety, expressing the need to bolster the nation's white population: "[w]e need population in Australia in order to give us this feeling of security and invulnerability which alone can permit a people to develop a civilisation".[33] According to Stephensen, an increase in the white population from under seven million to "at least twenty or thirty millions" would constitute "a number finally adequate for defence against any possible military invasion", and provide "the only means of holding Australia as a home for the white race", whilst also bringing "an increase of Australian national self-consciousness: in other words, a distinctive Australian culture".[34]

---

30 Diana H. Wyndham, "Striving for National Fitness: Eugenics in Australia 1910s to 1930s" (PhD thesis, University of Sydney, 1996), 7.

31 David Walker, *Anxious Nation: Australia and the Rise of Asia, 1850–1939* (St. Lucia: University of Queensland Press, 1999), 3–4; Stephen Garton, "Eugenics in Australia and New Zealand: Laboratories of Racial Science", in *The Oxford Handbook of the History of Eugenics*, eds. Alison Bashford and Philippa Levine (New York: Oxford University Press, 2010), 245.

32 Quoted in David Walker, "Race Building and the Disciplining of White Australia", in *Legacies of White Australia: Race, Culture and Nation*, eds. Laksiri Jayasuriya, David Walker and Jan Gothard (Nedlands, WA: University of Western Australia Press, 2003), 48.

33 Stephensen, *Foundations*, 185.

34 Stephensen, *Foundations*, 149, 188. Stephensen's statements suggest the close links between his version of cultural nationalism and the pro-fascist views he developed in the late 1930s. See

For proponents of the racial hygiene or eugenics movement, the answer to the population problem was to produce "a vigorous race of white settlers" – a solution that gave child-bearing national significance.[35] The women-led Racial Hygiene Association was involved in "positive eugenics" efforts designed to improve the quality of the white population through education and by encouraging citizens to make a careful selection of marriage partner. They also advocated "negative eugenics" strategies aimed at protecting the population against hereditary "degeneracy", arguing that the issuing of health certificates and pre-marital medical examinations should be made a legal requirement for marriage, so that individuals affected by syphilis, epilepsy or intellectual disability would be prevented from marrying and having children.[36] In addition, they campaigned for the institution of segregation colonies where people with intellectual disabilities and mental health conditions would be restricted from producing children.[37]

In the interwar years, the efforts of the Racial Hygiene Association and other Australian women's reform groups were focused mostly on increasing the health of the white population rather than on addressing issues of racial Otherness.[38] This is perhaps surprising given that there was relatively little legislative support for eugenic strategies targeting white degeneracy (such as mandatory sterilisation), in part because Australian regulation was directed more towards quarantining the nation from perceived external threats from Asia and managing its Indigenous populations.[39] Yet the aims of Australian women's movements to boost the health of the white population can nonetheless be understood in the context of ideas about race: as Jane Carey shows, the issue of mental deficiency was given such prominence because of the broader project of "white racial improvement for national progress".[40] According to David Walker, the task of producing a race of white Australians that could occupy the continent and be physically fitter than the British "conferred an importance upon Australia, a serious national, even global purpose, it did not otherwise possess".[41]

Munro, *Inky Stephensen*, 197–219; Ellen Smith, "White Aborigines: Xavier Herbert, P.R. Stephensen and the *Publicist*", *Interventions* 16, no. 1 (2014): 97–116.

35   Garton, "Eugenics in Australia", 245.

36   Ann Curthoys, "Eugenics, Feminism, and Birth Control: The Case of Marion Piddington", *Hecate* 15, no. 1 (1989): 73. See also Anne Rees, "'The Quality and Not Only the Quantity of Australia's People': Ruby Rich and the Racial Hygiene Association of NSW", *Australian Feminist Studies* 27, no. 71 (2012): 71–92; Jane Carey, "'Not Only a White Race, but a Race of the Best Whites': The Women's Movement, White Australia and Eugenics between the Wars", in *Historicising Whiteness: Transnational Perspectives on the Construction of an Identity*, eds. Leigh Boucher, Jane Carey and Katherine Ellinghaus (Melbourne: RMIT Publishing in association with the School of Historical Studies, University of Melbourne, 2007), 162–70.

37   Rees, "'Quality'", 71.

38   Carey, "'Not Only a White Race'", 167.

39   Garton, "Eugenics in Australia", 247–49.

40   Carey, "'Not Only a White Race'", 167–68.

41   Walker, "Race Building", 42.

In *Prelude to Christopher*, Dark similarly focuses her critique of eugenic discourse on ideas of population building and white physical and mental fitness. Nigel is a proponent of eugenics: a "practical idealist", he reads *The Science of Eugenics* and Havelock Ellis' *The Psychology of Sex*, and believes that "the business of human life should be decently ordered" (16, 22). Nigel tells Linda that she cannot have children because "[s]cientifically you don't – you *can't* come up to the standard" (81). The colony of Hy-Brazil – for which Nigel selects only people he has "passed ... as mentally and physically sound" – represents a eugenic solution based on strategies of education, segregation and selective breeding (43).[42] In some ways, Nigel's reforming efforts can be likened to those of Eric Dark who, from the mid-1930s onwards, became increasingly interested in the links between the medical profession and economic conditions. Eric published a series of articles in the *Medical Journal of Australia*, which were eventually collected and released as *Medicine and the Social Order* (1942). He read broadly about eugenic-related topics, including Australia's declining birth rate, the effects of miscegenation and the nature versus nurture debate.[43]

Yet Dark presents an implicit challenge to Nigel's eugenic principles by foregrounding the rights and agency of Linda, the abjected individual. Linda is treated by others with intense suspicion: Nigel's mother regards her daughter-in-law as "something hardly human" and Kay doubts that Linda could "ever feel such a human and pitiful emotion as loneliness", commenting, "Such people should be – locked up" (112, 126, 175). In a passage of interior monologue, Kay wishes for Linda's death, asking, "What has anyone to gain from her life – even she herself? Oh, and so much if she were dead!" (178). The Racial Hygiene Association expressed their eugenic ideas in similarly instrumentalist terms: in a presentation on venereal disease in Sydney in 1929, pro-sterilisation speaker Angela Booth stated that "[t]here are, on this earth, people who should never have been born, and Nature should have taken them away".[44]

Although Linda has a physical disability – "a limp that looked like a swagger" (19) – she is not associated with other factors that were often linked with mental degeneracy in the interwar years, such as working-class conditions, urban poverty

---

42   The racial purpose of Nigel's eugenic colony is communicated more explicitly in an early draft of *Prelude to Christopher*, in which Nigel recalls the reaction of his colleague Doctor Penleigh to the idea of establishing a colony on Hy-Brazil: "But the tropics! ... You can't build the ideal white race in a black man's country!" Dark subsequently crossed this section out in the handwritten draft. See *Prelude to Christopher*, Handwritten Manuscript (Chapter 9), Dark Papers, MLMSS 4545, Box 2.

43   Eric Dark's library included, for example, a copy of John Bostock and L.J.J. Nye, *Whither Away: A Study of Race Psychology and the Factors Leading to Australia's National Decline* (Sydney: Angus & Robertson, 1936). Eric's personal copy has an inscription from the authors, dated 23 September 1936. The Darks' Library Collection, Varuna, the National Writers' House.

44   Angela Booth, "Medical Prophylaxis and Venereal Disease", in *Report of Australian Racial Hygiene Congress*, 1929 (Sydney: RHA, 1929), 26, quoted in Carey, "'Not Only a White Race'", 165.

or lack of education. Instead, she is presented through the tropes of the dangerous Modern Woman, linked with sophistication, sexuality and professional competence.[45] Linda works as a biologist's assistant in her uncle's laboratory, and Nigel describes her brain as "beautiful": "her thoughts moved with the precision dear to all scientists, logical in their conclusions, sharpened with the tang of quick, rather cynical humour" (44). In contrast to Linda, Kay is presented as the wholesome Australian Girl whose health and productivity are valued by the settler-colonial nation-state.[46] As a nurse, Kay is associated with "the normal, the healthy, the decent and the orderly" (24). She fits the Aryan ideal, her face "fresh and fair, her blue eyes defensively steady", her hair a "golden gleam beneath her white veil" (24–25).

At times, Dark seems to endorse these highly determined cultural images of the healthy Australian Girl and the dangerous Modern Woman. As the novel progresses, however, it becomes clear that she is interested in contesting and undercutting such types. In a climactic final scene between Kay and Linda, Dark emphasises not only the physical but also the internal differences between the two women: parading her vital, healthy body in the mirror in front of Linda, Kay is revealed to have a "subtle and unrealised instinct of pure cruelty" (176). In contrast, Linda is associated with inner strength, prompting Kay to ask, "What had she – what could she have – that gave her mastery over youth, that gave her power to look at everything she didn't possess, and smile like that?" (176). The answer to Kay's question belongs to the romance tradition: love. For Linda, Nigel is the "one irrefutable proof that love lasted, that courage triumphed, that beauty reigned", and love "[t]he one indestructible vindication of [a] futile life" (29–30, 180). *Prelude to Christopher* draws on both popular romance and middlebrow women's fiction – forms that Dark knew well because of her experience of writing magazine stories for Australian periodicals in the 1920s and 1930s. The novel's central complication – that "Nigel, worshipper of normality, apostle of Eugenics, founder of a colony whose basis was to be the rearing of healthy children from untainted stock, was about to marry a potential lunatic" – reflects the classic romantic conundrum of lovers thwarted by a seemingly unbridgeable divide, recast in light of 1930s eugenic concerns (43). If we read Linda as a kind of Bertha Mason – the racialised "madwoman in the attic" in Charlotte Bronte's *Jane Eyre* – then Dark's questioning of the ways in which she is Othered anticipates the thinking through of these ideas in Jean Rhys' *Wide Sargasso Sea* (1965).[47]

---

45   Susan Carson, "Finding Hy-Brazil: Eugenics and Modernism in the Pacific", *Hecate* 35, no. 1–2 (2009): 130. For more on the cultural type of the Modern Woman, see Liz Conor, *The Spectacular Modern Woman: Feminine Visibility in the 1920s* (Bloomington: Indiana University Press, 2004); Alys Eve Weinbaum and Modern Girl Around the World Research Group, *The Modern Girl Around the World: Consumption, Modernity, and Globalization* (Durham, NC: Duke University Press, 2008).

46   On the cultural type of the Australian Girl, see Angela Woollacott, *To Try Her Fortune in London: Australian Women, Colonialism, and Modernity* (New York: Oxford University Press, 2001).

47   For key critical works exploring the concept of the madwoman in relation to *Jane Eyre*, see Sandra M. Gilbert and Susan Gubar, *The Madwoman in the Attic: The Woman Writer and the Nineteenth-Century Literary Imagination* (New Haven, CT: Yale University Press, 1979); Gayatri

It is perhaps surprising that *Prelude to Christopher* presents such a challenge to eugenic ideas, given Dark's close familial connection to medical reformers such as Piddington. Yet her apparent discomfort with eugenic discourse can be linked to the particular context of interwar liberalism. After the Great War, the "New Liberal optimism" of the early decades of twentieth-century Australia, which we saw demonstrated so clearly in *Slow Dawning* (1932), was in decline, undermined by an increasing scepticism about state power.[48] The growing threat of fascism abroad and conservative nationalism at home seemed to weaken Australian liberal intellectuals' faith in government, so that in the work of interwar liberals such as Meredith Atkinson, Clarence Northcott, F.W. Eggleston and Keith Hancock, there appeared to be a return to more conservative, traditional beliefs about the need to protect the individual from the state.[49] In Australia in the 1930s, as in other liberal democracies, there were fears that "all ideologies, even reformist liberalism" were "contaminated by the presence of totalitarian regimes".[50] As Mark Greif recounts:

> Serious arguments were proffered that the world was becoming totalitarian because the totalitarian model of the rule of men was more efficient and effective than the liberal state's manner of leaving men on their own, proposals that reinforced the 1930s intellectuals' habitual mistrust of liberalism or fears on its behalf.[51]

In his address to the 1935 Paris Congress of International Writers for the Defence of Culture, E.M. Forster, for example, spoke about the "insidious" power of "the dictator-spirit working quietly away behind the façade of constitutional reforms".[52]

Dark shared with British liberal intellectuals a deep concern about the threats to individual freedom posed by seemingly benevolent policies of efficiency and nation building. In fact, *Prelude to Christopher* marks a significant shift in her liberal thinking, as shown by the novel's ambivalence about the role of the scientific expert. As explored in the previous chapter, *Slow Dawning* (1932) reflects a number of New Liberal commitments: it emphasises the close connection between the actions of an individual woman character and the collective progress of womankind, and projects confidence in the reforming role of the medical expert.

Chakravorty Spivak, "Three Women's Texts and a Critique of Imperialism", *Critical Inquiry* 12, no. 1 (1985): 243–61.

48 Tim Rowse, *Australian Liberalism and National Character* (Melbourne: Kibble Books, 1978), 125.

49 Robert Darby, "'An Instinct for Freedom': Political Undercurrents in the Short Fiction of Marjorie Barnard", *Literature & History* 26, no. 1 (2017): 57, 61; Rowse, *Australian Liberalism*, 41, 76; Ian Tregenza, "Are We 'All Socialists Now'? New Liberalism, State Socialism and the Australian Settlement", *Labour History* 102 (2012): 95.

50 Nicolas Birns, *Contemporary Australian Literature: A World Not Yet Dead* (Sydney: Sydney University Press, 2015), 34.

51 Mark Greif, *The Age of the Crisis of Man: Thought and Fiction in America, 1933–1973* (Princeton, NJ: Princeton University Press, 2003), 5.

52 E.M. Forster, "Liberty in England", in *Abinger Harvest* (London: Edward Arnold & Co, 1936), 65–66.

While *Slow Dawning* champions this role, *Prelude to Christopher* calls it into question by pitting the values of instrumentalism and efficiency against the rights of the individual. The novel's striking ending, in which Linda commits suicide, is framed as a triumph of individual choice: to Linda, death is "the knowledge of the ace of trumps in her hands!" and an assertion that "this is my life – mine!" (118, 119). As Anne Maxwell suggests, Linda's choice to end her own life is "identified as the very last freedom available to those rendered worthless by the implacable eugenic system that Nigel subscribes to".[53]

It is not a coincidence that it was in the 1930s that Dark started to employ a multi-perspectival form of narration in her novels. This narrative style invites the reader to recognise the existence of multiple points of view, and to challenge versions of truth that claim epistemological certainty. Linda is first introduced to the reader through other characters' perspectives which frame her in negative terms; through Dark's use of irony and other destabilising techniques, the reader comes to question these narrative voices and view their perspectives as contingent and limited. Dark increasingly privileges Linda's narrative as the novel progresses: through passages of free indirect discourse and extended flashbacks, the reader comes to a deeper understanding of the *reasons* for Linda's unusual behaviour, including her traumatic past, longing for normality, and desire for children. Linda is aware that she is seen as "a kind of woman-monster" and internalises the fears of hereditary madness, believing she will one day find her brain "soft, rotting away beneath her hands!" (83, 118). The heightened emotional register of these passages works to align the reader's sympathy with Linda. Nigel comes to ask whether, "in his unwavering refusal to father children who might carry the germ of insanity in their blood, he had been wrong after all? Wickedly unjust – to Linda?" (90). These devices are akin to those of other interwar modernist writers who similarly adopted narrative and rhetorical strategies aimed at "testing moral and political norms, including the norms of critical thinking".[54] Forster, for instance, employed strategies of indirectness and complexity in his 1930s essays as a means of "reminding readers of the contingency and contestability of their beliefs".[55] Woolf's complex, non-linear narratives similarly involved, as she described it, "thinking against the current, not with it".[56]

Most contemporary reviewers commented on the strikingly modern style of *Prelude to Christopher*, rather than on the novel's thematic focus on eugenics. M.

---

53 Anne Maxwell, "Education, Literature and the Emotions: A Salute to Eleanor Dark's *Prelude to Christopher*", *JASAL: Journal of the Association for the Study of Australian Literature* 12, no. 1 (2012): 9.

54 Rebecca L. Walkowitz, *Cosmopolitan Style: Modernism Beyond the Nation* (New York: Columbia University Press, 2006), 2.

55 Paul B. Armstrong, "Two Cheers for Tolerance: E.M. Forster's Ironic Liberalism", *Modernism/modernity* 16, no. 2 (2009): 288.

56 Virginia Woolf, "Thoughts on Peace in an Air Raid" [1940], in *The Essays of Virginia Woolf*, 6, ed. Stuart N. Clarke (London: Hogarth Press, 2011), 244.

Barnard Eldershaw noted Dark's interest in science and medicine, writing that her novels were "approached in a scientific spirit" with "a touch of the research laboratory and the text-book about them"; however, Barnard Eldershaw overlooked the ways in which the novel interrogates ideas of scientific rationalism.[57] Instead they wrote, somewhat unfairly, that "science, and above all the science of medicine, holds glamour for the author".[58] At least one reviewer did draw attention to the humanist message of Dark's novel. The *Daily Telegraph* connected *Prelude to Christopher* to international questions such as "Shall the State forbid the individual to have children, in the interests of the community?":

> One's first impulse is to insist that, where there is any shadow of suspicion of hereditary insanity, parenthood should be prevented. And, from the community point of view, that argument is probably unanswerable. But the community is a mass of individuals, and to each one of those his or her own rights are quite as important as the public interest.[59]

The reviewer concluded with the hope that *Prelude to Christopher* would make the eugenist "consider the mentally unsound person not merely as a subject for scientific consideration, but as a human being with a strong appeal to human sympathy".

Stylistic Hybridity in *Prelude to Christopher*

In its openness to multiple styles, genres and cultural influences, *Prelude to Christopher* challenges notions of literary purity. Dark signals the intertextuality and internationalism of her novel by using the opening bars of Tchaikovsky's sixth symphony, *Symphonie Pathetique*, as an epigraph.[60] The cover of Stephensen's edition features the musical score set against a vibrant orange background, with the blurb claiming that *Prelude to Christopher* was "[n]ot a book for weaklings or sentimentalists" but "a matured work of art", and describing Linda as "an Ophelia of the twentieth century" (Fig. 2.2). The connection between *Prelude to Christopher* and *Hamlet* is made clear in Nigel's recollection of his first encounter with Linda:

> Her green dress reminded him vaguely of water-weeds, her black hair might have been wet, so smoothly and flatly shining it lay round her head and ears. Only her body and her perfect skin told of her youth; about everything else there clung

---

57   Barnard Eldershaw, *Essays*, 194.
58   Barnard Eldershaw, *Essays*, 194.
59   "Madness in the Family", *Daily Telegraph* (Sydney), 19 May 1934.
60   Dark played the symphony while writing the novel. According to Eric, "it gave her an emotional feeling that she could in some strange way transfer to her writing". Quoted in "Eric Dark for Eleanor Dark", in *A Writing Life: Interviews with Australian Women Writers*, ed. Giulia Giuffre (Sydney; Boston: Allen & Unwin, 1990), 105.

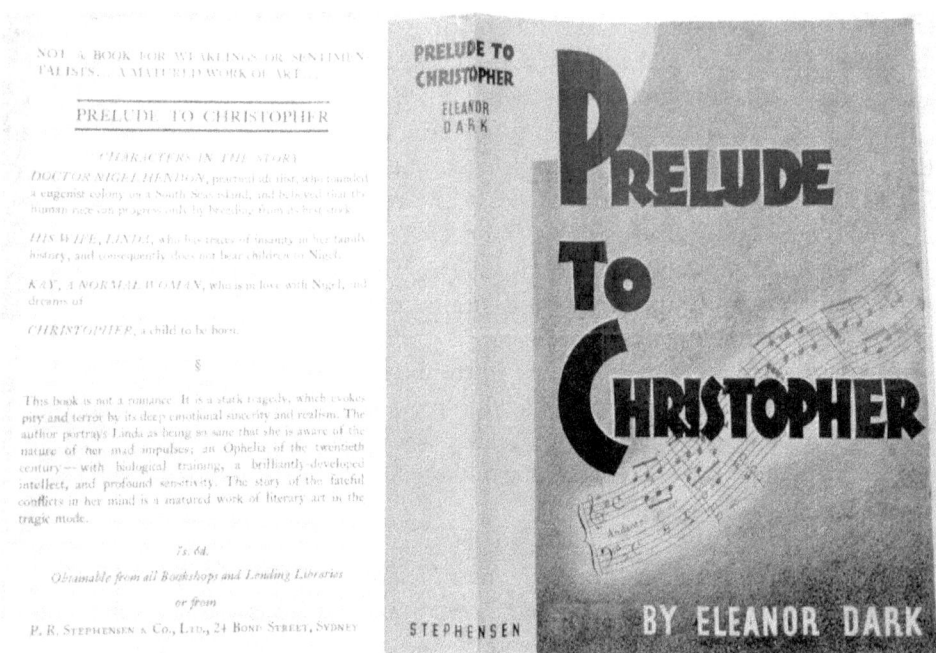

Figure 2.2 Book cover of the Australian edition of *Prelude to Christopher* (Sydney: P.R. Stephensen & Co., 1934). Eleanor Dark Papers. Mitchell Library, State Library of New South Wales. MLMSS 4545, Box 24.

something that vaguely insisted on experience, sophistication … her face seemed thin, almost gaunt, with high cheekbones, and pointed chin. Her mouth and whatever it told of were hidden defiantly behind the painted bow of her lips; above a straight nose, her green eyes watched, strangely brilliant, strangely restless. (16)

The references to "water-weeds" and "wet" hair in this extract create an implicit comparison between Linda and Ophelia, foreshadowing the former's eventual psychological breakdown and death. Dark also associates Linda with the archetypal *femme fatale* – a popular female type that circulated through both high and mass forms of culture, and linked women with decadence, independence, exoticism, uncontrolled sexuality and destruction.[61] Serpents and demons were often associated with the figure of the *femme fatale*: Linda is described by Doctor Marlow as "snake-like" and as "something forced underfoot, hated, feared, preserving its life with its subtlety, its gift for camouflage, its fangs" (66). Linda is also connected with ideas of witchcraft. She imagines herself as a "sorceress" with a "seething cauldron",

---

61   Lucas Tromly, "'Lady Tiger in a Tea Gown': Decadence, Kitsch, and Faulkner's *Femme Fatale*", *Mississippi Quarterly* 62, no. 3–4 (2011): 458–59; Ben Robbins, "Inscrutable Images and Cultural Migrations: Wartime Noir and the Compson Appendix", *Faulkner Journal* 28, no. 1 (2014): 62.

making "some odd concoction" of herbs for a "frightened client": poisons, love potions and "abortifacients" (29). As Nicole Moore points out, witchcraft represents a "premodern feminine science" that offers Linda an alternative lineage to the masculine discourse of modern science that has deemed her insane.[62] As a biologist who is also viewed as a "potential lunatic" (43), Linda is both an agent and a victim of modern science – a tension that Moore sees as crucial to Australian feminine modernism.[63]

At times *Prelude to Christopher* struggles to reconcile the competing images and ideas it puts into play. For example, the idea of woman as scientist sits uncomfortably alongside Dark's conception of woman as mother. As Modjeska and Moore both point out, Dark's critique of instrumentalism relies in part upon residual Victorian and essentialist understandings of femininity, in which women are associated with fundamental and supposedly natural imperatives such as the desire for children.[64] Dark argues through the women characters that eugenics ignores the "two most powerful urges of humanity – self-preservation and the reproduction of one's kind" (91–92). Linda's desire for maternity is expressed as her "primaeval right to bear a child", and in asserting this right she is "driven by the ancestral instincts of uncountable millions in a million generations" (91). The alignment of women with maternity echoes some of the ideas of Dark's father, Dowell O'Reilly, who believed that women's essential purpose was motherhood and that women had a closer connection to nature than men: "every man is a boy and every woman is a mother".[65]

Although the women characters are rarely allied in *Prelude to Christopher*, they are linked through their biological connection to nature and ability to think beyond masculine notions of scientific rationalism. Mrs Hendon observes, "human nature had proved itself too strong for his [Nigel's] theories … Never could you convince a woman that she must bear the children of a husband allotted to her by some scientific formula!" (108). Standing together at Nigel's hospital bed, Mrs Hendon, Kay and the hospital matron reflect on the foolishness of Nigel's ideals:

> Man! Absurd, pathetic creature … Absurd, pathetic Nigel, still clinging to his island with an unbelievable tenacity, craving still, after a lifetime of disillusionment, his short cut to a perfected humanity! Some thoughts like that lay dimly behind their simultaneous reaction.

---

62 Nicole Moore, "The Rational Natural: Conflicts of the Modern in Eleanor Dark", *Hecate* 27, no.1 (2001): 28.

63 Moore, "Rational Natural", 26.

64 See Drusilla Modjeska, *Exiles at Home: Australian Women Writers 1925–1945* (Sydney: Sirius Books, 1981), 219–20; Moore, "Rational Natural", 19–31.

65 Dowell O'Reilly to Mollie Miles, 25 April 1915, in *Dowell O'Reilly: From His Letters*, ed. Marie O'Reilly (London: Simpkin, Marshall, Hamilton, Kent & Co., 1927), 42; Frank Bongiorno, "'Every Woman a Mother': Radical Intellectuals, Sex Reform and the 'Woman Question' in Australia, 1890–1918", *Hecate* 27, no. 1 (2001): 54.

Some inherent sexual mistrust of short cuts – a mistrust born of endless generations that had watched the slow passing of ten moons, felt the deliberate unfolding of new life, watched the child's unhurried development through long years of brooding care. An instinct that some day, somehow, in *their* brains and bodies so irrevocably earth-chained, rather than in the soaring dreams of their menfolk, lay the ultimate salvation of the human race. (55–56)

Here, the "army of women" is not portrayed as a united collective advancing upon the promises of modernity, as in *Slow Dawning*, but as individual women who are nonetheless connected by their shared and evolutionary capacity for maternity. Their "inherent sexual mistrust of short cuts" means that the "natural", cyclical processes of the woman's body – "the slow passing of ten moons" of gestation – are placed in contrast with the fast-paced, artificial solutions provided by a scientific modernity that Dark genders as masculine.

In Dark's subsequent novels, she also attributes women, and particularly mothers, with a special role in challenging masculinised technological modernity. In *Return to Coolami*, Margery thinks thunderously of men's desire for war: "Let them not hold too cheaply the life which she is growing tired of producing for such a senseless purpose! … a day may come when she will say, 'No. I bear no more children into a world not fit to receive them –' And then what?"[66] In *Waterway* (1938), Lady Hegarty expresses similar anguish that, despite mothers' care for their sons, "some day they will be blown into small and bloody pieces by shell, or perhaps they will be gassed and their skins peel off … or perhaps they will fall, blazing, from the sky".[67] In *Lantana Lane* (1959), it is women who recognise that "the types of construction which most excite his [men's] enthusiasm are those which demand … excavation or demolition on a massive scale".[68] In each of these novels, gender is a key tactic by which Dark contests instrumentalism and articulates the problems with mid-century technological development – whether eugenics, war, nuclear power or the destruction of the natural environment – and yet this critique makes it difficult for her to explore fully the idea of woman as rational, scientific being.

Prelude to Christopher also draws significantly on the gothic mode. Linda's childhood is framed in gothic terms:

she had lived out her stormy, haunted childhood with her uncle's gently-spoken promise of ultimate lunacy peering at her from every shadow, lying in wait for her at every corner; the family tree which he had so painstakingly compiled and so beautifully set out on a great sheet of yellowish parchment, with the names of the "afflicted" in red ink, appearing like plague-spots here and there … (30)

---

66 Eleanor Dark, *Return to Coolami* (London: Collins, 1936), 200–01.
67 Eleanor Dark, *Waterway* (North Ryde, NSW: Angus & Robertson, [1938] 1990), 270. All subsequent references are to this edition and appear in parentheses in the text.
68 Eleanor Dark, *Lantana Lane* (London: Collins, 1959), 214.

The frightening house, malevolent uncle and use of terms such as "haunted", "lunacy" and "shadow" all invoke a sense of gothic melodrama, while the family tree represents eugenic fears of defective heredity. In the 1930s there was an international trend in gothic middlebrow women's novels, seen in the works of Daphne Du Maurier, Dodie Smith, Ivy Compton-Burnett and Agatha Christie. Modernist writers of the time also drew on the gothic mode: Djuna Barnes, William Faulkner, James Joyce and D.H. Lawrence showed a fascination with gothic images of the "unstable self", which Andrew Smith and Jeff Wallace trace to the influence of both psychoanalytic theory and the preoccupation with physical and mental degeneracy in Victorian novels such as Robert Louis Stevenson's *The Strange Case of Dr Jekyll and Mr Hyde* (1886) and H.G. Wells' *The Island of Doctor Moreau* (1896) – a work that also influenced Dark's novel.[69]

Prelude to Christopher can be read as a novel of ideas similar to those produced by Wells and Aldous Huxley. It absorbs the popular nature versus nurture debate that was in international circulation at the time, asking readers to consider whether Linda's eventual psychological unravelling is a product of her genetic makeup or treatment by others. The nature/nurture debate had special significance in Australia, where it underpinned important questions such as whether settler culture could adapt to a tropical climate and environment.[70] *Prelude to Christopher* ultimately comes to endorse a nurture view: despite the fact that Linda has been taught to regard "human beings as elaborated amoebae" and herself as "a sort of walking storehouse of accumulated insanity", Dark resists this biological determinism (81). It is not genetics that ultimately leads to Linda's psychological breakdown but the rejection and marginalisation she experiences within society. She becomes "all that they believed her to be" due to the "sideways glances" of "smug, sane people", with Dark writing, "[m]ad they called her – mad they made her" (64). It is an assertion that environmental conditions, rather than biological ones, are the key causes of insanity – a finding that is particularly poignant given the death of Dark's own mother, Eleanor Grace O'Reilly, in Callan Park Hospital for the Insane in 1914.

In *Brave New World*, published only two years before *Prelude to Christopher*, Huxley pits the humanist, individualistic values of John against the utilitarian, technocratic ethos of the World State, which employs scientific forms of control to regulate the processes of maternity and child-rearing. Both Huxley and Dark's novels involve the suicide of a central character as a means of resisting state control. Although *Brave New World* was banned as an import to Australia between late 1932 and early 1937, it nonetheless circulated quite widely,[71] and given Dark's admiration

---

69 Andrew Smith and Jeff Wallace, "Introduction: Gothic Modernisms: History, Culture and Aesthetics", in *Gothic Modernisms*, eds. Andrew Smith and Jeff Wallace (New York: Palgrave, 2001), 3, 4; Andrew Smith, "Vampirism, Masculinity and Degeneracy: D.H. Lawrence's Modernist Gothic", in *Gothic Modernisms*, 150; Carson, "Finding Hy-Brazil", 125.
70 Walker, "Race Building", 42.
71 Moore, *Censor's Library*, 99.

for Huxley's writing[72] it is possible that she obtained a copy. At the very least, the two authors articulated similar strands of liberal thought that involved a defence of the rights of the individual and opposition to eugenic discourse. The parallels between the two works suggest that Dark was able to write about subversive ideas at a time when they were largely censored in Australia, perhaps in part because the modernism of her writing was camouflaged amongst other genres such as romance fiction.

It is easy to see a connection between the rhetoric of eugenics and attempts to quarantine Australian literary culture from seemingly foreign styles such as modernism: as Pearse's essay demonstrates, these fears were articulated through the same language. The fact that Dark aligns *Prelude to Christopher* with a woman associated with disease and degeneracy seems particularly significant, as it suggests that she was pushing back against fears of both genetic abnormality and cosmopolitan, hybrid narrative styles. Dark's overseas publishers approached the novel's stylistic hybridity as a problem, suggesting that she return to more straight-forward romance plots with happy endings. It is only more recently that the "oppositions" and "transgressions" in *Prelude to Christopher* have started to be appreciated as "fit[ting] with writing now better than they did with most other Australian novels in the 1930s".[73]

The Quarantined Island

If Linda's perspective suggests the cruelty of trying to insulate culture from supposedly dangerous elements, then this point is also played out on a larger scale through the backstory of Nigel's failed eugenic colony, Hy-Brazil. Dark constructs the island as a complex and multi-layered site. Like many island utopias in Western fictions, it represents "the desire for singular, bounded objects of possession".[74] The name is drawn from the mythical island said to lie in the Atlantic Ocean west of Ireland, yet as in Wells' novel *The Island of Doctor Moreau*, Dark sets her fictional island in the South Pacific – a region where Australia played a sub-imperial role in the interwar period. As Victoria Kuttainen, Susann Liebich and Sarah Galletly show, in the interwar period the Pacific often operated in Australian culture "as an icon of modernity, signifying the conquest of space by speed, power, and stylish technology".[75] In setting the island in the Pacific, Dark represents the colonial

---

72 Susan Carson, "Conversations with the Land: Environmental Questions and Eleanor Dark", in *Land and Identity: Proceedings of the 1997 Conference University of New England Armidale New South Wales 27–30 September 1997*, eds. Michael Deves and Jennifer A. McDonnell (Association for the Study of Australian Literature, 1998), 192.

73 Brooks, "Rereading", 189.

74 Elizabeth McMahon, *Islands, Identity and the Literary Imagination* (London; New York: Anthem Press, 2016), 183.

desire to resolve the problems of modern Western society through projecting white fantasies onto a newly available, seemingly exotic location.

Dark had not travelled to the Pacific when she wrote *Prelude to Christopher*, although three years after the novel's publication she made brief stops at Auckland, Suva and Honolulu when travelling to America by ocean liner. It is likely that the setting of Hy-Brazil was influenced by images of the Pacific presented in stories, illustrations and advertisements that appeared in the periodicals in which Dark published her short stories, as well as in contemporary films and novels featuring the South Seas. Australian writers often used Pacific locations as sites of "the psychological quest, the testing ground on the limits of Western society".[76] Middlebrow magazines featured advertisements for leisure cruises with Pacific destinations, and published travel narratives set in Pacific locations. Fictional stories such as Vance Palmer's "Pacific Nights", published in *BP Magazine* in 1931, offered both entertainment and education; these narratives made readers more familiar with Pacific locations and strengthened Australia's consciousness of its geographical proximity to the Asia-Pacific, while often reinforcing ideas of white superiority.[77] Many of the stories in interwar magazines featured specific and realistic detail about Pacific locations and people, although others were set on fictional and seemingly uninhabited tropical islands like Dark's Hy-Brazil.[78]

In one sense, *Prelude to Christopher* participates in the exoticising of Pacific locations, depicting Hy-Brazil as an unspoiled Eden and projecting a narrative of Western utopia on to what is treated as the blank space of a South Seas island. Stephensen's Australian edition capitalised on the novel's Pacific setting, with the blurb describing Nigel as a man "who founded a eugenist colony on a South Seas island". The English edition similarly evoked a sense of romance and adventure through its cover illustration, which features boats moored in a cove in front of a cluster of buildings at the base of a snow-capped mountain – an image that evokes ideas of exploration and colonisation (Fig. 2.3).

Hy-Brazil also operates as a stand-in for Australia in Dark's novel. Suvendrini Perera argues that Australia exhibits an "insular imagination" an "unattainable desire for insularity" that is reinforced through its self-conception as "*the* island

---

75   Victoria Kuttainen, Susann Liebich and Sarah Galletly, *Transported Imagination: Australian Interwar Magazines and the Geographical Imaginaries of Colonial Modernity* (Amherst, NY: Cambria Press, 2018), 47.

76   Adrian Vickers, "Kipling Goes South", *Australian Cultural History* 9 (1990): 73.

77   Vance Palmer, "Pacific Nights", *BP Magazine*, June 1931, 29. See also Victoria Kuttainen and Sarah Galletly, "Making Friends of the Nations: Australian Interwar Magazines and Middlebrow Orientalism in the Pacific", *Journeys: The International Journal of Travel and Travel Writing* 17, no. 2 (2016): 43–44; Victoria Kuttainen, "Illustrating Mobility: Networks of Visual Print Culture and the Periodical Contexts of Modern Australian Writing", *JASAL: Journal of the Association for the Study of Australian Literature* 17, no. 2 (2017): 12; Anna Johnston, "Becoming 'Pacific-Minded': Australian Middlebrow Writers in the 1940s and the Mobility of Texts", *Transfers: Interdisciplinary Journal of Mobility Studies* 7, no. 1 (2017): 90.

78   Kuttainen, Liebich and Galletly, *Transported Imagination*, 248.

Figure 2.3 Book cover of the English edition of *Prelude to Christopher* (London: Collins, 1936). Eleanor Dark Papers. Mitchell Library, State Library of New South Wales. MLMSS 4545, Box 24.

nation, a singular territorial body girt by sea".[79] A similar desire for insularity can be seen in Nigel's hope that the island will offer an "antidote" to modern, urban conditions (9). He first learns about the island from a sailor he encounters at Sydney Harbour, after which:

> he could think of nothing but cliffs which shot up four hundred feet from a white thunder of surf; of a coastline which swept down to long curves of creamy beach, jagged promontories of foam-veiled rock, a tiny, almost land-locked harbour: of a little world almost exquisitely alone ... A little Eden ... (9)

Nigel's mental image of Hy-Brazil creates a ghostly doubling of the geography of Sydney: the island's "almost land-locked harbour" evokes that of Sydney Harbour – the originary site of British invasion in Australia in 1788. Nigel hopes to find a "little world – unpeopled", just as British colonists viewed Australia through the concept of *terra nullius* (10). After learning of the island's existence, Nigel:

---

79 Suvendrini Perera, *Australia and the Insular Imagination: Beaches, Borders, Boats, and Bodies* (New York: Palgrave Macmillan, 2009), 1, 8, 10.

walked faster … as though the elusive goal he sought were somewhere over there in the Gardens – or down by the bustling Quay – or across the harbour – or even out through the Heads, to sea. That thought of the sea brought him back with a queer little shock to the island. (11)

Here, Nigel first seeks a utopian solution within the city of Sydney, as signified by the iconic landmarks of the Royal Botanic Garden and Circular Quay. His subsequent conviction that the solution lies out "to sea" in the Pacific suggests the "elusive" nature of the colonial project itself, wherein the West seeks to locate a "little Eden" in each New World.

Underpinning the fictional plot of Hy-Brazil is a failed utopian experiment in Australia's history: the "New Australia" colony established by William Lane in Paraguay in the 1890s. Dark knew one of the colonists of New Australia: the poet Mary Gilmore. In *Prelude to Christopher*, Dark reveals herself to be somewhat sympathetic to such utopic visions, to the extent that Vincent Buckley included the novel in his account of a "strain of utopian humanism" in Australian literature.[80] Dark presents Hy-Brazil as a paradise where "[b]abies were born and crawled on green grass under a warm sun" (65). The island is framed as preferable to the alternatives of frenzied nationalism that Dark associates with the ANZAC campaign, and to the conditions of "incredible ignorance, incredible ugliness and futility" of the modern city (9). In particular, the novel seems sympathetic to Nigel's criticisms of Australia's involvement in a British war. Nigel compares the country sacrificing its best men to killing "magnificent prize cattle" and choosing instead to "breed … from the culls", using the discourse of eugenics to present an anti-imperial argument that would likely have resonated with Stephensen (110). Nigel's resistant form of nationalism is similar to that of Roger Blair in *Waterway*, who advocates the need for a fledgling nation to strengthen its own population, against "man-power wasted … genius flung away … potential fatherhood most tragically sacrificed" (63).

Yet *Prelude to Christopher* also calls into question the idea of the island utopia by showing the impossibility of forming a community that is quarantined from transnational forces, and by challenging the notion that white racial problems can be solved through acts of colonisation, migration and cultural quarantine. The novel's compressed temporal scale makes readers aware from the beginning that Nigel's social experiment somehow ended in failure – a narrative structure that, as Paul Giles notes, foregrounds questions of eugenics by placing the idea of an "open future" in tension with one predetermined by the past.[81] We learn through flashbacks that, despite Nigel's prohibition, Linda sought a lover on the island and

---

80 Vincent Buckley, "Utopianism and Vitalism in Australian Literature", *Quadrant* 3, no. 2 (1959): 43–45.

81 Paul Giles, *Backgazing: Reverse Time in Modernist Culture* (Oxford: Oxford University Press, 2019), 203.

became pregnant with a child whose existence would threaten the genetic purity of the colony. In an ironic twist, it is not Linda's child that brings about the colony's downfall but rather the settlers' choice to join British troops to fight in the Great War. When news of the coming conflict reaches the island, the members abandon Nigel's pacifist principles and sing, "*Rule, Britannia! Britannia rule the waves*", staging a violent riot that leads to the death of Linda's unborn child and brings an end to the social experiment (102). Dark frames the war as the ultimate form of insanity – one character describes it as "the brain-storm of a mad civilisation" – and it leads Nigel to realise that "somewhere beneath the soundness of these picked human beings ... a dark current ran silently, a blood-lust, a savagery" that renders each one "what Linda feared to be, a homicidal lunatic" (58, 60).

The collapse of the island utopia due to the arrival of the war is a complicated plot twist that is treated ambivalently due to Dark's anti-imperialist sympathies; however, it underscores one of the major points of the novel: that an island is not a bounded site but is rather implicated in international and imperial networks. When read as a commentary about Australia itself, Dark's narrative draws attention to the impossibility of quarantining settler culture from outside influences.

Prelude to Christopher and the Middlebrow

In its representation of an unstable and controversial heroine and its fragmented narrative style, *Prelude to Christopher* has less in common with middlebrow women's fiction than Dark's other novels. Nonetheless, it was mediated through both middlebrow and highbrow distribution mechanisms and cultural institutions. When *Prelude to Christopher* was published in London in 1936, it was selected as a London *Evening Standard* Book of the Month: a middlebrow cultural channel that was viewed as part of the novel's success by Australian reviewers and readers. In Australia, the novel received attention in periodicals that were linked to the distinctive forms of local middlebrow culture that started to emerge in the 1930s, including *All About Books* and *The Home*.[82] In her review for *All About Books*, a magazine which, according to David Carter, was a "distinctive manifestation of contemporary middlebrow cultural dispositions", Nettie Palmer emphasised the quality of *Prelude to Christopher* and claimed it "deserves the attention" of all readers.[83] Her review suggests the role of middlebrow book culture in drawing readers' attention to quality books amidst the proliferation of newly published works, and the efforts of Australian cultural commentators to construct a broad yet discerning national readership.[84]

---

82 David Carter, "The Mystery of the Missing Middlebrow or The C(o)urse of Good Taste", in *Imagining Australia: Literature and Culture in the New New World*, eds. Judith Ryan and Chris Wallace-Crabbe (Cambridge, MA.; London: Harvard University Press, 2004), 138.

83 Carter, *Always Almost*, 155; Nettie Palmer, *All About Books*, 12 June 1934.

In its connection to transnational ideas about psychology and the cosmopolitan Modern Woman, *Prelude to Christopher* also offered Australian women readers the opportunity to view themselves as modern – an aspiration which was connected closely with Australian middlebrow culture.[85] Dark's novel was reviewed in a number of magazines that were associated with the new market segment of women's culture, including the *Australian Women's Weekly*, Adelaide's *Housewife*, The Australian Woman's Mirror, the *Woman's Budget*, the *Sydney Morning Herald's* "Women's Supplement" and *The Home*. Many of these reviews drew attention to the modernity of Dark's novel. The reviewer in *The Home*, F.S. Burnell, celebrated Dark's representation of "a cultured and sensitive woman", finding Linda "compellingly real".[86] Burnell noted the internationalism of Dark's novel, reading it as a "study in morbid psychology" that reflected the current "world-neurosis during a trying period" and "the modern tendency to look unpleasant facts boldly in the face". Her description of Linda may well have appealed to readers of *The Home*, which was one of the places where modernist design first circulated in Australia, through the promotion of domestic décor and arts and crafts.[87] *The Home* targeted "an upmarket readership who were or wished to become sophisticated and highly mobile worldly moderns".[88] One of the ways in which it did this was by publishing and promoting the work of Australian writers linked with "cosmopolitanism, travel, and modernity", including Katharine Susannah Prichard, Henrietta Drake-Brockman, Vance Palmer, Jean Devanny and Dark.[89] Through publishing short stories by these writers, *The Home* promoted the idea of Australians taking "part in the world's stylish modern marketplace as residents of an 'Island Continent' connected to the world".[90] Dark's novel is described by Burnell as "the most distinguished achievement by an Australian writer that I at least have so far encountered".[91] Adjacent to the review is an advertisement for women's Dunlop Sport Shoes that features a relaxed-looking couple sitting opposite each other on reclining deck chairs, possibly evoking travel on a modern cruise liner (Fig. 2.4). As with the visual advertisement, the review of *Prelude to Christopher* offers Australian women readers a chance to participate in modernity through the discerning consumption of products, including books and shoes.

Prelude to Christopher was also reviewed in publications that can be associated with more elite formations of literary taste. *Desiderata* (1929–39), a small-circulation journal printed in Adelaide, is one of the few examples of a highbrow publication

---

84   David Carter, "Literary, but Not Too Literary; Joyous, but Not Jazzy: *Triad* Magazine, Antipodean Modernity and the Middlebrow", *Modernism/modernity* 25, no. 2 (2018): 260.
85   Carter, *Always Almost*, x.
86   F.S. Burnell, "Some Books", *The Home* 16, no. 3 (1 March 1935): 11.
87   Carter, "Mystery", 182.
88   Kuttainen, "Illustrating Mobility", 7.
89   Kuttainen, "Illustrating Mobility", 10–11.
90   Kuttainen, "Illustrating Mobility", 12.
91   Burnell, "Some Books", 11.

Figure 2.4 *The Home* 16, no. 3 (1 March 1935), 11.

in interwar Australia.[92] The journal used Dark's novel as part of its rallying cry for a more discerning Australian reading public:

It is encouraging that Australia has found a writer who has produced a wholly mature novel and that an Australian publisher has ideals and courage sufficient

---

92 *Desiderata* has been linked to both high modernism and the middlebrow. Nicole Moore describes it as a "small modernist art and literary journal", whereas David Carter associates the magazine's commitment to contemporaneity and its "modernising Anglocentrism" with the historical middlebrow. See Moore, *Censor's Library*, 124; David Carter, "Modernising Anglocentrism: *Desiderata* and Literary Time", in *Republics of Letters*, 85–98.

to issue the book. The next step, and one no less difficult, is to find a public with courage to read it.

> *Prelude to Christopher* calls for courage. Its theme is a pathological case which thousands would devour if presented in the journalese of our press, but offered as it is with power and the haunting terror of truth, will in all probability, and to our shame, be shunned by the novel-reading public with a chain-store mind, and ignored by more serious readers who "have no time for novels".
>
> Sad as this is, it is made sadder by the knowledge that in *Prelude to Christopher* Eleanor Dark has given us, if not the first, then the most mature piece of fiction yet written and published in this country.[93]

The reviewer's call for "more serious readers" with neither "a chain-store mind" nor a dismissive attitude towards novels shows how *Desiderata* sought to encourage a modern Australian literature – and a community of readers with the "courage" to appreciate it. It would appear that, in the mid-1930s, *Prelude to Christopher* could be aligned with both high forms of culture and the broad appeal of the middlebrow.

Prelude to Christopher and Racial Otherness

Prelude to Christopher has enjoyed renewed attention in Australian feminist and literary studies over the past two decades.[94] It was reissued in 1999 by Halstead Press, with a coda by Barbara Brooks framing the novel as part of "a continuing story … about taking risks, asking questions, about women … who refuse to conform".[95] Anne Maxwell finds in Dark's novel a "less biologically determined and more humane" philosophy that could well speak to a twenty-first century shaped by neoliberalism and economic rationalism.[96] Although Dark's novel is still largely unknown outside of Australia, it featured recently as part of a series in the *Paris Review* called "Feminize Your Canon", in which Emma Garman celebrates the "bold experimentalism" of a novel whose "central theme – utopianism and tyranny are two sides of the same coin – is [currently] being played out on the world stage".[97]

To what extent should this recuperation of Dark's novel extend to her treatment of issues of race? Dark's challenge to eugenics appears very prescient in the context of the rise of Nazism in the 1930s. Quite remarkably, *Prelude to Christopher* was

---

93   "*Prelude to Christopher*", *Desiderata*, 1 August 1934.
94   See, for example, Sarah Ailwood, "Anxious Beginnings: Mental Illness, Reproduction and Nation Building in 'Prelude' and *Prelude to Christopher*", *Katherine Mansfield Studies* 2 (2010), 20–38; Susan Carson, "From Sydney and Shanghai: Australian and Chinese Women Writing Modernism", in *Pacific Rim Modernisms*, eds. Mary Ann Gillies, Helen Sword and Steven Yao (Toronto: University of Toronto Press, 2009), 173–98; Moore, "Rational Natural", 19–31.
95   Brooks, "Rereading", 189.
96   Maxwell, "Education, Literature and the Emotions", 9–10.
97   Emma Garman, "Feminize Your Canon: Eleanor Dark", *Paris Review*, 9 January 2019. https://www.theparisreview.org/blog/2019/01/09/feminize-your-canon-eleanor-dark/.

published by the German press Tauchnitz in 1937, as part of their series of English-language classics, and it was also translated into German; Brooks asks, "what would readers there [in Germany] have thought?"[98] There are some significant limitations to Dark's critique, however, which any recuperation of *Prelude to Christopher* needs to avoid reproducing. Like *Slow Dawning*, Dark's second novel focuses almost exclusively on the professional middle classes, with working-class characters such as Linda's maid, Nance, playing minor and undeveloped roles. In one sense, Linda embodies the racialised fears of 1930s Australia – as critics have noted, she is associated with some of the stereotypical tropes of the Oriental Woman, including black hair, a white, painted face, silk robes and inscrutable facial expressions.[99] The link between Linda and Bertha Mason, of Jamaican creole origins, furthers this sense of Linda as the racialised Other. The fact that Dark aligns the reader's sympathies with this character therefore appears to suggest that she favours modernity, cosmopolitanism and alterity over isolationist, nativist visions of Australian culture. Yet Linda is nonetheless a white woman, and although her life is restricted, she has access to forms of education and mobility that would not have been available to many women of colour at the time.

Furthermore, Dark's novel tends to elide the issue of racial Otherness by conflating it with mental illness. This is demonstrated in a passage where Nigel laments that:

> [a] man who bred a sheep with infinite care would marry a tuberculous wife and rear an infected family; a man who grew his fruit trees undeviatingly true to type would beget a brood of half-caste children. A man … under-nourished, meagre both mentally and physically – still must have his wife, his child, his long, shadowy, dreadful line of foredoomed posterity. (22)

Nigel's sentiments echo those of Valerie who, in *Slow Dawning*, laments that a "drunken labourer who likes to carry syphilis from a prostitute" is able to "infect his wife and unborn children".[100] The inclusion of "half-caste children" in Nigel's list of hereditary factors suggests that Dark was aware of racial Otherness as something that preoccupied eugenicists, and to some extent tried to encompass it in her critique. Yet by creating a conceptual link between racial difference and other traits such as disease, physical disability and mental illness, she effectively obscures the histories of imperialism that informed what was then termed the "half-caste problem" – the perceived threat to white racial purity posed by children of mixed race. In the 1930s, scientists and social reformers proffered various eugenic-based solutions to this perceived problem, ranging from segregation, forced marriage,

---

98   Brooks, "Rereading", 188.
99   Carson, "Finding Hy-Brazil", 130.
100 Eleanor Dark, *Slow Dawning* (London: John Long, 1932), 91.

sterilisation and biological absorption into the white Australian population. This latter idea was based on a strand of eugenic thought related to adaptability to environment, and became widely accepted by the late 1930s, informing the policy of forced removal of Aboriginal children now known as the Stolen Generations.[101] The restrictions to non-white immigration that were enshrined in the 1901 *Immigration Restriction Act* (and which continued to be upheld in the years between the wars) were similarly underpinned by eugenic fears of "inferior" racial types – in this case, from Asia.[102] Dark treats Linda as metonymic of a variety of issues, including racial difference, in a strategy that both invokes the reader's sympathy for the marginalised Other and succeeds in concealing the notion of race from view.

Given that Dark was concerned about scientific management and control, why did she not make overt mention of the racial policies that affected Aboriginal Australians and restricted Asian immigration at the time of the novel's release? It is difficult to assess whether this omission was due to the controversial nature of these issues, or Dark's own lack of awareness or interest. *Prelude to Christopher* was published only five years after Katharine Susannah Prichard's *Coonardoo* (1929) which, in its representation of a romantic and sexual relationship between an Aboriginal woman and a white man, scandalised white Australian commentators.[103] Dark tackled some of these issues in *The Timeless Land* historical trilogy (1941–53), although by this time the idea of interracial relationships seemed to be less controversial.[104]

Other works that Dark published at the same time as *Prelude to Christopher* reveal that she was not simply reluctant to engage with contemporary forms of racism but was at times actively involved in the transmission of racist attitudes. Only months after *Prelude to Christopher* was first released, Dark published a detective story in the *Bulletin* – one of the first of her magazine tales to appear under her own name. The murderer in "Murder on the Ninth Green" is eventually uncovered as the Mayor, Torode, whom Dark reveals to have "negro blood in him".[105] Reinforcing common associations between mixed race, degeneracy and criminality, the detective Morris Bray states that Torode has "all the morbid sensitiveness of the nearly-white", prompting the narrator to reflect on "the indefinable taint of evil and uncleanness that so often goes with the mixing of

101 Russell McGregor, *Imagined Destinies: Aboriginal Australians and the Doomed Race Theory, 1880–1939* (Carlton, Vic: Melbourne University Press, 1997), 161. On the Stolen Generations, see National Inquiry into the Separation of Aboriginal and Torres Strait Islander Children from their Families (Australia), *Bringing Them Home: Report of the National Inquiry into the Separation of Aboriginal and Torres Strait Islander Children from Their Families* (Sydney: Human Rights and Equal Opportunity Commission, 1997).
102 See Carey, "'Not Only a White Race'", 166–67; Walker, *Anxious Nation*, 168–72.
103 See, for example, Cecil Mann, "*Coonardoo*", *Bulletin*, 14 August 1929, 2.
104 Brooks with Clark, *Eleanor Dark*, 349.
105 Eleanor Dark, "Murder on the Ninth Green", *Bulletin*, 12 December 1934, 30. All subsequent references to this story appear in parentheses in the text.

bloods which should not be mixed" (30). Torode commits the murder because the victim "roused the black in him" so that "his racial instinct went mad with terror" (30) – statements that suggest that Dark was willing to exploit the nature side of the nature versus nurture debate to provide a sensational conclusion to her story.

Dark's highly stylised detective story, which draws on the tropes of the golden age detective fiction she enjoyed reading, throws into question the extent to which her critique of eugenic discourse extends to those of non-white backgrounds – at least at this point of her writing. While *Prelude to Christopher* contests biological determinism through its treatment of mental illness, the lesser-known "Murder on the Ninth Green" relies upon the racist trope of the murderous, mixed-race man consumed by a deterministic "racial instinct". Perhaps the radical qualities of *Prelude to Christopher* have been somewhat overstated in recent accounts, or perhaps they extend only to white, middle-class subjects. I suggest that we can read the contradictions of *Prelude to Christopher* – and of Dark's body of work more generally – as representative of some of the broader complexities of settler colonialism and its modernisms. At times, settler modernist texts are able to disturb triumphal accounts of colonialism, national progress and white racial fitness; however, they also contribute to the dispossession of Aboriginal peoples, offering new ways for settler writers to represent their own desires for cultural belonging. Any emancipatory potential of these texts must therefore be weighed against the ways in which they also participate in the ongoing structures of settler colonialism, including settler society's claims to cultural legitimacy.

Conclusion: "Portrait of Linda"

This chapter began with Pearse's image of modernism as a virus that threatened to infect literary culture and travel across national borders. While 1930s commentators such as Pearse used this medicalised metaphor to warn against modernism, more recent scholars have utilised the same language to champion modernism's virus-like ability to resist eradication and to adapt to local conditions. In their examination of the "Antipodean modernisms" of Australia and New Zealand, Prudence Black and Stephen Muecke ask: "if indeed the European strains of the modernist 'virus' took hold in the Antipodes, did they not result in the development of local strains, indigenous versions of modernism, whose history remains unfinished and only partially described?"[106] Drawing on the intersections between postcolonialism and the new modernist studies of recent decades, these critics understand modernism as decentred and developing through processes of translation, adaptation and hybridisation across multiple contact zones. Yet it is

---

106 Prudence Black and Stephen Muecke, "Antipodean Modernisms: Australia and New Zealand", in *The Oxford Handbook of Modernisms*, eds. Peter Brooker, Andrzej Gąsiorek, Deborah Longworth and Andrew Thacker (New York: Oxford University Press, 2010), 961.

important to note that not all of the ways in which modernism "hybridised", adapted to local conditions or emerged in Australia (and other settler-colonial contexts) were positive. As Peter Kirkpatrick demonstrates in his study of the Jindyworobak poets, one of the tropes that "became viral" in settler Australian literature was the tendency of white artists to represent themselves through "forms of Aboriginal experience" – a kind of modernist primitivism wherein settler-colonial fantasies of belonging were expressed through the appropriation of Aboriginal cultures.[107] Another strategy was to elide the presence of First Nations peoples altogether, or – as is the case in *Prelude to Christopher* – to collapse Aboriginality with ideas pertaining to whiteness. These tactics of appropriation, displacement and erasure can be read as part of the contradictory logics of settler colonialism, as settler society seeks to eliminate native peoples – both literally and symbolically – and at the same time to claim indigeneity for settler-nationalist purposes.[108]

Both the positive potential and inherent problems of settler modernism are displayed in Prelude to Christopher. In one scene, Dark provides a description of an expressionist painting by Linda's lover, d'Aubert. Titled "Portrait of Linda", the artwork represents her as the serpent in the Garden of Eden. The canvas is "weirdly daubed with incoherent masses of colour", depicting "the unreal loveliness of some mythical country" (105–06): Hy-Brazil. Linda appears in "the right background of the picture where, in a tangle of shadow", she is "like a part of the shade itself", looking "incredibly furtive and apart" (106). Viewing this "masterpiece of camouflage", Doctor Marlow is struck by a strong impression of "evil" and "outcast uncleanliness" (106). This scene captures through modernist ekphrasis both the fear of the Other and its haunting, inescapable presence. If we take this Other to be mental illness, then d'Aubert's painting suggests that such elements already existed inside white culture. If we read the Other as modernism, then the image reveals that this style already operated within interwar Australia, "camouflaged" amongst other impulses such as cultural nationalism. In each case, rather than viewing such influences as threats, Dark reframes them as productive: in her work, the serpent becomes the generative influence, hidden amongst and subtly altering the textual canvas of the interwar period.

At the same time, another more insidious act of camouflage could be at work in this painting. Dark offers the middle-class white woman as the abjected figure of 1930s Australia, displacing and concealing the racial Other who was more likely to be affected by eugenic policies at the time. The white body is thereby offered as

---

107 Kirkpatrick, "Jindy Modernist", 99. See also Dan Tout, "Neither Nationalists nor Universalists: Rex Ingamells and the Jindyworobaks", *Australian Humanities Review* 61 (2017): 1–26; Smith, "White Aborigines", 97–116.

108 Patrick Wolfe, "Settler Colonialism and the Elimination of the Native", *Journal of Genocide Research* 8, no. 4 (2006): 389. See also Jeanine Leane, "Tracking our Country in Settler Literature", *JASAL: Journal of the Association for the Study of Australian Literature* 14, no. 3 (2014): 1–17.

a metonym for the black one in a troubling manoeuvre that suggests the ongoing attempt of settler culture – and its modernisms – to elide and supplant Indigenous sovereignty.[109] The fact that Dark's novel is able both to unsettle and reify notions of white cultural legitimacy is indicative of the complexities of the literary modernisms produced in settler-colonial contexts.

---

109 For discussion of a similar sleight of hand in Dark's later novel *Waterway* (1938), see Brigid Rooney, "Time's Abyss: Australian Literary Modernism and the Scene of the Ferry Wreck", in *Scenes of Reading: Is Australian Literature a World Literature?*, eds. Robert Dixon and Brigid Rooney (North Melbourne: Australian Scholarly, 2013), 109.

3

"Like the Lens of a Camera": Commercial Culture, Settler Belonging and Middlebrow Modernism in *Return to Coolami* (1936)

> [T]he eye only sees what it brings with it the power of seeing, and there is evidence to suggest that this is a hard country for the average outsider to see.
>> Eleanor Dark, "Australia and the Australians", 1944.[1]

> Fixed in a sweet meniscus, out of Time,
> Out of the torrent, like the fainter land
> Lensed in a bubble's ghostly camera ...
>> Kenneth Slessor, "Out of Time", 1939.[2]

The publication of *Return to Coolami* in New York in 1936 marked Eleanor Dark's entry into the American book market, and the beginning of a new kind of success and visibility which would culminate in the selection of *The Timeless Land* (1941) for the Book-of-the-Month Club. Her London publisher, William Collins, sent a copy of *Return to Coolami* to Macmillan New York, who forwarded Dark a two hundred and fifty dollar advance.[3] Yet the enthusiasm of English and American publishers for *Return to Coolami* was bittersweet for Dark. Collins and Macmillan both favoured it over the more experimental *Prelude to Christopher* (1934), which Dark continued to argue was her best book. Although he was "very interested" in *Prelude to Christopher*, Collins felt that "from a sales point of view ... it may not be quite so easy to handle as *Return to Coolami*".[4] He agreed to publish the earlier novel only after the more conventional *Return to Coolami* was first released. The more predictable love plot,

---

1   Eleanor Dark, "Australia and the Australians", in *Australia Week-End Book* 3, eds. Sydney Ure Smith and Gwen Morton Spencer (Sydney: Ure Smith, 1944), 13. All subsequent references to this essay appear in parentheses in the text.

2   Kenneth Slessor, *Selected Poems of Kenneth Slessor* (Sydney: HarperCollins, 2014), 105.

3   Barbara Brooks with Judith Clark, *Eleanor Dark: A Writer's Life* (Sydney: Pan Macmillan, 1998), 145.

4   W.A.R. Collins to Eleanor Dark, 12 March 1936, Eleanor Dark Papers, Mitchell Library, State Library of New South Wales, MLMSS 4545, Box 25.

happy ending and "benign subject matter" of Dark's third novel has thus been read as her attempt to satisfy the desires of her international publishers.[5]

American publication meant that Australian authors could reach a much larger readership and achieve higher sales than was possible in Australia. Yet Dark was increasingly aware that many of her contemporaries linked popular success in the American market with crass consumerism, artistic compromise and a lack of commitment to national culture.[6] Miles Franklin sent Dark a copy of a review of *Return to Coolami* from a San Francisco newspaper, writing, "Well received, and Mcmillan [*sic*], that puts you on a highbrow level where I cd nevair nevair climb."[7] In her reply, Dark dismissed *Return to Coolami* as a "punk book", quoting an American review that described it as "for the porch and hammock trade", and writing, "Anything less highbrow could hardly be imagined!"[8] She seems to have approached *Return to Coolami* as something of a joke: before sending the manuscript to England, she wrote an inscription on the front, "Dedicated to all young women who are looking for something suitable for their mothers to read", which she then crossed out.[9] Even though it won her the Australian Literary Society Gold Medal for the second time, Dark viewed *Return to Coolami* as primarily a strategic novel, writing to Franklin that if she hadn't written it, both *Prelude to Christopher* and *Sun Across the Sky* (1937) would "still be doing the rounds of publishers, unaccepted and despised!"[10] In 1941, Marjorie Barnard wrote to Dark after *The Timeless Land* was selected for the Book-of-the-Month Club: "American success *is* success, & should be profitable."[11] This was something of a backhanded compliment, and hinted that Dark may have sold out.

Return to Coolami utilises many of the same recognisably modernist narrative techniques as *Prelude to Christopher*, including a compressed time frame (in this case, reduced from four days to two), multifocal narration, frequent use of free indirect discourse, flashbacks and a focus on introspection. It is, however, less fragmented in its narrative style, and features more narrative action and fewer challenging themes than *Prelude to Christopher*. *Return to Coolami* also has stronger Australian content and a more recognisable bush setting. Although a number of Dark's novels challenge patriotic attachment, *Return to Coolami* expresses a fairly straightforward commitment to the settler nation, and absorbs a

---

5   Helen Gildfind, "The Difficult Business of Writing: The Story of *Return to Coolami*'s Publication", *Antipodes* 27, no. 2 (2013): 158. See also Drusilla Modjeska, "'A Hoodoo on that Book': The Publishing Misfortunes of an Eleanor Dark Novel", *Southerly* 57, no. 2 (1997): 73–96.

6   Richard Nile, "Literary Democracy and the Politics of Reputation", in *The Oxford Literary History of Australia*, eds. Bruce Bennett, Jennifer Strauss and Chris Wallace-Crabbe (Melbourne: Oxford University Press, 1998), 143.

7   Miles Franklin to Eleanor Dark, 15 September 1936, Eleanor Dark Papers, National Library of Australia, MS 4998, Binder 1.

8   Eleanor Dark to Miles Franklin, 19 September 1936, quoted in Brooks with Clark, *Eleanor Dark*, 150.

9   Brooks with Clark, *Eleanor Dark*, 144.

10   Eleanor Dark to Miles Franklin, 19 September 1936, quoted in Brooks with Clark, *Eleanor Dark*, 152.

11   Marjorie Barnard to Eleanor Dark, 18 August 1941, Dark Papers, NLA MS 4998, Binder 1.

number of ideas and images from 1930s cultural nationalism. In its combination of experimental narrative techniques, an accessible and romantic plot and nationalist themes, it provides the mixture of the seriousness and pleasure which was characteristic of middlebrow book culture,[12] and this no doubt made the novel much easier to fit into overseas book markets. In fact, *Return to Coolami* provides a very clear articulation of Dark's middlebrow modernist aesthetic.

It has been argued that *Return to Coolami* symbolises a move away from literary modernism, both in Dark's work and in Australian literature more generally. According to Drusilla Modjeska, modernism did not thrive in 1930s Australian literature as it did in the works of such visual artists as Grace Crowley, Dorrit Black, Margaret Preston and Grace Cossington Smith; instead, critics, publishers and agents, mostly from overseas, were "lined up against" the development of Australian literary modernism, so that novelists such as Christina Stead and Patrick White needed to leave the country in order to "shift into an idiom and aesthetic of modernism".[13] Modjeska argues "it is difficult to make any modernist claims at all" about *Return to Coolami*, as Dark made "huge concessions to ease of reading" so that "a jaunty journey and love's happy outcome replace psychosis, eugenics and suicide [in *Prelude to Christopher*]".[14] I want to suggest that *Return to Coolami* represents not the disappearance of modernism from the Australian literary scene but a kind of sideways move by Dark, and by a number of Australian writers, which involved actively negotiating the expectations of the British and American book markets along with other, more local concerns. Australian writers often had to make a variety of accommodations and perform complex balancing acts as they "negotiated the fault lines between national and international literary space", with such manoeuvres at times enabling them to reach broader cultural and geographical audiences.[15]

The pragmatism that Dark showed in navigating international markets could be interpreted negatively, as evidence of a mercenary mindset or lack of sincerity, or it could show her deep desire to have her work read by a broad audience. We can see a similar form of pragmatism in the work of English and American women writers who also negotiated the high middlebrow. Rebecca West, for example, published a number of short stories in the American weekly the *Saturday Evening Post*, in the late 1920s and 1930s, in a move that took advantage of international market opportunities for middlebrow fiction.[16] A certain level of pragmatism, Jaime

---

12 David Carter, "'Some Means of Learning of the Best New Books': *All About Books* and the Modern Reader", *Australian Literary Studies* 22, no. 3 (2006): 333.
13 Modjeska, "'Hoodoo'", 74.
14 Modjeska, "'Hoodoo'", 82, 85.
15 Robert Dixon, "Australian Fiction and the World Republic of Letters, 1890–1950", in *The Cambridge History of Australian Literature*, ed. Peter Pierce (Cambridge: Cambridge University Press, 2009), 244.
16 Margaret D. Stetz, "Sideways Feminism: Rebecca West and the *Saturday Evening Post*, 1928", *The Space Between* 9, no. 1 (2013): 72.

Harker suggests, is an attribute of the progressive middlebrow – texts which "kept a highbrow concern with serious issues while satisfying both the lowbrow's demand for accessibility and entertainment".[17] Writers of the progressive middlebrow, like Dark, employed a number of different strategies to "move their readers", mixing genres and drawing on popular forms such as romance.[18] It is this same pragmatism and broad appeal that Virginia Woolf criticised in her satirical essay "Middlebrow", as she described the middlebrow as "mixed ... rather nastily, with money, fame, power, or prestige".[19] And yet middlebrow writers were able to reach a much broader audience than experimental modernists, as they provided both "invitations to question dominant ideologies" and opportunities for escapism.[20]

Viewing the middlebrow as a positive attribute of Dark's work at times involves reading against her own statements. There are difficulties in calling any writer middlebrow, as it is "a posthumous designation" that many writers would resist.[21] This would no doubt have been the case for Dark, who was not always at ease with the accommodations she had to make to achieve publication and commercial success. Many middlebrow women writers in England and America experienced similar anxiety and battled it with a characteristic form of humour.[22] In this chapter, I consider Dark's comments about her writing as part of a discourse shaped by the fraught "battle of the brows" of the interwar years, rather than as evidence of a lack of cultural value in her work. In fact, *Return to Coolami* is a key work in Dark's oeuvre, and deserves an important place in Australian literary and cultural history, as it showcases the entanglements between literary modernism, mass consumer culture and settler nationalism that frequently characterised the work produced by settler writers and artists between the wars.

Modernism and its Relations

The substantial reassessments of global and regional articulations of modernism of the past few decades allow us to challenge Drusilla Modjeska's claim that *Return to Coolami* represents a retreat from modernist experimentation. Reappraisals of

---

17   Jaime Harker, "Progressive Middlebrow: Dorothy Canfield, Women's Magazines, and Popular Feminism in the Twenties", in *Middlebrow Moderns: Popular American Women Writers of the 1920s*, eds. Lisa Botshon and Meredith Goldsmith (Boston, MA: Northeastern University Press, 2003), 119, 131.

18   Jaime Harker, *America the Middlebrow: Women's Novels, Progressivism, and Middlebrow Authorship between the Wars* (Amherst: University of Massachusetts Press, 2007), 20.

19   Virginia Woolf, "Middlebrow" [1932], *Collected Essays*, vol. 2 (London: Hogarth Press, 1942), 115.

20   Christoph Ehland and Cornelia Wächter, "Introduction: '... All Granite, Fog and Female Fiction'", in *Middlebrow and Gender, 1890–1945*, eds. Christoph Ehland and Cornelia Wächter (Leiden; Boston: Brill Rodopi, 2016), 3–4.

21   Harker, *America*, 18.

22   Melissa Sullivan and Sophie Blanch, "Introduction: The Middlebrow – Within or Without Modernism", *Modernist Cultures* 6, no. 1 (2011): 3.

Australian modernity, for instance, have increasingly revealed interwar Australia's contemporaneity and internationalism, rather than its insularity and resistance to cultural innovation. In light of this, *Return to Coolami* can be understood as just one instance of the "vast confidence with which 'Australian' subjects engaged with modernity locally and internationally".[23] As David Carter and Roger Osborne show, from the late 1920s to the mid-1940s a number of "substantial novels" by Australian writers were published and reviewed in America, including Martin Boyd's *The Madeleine Heritage* (1928), M. Barnard Eldershaw's *A House is Built* (1929) and *Green Memory* (1931), Henry Handel Richardson's *The Fortunes of Richard Mahony* trilogy (1929–30), Katharine Susannah Prichard's *Coonardoo* (1930) and G.B. Lancaster's *Pageant* (1933).[24] *Return to Coolami* is part of this sequence (although Dark's greatest American success came later, with *The Timeless Land*) and its relationship to America helps to open up studies of interwar Australian literature beyond a purely national or imperial focus, to one that is "transnodal" in its investigation of the relationships between Australia, Britain and America.[25]

Furthermore, recent studies of vernacular modernisms draw attention to the close relationship between modernism and popular culture, allowing us to recognise modernist engagements even in a novel depicting "a jaunty journey and love's happy outcome". *Return to Coolami* points to the complex interconnection between modernism and popular culture, as Dark draws on experiences and metaphors related to cinema, photography and motor travel to represent visual perception. Although the relationship between commercial culture and experimental modernism can be seen in instances of metropolitan modernism – for example, through the connections between British modernist texts and the gothic genre, cinema and fashion[26] – it is possible that the link may be even more clearly demonstrated in instances of settler-colonial modernity. Robert Dixon and Veronica Kelly raise the possibility that Australian modernism was the product of popular and vernacular rather than elite expressions of culture.[27] A few case studies serve to make this point. The first is the work of Australian modernist photographers of the 1930s, Olive Cotton and Max Dupain. Cotton and Dupain

---

23 Robert Dixon and Veronica Kelly, "Australian Vernacular Modernities: People, Sites and Practices", in *Impact of the Modern: Vernacular Modernities in Australia 1870s–1960s*, eds. Robert Dixon and Veronica Kelly (Sydney: Sydney University Press, 2008), xx.

24 David Carter and Roger Osborne, *Australian Books and Authors in the American Marketplace 1840s–1940s* (Sydney: Sydney University Press, 2018), 231.

25 Carter and Osborne, *American Marketplace*, 12.

26 See Celia Marshik, *At the Mercy of their Clothes: Modernism, the Middlebrow, and British Garment Culture* (New York: Columbia University Press, 2016); David Seed, "British Modernists Encounter the Cinema", in *Literature and the Visual Media*, ed. David Seed (Suffolk; New York: D.S. Brewer, 2005); Andrew Smith and Jeff Wallace, eds., *Gothic Modernisms* (New York: Palgrave, 2001); David Trotter, "Virginia Woolf and Cinema", *Film Studies*, no. 6 (2005): 13–26.

27 Dixon and Kelly, "Australian Vernacular Modernities", xxi; Robert Dixon, *Photography, Early Cinema and Colonial Modernity: Frank Hurley's Synchronized Lecture Entertainments* (London: Anthem Press, 2013), xxx.

both relied on commercial employment as a source of income and used it as an "opportunity for experimentation",[28] just as Dark did in the stories she wrote for commercial magazines in the 1920s. Cotton and Dupain produced photographs for a wide range of advertising campaigns that spanned architecture, fashion and home appliances, often employing modernist photographic techniques to promote new products.[29] The photograph Dupain took for Amalgamated Wireless Australasia to advertise the Hoover vacuum cleaner (1937), for example, adopts a modernist approach to light and shadow that is reminiscent of the style of Hungarian photographer André Kertész (Fig. 3.1).[30] Cotton adopted a similar approach when commissioned to take a photograph for an advertisement for spectacle frames, with her work "Glasses" (circa 1937) emphasising the beauty and simplicity of the frames through the use of stark studio lighting and attention to patterns of shadow (Fig. 3.2). In these images, objects designed with modernist principles in mind are subjected to modernist photographic aesthetics, so that modernism and mass culture intermingle in advertisements that were circulated through such middlebrow channels as *The Home*.

The poetry of Kenneth Slessor also demonstrates the close relationship between mass consumer culture and modernism in the Australian case. Although Slessor's poetry is well established as an example of Australian high modernism, more recent studies show how his work developed through an interaction with popular modernity. The light verse that he wrote for the populist newspaper *Smith's Weekly* between 1928 and 1933 was crucial to the development of his poetry: as Peter Kirkpatrick explains, these verses acted as "a bridging medium between the poet's earlier *Vision* phase and the later, more mature collections".[31] Slessor's work as a film critic for *Smith's Weekly* also had a significant impact on his modernist style and subject matter. Philip Mead argues that the poem "Five Bells" "could not have existed … without his (and Australia's) specific historical experience of film and the cultural apparatus of the cinema".[32] Slessor was not alone in drawing on styles influenced by popular cinema; scholars have noted similar influences in the work of a number of other well-known modernists, including Virginia Woolf and William Faulkner.[33]

---

28 Helen Ennis, *Photography and Australia* (London: Reaktion Books, 2007), 75.
29 Isobel Crombie, *Body Culture: Max Dupain, Photography and Australian Culture, 1919–1939* (Melbourne: Images Publishing Group/National Gallery of Victoria, 2004), 135–37.
30 National Gallery of Australia, Notes on Max Dupain's "Advertisement for Hoover", https://cs.nga.gov.au/Detail.cfm?IRN=86635.
31 Peter Kirkpatrick, "When Skyscrapers Burst into Lilac", in *Kenneth Slessor: Critical Readings*, ed. Philip Mead (St. Lucia: University of Queensland Press, 1997), 177.
32 Philip Mead, *Networked Language: Culture & History in Australian Poetry* (North Melbourne: Australian Scholarly, 2008), 34.
33 See Ben Robbins, "Inscrutable Images and Cultural Migrations: Wartime Noir and the Compson Appendix", *Faulkner Journal* 28, no. 1 (2014): 55–77; Seed, "British Modernists", 48–73; David Trotter, "Virginia Woolf and Cinema", *Film Studies*, no. 6 (2005): 13–26.

Figure 3.1 Max Dupain. "Advertisement for Hoover", 1937. Gelatin silver photograph. National Gallery of Australia.

Return to Coolami demonstrates some of the convergences between modernism, the middlebrow and cultural nationalism. In Dark's novel, the avant-garde ideas and fragmented style of *Prelude to Christopher* are moderated to create a more accessible narrative for middlebrow readers. Perhaps surprisingly for a novel that achieved wider international circulation than Dark's previous works, *Return to Coolami* also features rich descriptions of the Australian rural landscape. In this sense, it can be linked with what David Carter has termed the "national middlebrow", a mode of writing that advocated "virtuous citizenship and 'nationed' modernity" in bestseller novels and popular non-fiction by Australian writers such as Frank Clune and Ernestine Hill, and in middlebrow magazines that promoted domestic and regional forms of tourism such as *Walkabout* (1934–74).[34] In blending modernist styles with regional commitments, *Return to Coolami* contributes to the growing body of scholarship

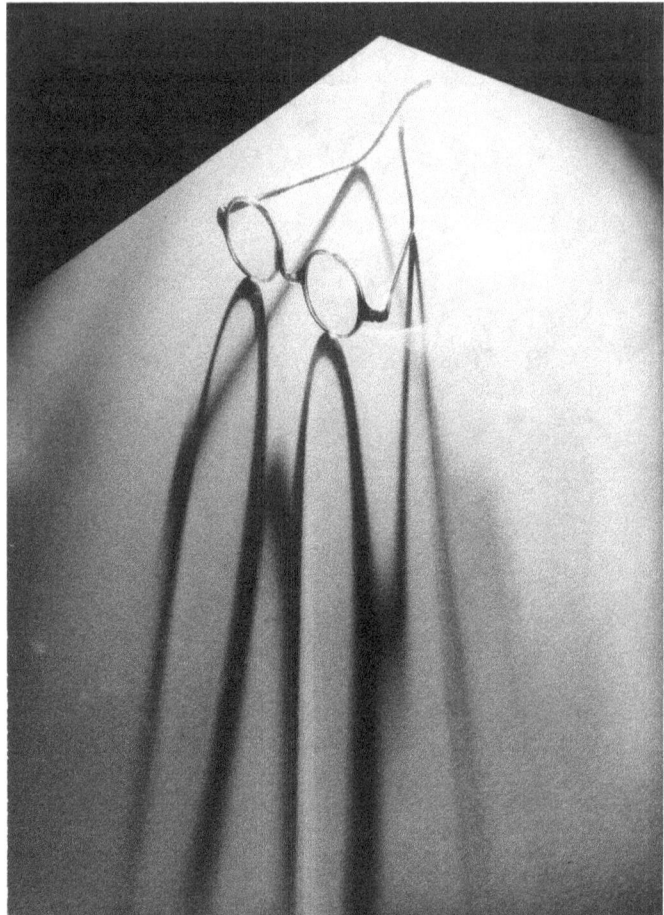

Figure 3.2 Olive Cotton. "Glasses", circa 1937. Gelatin silver photograph. Art Gallery of New South Wales.

in Australian literary studies that suggests that nationally focused writers were embedded in wider transnational movements and negotiated international aesthetics.

---

34   David Carter, "The Mystery of the Missing Middlebrow or The C(o)urse of Good Taste", in *Imagining Australia: Literature and Culture in the New New World*, eds. Judith Ryan and Chris Wallace-Crabbe (Cambridge, MA; London: Harvard University Press, 2004), 184; Robyn Greaves, "A 'Grim and Fascinating' Land of Opportunity: The *Walkabout* Women and Australia", *JASAL: Journal of the Association for the Study of Australian Literature* 14, no. 5 (2014): 3.

Return to Coolami and mass culture

The action of *Return to Coolami* takes place over two days, on a road trip from a fictional Sydney suburb, Balloo, over the Blue Mountains (Dharug and Gundungurra Country), to central-western New South Wales (Wiradjuri Country). The four main characters, Tom Drew, his wife Millicent, their daughter Susan and her husband Bret, are preoccupied with their pasts, which intrude upon the present day in the form of vivid memories. The novel follows the tangled love plot of a popular romance. Through the narrative developments, including two near-fatal accidents, all complications are resolved: Bret realises that he is indeed in love with his wife Susan, and they happily return to Bret's pastoral holding, Coolami. At the same time, Tom's materialistic suburban values are transformed into a true appreciation of the Australian outback. By the end of the novel, Tom and Millicent make plans to leave suburbia and purchase Wondabyne, a sheep station that neighbours Coolami.

As a novel that depicts a journey towards the interior of the continent, *Return to Coolami* locates the spiritual heart of the nation in the hinterland rather than the metropolis. This regional focus would have fitted well with state-based initiatives designed to encourage Australian citizens to explore non-urban environments, such as the Australian National Travel Authority (ANTA) which published *Walkabout*.[35] Dark seems conscious of her novel's relationship to domestic tourism. In one scene a character even launches into a parody of a tourism advertisement: "The Blue Mountains offer panoramic views of unparalleled magnificence. Nowhere else in the world are to be found scenes of more majestic splendour, while the bracing atmosphere, sparkling water, exquisite flora and intriguing fauna provide endless attractions for the tourist."[36] The novel's focus on non-metropolitan locations is perhaps surprising for a writer who, in *Waterway*, would celebrate the cosmopolitan modernity of Sydney. There are some glimpses of Dark as a writer of the city in *Return to Coolami*, captured by the description of the recently built Harbour Bridge as "this sudden miraculous beauty curving and spinning away over your head, this cobweb wizardry of steel, of soaring arches just touched by the first sunrays to a faint golden warmth" (26). It is an image that celebrates industrial modernity and resonates with the modernist photographs of the Harbour Bridge taken by Dupain in the mid-1930s. As in the work of many Australian modernist photographers, however, Dark's "embrace of modernity was selective rather than unequivocal".[37] Helen Ennis suggests that, for these photographers, it was not the city that inspired their 1930s modernism but rather other aspects such as "the 'primitive' and the natural world".[38] Similarly in *Return to Coolami*, the city is

---

35 Anna Johnston and Mitchell Rolls, *Travelling Home, Walkabout Magazine and Mid-Twentieth-Century Australia* (London; New York: Anthem Press, 2016), 3.

36 Eleanor Dark, *Return to Coolami* (London: Collins, 1936), 124. All subsequent references are to this edition and appear in parentheses in the text.

37 Ennis, *Photography*, 76.

linked with stultifying suburbia, and the characters escape it in favour of the mythic qualities of the bush.

Of all of Dark's novels, *Return to Coolami* is most engaged with the technological developments of interwar Australia, including, as one character remarks, "such luxuries as electric light and wireless and the talkies and, presently, television" (58). The novel refers to a number of elements of contemporary mass culture, including popular love songs and Hollywood icons. *Return to Coolami* also revels in the speed and mobility associated with the modern motor car, so that historian John Knott describes it as the "pre-eminent Australian evocation of motoring between the wars".[39] Dark enjoyed taking road trips to rural New South Wales with her family and friends (Fig. 3.3). It is likely that the road travelled by Bret and Susan was modelled on one such road trip to the Warrumbungle Range.[40]

Return to Coolami also has close links with popular cinema. Dark was an avid fan of the cinema: she had what she described as a "plebian passion for the screen".[41] She often attended the local picture palaces in Katoomba several times in one week. In the years between the wars, Australian cinemas mostly screened Hollywood films.[42] Dark's diary lists an impressive range of films that she viewed in the mid-1930s, including American features such as *China Seas* (1935), *Vanessa* (1935), *The Last Days of Pompeii* (1935), *Little Lord Fauntleroy* (1936), *Romeo and Juliet* (1936) and Laurel and Hardy; the British adventure film *Elephant Boy* (1937); and the German *Mädchen in Uniform* (1931).[43] In *Slow Dawning* (1932), Dark depicts Valerie going to the pictures to escape the pressures of her professional and personal life: she "fixed her eyes and her attention resolutely on the screen; it would be such a relief to lose oneself altogether for a little while".[44] The Darks' 1937 trip to America included a bus tour of Hollywood film stars' houses, showing how Australians' experiences of the United States were mediated through their encounters with cinema.[45] Dark also thought about her novels in relation to cinema: when trying to interest her American publishers in *Prelude to Christopher*, she suggested they send the manuscript to Bette Davis, whom she felt should play the part of Linda Hendon.[46]

---

38 Ennis, *Photography*, 63, 75–76.
39 John William Knott, "The 'Conquering Car': Technology, Symbolism and the Motorisation of Australia before World War II", *Australian Historical Studies* 31, no. 114 (2000): 15.
40 A. Grove Day, *Eleanor Dark* (Boston: Twayne, 1976), 53.
41 Eleanor Dark to Nettie Palmer, 1930s, quoted in Susan Carson, "Making the Modern: The Writing of Eleanor Dark" (PhD thesis, University of Queensland, 1999), 70.
42 Anne Rees, "Stepping Through the Silver Screen: Australian Women Encounter America, 1930s–1950s", *Journeys: The International Journal of Travel and Travel Writing* 17, no. 2 (2016): 50.
43 Eleanor Dark 1936–1939 diary, Dark Papers, MLMSS 4545, Box 21.
44 Eleanor Dark, *Slow Dawning* (London: John Long, 1932), 95.
45 Rees, "Stepping", 52.
46 Barbara Brooks, "Rereading *Prelude to Christopher*", in Eleanor Dark, *Prelude to Christopher* (Rushcutters Bay, NSW: Halstead Press, [1934] 1999), 186. Many years after the publication of *Return to Coolami*, Dark's publishers suggested that the novel had potential for television,

Figure 3.3 Unknown photographer. Eleanor Dark and her son Michael (Mick) Dark, undated. Eleanor Dark Collection, Varuna, the National Writers' House. © Jill Dark.

In *Return to Coolami*, Dark frequently uses flashbacks to move the narrative between past and present, in a way that both articulates experimental, modernist ideas about time, and would have been familiar to those who were used to film culture. Flashbacks were a popular device used in both the silent era of film and avant-garde films of the 1920s.[47] The disruption of linear chronology to return to past events was not unique to film, occurring prior to this in both literature and theatre; however, it took on a distinctive quality in cinema because of the "speed with which cinematic editing was able to cut decisively to another space and time", and in this way, the cinematic flashback was related to "modern notions of speed, movement, energy, [and] of the relativity of spatio-temporal relationships".[48] Dark's novel emphasises the speed with which a repressed memory can arise from the subconscious to disrupt the modern present. On the car journey, Susan re-encounters "a willow-fringed creek where she'd lunched once with Jim" and experiences "a whole remembered scene flung back at her with such brutal vividness that she seemed to feel suddenly on her lips the kisses he'd taken, [and] hear his very voice, ghost-like" (152). In this moment, the present rapidly collapses

---

although of Dark's works it is only the *Timeless Land* trilogy (1941–53) that has ever been televised. Gildfind, "The Difficult Business of Writing", 160.

47 Maureen C. Turim, *Flashbacks in Film: Memory and History* (New York: Routledge, 1989), 106; "The Trauma of History: Flashbacks upon Flashbacks", *Screen* 42, no. 2 (2001): 207.

48 Turim, *Flashbacks*, 3 6.

into the past in an emotionally charged landscape, as Susan literally sees and hears her past lover with the "vividness" of a talkie.

In many ways, *Return to Coolami* can be viewed as a modern, regional take on the American western. Dark frequently reminds readers that the passengers are travelling west and associates their journey with the "exciting tang of adventure" (18). She even alludes to the genre of the American western film in the novel, describing one character as having "an intriguing air of mixed Beau Brummel and Tom Mix!" (Mix was an American actor who commonly performed in westerns) (19). In 1934, the Darks invested in a film about Ned Kelly, which was shot in the Megalong Valley of the Blue Mountains. *When the Kellys Rode* (1934) is one of the bushranger films that Peter Limbrick argues were the antecedents of the "Australian western" – a genre which came into its own with *The Overlanders* in 1946.[49] As Peter Kirkpatrick and Limbrick both suggest, there are strong links between American and Australian versions of the western,[50] and perhaps this is one of the reasons why *Return to Coolami* appealed to American publishers.

American reviewers of *Return to Coolami* drew attention to both the novelty of the Australian setting and the surprising modernity of Dark's characters. The novel appeared to provide American readers with a vicarious form of travel to the Australian countryside, which, as one reviewer noted, was "a scene rarely visited by American readers".[51] Reviews featured titles such as "Poignant Story of Australian Countryside", "Discovery of Contentment in Australia", "Word Magic in the Antipodes" and "Australian Tale Holds Charm", drawing attention to the novelty of the setting.[52] The *Philadelphia Inquirer* noted: "There are no kangaroos, bushmen, nor pioneers in this story; it is a narrative of sophisticated, intelligent people."[53] One reviewer claimed that "[t]he four principal characters might be taking a trip from Knoxville to Atlanta, or Nashville, so far as the reader can notice any mannerisms which might be British or Australian".[54] A critic in the *Nashville Tennessee Banner* expressed surprise to find "this strange country inhabited by people very much like ourselves", claiming that Dark's characters could have come from "the middle stretches of Tennessee".[55]

---

49   Peter Limbrick, "The Australian Western, Or a Settler Colonial Cinema Par Excellence", *Cinema Journal* 46, no. 4 (2007): 71. To Dark's disappointment, *When the Kellys Rode* was censored in New South Wales due to the prohibition on representing bushrangers.

50   Limbrick, "Australian Western", 68–95; Peter Kirkpatrick, "Hellbound for Snowy River", *Meanjin* 73, no. 2 (2014): 32–41.

51   Ole H. Lexau, "Pleasant Trip", *Nashville Tennessee Banner*, 14 June 1936, from Eleanor Dark's album of newspaper clippings, Dark Papers, MLMSS 4545, Box 24. Other reviews mentioned in this chapter are also from this source, unless otherwise stated.

52   Hilton B. Greer, *Dallas Journal*, 8 June 1936; Sarah T. Dickson, *New York Herald Tribune*, 14 June 1936; *San Francisco Call Bulletin*, 6 June 1936; Pat Barnes, *Houston Post*, 21 June 1936.

53   Phoebe Gilkyson, "From Australia to a Far Distant Nebraska Farm", *Philadelphia Inquirer*, 11 July 1936.

54   McCortt, "Salt to Taste", *Middleboro News*, 11 June 1936.

55   Lexau, "Pleasant Trip".

These comments show how, in writing a novel that featured exclusively middle-class characters who were preoccupied with such modern problems as romance, divorce, leisure and the behaviour of the Modern Woman, Dark could invoke a sense of recognition from American readers. David Carter and Roger Osborne suggest that Australian historical sagas which were published in America, such as *The Timeless Land*, often produced a sense of "*unexpected* familiarity, almost a shock of recognition" for American readers.[56] The same appears to be true of *Return to Coolami*, although it is the modernity rather than the settler history of Australia that evokes parallels with America in these reviews. The fact that Dark was drawing on international cultural references and narrative structures such as the western, which circulated to Australia via American cinema, confirms the claim made by Jill Julius Matthews in her study of interwar Sydney that "[i]nternational modernity was gradually adapted and Australianised in Sydney then proudly performed to the rest of the country and returned to the world".[57]

Settler Vision

Cinema not only influenced the themes of Dark's work but also her aesthetics, providing her with the means of articulating multiple ways of seeing. As discussed in the previous chapter, she employed multi-perspectival narration in *Prelude to Christopher* to disrupt epistemological certainty and invite sympathy for a marginalised point of view. Dark also organised *Return to Coolami* around multiple characters' perspectives. Fusing modernist aesthetics with nationalist ideas, she drew on metaphors of vision offered by new forms of media, including cinema and photography, to express the cultural-nationalist discourse of settler indigenisation as a form of adjusted vision.

In an essay entitled "Australia and the Australians", published in 1944 in Sydney Ure Smith's *Australia Week-End Book*, Dark wrote that "the eye only sees what it brings with it the power of seeing, and there is evidence to suggest that this is a hard country for the average outsider to see" (13). This comment suggests the close connection between the concept of vision and claims of cultural legitimacy in Dark's work. Drawing on ideas expressed by other Australian writers, Dark used the metaphor of vision to convey the process of acclimatisation, describing settler culture in terms of those "whose vision has become adjusted" to the local environment (13). She argues in this essay that settler culture had, through a "slow, resistant merging with the ... environment", started to feel "at home" in the landscape, a process facilitated through the local production of art and literature (10, 12). This imagery allowed for a sharp distinction to be drawn between the

---

56   Carter and Osborne, *American Marketplace*, 269.
57   Jill Julius Matthews, *Dance Hall and Picture Palace: Sydney's Romance with Modernity* (Sydney: Currency Press, 2005), 1–2.

cultural products of "native-born" Australians and those of "outsiders" (13). D.H. Lawrence was one such "outsider", and Dark described his Australia-based, modernist novel *Kangaroo* (1923), as "one long, tormented effort to see" (13).

Dark's ideas about an "adjusted" settler vision were not unique: they can be understood within the broader framework of settler-colonial nationalism, in which settler culture seeks to distinguish itself from imperial culture, in part through claiming a sense of settler indigeneity.[58] The imagery that Dark used can be found in much earlier articulations of Australian cultural nationalism. A.G. Stephens, for instance, wrote in his introduction to the *Bulletin Story Book* (1901), "let us look at our country and its fauna and flora, its trees and streams and mountains, through clear Australian eyes, not through bias-bleared English spectacles".[59] In 1916, Australian expressionist painter Frederick McCubbin suggested that only "a native-born artist ... whose vision had never been disturbed by the schools of the old world" could accurately render the "difficult nuances" of the Australian natural environment.[60] In the interwar period, when cultural nationalism took on new energy, P.R. Stephensen drew on similar imagery to assert the cultural legitimacy of Australian writers and artists. Of English-born landscape painter Conrad Martens' paintings of Australia, Stephensen wrote, "Martens' colour is murky, his trees droop and spread like English trees; he painted our paddocks as if they were meadows; over his eyes there must have been a European film".[61]

The metaphor of settler belonging as an "adjusted" form of ocular vision occurs frequently in Dark's interwar novels. In *Waterway* (1938), the young writer Leslie Channon undertakes archival research in the Mitchell Library within the Public Library of New South Wales (now the State Library of New South Wales) and reflects that an "obscuring veil" clouded the vision of early convicts and settlers who sketched Sydney Harbour.[62] She marvels that these artists were "drawing, by some odd convention ... oaks and elms instead of gum trees!" (185). In contrast, Leslie's own vision has been adjusted by "a hundred and fifty years" of settler occupation (186–87). In her 1944 essay, Dark describes the development of Australian landscape painting in terms of an enhanced ability to "see" the natural environment:

58   Dan Tout, "Reframing 'Inky' Stephensen's Place in Australian Cultural History", *Settler Colonial Studies* 7, no. 1 (2017): 76; "Neither Nationalists nor Universalists: Rex Ingamells and the Jindyworobaks", *Australian Humanities Review*, no. 61 (2017): 3.

59   Quoted in Clifford Hanna, "Recollections through English Spectacles", *Australian Literary Studies* 9, no. 2 (1979): 236.

60   Quoted in Humphrey McQueen, "Place, Colour and Sedition: D.H. Lawrence's *Kangaroo*: A Study in Environmental Values", *Politics and Culture*, 3 (2006): n.p.

61   P.R. Stephensen, *The Foundations of Culture in Australia: An Essay Towards National Self Respect* (Gordon: W.J. Miles, 1936), 76.

62   Eleanor Dark, *Waterway* (North Ryde, NSW: Angus & Robertson, [1938] 1990), 185. All subsequent references are to this edition and appear in parentheses in the text.

Painters began to see the elusive beauty of unfamiliar forms, to capture on canvas the clear emptiness of the light, to paint heat, and loneliness, and distance. So, by degrees, we made friends with our country; we began to be at home. (12)

Dark represents a similar process in *Waterway* when Professor Channon visits the Art Gallery of New South Wales. Looking at a painting entitled "Bougainvillea, Townsville", Channon feels "a poignant stab of recognition"; another artwork, "In the Path of the Westerly", makes him think, "Yes, there were places in the Blue Mountains where you found gums just like that" (242–43). Although it is mostly "representational" and "conservative" art that allows Channon to "see ... his native land", Dark suggests that other, more modern works can also speak to the viewer: the paintings of artist character Lois Denning, with their dream-like, surrealist qualities, also contain "flashes of vision" (243, 245).

It was not only visual artists who could supposedly see "through clear Australian eyes", but also native-born settler writers. Dark argues in her essay that the bush ballads of Henry Lawson, while not "'poetry' in any sophisticated sense", were able to "light a spark of recognition in the minds of the people; to make them think, 'I've seen that place'" (11–12). Lawson's clear and accurate vision was "produced" by the land itself, whereas the vision of "outsiders" such as Lawrence is foreign and thus more occluded (11). Dark writes of *Kangaroo*, Lawrence "wanders through the pages of that book peering like a man half-blind, almost frantic with irritation because the beauty of other lands which he has seen hangs like a veil between him and a beauty which, here, he can only feel" (13).[63] Lawrence used the vision metaphor to great effect in his novel, writing about the "*invisible* beauty of Australia, which is undeniably there, but which seems to lurk just beyond the range of our white vision ... as if your eyes hadn't the vision in them to correspond with the outside landscape".[64] Dark was one of many interwar Australian writers and artists whose work was significantly influenced by Lawrence's vitalist ideas, and yet here she takes issue with his claim that the beauty of Australia was "invisible" to "white vision", staking a claim for Australian-born writers such as herself.

It is not surprising that settler Australian writers and commentators used vision as such an important metaphor for cultural legitimacy. The act of seeing has long been associated with that of knowing,[65] and at issue here is settler culture's ability

---

63 Susan Carson explores Dark's comments about *Kangaroo* in her paper, "Seeing a Hard Country: Lawrence's Australian Landscape", based on a presentation to the D.H. Lawrence Society of North America 12th international conference, Sydney, Australia, 29 June–3 July 2011. See also Susan Carson, "Conversations with the Land: Environmental Questions and Eleanor Dark", in *Land and Identity: Proceedings of the 1997 Conference University of New England Armidale New South Wales 27–30 September 1997*, eds. Michael Deves and Jennifer A. McDonnell (Association for the Study of Australian Literature, 1998), 191–93.

64 D.H. Lawrence, *Kangaroo*, ed. Bruce Steele (Cambridge: Cambridge University Press, [1923] 1994), 77. Italics in original.

65 Karen Jacobs, *The Eye's Mind: Literary Modernism and Visual Culture* (Ithaca, NY: Cornell University Press, 2001), 7; Martin Jay, *Downcast Eyes: The Denigration of Vision in*

to know and represent local landscapes in a way that is distinct from, and superior to, imperial (British) culture. Australian cultural nationalists in the interwar period saw themselves as postcolonial subjects involved in an anti-imperial struggle, and indeed they were fighting against material forms of cultural imperialism, including the dominance of English publishers over the local Australian book market. And yet, because settler nationalism not only operates against the original colonial power, but also through the ongoing, structural erasure of Indigenous presence, these claims for legitimacy were also part of "the unceasing process of ... dispossession".[66] As Peter Limbrick remarks, "no matter how much settlers choose to define themselves against the imperial authority that first set them in the colony, their situation in relation to indigenous [sic] populations has remained, structurally, one of colonization".[67] It is therefore possible to see the cultural-nationalist discourse of settler vision as one of what Terry Smith calls "the visual regimes of colonisation" – as part of a "quest to belong" that involved both the appropriation of Indigenous identity and the erasure of Aboriginal people's claims to Country.[68]

Ideas of settler indigenisation recur throughout Dark's work. In *Sun Across the Sky* (1937), the doctor, Oliver Denning, ponders what kind of people will emerge from the "strange blending of Northern race and southern climate", and imagines a people who are "[l]ean and brown – almost as lean and almost as brown as the people whose land they had stolen".[69] *Waterway* and *The Timeless Land* are similarly concerned with the "moulding process of the land" on settler identity.[70] In *Return to Coolami*, Dark presents a powerful image of a settler Australian who has become acclimatised to the natural environment. Bret's late mother is remembered for her cultivation of native plants at Coolami:

> Bret's mother had seen, Millicent thought, better than any one, the strange loveliness of an ancient land. She more than most of her countrymen had been able to escape a gospel of beauty handed down from generations which had dwelt on a milder and gentler soil. She had abandoned, somehow, an ancestral reverence for landscapes softly painted in lush greens for sappy, fragile flowers and the smooth charm of an unfailing fruitfulness. She'd seen new and more difficult beauty;

Twentieth-Century French Thought (Berkeley: University of California Press, 1993), 10. See also Simon Ryan, *The Cartographic Eye: How Explorers Saw Australia* (Cambridge; Melbourne: Cambridge University Press, 1996).

66 Anne Rees, "Reading Australian Modernity: Unsettled Settlers and Cultures of Mobility", *History Compass* 15, no. 11 (2017): 3. See also Patrick Wolfe, *Settler Colonialism and the Transformation of Anthropology: The Politics and Poetics of an Ethnographic Event* (London; New York: Cassell, 1999).

67 Peter Limbrick, *Making Settler Cinemas: Film and Colonial Encounters in the United States, Australia, and New Zealand* (New York: Palgrave Macmillan, 2010), 9.

68 Terry Smith, "Visual Regimes of Colonisation: European and Aboriginal Seeing in Australia", in *Empires of Vision: A Reader*, eds. Martin Jay and Sumathi Ramaswamy (Durham, NC: Duke University Press, 2014), 267; Jeanine Leane, "Tracking our Country in Settler Literature", *JASAL: Journal of the Association for the Study of Australian Literature* 14, no. 3 (2014): 2.

69 Eleanor Dark, *Sun Across the Sky* (London: Collins, [1937] 1946), 29–30.

70 Eleanor Dark, *The Timeless Land* (London: Collins, [1941] 1946), 81.

beauty that rioted opulently in a frothing mass of honey-scented gold … in a vast tree, dead, skeleton-white, lifting naked branches to the sky … (139)

Drawing on the imagery provided by other settler Australian writers, Dark depicts Bret's mother's affinity with the environment in terms of an ability to "see" a "new and more difficult beauty" – that is, an adjusted form of vision. Bret's mother rejects the "gospel of beauty handed down" by European landscape artists, instead demonstrating respect for Australia's distinctiveness by cultivating native flora. Her acclimatisation to Australian conditions is captured symbolically through the description of Coolami as "weathered to subdued greys, almost windowless so that it seemed like some vast rock flung there in prehistoric ages" (138). Millicent remarks that the house "might have grown there", providing a benign image of settler indigenisation that obscures the historical reality of dispossession (59). Dark makes reference to a range of native plants nurtured by Bret's mother, including "Silver Wattle", a "crooked Coolabah", and "boronia with feathery leaves" (138–39). The cultivation of these native plants seems to represent Dark's ideal conception of an ethical relationship between settler culture and the natural environment – an ideal influenced by her ecological and conservationist commitments, which were expressed through her support of the Blue Gum Forest campaign in the early 1930s and participation with Eric in local bushwalking and rock climbing activities.[71] Cultural-nationalist writers often used the nurturing of a plant as a key symbol of the development of a distinctive Australian culture. Artist Margaret Preston similarly used botanical motifs in her interwar paintings to suggest an indigenised settler modernist aesthetic. In symbolic terms, Bret's mother is revealed here as showing a commitment to cultivating local culture. On the one hand, Dark's horticultural imagery of roots and native plants reinforces nativist ideas of nationalism; on the other, it also suggests a writer grappling for language to convey settler culture's growing feelings of affinity to contested land, and may hint at more ecologically sensitive commitments that are expressed with much greater legitimacy in Indigenous representations of Country.[72]

Modern(ist) Vision

Dark's ideas about visual perception were evidently drawn from cultural-nationalist discourse, so in what sense were they also modern and modernist? Martin Jay and Karen Jacobs both connect artistic modernism with a preoccupation with vision and its capacity to "deliver reliable knowledge".[73] The modernist interest in vision has been linked to parallel developments in photography, and popular

---

71   Carson, "Conversations", 191.
72   For a discussion of the ecopoetic possibilities of *Return to Coolami*, see Kathleen Davidson, "Landscapes and Mindscapes: The Confluence of Modernism and Ecopoetics in Eleanor Dark's *Return to Coolami*", *Philament: A Journal of Literature, Arts, and Culture* 24, no. 2 (2018): 1–31.

and ethnographic film.[74] Modernist literary practices developed alongside "the emergence of parallel conventions in the cinema" such as simultaneity, multi-perspectivalism and montage.[75] The influence of cinema on Dark's modernist style has been noted in her use of cinematic flashbacks, sudden close-ups, cross-cuts between scenes and compressed timescales.[76] Her approach to vision also draws attention to other forms of material culture, including modern kinds of transport. Andrew Thacker argues that the motorcar, tram, bus and railway all created new forms of movement that altered ways of seeing, and that these "provided a key impetus to some of the experimental forms of modernist writing".[77]

In *Return to Coolami*, Dark's interest in the subjectivity of vision ("the eye only sees what it brings with it the power of seeing") is expressed through a number of modernist devices, including the novel's multifocal narrative style, use of interior monologue and striking ways of representing human consciousness. Dark's novel is also fascinated with mechanised ways of seeing, whether through the lens of a camera or from the window of a moving motor vehicle, and Dark embraces these vernacular, modern experiences as crucial metaphors for the settler relationship to the natural environment. If seeing operated as an important metaphor for belonging in interwar cultural-nationalist discourse, then technological innovations which altered and produced "new modes of organizing vision and sensory perception", including photography, cinema and motoring,[78] allowed writers such as Dark to express claims for cultural legitimacy in new and strikingly modern(ist) ways.

Return to Coolami employs a form of "camera consciousness", a term used by Lara Feigel to capture the ways in which modernist writers of the 1930s depicted human consciousness "itself as a camera or projector".[79] Christopher Isherwood's statement in *Goodbye to Berlin* (1939), "I am a camera with its shutter open," is a famous example of this camera consciousness.[80] Dark provides another instance of this trope when, in a climactic scene, Bret performs a precarious night-time climb

---

73   Martin Jay, "Scopic Regimes of Modernity", in *Vision and Visuality*, ed. Hal Foster (New York: New Press, 1999), 4; "The Disenchantment of the Eye: Surrealism and the Crisis of Ocularcentrism", *Visual Anthropology* Review 7, no. 1 (1991): 15; Jacobs, *Eye's Mind*, 3.

74   David Trotter, *Cinema and Modernism* (Malden, MA: Blackwell Publishers, 2007), 3–4, 10; Rebecca Sanchez, *Deafening Modernism: Embodied Language and Visual Poetics in American Literature* (New York: New York University Press, 2015), 29.

75   Seed, "British Modernists", 70; Keith Cohen, *Film and Fiction: The Dynamics of Exchange* (New Haven, CT: Yale University Press, 1979), 208.

76   Susan Carson, "A Girl's Guide to Modernism's Grammar: Language Politics in Experimental Women's Fiction", *Hecate* 30, no. 1 (2004): 180.

77   Andrew Thacker, *Moving through Modernity: Space and Geography in Modernism* (New York; Manchester: Manchester University Press, 2003), 7–8.

78   Miriam Bratu Hansen, "The Mass Production of the Senses: Classical Cinema as Vernacular Modernism", *Modernism/modernity* 6, no. 2 (1999): 60.

79   Lara Feigel, *Literature, Cinema and Politics, 1930–1945: Reading Between the Frames* (Edinburgh: Edinburgh University Press, 2010), 122.

80   Quoted in Feigel, *Literature*, 122.

of the mountain Jungaburra. Dark writes, "His whole widely roving consciousness suddenly narrowed, contracted like the lens of a camera, focused itself with a tremendous, an agonising intentness on that one stride ahead of him" (226). In this description, Bret's vision is figured as a wide-angled shot that is adjusted to a focused close-up, to convey the intensity of concentration required when navigating mountainous terrain. This is followed by another shift when, "with a click the lens of his consciousness was wide open again, collecting from everywhere, avidly, a medley of sensations, thoughts, emotions" (226–27). Dark's image of "the click [of] the lens of his consciousness" is a highly arresting one, and suggests that *Return to Coolami*, for all its adherence to a romance plot, should be considered seriously as an example of Australian modernist styles. David Trotter argues that modernist texts were fascinated with "the automatism of the camera's-eye view".[81] It is easy to see why a settler writer might have been attracted to the idea of a field of vision that, like the lens of a camera, could be adjusted to bring into focus the nuances of its distinctive environment. In this way, the idea of settler indigenisation is expressed through a strikingly modernist image.

Modernism and settler nationalism are revealed as mutually constitutive in this example, rather than as two opposing forces. Dark's use of the camera as a metaphor resonates with Slessor's image of Sydney "Lensed in a bubble's ghostly camera" in the poem "Out of Time" (1939). Both Dark and Slessor exhibit a camera consciousness that was influenced by and adapted from their experiences of international cinema. Yet Dark's description of Bret is also nationalist, providing a powerful depiction of vitalist masculinity at home in the Australian outback. Max Dupain's photographs similarly employed modernist forms in ways that naturalised ideas of vitalism, eugenics and nationalism. His photographs of human subjects reflected the "body culture" ethos of the 1930s, employing the techniques of the New Photography movement to showcase "a new homegrown generation of white Australians whose bodies were honed through time spent lying in the sun and swimming in the ocean".[82] In the case of the iconic "Sunbaker" (1937), these photographs would eventually come to be viewed as quintessentially nationalist images.

Seeing in Motion

Return to Coolami also reflects a modernist enthusiasm for seeing in motion. Dark's characters traverse the landscape at great speed, and the pleasure they take in mobility constitutes their modernity and mediates their sense of belonging in the landscape. As Enda Duffy argues in his study of modern speed, motoring demanded "new levels of visual alertness for seeing in motion", and the interaction

---

81 Trotter, *Cinema*, 5, 9.
82 Crombie, *Body Culture*, 26, 65.

between the human subject and the new "speed-producing machine" produced a new aesthetics of adrenaline.[83] Aldous Huxley wrote in 1931 of speed as "the one genuinely modern pleasure":

> The automobile is sufficiently small and sufficiently near the ground to be able to compete, as an intoxicating speed-purveyor, with the galloping horse ... When the car has passed seventy-two, or thereabouts, one begins to feel an unprecedented sensation – a sensation which no man in the days of horses ever felt. It grows intenser with every increase of velocity.[84]

Return to Coolami captures this modern pleasure of speed, picking up on an association between the motor car and modernity which had already appeared in Vance Palmer's *The Passage* (1930). Much of the action of *Return to Coolami* takes place inside Tom's car, a "Madison" tourer with a "lustrous olive-green ... bonnet, satin-smooth, mirror-bright" (8). Tom likens the speed of the automobile to magic, thinking:

> Forty-five and you hardly knew you were moving! Fifty. Fifty-five. A miracle really, this conversion of a few gallons of petrol into annihilated miles! A liquid, a vapour that could spin you like the carpet of Bagdad from Ballool to Coolami! (36)

Speed allows Dark's characters to traverse the landscape with great ease and in a relatively short amount of time – a point emphasised by the combination of the novel's compressed temporal scale with the range of geographical settings described. The modernist-inspired cover design of the American edition of *Return to Coolami* (Fig. 3.4) features the "silver-plated effigy on the radiator-cap" of Tom's car, along with horizontal lines which suggest the forward movement of the speeding vehicle (7). Dark associates the effigy's "lean, boyish-looking body – straining forward" with "eagerness ... adventure", so that the cover illustration reinforces the novel's vitalist celebration of speed, adrenaline and modern pleasure (7–8).

Dark portrays the process of observing the landscape from a car as a form of cinematic pleasure. Film scholars also make the connection between travel and the spectatorship of cinema.[85] As Robert Dixon notes in examining the work of Australian photographer and film maker Frank Hurley, "the automobile driver experiences it [the landscape] unfolding before him like a film".[86] Dark makes

---

83 Enda Duffy, *The Speed Handbook: Velocity, Pleasure, Modernism* (Durham, NC: Duke University Press, 2009), 7, 113.

84 Aldous Huxley, *Music at Night and Other Essays* (New York: Doubleday, Doran & Co., 1931), 227–28.

85 See Guiliana Bruno, *Atlas of Emotion: Journeys in Art, Architecture, and Film* (London; New York: Verso, 2002); Ellen Strain, *Public Places, Private Journeys: Ethnography, Entertainment, and the Tourist Gaze* (New Brunswick, NJ: Rutgers University Press, 2003).

this same point in *Return to Coolami* as the passengers observe and become acclimatised to the changing landscape from the luxurious comfort of the Madison. In one scene, Millicent watches the change of scene from the Blue Mountains to the flatter terrain of central-western New South Wales:

> The sudden transition from mountain to plain country was intriguing, Millicent thought, watching green, wet paddocks where for the last few hours she'd been seeing the bush and the blue depth and distance of far-away gullies. She … [was] glad to relax into her well-upholstered corner of the seat and watch the landscape absently from eyes half focused, seeing it only as a strip of moving, slightly hypnotising colour. (130)

Sitting in "her well-upholstered corner" and viewing the passing landscape as "a strip of moving … colour", Millicent could just as easily be in a modern picture palace. In describing Millicent's vision, Dark uses a number of technical terms related to the composition of a photograph or film shot, including "depth", "distance" and "focus". Even the phrase "sudden transition" evokes the fast cut from one scene to another in a film sequence. Millicent's eyes are "half focused" like the lens of a camera, providing another instance of camera consciousness whereby a settler character becomes attuned to the distinctive qualities of the bush landscape.

Adjusted Vision

Motoring had particular cultural meanings in a settler-colonial context such as Australia. In the first half of the twentieth century, Australia had one of the highest rates of automobile ownership in the world, with the car often representing mastery over the environment and the eradication of distance.[87] Anne Rees has recently argued that mobility was "a defining characteristic of the Australian modern", as "[r]eal and imagined mobilities across stolen land were (and are) essential for settlers to claim Australia as their own".[88] The connection between motor travel and settler belonging is showcased through the character development of Tom. Tom's initial, exploitative approach to the natural world is captured through his ostentatious villa in the fictional Sydney suburb of Ballool:

> The cypress hedge that he'd planted was growing well, and the pergola was fairly smothered in yellow roses. The lawn, he noticed with a slight frown, needed clipping round the edges … Here, he thought, looking along his own high brick wall towards the high brick walls of his neighbours, there was dignity, security.

---

86   Robert Dixon, "Shooting in Occupied Space: Frank Hurley in the Middle East, 1940–46", *History of Photography* 38, no. 1 (2014): 44.
87   Knott, "'Conquering Car'", 3, 26.
88   Rees, "Reading Australian Modernity", 3, 6.

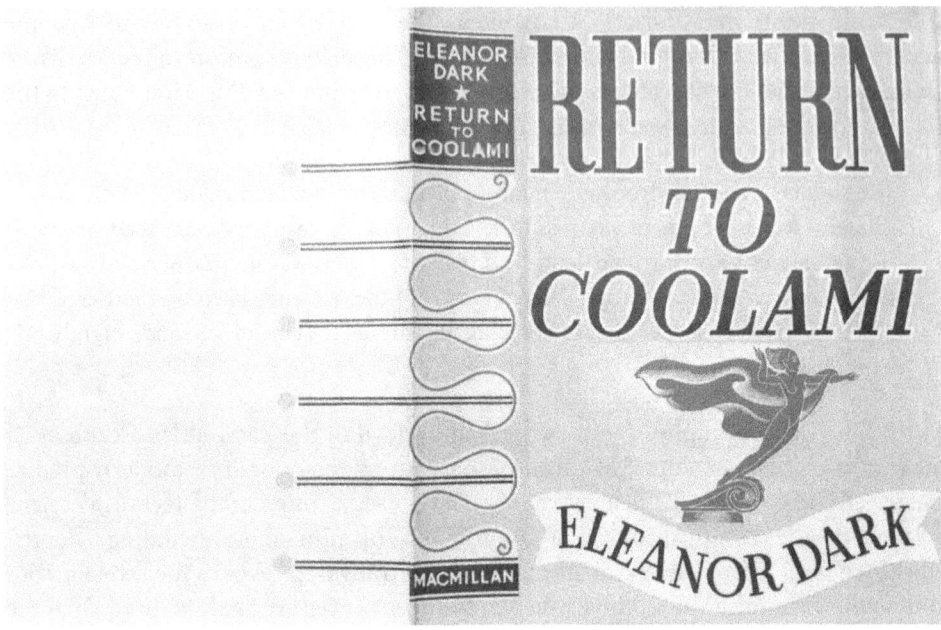

Figure 3.4 Book cover of the American edition of *Return to Coolami* (New York: Macmillan, 1936). Eleanor Dark Papers. Mitchell Library, State Library of New South Wales. MLMSS 4545, Box 24.

> Roads were smooth for the passing of costly cars; footpaths were well-kept; gardens … were properly looked after, they were assets … (15–16)

Dark provides a leftist critique of Tom's suburban values, pointing to his materialistic and exploitative approach to the environment. The inclusion of non-native plants in Tom's garden creates an implicit contrast with the pastoral property of Coolami. In contrast to Bret's mother, Tom is not interested in nurturing Australian culture or integrating into the environment, but rather is blinded by the materialism of suburbia. Tom is "[j]ealous" and "[f]iercely touchy" about the rural environment where his wife spent her childhood (20). On the car journey he responds to Aboriginal placenames with derision:

> Parramatta. It had a silly sound, a jabbering sound, the kind of sound that a child might make experimenting with vocal noises! And over there to his left still another – Kirribilli! Well, they sounded just exactly what they were – the language of savages! (19–20)

As a number of scholars have observed, Dark's novels frequently entangle different temporal scales of past and present, so that Sydney operates as "a palimpsest where the past and present coexist in an uneasy relationship".[89] In *Return to Coolami*, placenames evoking Aboriginal naming, such as Bullaburra, Kalangadoo and

Parramatta,[90] are used to register the presence of a precolonial past that breaks through the apparent surface of modernity, with Tom's lack of appreciation for it indicating his inability to perceive what Stephensen called the "Spirit of the Place".[91]

The car journey through the bush landscape exerts a powerful, vitalist force on Tom that involves an adjustment of visual perception and recognition of Australia's precolonial past. As Millicent reflects when standing at a Blue Mountains lookout, "a sight like that broke down your defences, opened your heart, made you in an instant mysteriously receptive" (76). Through traversing "that vast and adventurous expanse" of the outback – a journey made possible only by the speed and mobility of the motor vehicle – Tom comes to realise that his life has hitherto been confined to "a very little circle indeed" (204). He feels a "stirring of excitement in the mere thought of distance, an urge … for some sense of spaciousness" (235). In particular, it is the immersive quality of driving that provides him with access to the natural environment: as he slows down and begins "to look about him", Tom finds, "with eyes suddenly opened", a new kind of beauty:

> It was the sun doing things to the leaves. Turning a young gum sapling into something that dripped rubies. Flaming suddenly behind a dead leaf so that it became a topaz. Plunging into a bush with dark glossy leaves and finding purple there – bursting out again leaving streaks of silver in its wake … Every gum leaf, hanging motionless with its edge to the sun, looked burnished … (55)

The comparison of the native flora to jewels and precious metals conveys Tom's newfound discovery of the richness of the Australian bush, in contrast to the superficial wealth of owning "two cars and a house at Ballool and a cottage at the seaside" (138). This ability to "see … for the first time, his native bushland" is described as "a moment of perception, flashed and gone" (60). Tom reassesses his opinion of his Ballool home, and even develops an appreciation for the placenames he formerly derided, catching "for the first time a hint of music in outlandish names" (235). Dark's conception of an ethical form of settler belonging therefore encompasses an acknowledgement of Indigenous peoples' precolonial presence in

---

89   Harriet Edquist, "Ghosts of the Past: Mapping the Colonial in Eleanor Dark's Fiction", in *Mapping Different Geographies*, eds. Karel Kriz, William Cartwright and Lorenz Hurni (Berlin, Heidelberg: Springer, 2010), 254. See also Meg Brayshaw, "Trans-Scalar Sydney, Narrative Form and Ethics in Eleanor Dark's *Waterway*", *JASAL: Journal of the Association for the Study of Australian Literature* 17, no. 1 (2017): 1–10; Barbara Brooks, "*Waterway*: The Multilayered City; History, Economics and Dream", *Hecate* 27, no. 1 (2001): 11–18.

90   Dark used placenames associated with Aboriginal languages as an important symbol in her novels; however, she also invented or borrowed names in ways that would seem highly problematic today. In *Return to Coolami*, the name "Kerrajellanbong", which Bret explains means "the place in the shadow of the mountain", and "Coolami", which is said to mean "birthplace of heroes", appear to be words that Dark has invented to suggest Aboriginal naming (125, 126).

91   Stephensen, *Foundations*, 11.

and, to some extent, ongoing spiritual connection to the land, although it does not extend to supporting contemporary land rights.

It is significant that Tom's vision is adjusted as he travels along the Great Western Highway, a road which Dark depicts as one "of inconceivable glamour and romance" (205). In the interwar period, highways often functioned as a metaphor for progress, "imagined as a spatial superconductor for transporting vehicular traffic in an unimpeded, frictionless flow".[92] This particular road is also an important originary site of Australian colonialism, and Dark went on to describe the building of it in the final instalment of her historical trilogy, *No Barrier* (1953). In *Return to Coolami*, the road connects the modern characters to the colonial past: Bret marvels, "What a feat they'd performed, those chaps, those pioneers! Almost incredible that they should ever have got through at all!" (76). In a striking moment of cinematic vision, Tom imagines himself as part of Australia's settler history:

> He said to Bret:
> "Who made the Western Road?"
> Bret answered between puffs:
> "Chap called Cox. In six months from Penrith to Bathurst."
> "*Six months!*"
> "Six months with a gang of thirty. Mostly convicts, I think they were."
> [Tom] Drew stared down at the map. Perhaps because he'd had a long day and was beginning to feel tired, the black line of the road faded by some optical illusion into the moving winding strip that his eyes had been watching since early morning. The darkly shaded valleys, stretching out like talons towards it, became blue and luminous, incredibly deep, dreadfully remote, so that he had a brief sensation of vertigo, and a ridiculous momentary feeling that he, Tom Drew, in clothes with arrows on them, and chains about his ankles, was toiling perilously on a moving road that stretched like a tightrope with blue death on either side ... (205)

In this scene, Tom's vision moves from the topographical perspective of the highway as a "black line" on a map to a cinematic experience of the road as a "moving winding strip". Importantly, Tom imagines himself as part of this historical scene, costumed in the role of convict, seeing the road from the point of view of an actor within a film set, moving through what Benedict Anderson calls the "homogenous, empty time" of linear history.[93] The Tom who drives an expensive 1930s car is fused with a nineteenth-century convict "toiling perilously on a moving road" through the chronotope of the highway, creating a modernist sense of

---

92 Edward Dimendberg, "The Will to Motorization: Cinema, Highways and Modernity", *October* 73 (1995): 93.

93 Benedict Anderson, *Imagined Communities: Reflections on the Origin and Spread of Nationalism*, rev. edn (London; New York: Verso, 1991), 26.

synchronicity between past and present that is similar to the one that Brigid Rooney identifies in Dark's depiction of Sydney Harbour in *Waterway*.[94] Through a cinematic form of vision, Tom is able to imagine himself as part of a colonial drama, inscribed into the nation's history.

Middlebrow Modernist Time and Memory

Return to Coolami packages distinctly modernist concerns with time and memory in ways that are accessible and entertaining for middlebrow audiences, suggesting that middlebrow writing can be understood as "a domestication of modernist themes".[95] Drawing on a familiar trope in Australian literature, Dark depicted the journey into the physical interior of the Australian continent as an extended metaphor for a psychic journey into the tortured places of the unconscious. She links physical spaces with interior states in phrases such as the "unexplained territory in one's own mind" (131), a description that foreshadows Patrick White's "country of the mind" in *Voss* (1957).[96] Dark also imbues her characters' recollections with a highly visual, cinematic quality to convey the effects of subconscious memories on the present. Bret finds "in his memory a picture so bright, so detailed and clearly defined, that he wondered fleetingly that some unconscious self should have stored and guarded it so jealously" (258). Characters' memories are described as unfolding like a "sequence of pictures" (283), or as "a succession of scenes like the lights that waver across your ceiling at night from passing trams or cars" (128). The flickering strip of memory is reminiscent of the "strip of moving, slightly hypnotising colour" that Millicent observes from the car, suggesting that Dark used the same imagery to describe the interior vision of memory and the exterior vision of the landscape. There is a distinctly Bergsonian quality to this idea of the mind as "a kind of cinematograph inside us", an influence also seen in Slessor's poem "Last Trams" (1939), where, from a moving tram, human figures appear like the frames of a film reel: "Their faces brush you as they fly,/ Fixed in the shutters of a blink."[97]

Like Slessor's modernist poetry, Dark's novels frequently explore the subjective, lived experience of time: what Bergson describes as *durée*.[98] In *Return to Coolami*, after the car skids to the edge of a precipice, Bret wonders in relation to time, "what the devil was it? Absurd to contend that the minute or less during which they had

---

94   Brigid Rooney, "Time's Abyss: Australian Literary Modernism and the Scene of the Ferry Wreck", in *Scenes of Reading: Is Australian Literature a World Literature?*, eds. Robert Dixon and Brigid Rooney (North Melbourne: Australian Scholarly, 2013), 109.

95   Ehland and Wächter, "Introduction", 3.

96   Patrick White, *Voss* (North Sydney: Random House Australia, [1957] 2012), 451.

97   Henri Bergson, quoted in Seed, "British Modernists", 51; Kenneth Slessor, "Last Trams", in *Selected Poems*, 113.

98   See Henri Bergson, *Time and Free Will: An Essay on the Immediate Data of Consciousness* (New York: Dover Publications, [1889] 2012).

all been so close to death was the same as any minute during which they travelled uneventfully over an unremarkable half-mile!" (120). Bret's free indirect discourse raises an important, modern philosophical question about the nature of time, but does so in a way that is accessible because of its vernacular phrasing and connection to an exciting moment in the plot sequence. Similarly in *Waterway*, Dark likens the heightened consciousness brought about by the ferry collision to the widened focus of a camera lens or the rapid pace of a "movie-film":

> In such a crisis time is no longer the steadily moving vehicle of human consciousness, advancing unhurriedly in minutes as regular and unvarying as the tramp of soldiers on parade. A second expands, becomes monstrous, a minute stretches achingly into eternity … senses expand, widening their focus like the lens of a camera, recording avidly, and thought accelerates with the mad accuracy of a racing movie-film. (320)

Just as Virginia Woolf contrasts the clock time of Big Ben to the subjective experience of time in *Mrs Dalloway* (1925), so Dark distinguishes between the "regular and unvarying" forward trajectory of minutes to the "eternity" encompassed in a single moment of crisis.

Yet Dark also frequently undercuts the seriousness of her novels' investments in modernist ideas about time and memory. In *Return to Coolami*, after a lengthy passage of introspection, Bret laments that "[h]e couldn't … walk across a veranda without beginning to analyse his motives like some blasted be-spectacled highbrow dabbling in psychological bunk!" (270). In *Waterway*, after analysing her romantic feelings, Lesley thinks, "I'm going all D.H. Lawrence!" (204). Another character imagines a female modernist artist as "a lank and untidy female in a smock, a vague impression of jade earrings, cubist furniture, bare feet in 'arty' sandals, [and] a preposterous cigarette holder", before Dark undercuts this with a description of the much less pretentious artist character, Lois Denning (150). In these instances, highbrow culture operates more as a spectre conjured by Dark and associated with international culture, ostentation and inauthenticity, rather than as an actual, local Australian presence. David Carter notes a similar kind of rhetoric in the *Triad* – one of the Australian magazines in which Dark published short stories in the 1920s. The *Triad*'s editors claimed in 1924 that the magazine would be "literary, but not too literary", "entertaining, but not too consciously funny", "instructive, but not pedantic".[99] This "repeated rhetorical form ('X but not Y'; 'X but not *too* X') suggest[s] the work of positioning the editors had to perform, calibrating the magazine's range between two kinds of excess, staking a claim but also drawing a line".[100] Dark's middlebrow modernism was energised by similar tactics of

---

99 Quoted in David Carter, "Literary, but Not Too Literary; Joyous, but Not Jazzy: *Triad* Magazine, Antipodean Modernity and the Middlebrow", *Modernism/modernity* 25, no. 2 (2018): 256.
100 Carter, "Literary", 257.

balancing and mediating, and, as such, it was able to speak to Australian audiences who desired quality writing but did not want the exclusivity or alienation of "ultra-modernism", which they associated with the "faddishness, fraudulence, and oversophistication" of international highbrow culture.[101]

American reviews suggest that *Return to Coolami* was readily assimilated into the American middlebrow book market, where it was positioned between "summer reading" and more serious literature. A small number of reviews dismissed Dark's novel as light fiction, with one in the *New York Sun* claiming that "[f]eminine patrons of drug store circulating libraries will swoop joyously upon 'Return to Coolami' and have a splendid time snuffling over the sorrows of Susan".[102] This gendered critique of mass culture resonates with the dismissive comments made by Dark's father, Dowell O'Reilly, about the "Ladies' Circulating Library".[103] Most American reviewers, however, felt that *Return to Coolami* was "many cuts above the ordinary summer novel".[104] Using rhetoric that reflects the tendency of the middlebrow to seek to mediate between different levels of cultural value, the Fort Wayne *News-Sentinel* described Dark's novel as "not a heavy, but not a frivolous study of human life in picturesque Australia", and the *San Francisco Chronicle* recommended it to "those who find the average run of summer novels a bit disappointing in their similarity and long for something more unusual".[105] The *Pittsburgh Post Gazette* said that *Return to Coolami* "should find readers among two large groups – those who enjoy a literate story, and those who read fiction for the light it sheds on human emotions and behaviour" – a description that pitches the novel to a discerning middlebrow audience.[106]

Dark's novel appears to have helped Australia appear modern to itself as well. The pleasure that Dark's Australian readers seem to have taken in the way she packaged experimental literary techniques and modern ideas in entertaining and accessible narratives is demonstrated in a review of *Return to Coolami* in the *Bulletin*'s Red Page in 1936:

> Anyone who reads at all widely in current work must often be unfavourably struck by the apparent inability of our writing to come really abreast, not so much with the quality as with the kind of writing that is being done at the same time elsewhere in the world. We overtake the kind a considerable number of years in arrears. Perhaps the thing of greatest literary importance about Mrs. Dark's altogether fine novel is that this author, at least, steps completely over that time lag. Her novel is perfectly modern – in its diction, in its form, in its psychological concept of

101 Carter, "Literary", 260.
102 Rex Hunter, "Sorrows of Susan", *New York Sun*, 13 June 1936.
103 Dowell O'Reilly, "The 'Ta Ta!' Woman", *Bulletin*, 18 November 1915, 52.
104 Tom Shaw, Jr., "Book-Slants", *Greensboro Record*, 22 June 1936.
105 "Tells Story Neatly", *News-Sentinel* (Fort Wayne, Ind.), 20 June 1936; "Simple Story Adroitly Told", *San Francisco Chronicle*, 5 July 1936.
106 "Journey", *Pittsburg Post Gazette*, 30 June 1936.

character. It is a sterling piece of work in any case, but its modernness – by which is meant its being directly in tune, in the beat of the life-rhythm of this present time – gives it an importance in Australian literary effort which seems very great to-day, though this will depend entirely upon the extent to which its influence has effect.[107]

In this review, the "modernness" of Dark's writing is embraced as a sign that settler culture has overcome the "time lag" between it and what is happening "at the same time elsewhere in the world" – a view produced by the anxiety that those at a "[g]eographical distance" are necessarily culturally belated.[108] Yet the novel with which the reviewer demonstrates the contemporaneity of Australian writing is not an "ultra-modern" one, but one that combines an accessible narrative, nationalist themes and a romantic ending, with a compressed, two-day time frame, a focus on psychological introspection, and modern ideas about sexuality, birth control and divorce.[109] This suggests that, in conforming to some aspects of middlebrow taste, Dark's work was able to open readers up to more experimental literary devices and contemporary ideas.[110]

Modernist Timelessness

The fluid relationship between past and present in *Return to Coolami* allows for one of the central tenets of Dark's fiction to emerge – that of the "timelessness" of the Australian landscape. Tom reflects on "the strangeness of Time arrested, Time suspended", thinking, "[i]n the mountains the records of a thousand years were written across the cliff faces; and in the gullies ... you might walk under tree-ferns whose ancestors had been tree-ferns before you grew legs and came to live on dry land!" (290, 291). P.R. Stephensen drew on similar ideas in *The Foundations of Culture in Australia: An Essay Towards National Self Respect* (1936), writing about an environment "geologically so old that Time seems to have stood still here for a million years".[111] The discourse of primitivism is an established trope of literary

---

107 "Several Novels by Women", *Bulletin*, 22 April 1936, 2.
108 David Carter, *Always Almost Modern: Australian Print Cultures and Modernity* (North Melbourne: Australian Scholarly, 2013), viii.
109 Some Australian reviewers did feel that *Return to Coolami* was *too* modern. The reviewer in Sydney's *Labor Daily* connected it to "a form of modernism that a number of our authoresses strain so desperately to portray", writing that the introspection and self-analysis of the characters produced an effect of "complete nausea" on the reader. Such reviews tended to be in the minority. Will Hanley, "Marriage was a Continual Fight, Conversation Lolly Put Things Right", *Labor Daily*, 5 March 1936.
110 In contrast to the warm reception of *Return to Coolami*, some reviewers associated Dark's earlier novel, *Prelude to Christopher*, with the ultra-modern. One New Zealand review negatively compared it to "the work of many ultra-modern composers, artists and sculptors" because of its "abnormal" themes and style. "Fiction", *Wanganui Chronicle*, 28 July 1934.
111 Stephensen, *Foundations*, 11.

and artistic modernism;[112] however, it also had particular meanings in instances of settler-colonial modernity. By suggesting that a "timeless" and "primitive" continent existed prior to colonial invasion, Dark and other writers such as Stephensen and the Jindyworobak poets invoked a pre-imperial past that they felt could also provide settler culture with a post-imperial, nationalist future. In *Return to Coolami*, Tom reflects on the limitations of the imperialist narrative of Australia's beginnings, realising that "until now he had always felt that this land of his had been born out of the womb of Mother England in the year 1770 with Captain James Cook for midwife" (290). Moving through the landscape allows him to recover a sense of the nation prior to settler occupation, and this timeless environment is framed as available to modern settler characters.

The modernist slippage between past and present, and the way this reinforces settler claims to belonging, is demonstrated through Dark's depiction of the mountain Jungaburra. Bret reflects that it "had an almost insubstantial look as though it were something you were dreaming about rather than seeing", and thinks "[n]o wonder … the natives had called it Jungaburra – 'a spirit place'" (163). Millicent similarly reflects on Jungaburra as a "spirit place so utterly unchanged, dreaming its immortality away", reiterating the idea that the natural environment exists in a dream state that is outside of time. Dark's novel draws upon the colonial discourse of Aboriginal "Dreamtime", which involves the idea that Aboriginal cultures exist outside of time, implying a fundamental denial of contemporaneity that often operated "in the interests of European land claims".[113] As Maureen Perkins argues, due to the inherent connection between time and space, to "deprive Aboriginal people of temporality in dominant discourse was to deprive them of a land as well".[114] Although Dark shows a modernist interest in dream states and frequently brings past temporalities into the present, she nonetheless reinforces the idea that Aboriginal cultures operated outside of normative Western conceptions of time and is therefore unable to recognise Indigenous claims to sovereignty.

These ideas are conveyed through the name Jungaburra, which appears to be one that Dark invented to conjoin ideas of dreaming and Indigeneity. Perhaps Dark adapted the name from the actual location of Yungaburra in Queensland's Atherton Tableland; it also suggests a pun on the name of Carl Jung, who emphasised dreams as a means of connecting with the unconscious. The fact that it also sounds like an Indigenous word demonstrates the entanglement of ideas of psychology, nationalism and primitivism in the novel. It is significant that it is on this mountain that Bret realises his love for Susan, for it shows Dark's idea that the mythic, transformative qualities of the natural environment were accessible not only to the

---

112 See Marianna Torgovnik, *Gone Primitive: Savage Intellects, Modern Lives* (Chicago: University of Chicago Press, 1990).
113 Maureen Perkins, "Timeless Cultures: The 'Dreamtime' as Colonial Discourse", *Time & Society* 7, no. 2 (1998): 337.
114 Perkins, "Timeless Cultures", 349.

"natives" who named it (and who are curiously absent from contemporary life in the novel) but also to modern settler Australians. In the shadow of Jungaburra, Bret experiences "a feeling that all the time between then and now was an illusion" (213). Bret and Susan are framed as the beneficiaries of this "spirit place", and this mythic collapsing of past and present is depicted as a seamless transaction that obscures any contestation over land ownership in the present. Dark's ideas about time were not only strikingly modernist, then, but also facilitated settler claims to belonging.

Settler nationalism also involves asserting a distinction between the interests of settler and imperial cultures. Dark uses the unstable relationship between past and present to provide an anti-imperialist response to the Great War. The war operates as an important catalysing event in Dark's interwar novels, associated with trauma, the mass slaughter of young Australian men and a misguided allegiance to Empire.[115] Susan's brother Colin enlists because of "second-hand ideas, mostly poetical and all so very out of date", and faces "an orgy of organised and nauseated killing" (24–25). As a returned veteran, Colin is driven to alcoholism and domestic violence. Through Millicent's reflections, the reader is made aware that Colin experiences nightmares: "[t]hings that crowded on him in the night and tortured him and flung him, shuddering and wet with perspiration, out of frightful sleep" (24). These descriptions of shell shock reflect ideas about war neuroses propounded by Sigmund Freud in seminal essays such as "Mourning and Melancholia" (1918). Through showing the psychological effects of war trauma on an Australian character, Dark not only exposes readers to international ideas about repressed memories, but also expresses resistance to Australia's involvement in British war interests. She describes the horrors of war as "fiercely photographed on the ... memories" (166) of Australian veterans such as Colin – an image that links trauma and memory with new visual technologies of photography, just as Freud did in *Civilisation and its Discontents* (1930),[116] while also calling attention to the injustice of Australian soldiers' involvement in imperial struggles.

Ambivalence About Modernity

Although *Return to Coolami* is more enthusiastic in its embrace of mass consumer culture than Dark's other novels, it nonetheless displays her characteristic ambivalence about some aspects of technological development. Dark ultimately draws on the new, modern and mass-produced pleasures of motor travel and cinema to stage a return to what she saw as the mythic, timeless and premodern qualities of the Australian environment. This deep ambivalence is registered in the contradictory meanings that she associates with the Madison car: it is a symbol

---

115 Eric Dark served in the Great War and was gassed and badly wounded at Passchendaele.
116 For an exploration of the relationship between trauma, memory and the photograph, see the work of trauma theorist Cathy Caruth.

of Tom's materialistic values; a source of modern speed, mobility and pleasure; and a magic time machine that is capable of transporting characters into a more authentic past, "less a mechanical means by which they voluntarily travelled, than a mysterious and omnipotent force bearing them, passive, tranced and pleasantly comatose, towards some destiny which they would not ... avoid" (306). The car not only takes the passengers forwards in time, towards "a future coming endlessly upon them", but also into the past, as the placenames associated with Aboriginal languages evoke "something you had forgotten a thousand years ago and to which you were returning now, not only in miles along a road but in spirit through a dissolving barrier of time" (290, 307).

We have traced this same sense of ambivalence about modernity in Dark's work over the previous chapters of this book. In her futuristic story "How Uncle Aubrey Went to London" (1928), Dark cautioned the reader against faddish attempts to navigate international travel through ultra-modern forms of speed and mobility. In *Return to Coolami* as well, Dark sought to curb some of the excesses of technological modernity. Australian modernist photographers displayed similarly ambivalent attitudes about industrial modernity in the interwar period. Even as they employed modernist forms, Max Dupain, Olive Cotton and Harold Cazneaux often turned to natural locations such as the beach and country towns, to provide a seemingly authentic alternative to what they saw as the frenzy and decadence of modern city life.[117] This quality of ambivalence was much less apparent in their commercial work, which, for obvious reasons, promoted the consumption of modern products.[118] Taken together, their private and commercial work represents a blend of enthusiasm about and resistance to technological modernity that can be likened to Dark's ambivalent position. A similarly conflicted attitude can be found in Kenneth Slessor's poetry. Although his more famous, mature poems often display a modernist pessimism, the light verses he produced for *Smith's Weekly* offer "another, more social side of his modernism", and take pleasure in the "new sensory or imaginative pleasures" of mass consumer culture.[119]

As in *Prelude to Christopher*, in *Return to Coolami* Dark's critique of technological progress relies upon an opposition between masculinity and femininity, wherein men are linked with destruction, and women with creativity and motherhood. This is articulated by Colin's wife Margery:

Men still like to smash and women still like to create, but surely, surely, it was no longer necessary that man should expend his destructive force, every year more diabolically ingenious, on the life which woman was still faithfully renewing after the fashion of uncountable ages ago? ... Did he really think it more interesting to

---

117 Ennis, *Photography*, 63–64.
118 Ennis, *Photography*, 82.
119 Peter Kirkpatrick, "Slessor's Darlinghurst Nights: Troping the Light Fantastic", in *ASAL Annual Conference Proceedings, 3–8 July 1994* (Association for the Study of Australian Literature, 1994), 8, 10.

pick a quarrel with his fellow man than to pursue his quite reasonable argument with, say, a typhus germ to its victorious conclusion? Did he really prefer sinking under the ocean for the purpose of ambushing and drowning some hundreds of human beings, to cruising about in a new world of smothered light and sound, still virtually unexplored – the last remaining mystery-land of his globe? …

Hasn't he, her heart cried despairingly, enough to do? … the air to turn somersaults in, the bed of the ocean to explore, the vast unknown forces of electricity, atomic energy to harness, the whole universe of suns to conquer … (199–200)

The selective nature of Dark's embrace of modernity is given strong expression in this passage. While denigrating technological developments she links with violent masculinity, including "diabolically ingenious" ways of waging war, Dark champions more progressive causes such as the curing of diseases through medicine, geographical exploration and scientific experiments that can be employed for the common good – aspects of modernity which she associates with a more humane and peaceful society.

As the above passage demonstrates, at this stage of her writing Dark still felt that science, technological development, geographical expansion and mass consumer culture had some positive resonances. Although *Return to Coolami* does not embrace mass culture in its entirety, it does associate some aspects of it with the "adventure of modernity" and the "romance of the modern", and hence Dark was able to use such experiences as cinema and motor travel as available metaphors for representing settler belonging.[120] By the post-Second World War period, Dark's ambivalence about vernacular modernity seems to have largely transformed into a deep-seated anxiety about the negative effects of mid-century consumer culture. In *No Barrier*, she no longer associates the Great Western Highway with "glamour and romance", as she does in *Return to Coolami* (205), but treats it as a symbol of capitalist greed and urban expansion. The wealthy gentry use the highway built by William Cox as a route to the fertile land west of the mountains, so that the thoroughfare becomes symbolic of their moral bankruptcy: "their wealth, their greed, their cruelty and their arrogance".[121] This class-based critique can be read as part of Dark's reaction to the rapid capitalist development of postwar reconstruction, and her increasing sense of alienation from Menzies-era Australia.[122]

The final novel that Dark published, *Lantana Lane* (1959), presents an even stronger statement against urban expansion, scientific development and mass

---

120 Matthews uses these phrases to describe the enthusiastic way that Sydney embraced international modernity in the interwar period, in *Dance Hall*, 2, 5.

121 Eleanor Dark, *No Barrier* (London: Collins, 1953), 162.

122 See Susan Carson, "Surveillance and Slander: Eleanor Dark in the 1940s and 1950s", *Hecate* 27, no. 1 (2001): 32–43.

consumer culture. Whereas in *Return to Coolami*, speed and mobility operate as vehicles for settler belonging, in *Lantana Lane* the small-scale farmers of Queensland's Sunshine Coast hinterland associate it with a lack of neighbourliness, as those travelling on the highway are distinguished only by "the flash of sun on their paint and chromium".[123] The novel registers a mid-century sense of exhaustion with the promises of modernity, reflecting a broader cultural shift in which the "initial enthusiasm" about speed and the mastery of space in the interwar years gave way to "dystopian skepticism" in the 1950s.[124] Science is also reframed as a significant threat to the development of liberal humanist culture, associated with chemical sprays, the atom bomb and the destruction of the natural environment in a "bulldozer age". Dark's narrator wonders satirically whether scientists will "toss off … a machine to deliver works of art as needed – and not unsettling ones, either, like those we have been compelled to put up with in the past" (143). A similar anxiety about the banality and insidiousness of mass culture was expressed by a number of mid-century Australian writers and artists, registered in the use of satire in such examples as Barry Humphries' parodic character Edna Everage, Robin Boyd's *The Australian Ugliness* (1960) and White's play *The Season at Sarsaparilla: A Charade of Suburbia* (1962).[125] The embrace of popular modernity in *Return to Coolami*, although never unequivocal, therefore belongs to the particular cultural moment of the interwar years, in which mass culture could still be associated with utopic potential rather than with what White went on to describe as "the march of material ugliness".[126]

Conclusion

Return to Coolami did not signal the end of modernism, either in Dark's work or in Australian literary culture. Rather, modernism emerged in Australia in more covert ways: expressed in commercial advertisements, middlebrow romance novels or depictions of settler nationalist desires. Furthermore, the fact that Australian writers had to navigate the tastes and expectations of book markets in Britain and America did not necessarily spell the end of literary modernism in Australia. Instead, it contributed to sideways expressions of modernism such as Dark's distinctive form of middlebrow modernism. While Dark may have been frustrated by the kinds of accommodations she had to make in writing *Return to Coolami*

---

123 Eleanor Dark, *Lantana Lane* (London: Collins, 1959), 10. All subsequent references are to this edition and appear in parentheses in the text.

124 Dimendberg, "Will to Motorization", 94. See Melinda Cooper, "'[W]hen the Highway Catches Up with Us': Negotiating Late Modernity in Eleanor Dark's *Lantana Lane*", *Queensland Review* 23, no. 2 (2016): 214.

125 Susan Sheridan, "Thea Astley: A Woman Among the Satirists of Post-War Modernity", *Australian Feminist Studies* 18, no. 42 (2003): 262.

126 Patrick White, "The Prodigal Son", in *Patrick White: Selected Writings*, ed. Alan Lawson (St. Lucia: University of Queensland Press, 1994), 270.

and ensuring publication for her preferred novel, *Prelude to Christopher*, these same manoeuvres mean that *Return to Coolami* provides fascinating insight into the ways in which Australian writers of the interwar period conjoined modernist experimentation with cultural-nationalist ideas, drew on images from mass consumer culture and negotiated middlebrow taste. *Return to Coolami* is therefore a crucial novel both within Dark's oeuvre and in the history of Australian modernism more generally, as it is here that we see her distinctive middlebrow modernist style begin to emerge.

4

"The Everlasting Voice of Man": Modernist Aesthetic Utopianism and *Sun Across the Sky* (1937)

> Only connect! That was her whole sermon. Only connect the prose and the passion, and both will be exalted, and human love will be seen at its height. Live in fragments no longer. Only connect ...
>
> E.M. Forster, *Howards End*, 1910.[1]

> It is a breach in continuity that threatens: what has been inadvertently dropped may be irrecoverable or forgotten.
>
> F.R. Leavis, *Mass Civilisation and Minority Culture*, 1930.[2]

> Only the everlasting voice of man chanting his past and challenging his future. Only that voice to keep awake his faith in himself which, by now, he might so very easily have lost!
>
> Eleanor Dark, *Sun Across the Sky*, 1937.[3]

In 1934 and 1935, Eleanor Dark wrote the draft of a novel entitled "Gnome in Sunlight", which was published as *Sun Across the Sky* in London and New York in 1937.[4] At the same time, Eric Dark was engaged in an intensive period of reading about society and politics, prompted by the poverty he encountered while working as a general medical practitioner in Katoomba during the Depression. In Eleanor's words, Eric "began to look for reasons for a condition that allowed hundreds of thousands of people to suffer want in a country that was producing more than

---

1   E.M. Forster, *Howards End* (London: Penguin, [1910] 1989), 188.
2   F.R. Leavis, *Mass Civilisation and Minority Culture* (Cambridge: Minority Press, 1930), 14.
3   Eleanor Dark, *Sun Across the Sky* (London: Collins, [1937] 1946), 139. All subsequent references are to this edition and appear in parentheses in the text.
4   Barbara Brooks with Judith Clark, *Eleanor Dark: A Writer's Life* (Sydney: Pan Macmillan, 1998), 164.

enough to feed, clothe and shelter them all".[5] Eric read government reports, the works of Karl Marx and of British Fabian socialists H.G. Wells and George Bernard Shaw. His investigation caused him to shift his politics from the right to the left, and he became active in the left wing of the Labor Party.[6] As Eleanor had always considered herself a socialist, she did not experience as radical a shift in her beliefs as Eric; however, *Sun Across the Sky* and *Waterway* (1938) nonetheless respond to the deep sense of social and ideological crisis associated with the Depression, and the growing threat of fascism overseas and authoritarian government at home. In the same year that *Sun Across the Sky* was released, Eric published the first of a series of articles in the *Medical Journal of Australia*. These essays, which Eleanor typed, explore the interconnections between the health of the individual and that of the broader political and economic structures of society, and were eventually collected and published as *Medicine and the Social Order* (1942). While husband and wife obviously influenced each other's thinking,[7] the broader point is that both were participating in an international response necessitated by the political and economic conditions of the mid to late 1930s. In particular, the Darks were searching for answers to what appeared to be an unprecedented crisis of liberal humanism. At best, liberal humanism seemed no longer to possess the power to explain the social catastrophes that occurred in the 1930s; at worst, it seemed directly to have contributed to these events.

This chapter will explore *Sun Across the Sky* in the context of the international response to the crisis of liberal humanism and examine the intersection of Dark's ideological position with her middlebrow modernist style. *Sun Across the Sky* draws on an extremely elevated discourse about culture and frequently looks back to great Western humanist traditions, as well as to formative Australian ones, in order to locate a legacy that will carry humanity into the future. Why would a writer facing a global crisis in liberal humanism articulate such a robust defence of its claims? The investment of *Sun Across the Sky* in liberal humanism could be read as a sign of the novel's nostalgic or belated quality; however, I will argue that it is part of its contemporaneity and internationalism. Like many intellectuals of the 1930s, Dark sought to resolve the social crises of the period through the realm of culture and art. This attempt to invest art with a totalising significance is what David Carter calls "aesthetic utopianism", which aims at restoring unity between the individual and the social sphere through artistic and cultural rather than programmatic or political means.[8] It reflects a specific discourse about culture wherein its fundamental purpose

---

5   Eleanor Dark, quoted in Jean Devanny, *Bird of Paradise* (Sydney: Frank Johnson, 1945), 254.
6   See Devanny, *Bird of Paradise*, 253–54; Susan Carson, "Pathology and Modernity: Medical Discourses and its Fictions", paper presented to North Eastern Modern Language Association Conference, Boston, USA, February 2009, 5; "Surveillance and Slander: Eleanor Dark in the 1940s and 1950s", *Hecate* 27, no. 1 (2001): 33; Barbara Brooks, "*Waterway*: The Multilayered City; History, Economics and Dream", *Hecate* 27, no. 1 (2001): 13–14.
7   Eleanor Dark pointed out the connection between her writing and Eric Dark's *Medicine and the Social Order*, in Devanny, *Bird of Paradise*, 251.

is to "reconcile divisions within the individual and society which are invoked as symptomatic of industrial/technological civilisation"; that is, "to reclaim 'full human beings'".[9] Carter suggests that M. Barnard Eldershaw's *Tomorrow and Tomorrow and Tomorrow* (1947; 1983) and Dark's *The Little Company* (1945) are prime Australian examples of aesthetic utopianism, as both feature characters who are authors and suggest that the novel form can "reconnect the individual and the social, the humanist and the materialist".[10] Although Carter does not examine *Sun Across the Sky* in this light, it is nonetheless Dark's first attempt to reconcile the deep divisions of the 1930s through the realm of culture.

The aesthetic solutions that Dark offers in *Sun Across the Sky* not only have national significance, as Patrick Buckridge demonstrates in exploring the novel as an example of Australia's state of "canonical anxiety" in the 1930s and 1940s,[11] but were also part of a broader, international search for cultural continuity in a period of world crisis. Dark's aesthetic utopianism resonates with that of British cultural critics of the Cambridge school, such as F.R. Leavis, who argued that literature could provide a means of connecting the past and present in a period where society faced "a breach in continuity".[12] As with these critics, who looked to literature and particularly poetry to provide a way forward in a time of crisis, *Sun Across the Sky* asks whether poetry and visual art – "the everlasting voice of man chanting his past and challenging his future" (139) – would be powerful enough to resist modern capitalism and carry humanity into the uncertain future. Dark answers this question in the affirmative, concluding the novel with "the promise of another sunrise – another day" (192). Her aesthetic utopianism is prescient in that it looks to a then relatively obscure cultural figure – the Australian symbolist poet Christopher Brennan – as the focus of a poetic tradition which Dark hoped would lead the nation into a liberal future.

Dark's aesthetic utopianism is also *modernist* in its expression. Her defence of liberal humanism is conveyed through modernist narrative techniques, including signature devices such as the one-day temporal scale and a focus on introspection. These modernist aesthetics are important, as they suggest the interconnections between modernism and liberal humanism, and thus challenge the traditional notion that liberal humanism was incapable of experimental expression. This study thereby contributes to the small but growing body of research which points to the potential connections between liberalism and modernism.[13] In particular, studies

---

8   David Carter, *Always Almost Modern: Australian Print Cultures and Modernity* (North Melbourne: Australian Scholarly, 2013), 196.
9   Carter, *Always Almost*, 196.
10   Carter, *Always Almost*, 192–94. *The Little Company* is discussed in greater detail in Chapter 5.
11   Patrick Buckridge, "'Greatness' and Australian Literature in the 1930s and 1940s: Novels by Dark and Barnard Eldershaw", *Australian Literary Studies* 17, no. 1 (1995): 30.
12   Leavis, *Mass Civilisation*, 14. See also Francis Mulhern, *The Moment of "Scrutiny"* (London: NLB, 1979); Raymond Williams, *Culture and Society* 1780–1950 (London: Chatto & Windus, 1958).

of the work of E.M. Forster have illuminated these conjunctions, helping us to reconsider the politics of modernism "outside the poles of extreme right and left politics" and showing that far from being homogenous, modernists expressed complex and conflicting ideological positions.[14]

Sun Across the Sky registers a shift in Dark's work, from the more willing embrace of mass consumer culture in Return to Coolami (1936), to a greater emphasis on elite expressions of visual art and poetry. Perhaps this shift indicates Dark's increasing desire to distinguish herself as the writer of serious novels; perhaps, after gaining a certain degree of acceptance from her English and American publishers with Return to Coolami, she was now able to write more of what she wanted. Due to its emphasis on high culture, Sun Across the Sky is more difficult to categorise as middlebrow than some of Dark's other works. The novel draws extensively on vitalism which, in its belief that "there was a vital life force accessible only to an artistic or spiritual elite", conflicted with the democratic values of the middlebrow.[15] The novel also contains one of Dark's most searing portrayals of the popular writer and the commodification of literature for mass markets, and in this way it reverberates with Leavis' criticisms of the "levelling-down" which he linked with mass production and the creation of the middlebrow.[16] Australian cultural nationalists expressed similar views: P.R. Stephensen, for instance, argued in the mid-1930s that the "mechanics of marketing" and "salesmanship" were causing cultural mediocrity.[17] Yet, as in all of Dark's novels, we can trace elements of mass culture in the modernist aesthetics of Sun Across the Sky, including the conventions of popular romance and narrative techniques influenced by cinema. The novel also demonstrates the ongoing influence of the middlebrow on Dark's work. It focuses predominantly on middle-class characters and attempts to resolve social problems through a plotline involving romantic coupling. There is also an attempt to portray a more democratic array of perspectives, which reflects Dark's increasing awareness of the class and economic conflicts of the 1930s. She tries to connect the liberal freedoms which she associates with high culture to the

---

13 See, for example, Amanda Anderson, "Liberal Aesthetic", in Theory after "Theory", eds. Jane Elliott and Derek Attridge (New York: Routledge, 2011), 249–62; Janice Ho, "The Crisis of Liberalism and the Politics of Modernism", Literature Compass 8, no. 1 (2011): 47–65.

14 Ho, "Crisis", 59. See also Brian May, The Modernist as Pragmatist: E.M. Forster and the Fate of Liberalism (Columbia: University of Missouri Press, 1997); David Medalie, E.M. Forster's Modernism (London: Palgrave Macmillan, 2003); John J. Su, "The Beloved Republic: Nostalgia and the Political Aesthetic of E.M. Forster", in Modernism and Nostalgia: Bodies, Locations, Aesthetics, ed. Tammy Clewell (London: Palgrave Macmillan, 2013), 198–215.

15 David Carter, "Literary, but Not Too Literary; Joyous, but Not Jazzy: Triad Magazine, Antipodean Modernity and the Middlebrow", Modernism/modernity 25, no. 2 (2018): 266, n47.

16 F.R. Leavis, For Continuity, Essay Index Reprint Series (Freeport, NY: Books for Libraries Press, [1933] 1968), 18.

17 P.R. Stephensen, The Foundations of Culture in Australia: An Essay Towards National Self Respect (Gordon, NSW: W.J. Miles, 1936), 105. See Robert Dixon, "Australian Fiction and the World Republic of Letters, 1890–1950", in The Cambridge History of Australian Literature, ed. Peter Pierce (Cambridge: Cambridge University Press, 2009), 239.

experiences of the working classes; as we will see, the result is an uneasy attempt to reconcile class divisions through the realm of culture.

"Writers of the Individualistic and Liberalizing Type"

In the mid-1930s, Australian writers and artists expressed fears about the growing spirit of illiberalism that they perceived both overseas and at home. These figures were alarmed about the spread of fascism in Italy and Germany, responding with fear to reports of state censorship and the exile of writers in Europe.[18] They were also disturbed by what seemed to be the growing conservativism of a series of Australian governments, fearing parallels between the Australian situation and what was occurring overseas. Dark was involved in the Fellowship of Australian Writers (FAW) which started actively to campaign against censorship in the mid-1930s, galvanised by such events as the government's efforts to prohibit the visit of Czech writer Egon Kisch in late 1934, and to ban Clifford Odets' anti-Nazi play, *Till the Day I Die*.[19] The literary bans and police raids on bookshops which led Cecil Mann to report that "Australia remains a joke" in 1930, started to take on a more sinister aspect as evidence of a growing authoritarianism.[20]

Australian writers responded to the social and political crises of the mid-1930s in a variety of ways. Nettie Palmer sought solutions within democratic liberalism and cultural nationalism, and supported internationalist socialist struggles in Spain.[21] Amongst Dark's generation, a number of writers, including Jean Devanny and Katharine Susannah Prichard, confirmed their commitment to communism, which appeared to offer a systemic explanation of the current crisis as a collapse of capitalism. In contrast, P.R. Stephensen and W.J. Miles expressed increasingly pro-fascist and anti-Semitic views in their newspaper the *Publicist* (1936–42), which Stephensen used to make appeals for the formation of a Sydney chapter of the Australia First Movement, the foundation of which led to his internment in 1942.[22]

Marjorie Barnard and Eleanor Dark, who had both expressed strong commitments to liberalism, faced uncertainty about their beliefs in the late

---

18   Drusilla Modjeska, *Exiles at Home: Australian Women Writers 1925–1945* (Sydney: Sirius Books, 1981), 12.

19   Craig Munro, *Inky Stephensen: Wild Man of Letters* (St. Lucia: University of Queensland Press, 1992), 150–51; Nicole Moore, *The Censor's Library: Uncovering the Lost History of Australia's Banned Books* (St. Lucia: University of Queensland Press, 2012), 125; Robert Darby, "'An Instinct for Freedom': Political Undercurrents in the Short Fiction of Marjorie Barnard", *Literature & History* 26, no. 1 (2017): 57.

20   Cecil Mann, "Australia Remains a Joke", *Bulletin*, 21 May 1930, 2. For a discussion of Australian writers' anti-censorship protests in this period, see Moore, *Censor's Library*, 123–29.

21   Modjeska, *Exiles at Home*, 12–13. See also Deborah Jordan, "'Written to Tickle the Ears of the Groundings in Garden Cities': The Aesthetic of Modernity: Vance and Nettie Palmer and the *New Age*", in *Impact of the Modern: Vernacular Modernities in Australia 1870s–1960s*, eds. Robert Dixon and Veronica Kelly (Sydney: Sydney University Press, 2008), 91–108.

22   See Munro, *Inky Stephensen*, 197–219.

interwar period. By this time, the positive view of the state associated with New Liberalism was increasingly regarded as obsolete by liberal thinkers around the world.[23] In 1935, the historian George Dangerfield declared "the strange death of liberal England", a statement which seemed to describe the state of ideological crisis across Europe.[24] British liberals expressed anxiety about whether their values could flourish in the event of a second global war. In his address to the Congress of Writers in Defence of Culture in Paris in 1935 (an event which Christina Stead and Nettie Palmer both attended), E.M. Forster articulated the fragility of a liberal humanist ideological position:

> If there is another war, writers of the individualistic and liberalizing type, like myself and Mr. Aldous Huxley, will be swept away … This being so, my job, and the job of those who feel with me, is an interim job. We have just to go on tinkering as well as we can with our old tools until the crash comes … After it – if there is an after – the task of civilization will be carried on by people whose training has been different from my own.[25]

The same doubts about the future of liberalism were experienced by Australian liberal thinkers. Barnard, who described herself as a "19th century liberal", influenced by the "Gladstonian" liberalism of her Sydney University history professor George Arnold Wood, felt that, with "war inexorably advancing towards us", her liberal position had become "inadequate".[26] Like Eric Dark, Barnard read widely in search of answers, and yet she "could find nothing between Christian pacifism and communism that offered … [her] the intellectual support … [she] needed to face the ominous future".[27] Instead, Barnard and fellow writer Flora Eldershaw expressed their suspicions about the authoritarian trends of the 1930s through defending artistic and personal freedom and opposing state censorship, principally through their involvement in the FAW. Eldershaw was active in the Labor Party, and Barnard joined the pacifist Peace Pledge Union, as well as a local branch of the Labor Party (although she later denied joining the latter).[28] Neither joined the Communist Party, although they had a number of friends who were members, and were sympathetic to its causes.

Dark seems to have found a renewed significance in classical liberal humanism's ideas of individual freedom and self-expression in this period of state

---

23 Mulhern, *Moment*, 11–14.
24 George Dangerfield, *The Strange Death of Liberal England* (New York: Capricorn Books, [1935] 1961); Ho, "Crisis", 49.
25 E.M. Forster, "Liberty in England", in *Abinger Harvest* (London: Edward Arnold & Co, 1936), 67.
26 Marjorie Barnard, "How *Tomorrow and Tomorrow* Came to Be Written", *Meanjin* 29, no. 3 (1970): 328.
27 Barnard, "How *Tomorrow*", 328.
28 For more on Marjorie Barnard's and Flora Eldershaw's respective political commitments in this period, see Maryanne Dever, "'No Time is Inopportune for a Protest': Aspects of the Political Activities of Marjorie Barnard and Flora Eldershaw", *Hecate* 17, no. 2 (1991): 9–21.

censorship and encroaching authoritarianism. She also responded to the social crises of the 1930s by attempting to make her novels more capacious: in *Sun Across the Sky*, *Waterway* and *The Timeless Land* (1941), she presents a broader cross-section of society than in her earlier interwar novels. The optimism of *Sun Across the Sky* might appear surprising given its context, but it is part of a series of works by liberal writers of Dark's generation that express confidence in Australia's possible future role as a bastion of progressive values. The impending global crisis seemed to invest Australia with even greater cultural significance. M. Barnard Eldershaw concluded their non-fiction work *My Australia* (1939) with the hope that, "If Australia has anything to give the world, it is the picture of a people growing, developing, progressing, without violence, working together in a world not yet defaced by irremediable hatreds and divisions towards a goal in which we all can share."[29] Dark similarly wrote of Australia, "whatever the world may require of us in the future, I think we shall be ready – on the side of Demos".[30] Frank Dalby Davison, in his anti-fascist pamphlet *While Freedom Lives* (1938), expressed hope for "a new age born with as little further darkness and bloodshed as may be possible", framing Australia's cultural and geographical isolation from Europe as a virtue: "it grows increasingly clear that a moment will come when we can look only to ourselves for strength and wisdom."[31] According to these Australian expressions of liberal humanism in the late interwar period, Australian culture could provide the very peace-loving, democratic values that the world most needed in a period of rupture and crisis.[32] This sense of optimism was much less visible in the work of an earlier generation of Australian cultural nationalists, including Vance Palmer, Louis Esson, Frank Wilmot and Frederick Sinclaire – writers whom David Walker argues turned from "dream to disillusion" in the interwar period, as their prewar hopes for a transformed culture failed to materialise.[33] The aesthetic utopianism of *Sun Across the Sky* therefore reflects a particular cultural moment which involved fears about the continuity of liberal values, anxiety about the growing authoritarianism of Australia's government, greater attention to class injustice and a tentative sense of optimism about Australia's potential role in championing liberal ideals.

Sun Across the Sky is an under-examined novel in Dark's oeuvre, just as her liberal humanism is an under-examined aspect of her engagement with modernity. As already seen, Dark's liberal humanist commitments were viewed as conservative and bourgeois by contemporaries such as Devanny who expressed more radical

---

29   M. Barnard Eldershaw, *My Australia* (London: Jarrolds Publishers, 1939), 309–10.
30   Eleanor Dark, "Australia and the Australians", in *Australia Week-End Book* 3, eds. Sydney Ure Smith and Gwen Morton Spencer (Sydney: Ure Smith, 1944), 19.
31   Frank Dalby Davison, *While Freedom Lives* (Sydney: Tomalin & Wigmore, 1938), 9, 12.
32   P.R. Stephensen expressed a similar view: "If Europe is determined to go smash in an unprecedentedly insane machine-and-poison war ... might Australia in that event ... become the sole repository of what were once European culture, ideals of decency, and civilisation?" Stephensen, *Foundations*, 88.
33   David Walker, *Dream and Disillusion: A Search for Australian Cultural Identity* (Canberra: Australian National University Press, 1976).

political commitments. More recently, critics whose work reflects post-1980s critiques of liberal humanism have again associated Dark's ideological views with conservativism and naiveté.[34] Yet we are currently seeing a reinvigorated defence of the idea of the human in some areas of the arts, as particular literary scholars and philosophers search for forms of humanism that withstand postcolonial, Marxist and feminist critique.[35] Rather than dismiss liberal humanism completely as "a singular, uncontested phenomenon" that is "naïve and uncritical ... a conceited, bourgeois ideology", critics such as Emily Apter, Andy Mousley and Amanda Anderson seek to uncover and salvage its more radical forms.[36] In re-examining Edward Said's humanism, Apter searches for other kinds of humanisms which, in Said's words, allow one to "reach beyond identity to something else" that "puts you in touch with others more than one normally is".[37] Eileen Joy and Christine Neufeld similarly suggest that, notwithstanding humanism's "long and troubling history", the "*possibility* of a recuperated and recuperative humanism" remains important, particularly in an age of neoliberal efficiency and instrumentalism.[38] Anderson similarly argues that liberalism is more complex in its stances, aesthetics and aims than anti-humanist critiques allow.[39] A recent Australian example of this recuperated interest in the political implications and literary expressions of humanism is Brigitta Olubas' monograph on Shirley Hazzard, which explores Hazzard as a "cosmopolitan humanist" who offers "a forceful and distinctive moral voice".[40]

Sun Across the Sky and the Artist

Sun Across the Sky follows a number of interconnected characters who live in Thalassa, a coastal town near Sydney, over the course of one day.[41] Oliver Denning, a humane and vigorous local doctor, connects most of the stories, and although

---

34 See, for example, Modjeska, *Exiles at Home*, 13; Marivic Wyndham, *"A World-Proof Life": Eleanor Dark, A Writer in Her Times 1901–1985* (Sydney: UTS ePress, 2007), 5.
35 This new or recuperated form of humanism has been called "literary humanism", "critical humanism", "new humanism", "emancipatory humanism" and "Saidian humanism". See, for example, Anderson, "Liberal Aesthetic", 249–62; Emily Apter, "Saidian Humanism", *Boundary 2* 31, no. 2 (2004): 35–53; Martin Halliwell and Andrew Mousley, *Critical Humanisms: Humanist/ Anti-Humanist Dialogues* (Edinburgh: Edinburgh University Press, 2003); Eileen A. Joy and Christine M. Neufeld, "A Confession of Faith: Notes toward a New Humanism", *Journal of Narrative Theory* 37, no. 2 (2007): 161–90; Andy Mousley, *Re-humanising Shakespeare* (Edinburgh: Edinburgh University Press, 2007).
36 Mousley, *Re-humanising Shakespeare*, 13–14.
37 Edward Said, quoted in Apter, "Saidian Humanism", 35, 42.
38 Joy and Neufeld, "Confession", 173.
39 Anderson, "Liberal Aesthetic", 250.
40 Brigitta Olubas, *Shirley Hazzard: Literary Expatriate and Cosmopolitan Humanist* (Amherst, NY: Cambria Press, 2012), 42, 248.
41 Thalassa is the Greek word for sea.

the narrative is focalised through a number of other characters as well, it is Oliver's perspective that is most privileged. On his car journeys between visiting patients, Oliver contemplates a diverse range of philosophical and social issues, including love, art, morality and class. One of his patients is the capitalist autocrat Sir Frederick Gormley, who has turned Thalassa from a fishing settlement called Murragoondah into "the most flourishing tourist resort in the state" (5–6) – a setting that shares much in common with that of Vance Palmer's novel *The Passage* (1930), in which a fishing community based on Caloundra is similarly threatened by the creation of a commercial resort. Patrick Nicholas Kavanagh, whom Dark based on the Australian poet and University of Sydney professor Christopher Brennan, represents the antithesis of capitalism: Kavanagh is eccentric, brilliant and cares nothing for financial gain, whereas Gormley is scheming and amoral.[42] Kavanagh and Gormley wage battle over the fishing village, a piece of land owned by Kavanagh. Gormley hopes to purchase it in order to expand his resort, while Kavanagh shows no interest in selling and is occupied by higher goals of artistic creativity.

The novel begins with sunrise. Gormley gloats over Thalassa from his house on top of a hill and ponders how he can engineer the destruction of the fishing village; Oliver wakes to the sensual memory of an evening spent with artist Lois Marshall two months before. Oliver is married to Helen, a woman who suffers from neurosis and fears sexual intimacy. One of the driving tensions of the novel is whether Oliver will leave Helen to be with Lois, who is framed as his natural companion. Over the course of the day, Oliver comes to the realisation that joy and personal authenticity are more important than following societal convention, and this leads him to choose a more vital life with Lois, rather than continue his marriage with Helen. In the meantime, Gormley forces a subordinate, Tinker Strom, to light a bushfire that will destroy the fishing village. The fire leads to the inadvertent death of Kavanagh. In a heroic gesture, Oliver saves Kavanagh's poetry manuscript for posterity. Gormley flees the town and is killed in a car collision with Strom. The sense at the end of the novel is one of cosmic restoration: Gormley is killed by his own capitalist greed, Oliver and Lois have found companionship and a vitalist joy in each other, and Kavanagh's genius, although unacknowledged by most, will survive through his poetry.

Dark's representation of Kavanagh draws on the discourse of the artist as visionary – an idea that was prominent in a number of modernist novels such as Virginia Woolf's *To the Lighthouse* (1927). His genius is given almost mythic status:

> Vast stores of the knowledge of mankind and half its tongues were ranged behind his massive forehead. Mathematically exact, his memory recorded and fetched forth at his bidding facts trivial and facts portentous. Poetry flowed from him

---

42 See Axel Clark, *Christopher Brennan, A Critical Biography* (Carlton, Vic: Melbourne University Press, 1980).

unendingly, Latin hexameters, the folk songs of Germany, the French of Mallarme, the ageless beauty of Biblical prose, and through it all there burned incessantly the vital spark of his own genius. (97)

Dark establishes the link between Kavanagh and Brennan through references to the symbolist literary tradition, and through the novel's epigraph, which is drawn from Brennan's poem "The Twilight of Disquietude" (1913). The connection seems to have been obvious to some Australian readers at the time: one contemporary Sydney reviewer wrote that Kavanagh "is a transmogrified Christopher Brennan – our vagrom literary giant at whose feet Miss Eleanor O'Reilly doubtless used to sit".[43] Brennan was indeed a friend of Dark's parents, Dowell and Eleanor O'Reilly. Dowell met Brennan at the University of Sydney in 1889, and the friendship continued throughout their lives, although it was sometimes strained.[44] When Dark visited her father in Woollahra when home from boarding school, she encountered Brennan, as well as other prominent cultural figures such as Lionel Lindsay and Julian Ashton.[45] Less than a year after Dark's mother's death, Brennan gave Eleanor a copy of his new collection, *Poems* (1914), inscribed "To Pixie O'Reilly this copy that should have been her mother's".[46] Dark also inherited two signed copies of Brennan's *XXI Poems: Towards the Source* (1897), addressed to her mother and father, respectively.[47]

Why did Dark use a relatively obscure poet from her father's generation to represent artistic genius in a novel set in the 1930s? By the time *Sun Across the Sky* was published, Brennan had been dead for five years and O'Reilly for fourteen. Nonetheless, to Dark, Brennan represented the possibility of an Australian literary tradition based on the values of liberty and self-expression which, in the 1930s, had yet to be fully acknowledged by academics or the reading public. Patrick Buckridge notes that, given the significant anxiety within 1930s Australian literary culture about mediocrity and a lack of tradition, *Sun Across the Sky* is remarkably hopeful about the potential of Australia to produce great art.[48] The nationalist arguments

---

43 Adam McCay, "Novels of Eleanor Dark", *The Sun*, 3 October 1937, 16, from Eleanor Dark's album of newspaper clippings, Eleanor Dark Papers, Mitchell Library, State Library of New South Wales, MLMSS 4545, Box 24. Other reviews mentioned in this chapter are also from this source, unless otherwise stated. Dark was anxious to preserve the connection between her novel and Brennan's poetry. When Collins and Macmillan rejected the title "Gnome in Sunlight", she recommended a variety of other titles derived from lines of Brennan's poems. These were also rejected, and the title "Sun Across the Sky" was eventually agreed upon. See correspondence between Dark and her publishers in the Dark Papers, MLMSS 4545, Box 25.

44 See Helen O'Reilly, "The Poet in her Past: Eleanor Dark and Christopher Brennan", *Southerly* 75, no. 2 (2015): 217–23; H.P. Heseltine, "'Cyrus Brown of Sidney Town': Christopher Brennan and Dowell O'Reilly", in *Bards, Bohemians, and Bookmen: Essays in Australian Literature*, ed. Leon Cantrell (St. Lucia: University of Queensland Press, 1976), 136–52.

45 O'Reilly, "The Poet", 218.

46 Dated "Easter 1915". This copy is kept in the Eleanor Dark Collection, Varuna, the National Writers' House.

47 Eleanor Dark Collection, Varuna, the National Writers' House.

of Dark's contemporaries were often focused on the novel form rather than poetry, and stressed the absence of or need for an Australian tradition: Nettie Palmer, for example, argued in her book *Modern Australian Literature 1900–1923* (1924) that interwar Australia had no great literary tradition, as "in our literary history … promising movements tend to run into sand".[49] It was not until the 1940s and 1950s, with the advent of *Meanjin* and the major statements of Australian nationalism by Vance Palmer, A.A. Phillips and Russel Ward, that the "*presence* of an Australian tradition comes to replace that sense of its loss or absence which had produced earlier nationalist arguments".[50] It is striking, then, that *Sun Across the Sky* expresses such a sense of confidence about the existence of a great humanist tradition in Australian culture. Dark locates this tradition not in the nationalist-democratic values of Henry Lawson, Banjo Paterson, Joseph Furphy and the *Bulletin* school, which cultural nationalists frequently championed, but in the more individualist and vitalist strand of Australian poetry associated with Brennan. In this way, her novel anticipates the elevation of Brennan that came about in the 1950s and 1960s, in the work of figures associated with the beginning of institutional Australian literary studies, including G.A. Wilkes and Vincent Buckley, and which led to a redrawing of the literary map to favour a "metaphysical" Australian canon traced from Brennan to Patrick White.[51]

Dark also includes visual art in this humanist tradition, using Lois Marshall to suggest that a younger generation of artists will take up the mantle of an earlier one. Lois represents a more modern conception of the artist: she is a woman, a professional artist and a mother, has at least one of her paintings hung in a public gallery and paints in a separate studio in the garden that is reminiscent of Dark's own studio at Varuna, which was built near the main house in the mid-1930s. Lois is also financially secure, surviving on the royalties of her late husband's popular novels. Together, the poetry of Kavanagh and the artwork of Lois represent:

> the voice … fashioned out of the past of mankind for the future of mankind …
> Only that voice to keep awake his faith in himself which, by now, he might so very
> easily have lost! Only his own voice struggling to its expression through words or

---

48 Buckridge, "'Greatness'", 31, 34.

49 Nettie Palmer, *Modern Australian Literature, 1900–1923* (Melbourne: Lothian Book Publishing Company, 1924), 57.

50 David Carter, "Critics, Writers, Intellectuals: Australian Literature and its Criticism", in *The Cambridge Companion to Australian Literature*, ed. Elizabeth Webby (Cambridge; Melbourne: Cambridge University Press, 2000), 269–71.

51 See G.A. Wilkes, *New Perspectives on Brennan's Poetry* (Sydney: Halstead Press, 1953); Vincent Buckley, "The Image of Man in Australian Poetry", in *Essays in Poetry, Mainly Australian* (Carlton, Vic: Melbourne University Press, 1957), 1–27; "Utopianism and Vitalism in Australian Literature", *Quadrant* 3, no. 2 (1959): 39–51. For more on the idea of a "metaphysical" Australian literary canon, see John Docker, *In a Critical Condition: Reading Australian Literature* (Ringwood, Vic: Penguin, 1984).

through music or through form, so that for every snarl of the beast which rose in him there came returning always the answering paean of his godhead. (138–39)

According to this passage, the purpose of art is to provide a sense of cultural continuity. Dark acknowledges that humankind's faith in itself is precarious, that it could "so very easily have [been] lost", registering the fragility of liberal humanism in the 1930s period. Yet as long as the artist can continue to express their ideas with complete freedom, then a link will be sustained between past tradition and the future, keeping violence and repression (the "snarl of the beast") at bay. In this way, Dark's utopian vision relies upon a continuous tradition of liberal and humanist values, not through political solutions but in the realm of art. Her emphasis on poetry resonates with that of British cultural critics who took up the ideas of Matthew Arnold to suggest that poetry could provide a vital social role in a period where "social changes … have virtually broken continuity".[52] As with the Cambridge school, Dark's understanding of culture in *Sun Across the Sky* is distinctly Arnoldian in its emphasis on "the best which has been thought and said in the world".[53]

Vitalism and Art

Sun Across the Sky also shows the strong influence of vitalism on Dark's work. She associates the artistic genius of both Kavanagh and Lois with Henri Bergson's concept of *élan vital*: the idea that life is fuelled by creative energy and a vital force that can be accessed through instinct and intuition.[54] Dark frequently uses imagery of electricity and fire to describe those who are receptive to life's vitality: Oliver has an "air of electric vitality"; Lois is "flooded by creative force as a vast machine is flooded with electric power"; and Oliver's brain is "a tinder" from which Kavanagh's "genius could strike fire" (22, 28, 42). She also imbues the natural environment with a sense of *élan vital*, writing about "an obscure force in all life which was still mystery" (137). The vitalist ideas of Bergson were filtered through to Australians in large part through the writings of D.H. Lawrence – the writer whom F.R. Leavis championed for his expression of aesthetic values.[55] Lawrence portrayed the individual in terms of organic unity, writing in 1936 that "[t]o be alive, to be man alive, to be whole man alive: that is the point".[56] The Darks were drawn by

---

52 Leavis, *For Continuity*, 49; Mulhern, *Moment*, 28, 36; Williams, *Culture*, 254.
53 Matthew Arnold, in *Matthew Arnold, Prose Writings: The Critical Heritage*, eds. Carl Dawson and John Pfordresher (London; Boston: Routledge, 1979), 282.
54 See Henri Bergson, *Creative Evolution*, trans. Arthur Mitchell (New York: H. Holt and Company, [1907] 1911).
55 Isobel Crombie, *Body Culture: Max Dupain, Photography and Australian Culture, 1919–1939* (Melbourne: Images Publishing Group/National Gallery of Victoria, 2004), 19–20.
56 D.H. Lawrence, "Why the Novel Matters", in *Phoenix: The Posthumous Papers of D.H. Lawrence*, ed. Edward D. McDonald (New York: The Viking Press, 1936), 538.

this idea of the unity of mind, body and spirit. In *Medicine and the Social Order*, Eric asserted the importance of approaching a patient as "the whole man", writing, "Health is the well-being … of the whole man, physical, mental and moral."[57] In *Sun Across the Sky*, Oliver reflects on the "temptation to … make opposite or even conflicting elements of what were really complementary parts of a whole", suggesting that an individual is "not a spirit within a body, or a body enclosing a spirit, but a complete and miraculous entity whose ultimate genius is its awareness of itself" (54–55).

Vitalism was at its peak in Australian bourgeois thought in the final decades of the nineteenth century, when it made a significant impact on Australian progressive thinkers; however, it was given new energy in the interwar years by the Sydney-based literary journal *Vision* (1923–24), inspired by Norman Lindsay and edited by Jack Lindsay.[58] *Vision* was highly idiosyncratic in its views, expressing strong antipathy towards modernism, and defending beauty and creativity, which it associated with vitalism.[59] Dark's library includes a copy of the second issue of *Vision*; her parents knew Norman Lindsay, and she was also connected to him through her association with Stephensen, and through her membership of the Sydney-based Yabber Club.[60] Through Stephensen, she was also linked indirectly to Lawrence, whose work Stephensen had published in London. As explored in the previous chapter, Dark was critical of Lawrence's representation of Australia in his novel *Kangaroo* (1923); however, she also seems to have been significantly shaped by his vitalist ideas, as were a number of her contemporaries, including Katharine Susannah Prichard, Stephensen and the founder of the Jindyworobak movement, Rex Ingamells.

In *Sun Across the Sky*, Dark seems to allude to the Lindsay vitalist tradition through a number of references to classical and pagan mythology.[61] She links Kavanagh to Orpheus, Pan and Dionysus, and to "Imps, devils and satyrs" (23, 64, 97). Lois' paintings feature gnomes and Oliver imagines Lois and her daughter Chloe as nudists, "capering about their garden, across the green lawn and through the gum trees, and over the rocks like a pair of jolly elves" (47) – an image that evokes the gardens of Norman Lindsay's Faulconbridge home, with its sculptures of mythic creatures in a bush setting. The generation of Australian visual artists whose work featured pagan and classical images included Sydney Long, D.H. Souter, Ernest Moffit and Norman and Lionel Lindsay; these images also featured in the early poetry of Kenneth Slessor, who was a co-editor of *Vision*. Dark would have been aware of the presence of this vitalist tradition in Australian art and poetry,

---

57 Eric Payten Dark, *Medicine and the Social Order* (Sydney: E.P. Dark, 1942), 8.
58 Michael Roe, *Nine Australian Progressives: Vitalism in Bourgeois Social Thought, 1890–1960* (St. Lucia: University of Queensland Press, 1984), 17.
59 Carter, *Always Almost*, 6.
60 Pamela Bell, "Art That Never Was: Representations of the Artist in Twentieth-Century Australian Fiction" (PhD thesis, University of Sydney, 2003), 46.
61 Bell, "Art", 61.

although by the time she wrote *Sun Across the Sky*, this tradition mostly belonged to an earlier generation of artists.

Given that the vitalism of the Lindsay *Vision* school was so avowedly anti-modernist and masculinist in its expression, it seems surprising that Dark drew on it for ideas about creativity. To some extent she attempts to modernise its ideas by applying them to a female artist character who is also a mother. Dark frames maternity as a creative and energising pursuit: when Chloe is born, Lois feels a "peace, an utter and miraculous freedom" and no longer experiences the desire to paint (74). In this way, Dark modifies the vitalism of *Vision* by offering a much more positive representation of a woman as a professional artist.[62] She also shows greater openness towards modernism than did the *Vision* school. There are some descriptions of Lois' art which seem to link it with surrealism and impressionism: in Waterway, where Lois appears again as a central character, her paintings are described as "like dreams, as if she's not properly awake, flashes of vision disconnected from reality",[63] and in *Sun Across the Sky*, we are told that her artworks are "unfamiliar in form", with an "engaging vigorousness of line and colour" (75). Yet in *Waterway*, Lois' friend Professor Channon is anxious to distinguish her work from that of "the moderns":

> The moderns, he thought with the prejudice of age, were other-worldly in the sense that their works were foreign to all human conceptions; but the other-worldliness of Lois' work lay in her capacity to present a new, an entirely fresh and original conception of familiar things. (245)

At the same time, Lois' work does not sit easily with that of the "conservatives", whose "representational" landscape paintings Channon prefers (243, 245).

The fact that Lois' paintings contain both modernist and more traditional elements is striking, given the context of an extremely polarised atmosphere in the Australian art world at the time *Sun Across the Sky* and *Waterway* were published. The conflict between the conservative landscape school and the modernists coalesced around key events, including Robert Menzies' formation of the conservative Australian Academy of Art in 1937, and the response from avant-garde artists in Melbourne in forming the Contemporary Art Society.[64] In the year following *Waterway*'s publication, the art establishment of New South

---

62 As Patrick Buckridge points out, although Dark does challenge masculine representations of the artist through Lois, her depiction of Kavanagh reinforces "the patriarchal nature of the discourse of greatness", associating the artist with typically masculine qualities such as "power, independence, individuality, vitality, [and] self-denial". Buckridge, "'Greatness'", 34.

63 Eleanor Dark, *Waterway* (North Ryde, NSW: Angus & Robertson, [1938] 1990), 245. All subsequent references are to this edition and appear in parentheses in the text.

64 See Richard Haese, *Rebels and Precursors: The Revolutionary Years of Australian Art* (Ringwood, Vic: Allen Lane, 1981); Ann Stephen, Andrew McNamara and Philip Goad, *Modern Times: The Untold Story of Modernism in Australia* (Carlton, Vic: Miegunyah Press, 2008).

Wales and Victoria would denounce the *Herald* Exhibition of French and British Contemporary Art in strident, reactionary terms.[65] How then can we account for the way that Dark blends different, even opposed aesthetic traditions in her novels of this period? Some scholars have suggested that Dark knew very little about modernist art and the debates surrounding it in 1930s Australia.[66] This seems unlikely, given that her stepmother and two brothers were artists, and that she published in periodicals which featured articles on and examples of modernist art, including *The Home* and *Art in Australia*. Dark's friends the Evatts were art collectors who supported the Contemporary Art Society and opposed the Australian Academy. Mary Alice Evatt, whom Dark knew from Redlands, was a modernist painter, and brought the artist Grace Crowley to visit Dark in January 1937.[67] When Mary Alice's husband, the New South Wales judge H.V. Evatt, read *Waterway*, he wrote to Dark with concern about the fact that she had expressed "points of view which are not only erroneous but would, in Europe at least, suggest a complete lack of touch with the almost universally recognised position of the modern painters".[68] While Channon's anti-modernist position in *Waterway* may not suggest a very nuanced understanding of modern art, it does fit with the rhetoric about literary value found in the same Australian, middlebrow magazines in which Dark published her poetry and short stories: it operates as a claim to a more sensible space somewhere between pretentious, international modernism and a parochial or outdated conservativism, wherein a writer can present a "fresh and original conception of familiar things" without alienating or patronising readers (245). Dark's inclusion of a range of aesthetic styles in her conception of great art reflects the fact that, in the 1920s and 1930s, there was little within the Australian literary scene to equate to the existing high modernist Australian artistic culture championed by the Evatts.

If *Sun Across the Sky* is not particularly interested in distinguishing between the types of art that polarised the 1930s Australian art world, then it *is* concerned with the elemental creative spark that Dark seemed to associate with all great artists. She is more interested in establishing a continuous tradition of great art that will stretch from the past into the future, thereby providing an unbroken line through the current crisis, than in differentiating between styles. This "everlasting voice of man" is what Dark offers in the face of social fragmentation (139). When Kavanagh dies at the end of the novel, his legacy is passed on to Lois – a point made clear by the fact that Oliver gives instructions that Kavanagh's manuscript should be taken to her after it is saved from the burning house. The fact that Kavanagh and Lois work in different mediums does not seem to matter here: Dark associates both with

---

65 See Eileen Chanin, Steven Miller and Judith Pugh, *Degenerates and Perverts: The 1939 Herald Exhibition of French and British Contemporary Art* (Carlton, Vic: Miegunyah Press, 2005).
66 Bell, "Art", 46; Brooks with Clark, *Eleanor Dark*, 203.
67 Brooks with Clark, *Eleanor Dark*, 203.
68 H.V. Evatt to Eleanor Dark, 7 August 1938, Eleanor Dark Papers, National Library of Australia, MS 4998, Binder 1.

the unbroken "voice" of human achievement that represents humankind's greatest hope for a future based on the values of liberty and self-expression.

Mass Civilisation

The distinction with which *Sun Across the Sky* is most concerned is that of the true artist who pursues creative expression as an end rather than a means, versus the commercial writer who is driven by opportunism and the fluctuating demands of the market. Dark's great artist characters are disinterested in financial gain: Kavanagh appears dishevelled and lives a bohemian existence amongst the fisher-folk; Lois too is uninterested in material concerns and frequently forgets to eat. In contrast, Lois' late husband Kit, a popular writer who achieved success as a novelist after writing for periodicals, is revealed as commercially motivated. We learn through Lois' recollections that Kit was a formulaic and derivative writer, motivated by "a steadily increasing stream of cheques" (27):

> She didn't know quite when she had begun to suspect that to Kit fame and fortune were less the rewards of art, than art a mechanism by which you won ... fame and fortune. That had horrified her ... He would come home, she remembered, with an armful of magazines, and for hours with a notebook and pencil he would pore over them. Then, unerring in his chameleon-like flair for assuming the colour of the periodical he was "after", he would construct in due course a pretty and sentimental tale for *The Woman's Idle Hour*, a virile and absorbing "yarn" for *Man and Action*, an austere political article for *The Conservative*, a grim psychological study for *Highbrows*, and a bit of cheerful nonsense for *The Merry Heart*.
>
> And cheques would come in. Three pounds, half a guinea, eight pounds, seven and sixpence, five guineas ... (73)

Dark is highly critical of the "technical ingenuity" of the commercial hack: Kit has "neat indexed note-books full of plots, titles, sentences or phrases", which he uses to "delight ... the palate of the reading public" (27, 75). He is criticised not so much for his affiliation with a particular kind of culture, but for his "chameleon-like" ability to write for a variety of markets, including highbrow and popular ones. In this way he is aligned with the mass forms of marketing and standardisation which Dark humorously parodied in her early story "The Book, the Bishop and the Ban", and which British cultural elites F.R. Leavis, Q.D. Leavis and Virginia Woolf famously associated with the formation of middlebrow taste. In particular, it is Kit's lack of sincerity with which Dark most takes issue. She later told Jean Devanny when speaking self-deprecatingly about *Slow Dawning* (1932), "A book can't be made convincing to the reader unless the writer believes in it himself."[69]

---

69   Eleanor Dark, quoted in Devanny, *Bird of Paradise*, 249.

We can see a strong opposition emerging in *Sun Across the Sky* between Dark's conception of a "craftsman", which Oliver describes as "just a clever fellow with his tools", and a true artist, who is "a creator of creations" (159). In contrast to Kit's "clever" approach, Lois' paintings "flamed into life", are "unfamiliar in form", and express the "freshness and intensity of her released emotions", and in this way they represent Dark's desire for cultural authenticity unsullied by the commercial realm – a desire which was key to literary modernism (75).[70] Kit is eventually killed off in a bizarre plot twist involving an accident with a vacuum cleaner, freeing Lois to pursue her art with financial independence. It provides an interesting plot parallel with the death of E.M. Forster's working-class character Leonard Bast by a falling bookcase in *Howards End* (1910): while Bast is killed by the high culture that he hopes to master, Kit is killed by a machine that represents the banality of the mass culture that he tries to exploit.

The irony is that Dark drew so much on both popular culture and middlebrow marketing herself. Like Kit, she wrote for a variety of magazines, adapting her style to suit the target audience of the particular publication. *Sun Across the Sky*, like all of Dark's novels, features the conventions of popular romance, including a love triangle between Oliver, Lois and Helen. Surely Dark's experience of trying to satisfy the demands of both overseas and local publishing markets, as detailed in the previous chapters, would have illuminated the material constraints placed upon the artist operating from a colonial context; however, in *Sun Across the Sky* her artist-geniuses are represented as completely autonomous in their artistic endeavours.

Reviewers in Australia, England and America found Dark's artist characters to be unconvincing. In a review of *Sun Across the Sky*, ironically titled "A Pair of Geniuses", the *New York Times* suggested that Dark's power as a novelist was "a very long way below her ambitions", as she "failed to make the reader believe that her two geniuses, Patrick Nicholas Kavanagh, the poet, and Lois Marshall, the painter, were really as wonderful as she repeatedly insists".[71] Another, particularly negative, American review described *Sun Across the Sky* as an "hysterical argument for the right of the artist to throw aside the bonds of convention and free himself from the petty rules imposed by morals".[72] Yet another seized upon Dark's distinction between the artist and craftsman to make the point: "Miss Dark [*sic*], you see, is a very skilful craftsman; she is not an artist."[73] The reviewer categorised Dark's novel as an instance of "holiday reading": a "book to be read once, when the mind is weary and needs diversion, and then laid aside". This description of the novel's

---

70   Elizabeth Outka, *Consuming Traditions: Modernity, Modernism, and the Commodified Authentic* (Oxford: Oxford University Press, 2009), 16.

71   Louise Maunsell Field, "A Pair of Geniuses", *New York Times*, 14 November 1937.

72   A. N., "Book Makes Weak Plea for Artists' Freedom", *Cleveland Plain Dealer*, 19 December 1937.

73   Roberta Aldred, "For Diversion", *News-Sentinel* (Fort Wayne, Ind.), 6 November 1937.

ephemeral quality must have been particularly galling for Dark, given her efforts to explore the enduring nature of art and literature in *Sun Across the Sky*.

The Middlebrow Cultural Critic

Dark's characterisation of Oliver suggests that her aesthetic utopianism may also have an inadvertent middlebrow quality. As a middle-class doctor, Oliver is neither an artist nor a university-trained poet, yet he nonetheless discerns the essential truths offered by great art. He represents the cultural role of middle-class public intellectuals such as Eric Dark, rather than university-trained elites. Oliver's interpretations of Lois' paintings convey social and moral truths that Dark evidently believed were important for the time: for instance, he interprets her image of a gnome emerging from a cave and touching sunlight for the first time as a vision of future humanity no longer exploiting the natural resources of the earth for capitalist gain, but rather learning to "absorb it" and be "part of it" (162).

The fact that Oliver is framed more as a middlebrow cultural critic than a university-trained specialist suggests not only the ongoing presence of the middlebrow in Dark's writing, but also the particular institutional conditions of interwar Australian cultural life. In 1930s England, cultural critics aimed to form an intelligentsia of specialists: a "minority capable not only of appreciating Dante, Shakespeare, Donne, Baudelaire, Hardy (to take major instances) but of recognising their latest successors constitute the consciousness of the race (or of a branch of it) at a given time".[74] The function of this "minority" would be to "watch over and guide the progress of society at large", through elucidating the human values in literature (specifically, European and English literature).[75] Their cultural program was closely linked to the development of the English Tripos system at Cambridge University.[76] In Australia, although there were academic systems in place for the canonisation and teaching of English literature, there were no comparable ones for teaching and preserving the national literature in universities until the 1950s.[77] In fact, those advocating an indigenous Australian literature frequently positioned themselves against professors of English in Australian universities who "saw their main task as maintaining an unbroken cultural linkage with England".[78] In 1935, G.H. Cowling, Professor of English Literature at the University of Melbourne, wrote a rejoinder to Vance Palmer's article on "The Future of Australian Literature"

---

74 Leavis, *Mass Civilisation*, 13.
75 Mulhern, *Moment*, 33.
76 Mulhern, *Moment*, 3–4.
77 Buckridge, "'Greatness'", 30. See also Leigh Dale, *The English Men: Professing Literature in Australian Universities* (Canberra: Association for the Study of Australian Literature, 1997), 143–65; Robert Dixon, "Introduction", in *Authority and Influence: Australian Literary Criticism 1950–2000*, eds. Delys Bird, Robert Dixon and Christopher Lee (St. Lucia: University of Queensland Press, 2001), xv–xvii.
78 Dale, *English Men*, 1.

in the Melbourne *Age*, and expressed the view that Australia lacked tradition because "[t]here are no ancient churches, castles, ruins … this means that we can never hope to have a Scott, a Balzac, a Dumas … nor a poetry which reflects past glories".[79] Cowling's article energised Stephensen to write a response, which eventually developed into *The Foundations of Culture in Australia: An Essay Towards National Self Respect* (1936). Miles Franklin commented that Cowling's arguments were characteristic of the "small-grade Britons" who worked in Australia's universities.[80]

The result of these institutional differences between the English and Australian situation was that, in Australia, those advocating a national literature had to operate mostly outside of the universities, in commercial, middlebrow culture.[81] Stephensen, the Palmers, Marjorie Barnard, Flora Eldershaw and Dark expressed many attitudes typically associated with middlebrow culture, including reservations about modernism, elitism and specialisation.[82] Cultural nationalists adopted an anti-elitist rhetoric: Stephensen, for instance, described Australia's "pathetic intelligentsia, particularly the feeble 'university' type", as those who "read T.S. Eliot, longing for the 'sophisticated English' culture which they imagine that this Bostonian émigré represents".[83] The anti-imperialist nature of these critics' resistant nationalism complicates their relationship to British university critics, as does their commitment to disseminating culture to a broad national audience.

Sun Across the Sky reflects this ambivalence, advocating high culture but also emphasising the role of the sensitive but untrained middle-class professional in its dissemination. Dark clearly disagreed with Cowling that Australia was incapable of producing "a poetry which reflects past glories", pointing to Brennan as a key example of a continuous Australian tradition. In *Waterway*, she writes that "Genius … does not need circles or self-conscious intelligentsia" but rather "asks only to feel the thrusting urge of growth about it – a clamour and a flood of life" (116). In this way, an intuitive embrace of great art and a vitalist response to environment could afford the basis of a continuous tradition: as Oliver expresses it in *Sun Across the Sky*, "it didn't seem worth bothering about, that he … did not happen to be an artist … You only had to live with joy and die with undiminished zest, and

---

79 G.H. Cowling, "The Future of Australian Literature", *Age*, 16 February 1935, 6.
80 Miles Franklin to Hartley Grattan, 14 March 1935, quoted in Munro, *Inky Stephensen*, 152. David Carter points out that, although Cowling worked as a university professor, the reviews that he wrote for the periodical *All About Books* reveal a "generalist" attitude towards the literary marketplace, in which "good literature" is associated with "sincere emotion, unity of purpose, sympathetic characters and a good story". See Carter, *Always Almost*, 163–64. Even if this is so, Stephensen and Franklin appear to have believed that Cowling represented highbrow, Anglophile and traditionalist tastes.
81 David Carter, "Modernity and the Gendering of Middlebrow Book Culture in Australia", in *The Masculine Middlebrow, 1880–1950: What Mr. Miniver Read*, ed. Kate Macdonald (New York: Palgrave Macmillan, 2011), 143.
82 Carter, "Modernity", 143; *Always Almost*, 147.
83 Stephensen, *Foundations*, 110–11.

the infinitesimal line of your existence would lie clearly and harmoniously in the vast pattern of the cosmic scheme" (153). In considering the emergence of an indigenised settler Australian race, Oliver wonders,

> whether the background of warmth and colour ... were building up in them ... slowly and imperceptibly, that passion and romance, that ebb and flow of intense emotion, that fierce love of life for the sake of living which is the true environment of all great art. Preparing carefully a soil which would some day bring great beauty to a triumphant blossoming ... (29–30)

In this passage, Dark attempts to provide a democratic basis for her aesthetic utopianism, suggesting that Australia provides the "true environment" for "all great art". It is an idea that invests Australia with an important role in a global context. In *Sun Across the Sky*, the first shoots of this "triumphant blossoming" already exist in figures such as Kavanagh, and will be continued by the artists and middle-class intellectuals of Lois and Oliver's generation. In contrast to Dark's sense of optimism, critics of the Palmers' generation tended to express the view that Australia had failed to produce a truly national people: Nettie Palmer reflected in 1937 that "we have no sense of ourselves as a people, with a yesterday and a to-morrow".[84]

Mapping the Community

One of the purposes of modernist aesthetic utopianism was to "reconnect the individual and the social" in a period where liberalism seemed no longer to provide satisfactory explanations for the relationship between the two.[85] *Sun Across the Sky* was Dark's first attempt to write a novel that would offer a more complete representation of a whole community. It features characters from a variety of classes, including capitalist business owners, the professional middle classes and the working classes. Dark tries to connect the lives of these characters to the social fabric of a small-town community and to the wider world and, in this way, she draws on the tradition of Victorian novels such as George Eliot's *Middlemarch* (1871–73) and Charles Dickens' *Bleak House* (1852–53), which similarly sought to show the relation of the organic community to the broader national whole.[86]

---

84 Nettie Palmer, 13 November 1937, in *Nettie Palmer: Her Private Journal "Fourteen Years"*, *Poems, Reviews and Literary Essays*, ed. Vivian Smith (St. Lucia: University of Queensland Press, 1988), 241. See Walker, *Dream and Disillusion*, 165–67.

85 Carter, *Always Almost*, 193.

86 In *Middlemarch*, George Eliot uses the image of society as a woven cloth to connect individual strands of human story into the organic community of a provincial Midlands society in England, and to the nation and world. See Chapter 2 in J. Hillis Miller, *Reading for Our Time: "Adam Bede" and "Middlemarch" Revisited* (Edinburgh: Edinburgh University Press, 2012). Dark uses the same metaphor in *Waterway*, depicting the community of Watsons Bay as a "small

In *Sun Across the Sky*, Dark uses the highly compressed, modernist one-day time frame to narrowly focus the narrative so that interconnections between characters become visible within a limited temporal scope. She creates a sense of simultaneous action through moving between various scenes focalised through differing characters' perspectives – a technique that is similar to the editing device of cinematic cross-cutting. For example, Dark ends one scene with Oliver turning towards the door of his bedroom and seeing Helen, followed by another describing Tinker Strom driving from Sydney to Thalassa to start the fire on Gormley's orders, and then depicts a separate scene involving Gormley waiting for news of the fire. The narrative then returns to Oliver and Helen, beginning just as Oliver turns towards the door. As there is no gap of time between the two scenes involving Helen and Oliver, the implication is that the scenes between them are occurring simultaneously: they are spliced between these other scenes. These moments of synchronicity increase and intensify as the novel continues towards the climax of the fire, allowing the reader to note the causal relationships between events and characters.

Dark also suggests the interconnection between local community and world by using Thalassa as a microcosm for a global totality. Dark provides synoptic views which usually involve characters looking down at the town from a significant height. These are examples of what Jon Hegglund calls the "situated eye": "a perspective distant enough to survey a valley, town or coastline, but still attached to a material, embodied human identity", which allows the writer to "mediate between a scale of knowable human perception and the abstraction of cartographic overview".[87] Hegglund traces an instance of this in *Howards End* when the narrator describes the view of England from the Purbeck Hills: Forster writes that, from this vantage point on the coast of south-central England, "the imagination swells, spreads and deepens, until it becomes geographic and encircles England".[88] It is a scene that registers the interconnection of a pastoral location with larger scales of city, nation and world, in an era when faster forms of rail and motor travel, and increased urban development, brought a greater sense of the region's proximity to these scales.[89]

In a similarly panoptic moment, Oliver looks out from his veranda towards Lois' house and connects the lives of those in Thalassa to what is happening across the globe:

> He could see a patch of her red roof through the trees, and his eyes fastened on it with a kind of hunger … His eyes seemed forced away from the speck of red

---

group of interwoven lives" which are "touching, running parallel for a little while, closely woven, breaking away" (13).

87   Jon Hegglund, *World Views: Metageographies of Modernist Fiction* (New York: Oxford University Press, 2012), 56.
88   Forster, *Howards End*, 171; Hegglund, *World Views*, 56.
89   Hegglund, *World Views*, 72, 76.

between the trees, to travel with a kind of bitter eagerness over the whole of this tiny microcosm in which he worked. What was its destiny? Where were they going, these strange, foolish, magnificent creatures, and the others like him, all over the tormented globe? (137)

In this passage Dark, like Forster in *Howards End*, moves the narrative focus from the local to a more abstract view in order to connect a subnational region to "larger global space".[90] In jumping from the proximate to the struggles of humanity "all over the tormented globe", Dark seems to skip over the scale of the continental nation. Forster's novel can be read as expressing similar fears about the region being "merely folded into a territorial nationalism", and in this way the "situated eye" can question and defamiliarise "the perceived organicism and 'givenness' of the nation", registering a specifically modernist scepticism about the role of the nation-state.[91]

Dark was acutely aware of the interconnections between the local community and the broader world in the 1930s. Oliver reflects on the compression of time and space in the modern world:

> Now when our thoughts, the records of our doings in pictures and in sound, our bodies themselves, flash about the surface of the globe borne by the mechanisms our brains have contrived ... we are no longer hundreds of small communities but one vast community; we cannot avoid each other, we cannot live alone in our beloved spot, for we have annihilated the space which made it solely ours. (96)

This is a striking evocation of the shrinking of time and space in modernity.[92] As we have seen, Dark attributed a similar feeling to the moment when, as a teenager, she witnessed the arrival of the first flight from England to Australia, and felt that "nations could never again be separate as they had been before" – a realisation which "became a conviction as the years passed".[93] Dark clearly experienced strong affective attachments to local place, as expressed in her evocation of the bush landscape in *Return to Coolami*; however, she also hoped for a world united by liberal values rather than divided by national exceptionalism. Oliver expresses this hope: although he shares "those threads of feeling which bind a man to the place he knows", he is also aware that:

---

90 Hegglund, *World Views*, 56.
91 Hegglund, *World Views*, 6–7, 55–58.
92 See Stephen Kern, *The Culture of Time and Space, 1880–1918* (Cambridge, MA: Harvard University Press, 1983).
93 Eleanor Dark, unpublished note, quoted in Susan Carson, "Paris and Beyond: The Transnational/National in the Writing of Christina Stead and Eleanor Dark", in *Transnational Ties: Australian Lives in the World*, eds. Desley Deacon, Penny Russell and Angela Woollacott (Acton, ACT: ANU Press, 2008), 236.

Buried there in the steady glow of the Englishman's love for his flowering lanes, of the Italian's love for his vineyards, of the Arab's love for his desert, of his own instant emotional response to this quiet place of flickering shadows and hot aromatic scents, there lay sparks of that lovely and dangerous and ill-directed flame called patriotism. (95–96)

Dark's awareness of the dangers of patriotism reflect the specific fears of the 1930s, when Australian intellectuals associated the increase in conservative nationalism at home with the spread of fascism abroad.[94] It is a fear that became a reality in the attitudes of Stephensen, whose cultural nationalism was increasingly expressed in pro-fascist terms at this time. Instead of a defensive nationalism, Dark advocates a cosmopolitan humanism which she associates with artists and scientists. These cultural figures, Dark suggests, are concerned with something of fundamental and transcendent significance: the human spirit. When Oliver and Lois reappear in *Waterway*, now married, they represent the ideal partnership of art and science (to some extent, representing Eleanor and Eric's similar alliance). In *Waterway*, Professor Channon argues that scientists and artists have a unique role in helping humankind think beyond the limits of parochial patriotism:

The scientists and the artists, at least, are already from the very nature of their callings, from the deepest mainsprings of the spirit, super-national in their outlook and their creed. They, and not diplomats trained from the nursery to think in terms of "my government", can, and ultimately will, lead us into peace.[95] (78–79)

For Dark, artists and intellectuals carry the hope of humanity, not because they offer political solutions, but because they pursue the very liberties that she believes will eventually bring about peace. She was interested in ways of thinking which were "super-national" – by which she seems to mean supra-national or transnational. The idea that it is artists and scientists, and not politicians or diplomats, who will *"lead us into peace"*, suggests a retraction from the state-based solutions of New Liberalism, to a more classical form of liberal humanism based on freedom of expression.

The Threat of the Global

Dark's hopes for a more capacious, cosmopolitan humanism are also presented in tension with her leftist awareness of the material effects of global capitalism on the local community. While Thalassa is in one sense a microcosm of the broader world, it is also under threat from larger global and national forces. Dark points

---

94 Carter, "Critics", 269.
95 Italics in original.

to the interconnection between Thalassa and the larger economic conditions of the Depression: as Gormley reflects, "Things were easing up a bit – people were beginning to spend again, and it only needed a few scorching days to send their cars tearing down in hundreds along the fine concrete road to Thalassa" (6). Thalassa is very much a region of a larger whole: its existence as a leisure resort depends upon the improved global economic conditions, and it has been built for the leisure classes from Sydney rather than the local fisher-people. In this way the novel shares similarities with other Australian works from the interwar period that also draw attention to the negative effects of urban development, including Vance Palmer's *The Passage*, and Frank Davison and Brooke Nicholls' travelogue *Blue Coast Caravan* (1935), which was written in response to soil erosion and deforestation in Queensland.

It is unclear whether Dark based Thalassa on a particular Sydney suburb. Unlike Watsons Bay in *Waterway*, it does not seem to correspond to any actual coastal town near Sydney. Helen O'Reilly has argued that Thalassa is Newport, the suburb on Sydney's northern beaches where Brennan lived from 1917, speculating that Dark may have visited there during her time at Redlands.[96] Dark's brother Brien ("Bim") O'Reilly produced a topographical map of Thalassa for use in the novel (Fig. 4.1), although Collins and Macmillan were hesitant about including it and, to Dark's disappointment, it was eventually left out of both the English and American editions. The geography of the bay shown in this map bears some resemblance to Newport; however, it has some additional elements, such as a lagoon, suggesting that it is in fact a composite of the many coastal landscapes that Dark and her brother knew through staying with their father and stepmother in Vaucluse, and through family beach holidays. Many of these towns were in the process of being transformed into tourist locations in the 1920s and 1930s, as was Dark's home of Katoomba. Through setting *Sun Across the Sky* in a town that is in the process of redevelopment, Dark registers resistance to the ways in which aggressive capitalism was reshaping and destroying the natural environment.

Dark uses the geographical landscape of Thalassa to portray the struggle between modern capitalism and humanist values. Gormley lives in a "huge and ostentatious house on the top of the hill": standing on the rooftop tower, he looks down at Thalassa "like a bright map below him, neat and alive and orderly with its rows of red-roofed houses, its brisk, small shops, its concrete roads, from which petrol bowsers sprouted like exotically-coloured growths" (6, 23). The physical height of Gormley's house represents his social power: he is wealthy but a cultural philistine, embodying Q.D. Leavis' point that "the people with power no longer represent intellectual authority and culture".[97] The threatened fishing village which Gormley seeks to destroy is "huddled on the uninviting sandy flats at the southern

---

96   O'Reilly, "Poet", 217. Newport was also the location for a number of Max Dupain's most iconic modernist and vitalist photographs, including "At Newport", 1952.
97   Q.D. Leavis, *Fiction and the Reading Public* (London: Chatto & Windus, 1932), 199.

Figure 4.1 Brien O'Reilly. Map of Thalassa. Drawn for inclusion in *Sun Across the Sky* (1937). Eleanor Dark Collection, Varuna, the National Writers' House.

end of the town", existing on the literal periphery of the "model tourist resort" (7, 58). Gormley hopes to transform the village into a "recreation reserve" with a "cricket pitch, football field … refreshment kiosk, and so on", all of which will "fetch fancy rents" and strengthen his monopoly of the town (8).

As part of her critique of capitalism, Dark alerts the reader to the layered histories that exist beneath Gormley's superstructure. The resort has "risen … in brick and concrete, in steel and petrol and all modernities from Murragoondah, the hidden gully whose only noise had been the thunder of its surf" (23). Gormley reflects that the beach at Thalassa:

> had been here before the town, it had been here before himself, before even the oldest inhabitant of the fishermen's settlement at its southern end. It had been here in days so remote that no living person remembered them at all; in days when lean, black-skinned people had listened by camp-fires to its thundering surf, and called it Murragoondah, "noisy water". (6)

As in many of her novels, Dark reminds readers of the older histories that underpin the settler-colonial nation. In particular, she draws attention to the precolonial Aboriginal past, insisting upon a prior presence in the land that is both authoritative and always positioned at an historical distance. Dark links Aboriginal people with a deep-seated respect for the ecological environment which she believes has been threatened by Western capitalist development. Because she invests so much in the dying race trope, however, she suggests that future iterations of this ethical relationship depend not so much on Aboriginal people, who belong to a lost past ("days so remote that no living person remembered them at all"), but on enlightened settler Australians such as Oliver and Lois, who relate to the natural environment in a non-exploitative manner.

The Limits of Aesthetic Utopianism

What were the political implications of Dark's aesthetic utopianism? Although her representation of the physical environment of Thalassa shows a willingness to engage with some of the material effects of capitalism, the novel's aesthetic solutions and reliance on coincidence and accident ultimately undermine this engagement. Gormley's death restores balance on an ideological but not a material level, as the fire destroys much of the fishing village, and the future of the fisher-folk is unclear. The material and class-based struggles over land ownership are not so much resolved as displaced onto the cultural project of art, which is represented by the saving of Kavanagh's manuscript. This sublimation of the struggle over material property in favour of intellectual and artistic property is perhaps symptomatic of aesthetic utopianism's lack of material and political solutions.

The more democratic array of characters in *Sun Across the Sky* indicates Dark's desire to address the increasing urgency of the social questions of the 1930s; however, her aesthetic utopianism relies upon a conception of culture that is allied with artists and middle-class intellectuals and difficult to reconcile with class-based problems and the racial issues endemic to settler society. Although *Sun Across the Sky* does open up the narrative to several working-class characters, they tend to play minor roles, and towards the end of the novel Dark seems to lose sight of them altogether. Furthermore, her characterisation of the working classes rests on a form of modernist primitivism that associates the fisher-folk with the premodern. Dark frames them as the natural descendants of the Aboriginal people who used to inhabit Murragoondah: like the "lean, black-skinned people", the fisher-people also walk barefoot and display "a joy primitive and unashamed" (70). Dark views their "primitive" qualities in characteristically modernist terms, suggesting that it is something that has been lost by "civilised" society. In a passage of free indirect discourse, Oliver reflects of the fishing village:

> there in the bare-floored huts, and the sandy lanes, and the littered backyards knee-high with grass and weeds, some message of the *genius Loci*, some accumulated essence of community thought told you that there was no yesterday and no to-morrow, and you walked the more lightly for it, like an animal, the burden of time lifted from your shoulders. (60)

This depiction anticipates Dark's treatment of the Eora people in *The Timeless Land*, whom she describes as living without a conception of time. Both Indigenous cultures and the fisher-folk are framed as existing outside of the "burden of time" – a positive state that is threatened by catastrophic encounters with capitalism, whether in the form of colonial invasion or 1930s urban redevelopment. Dark's romantic representation of the fishing village resonates with the arguments of 1930s British critics that the organic society of the pre-industrial era was threatened by mass culture and industrial modernity. In *Culture and Environment* (1933), F.R. Leavis and Denys Thompson described members of English agricultural communities in Arcadian terms, suggesting that their proximity to "human nature" and "the natural environment" was something that modern society had almost lost.[98] Dark locates authentic vernacular culture in the Australian fishing village, as does Vance Palmer in *The Passage*. Perhaps due to the lack of a continuous pre-industrial white Australian tradition – what Palmer decried as Australia's want of a "peasant population to cling passionately to their few acres, throw down tenacious roots, and weave a natural poetry into their lives" – Dark frames the fisher-folk as the cultural and spiritual descendants of Aboriginal Australians, depicting them as new types of "white Aborigines".[99] *Sun Across the Sky* therefore reflects the broader tendency of 1930s settler Australian writers to express their hopes for settler belonging by identifying with Aboriginal figures' claims to cultural legitimacy.[100]

The problems of linking settler-colonial belonging with Aboriginal culture are now well established. Not only does this gesture essentialise and romanticise a diverse body of Aboriginal beliefs and customs, it also displaces the primary settler/Indigenous conflict onto struggles between different types of settler Australians. A number of Dark's novels contain contested pieces of land, such as the fishing village of Thalassa, the land that Johnny Prentice appropriates in *Storm of Time* (1948) and *No Barrier* (1953) and the lane threatened by redevelopment in *Lantana Lane* (1959). Through framing these conflicts as crises between capitalism and more ethical, humanist settler communities, there is an erasure of Indigenous struggles over land rights, or, at best, a displacement of them onto the distant past.

If Dark's aesthetic utopianism was incapable of addressing these racial conflicts, then it also struggled to engage adequately with class-based struggles. Her growing awareness of class issues posed an inevitable challenge to her aesthetic utopianism: if artists and intellectuals will save humankind, then what does that mean for people who do not have access to cultural capital? There is an uneasy tension in *Sun Across the Sky* between the idea that art exists for the benefit of all humankind, and a leftist acknowledgement that art and culture are unevenly distributed. On Kavanagh's death, Oliver worries that the poet's genius is not nationally recognised, thinking, "all over a continent people go on toiling and grubbing like gnomes in

---

98 F.R. Leavis and Denys Thompson, *Culture and Environment* (London: Chatto & Windus, 1933), 34.

99 Vance Palmer, "Battle", *Meanjin Papers* 1, no. 8 (1942): 5. The term "white Aborigines" comes from Ian McLean, *White Aborigines: Identity Politics in Australian Art* (Melbourne: Cambridge University Press, 1998).

100 Ellen Smith, "White Aborigines: Xavier Herbert, P.R. Stephensen and the *Publicist*", *Interventions* 16, no. 1 (2014): 104.

the underground caverns of their own unlighted spirits, never knowing that a little warmth has gone out of that lovely radiance which they cannot value because it is not to be possessed" (174–75). Lois' painting is reframed here as an allegory of unenlightened Australians failing to grasp the full meaning and significance of true culture. The phrase "all over a continent" is one of the rare times when *Sun Across the Sky* makes an explicit reference to the continental nation, and it expresses an anxiety about the limits of an aesthetic solution to social problems. Dark attempts to resolve this through Oliver's heroic feat of saving Kavanagh's poetry manuscript. She frames this as a redemptive act that will contribute to the future of humankind despite the lack of regard for great art shown by the general population:

> No, they hadn't cared about Kavanagh. They hadn't even known about him. But he had lived, and whether they knew it or not, he had added a little to the stature of mankind. They walked because of him with their heads a little nearer to the sky … (190)

This description of Kavanagh's poetry adding "a little to the stature of mankind", whether or not people are aware of it, sidesteps the issues of material distribution and uneven access to culture. It is here that we see the limits of Dark's aesthetic utopianism: in its investment in high art, it lacks a material or institutional basis that would enable it to connect culture to politics.[101]

The Ethics of the Middlebrow Novel

As we have seen, despite Dark's attempts to connect the individual to the social, *Sun Across the Sky* is much more comfortable with the individual scale than with the collective, political or material. Dark's main interest is on what Emmanuel Levinas calls the ethical realm of the face-to-face, in which "[t]he relation with the Other … [is] an ethical relation".[102] This preference for the ethical over the political realm is captured in another instance of the situated eye. From atop a hill, Tinker Strom looks through a pair of binoculars at the fishing village that he will soon destroy through an act of arson:

> He lifted the glasses to his eyes, focused them with care and deliberation. The scene sprang sharply into life; it came near to him, and was no longer a distant view, but a place. He saw that there were narrow paths winding through the blackberries, and he knew that children had trodden them, and that they were labyrinthine ways of adventure and delight … He saw three little boys with their trousers rolled up

---

101 Francis Mulhern makes the same criticism of the British cultural critics of the Cambridge School, in Mulhern, *Moment*, 95.

102 Emmanuel Levinas, *Totality and Infinity: An Essay on Exteriority*, trans. Alphonso Lingis (Pittsburgh, PA: Duquesne University Press, 1969), 51.

to their thighs, sailing some kind of a boat, and a dog yelping and scratching on the bank near-by … He could see two women gossiping over a fence … In the slowly-moving circle of the clearly-visible, but silent little world the whole life of a community was caught up with a queer, a poignant intimacy. Strom stared at it sombrely. These people were not strangers; nor were they friends. He looked at them with the passionless despair, the cold, helpless sense of a common doom which an airman about to drop bombs upon a town might feel. If those sensations which were so welding his face into immovable lines of agony could have been translated into words, he might have said: "Not you the victims and I the destroyer, but all of us standing on the edge of annihilation. There can be no action of mine for your injury which will not quite as surely and still more dreadfully harm myself." (141)

In this passage, Strom's initial "distant view" allows him to think about the inhabitants of Thalassa in an abstract and detached way; however, it is the close-up perspective, facilitated through the magnifying power of the binoculars, which brings them "near to him", creating a sense of intimacy and compassion, and demanding an ethical engagement. Dark contrasts the more ethical encounter of the face-to-face with the aerial perspective of "an airman about to drop bombs upon a town", with the effect that the personal and proximate is privileged as the site of ethical contact. Dark's abiding interest in the scale of the individual human person is suggested through the voice of the narrator, which reminds the reader that, in harming the people of Thalassa, Strom will ultimately be doing damage to himself. It is an idea that echoes Oliver's reflection that "only yourself could save you, only yourself could destroy you" (153). The passage ultimately privileges the inter- and the intra-personal over the larger scale. It is an ethics that has strong connections to the middlebrow novel, which, in its focus on personalism, often provides solutions "to serious social problems [which] involve … the moral, ethical, and spiritual rehabilitation of the individual subject alone".[103] Dark faced difficulty in translating her ethics into a politics, instead using her novels to offer her readers opportunities to consider their own ethical choices in response to the thoughts and actions of her characters.[104]

Dark did hope that individual ethical encounters, when aggregated over time, would have a wider impact and produce a more liberal society. This hope rests on

---

103 Janice Radway, *A Feeling for Books: The Book-of-the-Month Club, Literary Taste, and Middle-Class Desire* (Chapel Hill: University of North Carolina Press, 1997), 13.

104 Robert Dixon reads Shirley Hazzard's *The Transit of Venus* (1980) in terms of this same difficulty of translating ethics into politics (a criticism levelled at Emmanuel Levinas by Jacques Derrida). See Robert Dixon, "Returning to the Scene of the Crime: On Re-reading *The Transit of Venus*", in *Shirley Hazzard: New Critical Essays*, ed. Brigitta Olubas (Sydney: Sydney University Press, 2014), 86–87; John D. Caputo, "Adieu – sans Dieu: Derrida and Levinas", in *The Face of the Other and the Trace of God: Essays on the Philosophy of Emmanuel Levinas*, ed. Jeffrey Bloechl (New York: Fordham University Press, 2000), 282.

an evolutionary approach to social progress which David Carter links to interwar expressions of aesthetic utopianism.[105] Eleanor and Eric both expressed the idea that society had become infected by the disease of modern capitalism; however, while Eric outlined a specific program of social reform in *Medicine and the Social Order*, Eleanor resisted such solutions. In one scene in *Sun Across the Sky*, after a lengthy rumination on the sicknesses of humankind, including capitalism, the destruction of the natural environment and sexual repression, Oliver retreats to the scale of the face-to-face: "you must be thankful that work was always at your hand, and that in your work your mind came cleanly away from the sickness of humanity which you couldn't cure, to the sickness of one single human being whom you probably could" (34).

Dark was reluctant to acknowledge liberalism as a key contributor to the current economic and social crises. Instead, she framed the crisis as an aberration that would pass over time:

> Laws of society, laws of economics! Spoken of with bated breath, great images set up and worshipped by man who made them, by man whom they now enslave. "Born free yet everywhere in chains!" Chains of his own forging, chains which, from the cradle to the grave he busily fastened on himself and his children and his children's children …
>
> But that could not be. Such a struggle of mankind out of primeval chaos, could not end in defeat. Somehow before it was too late he would win back his faith in himself, would become great in that faith, so that with the wisdom painfully learned through centuries, and with the strength to break his chains, he would not break but patiently unravel them, knowing knowledge to be a greater thing than force …
>
> At such a time he would look back incredulously at a strange period in history when man had made laws and allowed them to bully him. When he had created counters and allowed their value to fluctuate so that his whole life was black with misery and confusion. When he had flung fruit into rubbish tips, and burned wheat fields, and starved in the streets. When he had divided the world into sections and peopled each section with a different kind of man speaking a different language and seeking different ideals, so that they grew jealous and fearful and killed each other and mutilated the earth in recurring orgies of rage and hatred.
>
> A long, long time! Many generations and much agony, most likely … (33–34)

Here, Oliver echoes some of Eric's criticisms of the folly of capitalism, which involved "the ploughing-in of crops … and the destruction of wheat while millions of human beings desperately need these things".[106] Eric saw these as evidence of the fundamental inability of a system "motivated only by profit" to evenly distribute

---

105 Carter, *Always Almost*, 197.
106 Eric Dark, *Medicine*, 55.

goods,[107] and in this way *Medicine and the Social Order* reflects the tendency of 1930s intellectuals to feel "that the crisis … [was] *total*, not the result of bad management but of a system fundamentally rotten from its ethics to its economics".[108] In contrast, Dark frames the current crisis as an anomaly, "a strange period in history" caused not so much by liberalism but by the failure of humans to fully grasp their own innate freedom. The paraphrasing of Jean-Jacques Rousseau's statement "Man is born free and everywhere he is in chains", suggests that humans will progress out of the current situation by coming to a realisation of their own liberal freedoms. In this way, Dark tries to disentangle economic liberalism from ideological liberalism, rather than seeing them as mutually implicated. The process by which humankind will free itself from its current captivity is framed as a "long, long time!" involving "[m]any generations and much agony", and yet it must also occur "before it was too late". *Sun Across the Sky* sits in the uncomfortable interstitial space between the kind of slow, organic change that comes from liberal politics, and the demands of an oncoming tide of historical catastrophe.

Conclusion

This chapter reads Dark's modernist aesthetic utopianism as part of an international attempt to use culture to resolve the mass social crises of the late interwar period. Like British liberal writers such as E.M. Forster and cultural critics such as F.R. Leavis, Dark sought, above all, to find a means of connecting past and future. Her aesthetic utopianism relied upon an evolutionary approach to culture that resisted programmatic and political solutions, and, as such, she struggled to translate ethics into politics. *Sun Across the Sky* communicates its aesthetic solutions in ways that reflect Dark's context of settler-colonial modernity, as seen in the suggestion that Australia would play a unique global role in preserving liberal values.

To investigate Dark's liberal humanism in this mid to late 1930s period is not to suggest that her position was a completely coherent or successful one. In fact, as this chapter has shown, *Sun Across the Sky* achieves limited success in resolving the ideological and political crises faced by Dark's generation. It is difficult to translate aesthetic utopianism into politics, as it "cannot envisage … a political theory or a set of institutions through which social re-organisation might be articulated"; instead it offers an "ethical language which has as its *telos* the formation of the 'exemplary persona' of the literary intellectual".[109] By displacing the social problems of the age onto the aesthetic realm of art and the individual personality of the artist or intellectual, Dark fails adequately to respond to the very social crises that she introduces into the novel. A similar inability to connect culture to politics was

---

107 Eric Dark, *Medicine*, 56.
108 Carter, *Always Almost*, 192.
109 Carter, *Always Almost*, 196, 200.

also the main flaw of the British critics who expressed their ideas in the journal *Scrutiny*.[110] The continuity that *Sun Across the Sky* achieves is highly tenuous, therefore, and in this way it demonstrates the fragility, even the unsustainability, of the liberal humanist position in the late 1930s period.

Could culture put the world back together? The answer that Dark provides in *Sun Across the Sky* is that art and poetry can awaken a deep sense of human freedom without resorting to authoritarian means. Would this kind of aesthetically inspired utopianism, with its evolutionary basis, its rejection of the mass consumer market and its inability to deal with class and race-based issues, offer an adequate response to imminent global catastrophe? *Sun Across the Sky* already shows signs of strain, as Dark tries to stretch her novel writing for new social purposes but is limited by both her preference for the individual scale and reluctance to move away from liberal ideas. As we will see in the following chapter, in her next novel, *Waterway*, Dark's evolutionary teleology comes under significant pressure, as the threat of global catastrophe seems to demand much more immediate, political solutions than aesthetic utopianism.

---

110 Mulhern, *Moment*, 5.

5

"The Vast, the Bewildering, the Menacing Problems of all Humanity": Regional Cosmopolitanism and the Political Middlebrow in *Waterway* (1938)

> [Writers must] give up their poetic solitudes and soft self-probings to study worldly subjects, enter the political arena, take lessons from workmen and use their pen as a scalpel for … cutting through the morbid tissues of the social anatomy.
> Christina Stead, "The Writers Take Sides", 1935.[1]

Eleanor Dark's novel *Waterway* (1938) was released in London and New York in the year of Australia's Sesquicentenary celebrations, and only one year prior to the outbreak of the Second World War.[2] The novel registers the pressure of large-scale world issues, including economic depression and the likely threat of war in Europe, in a way that was unprecedented in Dark's writing up to this point. Breaking into *Waterway*'s modernist introspection and middlebrow romantic plotline are two dramatic climaxes that occur in Sydney within the scope of one day, and which are invested with far-reaching social significance: a protest staged by disaffected, unemployed workers, and a ferry accident based on the historic sinking of the *Greycliffe* in Sydney Harbour on 3 November 1927, recast in a contemporary setting. In the maritime accident on which Dark drew, the Union Steamship Company liner the *Tahiti* collided with a local commuter ferry near the suburbs of Vaucluse and Watsons Bay, when passing by near the Heads, en route to New Zealand. Resulting in the death of forty passengers, including six schoolchildren, this event represents a horrifying collision of the local with the global. In *Waterway*, the characters from the professional middle classes are caught up in these climaxes

---

1   Christina Stead, "The Writers Take Sides", *Left Review* 1, no. 2 (July 1935): 435. Stead wrote this report about the First International Congress of Writers for the Defence of Culture, which she attended in Paris in June 1935. See Hazel Rowley, *Christina Stead: A Biography* (Carlton, Vic: Miegunyah Press, 2007), 154–62.

2   Dark timed the release of *Waterway* so it would coincide with the year of the Sesquicentenary celebrations. She entered it in the Commonwealth Sesquicentenary Literary Competition, which was won by Xavier Herbert's *Capricornia* (1938).

and forced to confront the urgent demands of the age in a way that registers Dark's growing awareness of the political implications of the late interwar period.

Even more so than in *Sun Across the Sky* (1937), in *Waterway* Dark is interested in the relationship between the personal realm and larger, global realities. Like Christina Stead's *Seven Poor Men of Sydney* (1934), which is also set in Watsons Bay, *Waterway* is a novel of ambitious scope. One character, Lesley Channon, reflects that it is impossible to "divorce her personal problems from the vast, the bewildering, the menacing problems of all humanity, with which they seemed so alarmingly entangled".[3] Using imagery that is reminiscent of George Eliot's description of the organic community as "threads of connection" in *Middlemarch* (1871–72), Dark describes the community of Watsons Bay as "that small group of interwoven lives … lovely and horrible like the Medusa's head – a matted tangle of innumerable interwoven lives" (17).[4] These lives are "touching, running parallel for a little while, closely woven, breaking away, so that you could never, at whatever point you chose, study a life solely your own, but always a life thrumming and alive with contacts, reacting to them in harmony or discord like the strings of a violin" (13). The metaphors of weaving and entanglement emphasise interrelationship and connection, indicating Dark's awareness of the larger social fabric into which the primary liberal humanist subject – the individual – was connected. As in Eliot's novel, Dark's social vision relies upon a "complex interdependency" between individual lives and the larger social entities of community and nation, indicating Dark's debt to the older, pre-Marxist form of utopian socialism on which Eliot also drew.[5] Socialism "insists that, morally and epistemically, the individual must be understood as a constitutive part of a larger communal entity".[6] Dark sought to make these connections evident by rendering her characters' individual choices, actions and relationships as symbolic of larger ideological and political struggles, thus using the personalism of the middlebrow novel and the narrative techniques of modernism to connect readers to larger social issues.

Dark was not alone in her attempt to use the middlebrow novel as a political vehicle. The same can be said of male political middlebrow authors of the period, such as George Orwell, J.B. Priestley and John Galsworthy, whose social criticism and "mixture of middlebrow social conservativism and radical populism", Anna Vaninskaya argues, can be traced back to Edwardian writers such as G.K. Chesterton and H.G. Wells.[7] Dark was an avid reader of these Edwardian and

---

3   Eleanor Dark, *Waterway* (North Ryde, NSW: Angus & Robertson, [1938] 1990), 189. All subsequent references are to this edition and appear in parentheses in the text.

4   George Eliot, *Middlemarch: A Study of Provincial Life*, ed. Rosemary Ashton (New York: Penguin, [1871–1872] 1994), 95.

5   Mark Allison, "Utopian Socialism, Women's Emancipation, and the Origins of *Middlemarch*", *ELH* 78, no. 3 (2011): 721.

6   Allison, "Utopian Socialism", 723.

7   Anna Vaninskaya, "The Political Middlebrow from Chesterton to Orwell", in *The Masculine Middlebrow, 1880–1950: What Mr. Miniver Read*, ed. Kate Macdonald (New York: Palgrave Macmillan, 2011), 164, 170.

interwar writers, and in *Waterway* she expands her writing from the feminine middlebrow form of earlier works, to engage with the realm of the political middlebrow. It was a move that took her outside of the expected purview of the woman writer and incurred negative reactions from some critics. In 1951, G.A. Wilkes criticised what he saw as Dark's attempts to "become an 'intellectual' novelist" in *Sun Across the Sky* and *Waterway*, making the claim "Mrs Dark is no thinker".[8] Yet other women writers in Australia, England and America were also seeking to use the "individual appeals" of the middlebrow novel to address political issues.[9] British women writers with leftist politics such as Winifred Holtby and Storm Jameson were connecting the conservativism of the middlebrow to the political context of the 1930s in novels such as *South Riding* (1936) and *The Mirror in Darkness* trilogy (1934–36).[10] Like these writers, Dark appealed to her readers' emotions, not only to invite them to identify with her characters, but to provide narratives that addressed contemporary social and political issues.

Examining *Waterway* as an example of the political middlebrow allows us to recognise continuity between Dark's 1930s, more recognisably modernist novels and her historical fiction. As we will see in the following chapter on *The Timeless Land*, there are some strong connections between the novels that Dark wrote in the mid-1930s, including *Sun Across the Sky* and *Waterway*, and her historical fiction, including an interest in the relationship of the middle-class intellectual to the working classes, the attempt to locate a more humanist basis for Australian society and a sustained modernist engagement with the nature of time and the possibilities afforded by multiple points of view. Furthermore, the fact that *Waterway* draws on the ideas and images of Victorian realist novels such as *Middlemarch* suggests the close relationship between Dark's modernism and the narrative mode of realism, reinforcing Joe Cleary's point that "nineteenth-century realism already contained latent modernisms that broke strongly to the fore … in conditions of systemic crisis and that twentieth-century modernisms may equally have retained latent realisms".[11] Rather than approach Dark's so-called modernist and historical novels as radically different, we can see that Dark experimented with different forms and narrative techniques to reach broad audiences and address the political realities of the late interwar period and that, as in the work of her contemporaries Christina Stead and M. Barnard Eldershaw, this often involved merging modernist and realist strategies.[12]

---

8   G.A. Wilkes, "The Progress of Eleanor Dark", *Southerly* 12, no. 3 (1951): 142.
9   Kristin Ewins, "'Revolutionizing a Mode of Life': Leftist Middlebrow Fiction by Women in the 1930s", *ELH* 82, no. 1 (2015): 262.
10   Jaime Harker, *America the Middlebrow: Women's Novels, Progressivism, and Middlebrow Authorship between the Wars* (Amherst: University of Massachusetts Press, 2007), 18.
11   Joe Cleary, "Realism after Modernism and the Literary World-System", *Modern Language Quarterly* 73, no. 3 (2012): 268.
12   For a discussion of the relationship between modernism and realism in the work of Christina Stead, see Fiona Morrison, *Christina Stead and the Matter of America* (Sydney: Sydney University Press, 2019), 6–7.

There is a recognition in *Waterway* that the evolutionary teleology and incrementalism of liberal humanism may not be enough to confront the rapid pace of the oncoming social crises. Dark was more willing to engage with the political and material implications of 1930s social crises in *Waterway* than in *Sun Across the Sky*; however, as in the earlier novel, she struggles to find a means of translating the ethical encounter between individuals into the realm of politics, and to reconcile the novel's nationalist and cosmopolitan commitments. The result is a valiant, at times compelling, but also unresolved attempt to use the middlebrow novel, the tactics of modernism and the framework of liberal humanism to tackle the political issues of the late interwar period.

Cosmopolitan Humanism

Over the course of one day, *Waterway* follows the interconnected lives of a diverse range of characters who live in Watsons Bay and travel to and from the city. As in *Sun Across the Sky*, the characters are drawn from a variety of social classes. The upper class is represented by a number of families from fashionable Sydney society, including the Sellmans, Hegartys and Manning-Everetts. These families have made their fortunes through trade and are used to represent crass capitalism without social conscience. In contrast, Dark associates the characters from the professional middle classes with culture and gives them a strong interest in political analysis. These characters include doctor and artist couple Oliver and Lois Denning (who first appeared in *Sun Across the Sky*); retired academic Professor Channon; his daughter Lesley, a freelance journalist; his daughter Winifred, an intelligent and well-educated woman who is trapped in a loveless and stifling marriage to Arthur Sellman; Roger Blair, a cultural-nationalist writer and editor; and the harbour pilot Ian Harnet. Dark also includes Jack Saunders, an unemployed and disenchanted labourer, who represents her most detailed engagement with working-class experience to this point of her writing.

Waterway is much more explicitly engaged with contemporary political events than Dark's prior novels, as though the politicised environment of the late 1930s is literally breaking into her writing. David Carter argues that this openness to "'facts', political rhetoric, and utopian discourses" is characteristic of novels of the period, as the social crises experienced in the 1930s meant that "[c]onventional plots and characterisation were transformed" and "forced into formal experiment", producing "expanded forms of fiction" in such Australian examples as Dark's *Waterway* and *The Little Company* (1945), M. Barnard Eldershaw's *Tomorrow and Tomorrow and Tomorrow* (1947; 1983) and Frank Hardy's *Power without Glory* (1950).[13] In *Waterway*, Dark's middle-class characters discuss Lenin, socialism, economics and

---

13   David Carter, *Always Almost Modern: Australian Print Cultures and Modernity* (Melbourne: Australian Scholarly, 2013), 168–71.

unemployment. Roger claims that "[e]verybody of any intelligence is a Socialist nowadays", reflecting Dark's ongoing affiliation with socialism, if not communism (63). The characters are depicted as voracious readers: Winifred reads about pacifism and Oliver about economics, stating, "One's almost driven, these days, to hunt for something that promises even a glimmer of stability" (134). They are searching for answers to the central question of the late interwar period: "*If we don't find the true causes of this thing and destroy them it will happen all over again*" (192).[14]

What are the "true causes" of the social crises that marked the mid to late 1930s? Underpinned by a Christian-inflected form of liberal humanism, Dark suggests that both the cause and the solution lie inside each individual human person. According to Professor Channon, who is writing a book about humankind's "universal religion", titled "The Sapience of Homo Sapiens", humanity's "search for salvation must begin – and end – within", as "in your own being you carry your own destruction or salvation" (290). According to such an individual solution, structural economic or political systems do not go "far enough" in pointing to the essential problem. Discussing a book on economics, Channon tells Oliver, "There are hundreds of books like it being turned out now – all sound, all sincere, all true – as far as they go. But you won't find your stability in any of the 'systems' they dissect or advocate" (135). Instead, Channon suggests that humanity should unite through a common conception of its own intrinsic "infallibility" (290). The concept of humans carrying their own "destruction" resonates with the Christian doctrine of sin, although Dark is quick to distinguish Channon's philosophy as a secular one: he views Jesus not as divine but as "a not impossible standard of human behaviour and of human thought, a demonstration to man that godhead is innate within himself" (303–04).

Dark appears to have been drawn to this form of liberal humanism because it offered the potential for a cosmopolitan ethic that avoided the kinds of systems and defensive nationalist positions she increasingly associated with fascism and authoritarianism in the late 1930s. In order to elucidate this view, she stages a debate between Channon's liberal humanism and the cultural nationalism of Roger Blair, who acts as a mouthpiece for P.R. Stephensen's ideas about national culture. Roger is editor of *The Free Voice*, a magazine dedicated to "the fostering of a national consciousness" (76) – a description that resonates with Stephensen's creation of the *Australian Mercury* in 1935.[15] Roger believes that the nation is at risk of losing its "blessed isolation" due to the consumption of "cheap syndicated trash", which promotes "an American film star ... a Paris-trained mannequin" above "the real wealth of the soil, of man-power, of brain-power" (76–77, 80). Like proponents of provincial or defensive nationalisms, Roger attempts to quarantine

---

14   Italics in original. This is the case for all italicised quotations from *Waterway*.
15   In fact, *The Free Voice* or *The Voice* was the title of one of the journals Stephensen tried to start while in London (in 1930). See Craig Munro, *Inky Stephensen: Wild Man of Letters* (St. Lucia: University of Queensland Press, 1992), 101–02.

Australia from American mass culture.[16] He regrets that his landlady's daughter's "petal-smooth and sun-tinted face" is distorted by "shoddily 'fashionable' clothes ... the formal corrugations of a 'perm.,' ... greasy unguents ... stilt heels" and asks, "[h]ow were you to impose culture upon people of this mentality, concerned only with clothes ... and the latest Clark Gable talkie?" (18). Here, Dark mimics the attempts of cultural commentators to keep "true culture ... unsullied by the vulgar claims of commerce", which they frequently expressed in terms of a critique of feminised modernity.[17]

In characteristically middlebrow fashion, Dark moderates some of the more extreme elements of Roger's defensive nationalism. She frames him as a slightly comical, hyperbolic figure: in one scene, Roger's preoccupation with the lofty question of how "we can awaken a national consciousness" is satirised, as a "knock on the door sent him leaping for his trousers" (80). Similarly, in a romantic scene between Roger and Lesley in the Botanic Garden, Lesley responds to Roger's political pronouncements with amusement, feeling "her lips move involuntarily into a smile with which she usually listened to Roger's dissertations' (201). When Roger proposes to Lesley in the same scene, and raises the question of having children, she responds with a "half-hysterical shriek of laughter" to his didactic statement, "This country must be populated. We must have at least ten million," saying, "Roger, I'm not a microbe" (203). While Roger articulates a nationalist message of "populate or perish", Lesley offers a moderating view that represents the voice of the settler-colonial woman who was expected to fulfil these masculine ideas.

Dark also uses Professor Channon's cosmopolitan humanism to moderate and challenge Roger's cultural nationalism. In a letter to Roger, Channon argues that a commitment to global humanity should trump patriotism:

> Love of one's own country is, or has been, a natural emotion, but we must grow out of it. Its danger lies in the fact that it reaches a certain pitch, it embraces a certain conception – and then it attempts to remain static. But love is a living thing ... and like every living thing it must grow or it must decay. It must deepen, strengthen, enlarge, until it embraces far more than one country, one people, one ideal ... the spirit, finally, is the one thing that can't be stifled ... it is not national, or even international, but super-national. (78–79)

Whereas Roger is primarily concerned with the problem of developing a national culture, Channon argues that the problems of the modern age – and its solutions – are universal ones, as they concern the human spirit.[18] This debate between cultural

16 See Robert Dixon, "Home or Away? The Trope of Place in Australian Literary Criticism and Literary History", *Westerly* 54, no. 1 (2009): 12–17.

17 Jill Julius Matthews, *Dance Hall and Picture Palace: Sydney's Romance with Modernity* (Sydney: Currency Press, 2005), 19–20; Andreas Huyssen, *After the Great Divide: Modernism, Mass Culture, Postmodernism* (Bloomington: Indiana University Press, 1986), 44–62.

nationalism and supra-nationalism in *Waterway* picks up on broader intellectual arguments in 1930s Australia. In the same year that *Waterway* was published, the American Australianist C. Hartley Grattan, when writing about an "Australian literary tradition", noted "a constant struggle" between the isolationist nationalism expressed by Stephensen and the "supra-nationalism" of other Australian commentators.[19] Grattan associated supra-nationalism with Randolph Hughes, the Australian-born literary critic living in England, who had written a scathing review of Stephensen's *The Foundations of Culture in Australia* (1936) in the English periodical *The Nineteenth Century and After*. Grattan sought to provide an accommodation between the two positions of isolationist nationalism and supra-nationalism, writing, "Without for a moment giving grounds for a suspicion that I favour cultural 'isolationism', it seems to me that all sound culture is somewhere rooted in national earth. The supra-national culture must be constructed out of elements which were, at their birth, of national origin."[20]

These debates had significant political implications in the mid to late 1930s, when Australia was facing the likelihood that it would be asked to fight for Britain in the event of another European war. Stephensen argued against Australia's involvement in British war interests, writing that "[o]ur first concern, as Australians, is to consider what may happen *in Australia* whether or not things go smash elsewhere".[21] Although Dark also expressed anti-imperialist views, she felt uncomfortable about strident articulations of nationalism. She represents Roger as a fairly benign figure in *Waterway*, drawing on Stephensen's nationalist arguments from the mid-1930s; however, the pro-fascist and anti-Semitic views that Stephensen increasingly expressed in the *Publicist* in the late 1930s must surely have alarmed her, exacerbating her fears about the dangers of nationalism.[22] At the time of writing *Waterway*, Dark was thinking deeply about the threat of fascism, and contributed an essay to "Writers in Defence of Freedom", the collection compiled by the New South Wales FAW, in which she examined Hitler's ideas about women, referencing *Mein Kampf*.[23] She was also reading about the League of Nations,

18   As noted in the previous chapter, although Dark uses the term "super-national" to describe an ethic that can "*embrace … far more than one country*", it seems likely that she meant supra- or transnational.

19   C. Hartley Grattan, "On Australian Literature, 1788–1938", *The Australian Quarterly* 10, no. 2 (1938): 33. Dark had a copy of this edition of the journal. Stephensen brought Grattan to visit Dark in 1937, before she left for her trip to America. Grattan recommended a number of American books for her to read, including F. Scott Fitzgerald's *Tender is the Night* (1934). Barbara Brooks with Judith Clark, *Eleanor Dark: A Writer's Life* (Sydney: Pan Macmillan, 1998), 193; The Darks' Library Collection, Varuna, the National Writers' House.

20   Grattan, "Australian Literature", 33.

21   P.R. Stephensen, *The Foundations of Culture in Australia: An Essay Towards National Self Respect* (Gordon, NSW: W.J. Miles, 1936), 90.

22   See Munro, *Inky Stephensen*, 197–219. Randolph Hughes also expressed pro-fascist views, in his 1936 pamphlet entitled "The New Germany".

23   The FAW collection, "Writers in Defence of Freedom", includes essays by Marjorie Barnard, Flora Eldershaw, Jean Devanny, Miles Franklin, Leonard Mann, Brian Penton, Vance Palmer,

encouraged by her friend H.V. Evatt who would go on to play a key role in the establishment of the United Nations at the San Francisco Conference in 1945 as Australia's Foreign Minister. Dark wrote in 1940 that the "realisation that 'Patriotism is not enough' and that one's loyalties must be human loyalties rather than national" was now "obviously necessary".[24]

Regional Cosmopolitanism

The debate between cosmopolitan humanism and cultural nationalism is not fully resolved in *Waterway*: like a number of issues in the novel, it remains suspended. Dark struggles to reconcile the evolutionary teleology of Channon's cosmopolitan humanism with the urgency of the ensuing global conflict, and to balance a commitment to a "universal religion" with the particular, strategic nationalism of a settler-colonial nation (290). Channon's attempts to articulate a faith in humankind's "infallibility" exist in tension with his likely death from cancer (290). He is portrayed as "[s]truggling for enough faith still to look forward": his thoughts are "disintegrating, fading", and, at one point, "with a movement of despair, [he] tore his pages across and across" (238, 305). The fact that Channon is ultimately killed and the manuscript of his unfinished book destroyed in the climactic ferry crash suggests that Dark was unsure as to whether his cosmopolitan ethics might translate into programmatic politics. Her depiction of the crash, relayed through multiple, simultaneous narrative perspectives, emphasises the comparative sizes of the international mail steamer and the much smaller local vessel: the *Neptune*, described as "inconceivably vast", cuts through the ferry "as if she were no stronger than a matchbox" (316, 319). The nature of the accident as a violent collision between the global and the local throws Channon's vision of a cosmopolitan ethic capable of embracing the whole world into further question.

In *Waterway*, Dark also struggles to reconcile cosmopolitan humanism with the idea of the nation. At the same time that she seeks to moderate strident and defensive articulations of nationalism, she never fully retreats from her investment in the settler nation. Robert Dixon distinguishes between the "polemical nationalism" of Roger and the "place-based patriotism" expressed by other characters such as Oliver, arguing that it is not national attachment that Dark rejects but "nationalism as a critical dogma".[25] In particular, Dark remained committed to the anti-imperialist, resistant quality of Australian cultural

---

Brian Fitzpatrick, Dymphna Cusack and Eleanor Dark, and expresses opinions that range from communist to pacifist. Dark's essay is called "Women and Fascism". The collection was never published.

24   Eleanor Dark to W.A.R. Collins, 29 July 1940, Eleanor Dark Papers, Mitchell Library, State Library of New South Wales, MLMSS 4545, Box 25.
25   Robert Dixon, "Australian Literature, Scale and the Problem of the World", (unpublished manuscript, 2018), Microsoft Word file.

nationalism. As we have seen, her 1930s fiction frequently drew attention to the traumatic effects of the Great War, depicting it as a senseless waste of life that unjustly involved Australian soldiers in a European conflict. Her views resonated with those of Stephensen: his first column in the *Publicist* in 1936 featured satirical recruitment posters asking for half a million Australians "for use in Europe as soil-fertiliser" and to act as "lethal-gas inhalers".[26] In *Waterway*, Roger recalls being drawn into the war by "all the usual dope ... Flags and glory, King and Country" and asks, *"what the hell did it have to do with us, anyhow?"* (204–05). Jack Saunders also expresses resistance to being drawn into another "of their bloody European wars!" (146).

Dark's cosmopolitanism therefore accommodates strategic attachments to national territory. As Jon Hegglund points out, "Anticolonial nationalisms, in particular, have needed to fight their struggles on the terrain of cartography, precisely because a bounded place on the map – a territorial nation-state – is the only form through which sovereignty and self-determination can be realized in the post-Versailles world."[27] Dark's own experiences suggest that she felt both the allure of internationalism and the pull of more regional commitments. In 1937, she left the Australian continent for the first and only time, travelling to the United States and Canada on the ocean liner the *Niagara*, as part of Eric's tour of overseas hospitals. The ship made stops at Auckland, Suva and Honolulu, giving Dark her first glimpse of Australia's Pacific neighbours. The Darks travelled to a number of American cities, including Los Angeles, Kansas City, Chicago, Cleveland and Washington. While in New York, Dark visited the office of Macmillan and was impressed by their treatment of her. She particularly liked Yosemite National Park and the Canadian Rockies, revelling in the sense of space after what she described as the "sardine-like humanity" of New York.[28] On the journey home she mingled with other international travellers. After a total of three months away, she was thoroughly relieved to arrive home in Sydney. She wrote in her journal of the last day of the voyage: "Up at the crack of dawn to see first of coastline! Stayed on deck till inside Heads."[29] The location of Sydney Harbour seems to take on special significance in this moment, not in spite but because of her experience of international modernity. Her enthusiasm at arriving home is similar to that of Winifred in *Waterway*, who Ian Harnet recalls:

---

26 Quoted in Munro, *Inky Stephensen*, 170.
27 Jon Hegglund, *World Views: Metageographies of Modernist Fiction* (New York: Oxford University Press, 2012), 83.
28 Eleanor Dark to Mollie O'Reilly, 4 September 1937, quoted in Susan Carson, "Paris and Beyond: The Transnational/National in the Writing of Christina Stead and Eleanor Dark", in *Transnational Ties: Australian Lives in the World*, eds. Desley Deacon, Penny Russell and Angela Woollacott (Acton, ACT: ANU Press, 2008), 235.
29 Eleanor Dark, 23 October 1937, from 1936–1939 diary, Dark Papers, MLMSS 4545, Box 21.

standing at the window and looking down at the Quay and the ferries and the people, turning round to say to him eagerly: "How good it smells! The salt water – and there's a man down there selling brown boronia! I've missed it all dreadfully – I've been abroad you know ..." (37–38)

This description captures both the allure of international modernity, with its "salt water" and opportunities for travelling "abroad", and a strong attachment to local place, represented through Winifred's attraction to the native plant of "brown boronia". Dark appears to have been able to balance these two commitments, suggesting that any global perspective is "mediated by a situated perspectivalism" – that is, it assumes a position from "*within* a national identity".[30]

The accommodations that Dark makes between cosmopolitan humanism and more nationalist and place-based commitments raise larger debates about the meaning of cosmopolitanism. Although Dark's flexible attachments were shaped by the specific conditions of the interwar period, they nonetheless provide insight into how an individual might seek to balance a commitment to the world with more local affiliations. The idea of regional cosmopolitanism challenges the idea that worldly attachment necessarily involves a rejection of the region or nation.[31] Instead of a sense of detached universalism, wherein local or national commitments are subsumed by the global, regional or flexible forms of cosmopolitanism suggest multiple sites of affiliation.[32] Neal Alexander and James Moran argue that modernist writers were able to express nuanced commitments to both region and world through their experimental aesthetics, as "spatial complexity is often intrinsic to the very forms and styles of individual modernist texts", which are "located within, and shuttle restlessly between, multiple and overlapping spatial frames: local, regional, national, and international".[33] *Waterway* similarly suggests that one can be ethically committed to, and move between, local, national and global scales, although the novel also registers tensions between these diverse commitments and suggests the difficulty of reconciling them on a political level.[34]

---

30   Hegglund, *World Views*, 15.
31   See Jessica Berman, "Toward a Regional Cosmopolitanism: The Case of Mulk Raj Anand", *MFS: Modern Fiction Studies* 55, no. 1 (2009): 142–62.
32   Rebecca L. Walkowitz, *Cosmopolitan Style: Modernism Beyond the Nation* (New York: Columbia University Press, 2006), 9.
33   Neal Alexander and James Moran, "Introduction: Regional Modernisms", in *Regional Modernisms*, eds. Neal Alexander and James Moran (Edinburgh: Edinburgh University Press, 2013), 6–7.
34   Dark's regional cosmopolitanism shares some similarities with the "strategic provincialism" that Robert Dixon and Brigid Rooney associate with Nettie Palmer. As in Palmer's work, *Waterway* "'knows' the wider world", yet invests in regional commitments to the nation and the local community for strategic and often anti-imperialist purposes. See Robert Dixon and Brigid Rooney, "Introduction: Australian Literature, Globalisation and the Literary Province", in *Scenes of Reading: Is Australian Literature a World Literature?*, eds. Robert Dixon and Brigid Rooney (North Melbourne: Australian Scholarly, 2013), xxv.

An extended passage from *Waterway* captures both the flexible commitments of modernist regional cosmopolitanism and the tensions that exist between its sometimes competing affiliations. Channon is prompted by news of his terminal illness, and the ominous international headline, *"Failure of Peace Talks"*, to imagine the world from a global perspective, "as if on a gigantic pair of wings, he seemed to feel himself lifted away from the earth – to be seeing it from an incredible distance, and with an incredible, an all-embracing comprehension" (119). Dark writes:

> he saw the globe of the world spinning beneath him, in sun and in shadow, with calm oceans and stormy oceans, with long wastes of white at either pole, and the lush green of tropical growth about its middle like a bright sash … from this vast distance humanity and its little preoccupations were not even visible. There was, perhaps, here and there a greyness, clinging and unwholesome like a mildew; the patches where parasitic man had lived longest and most densely, where he had built and torn down again … spawning endlessly so that at last the soil to which he was born could no longer support him and he went out to infect fresh lands …
>
> *Failure of Peace Talks.* Well, presently perhaps, that greyish patch which was Europe would burst into smoke and flame. And what then? … whatever happened the world would go on spinning, half in sun, half in shadow, with calm oceans and stormy oceans, with white wastes at either pole, and the bright sash of tropical green about its middle. It was even conceivable that the tenacious parasite which had infested it for thousands of years might vanish quite away…
>
> He found himself struggling against this thought even as his brain formed it. From the terrible and solitary heights in which impending death held him captive, he saw a great island continent alone in its south sea, and he knew that somewhere in it there was a street and a house at whose garden gate there stood the shell of an old man with a newspaper in his hand. Godlike in his aloof omniscience, seeing all the world spread out below him, he desired nothing but to return to that shell of humanity, old as it was, doomed as it was, to return and be part of it as he had always been, struggling with the complications of its communal life, part of that life, whether it marched to survival or to death. (120–21)

This striking passage has a "polytopic" or "trans-scalar" quality,[35] as the narrative follows Channon's thinking from the quotidian details of his existence in a Sydney harbourside suburb, to the "incredible distance" of a detached planetary perspective, moving to a focus on Australia ("a great island continent alone in its south sea"), and then staging a return to "the shell of an old man with a newspaper in his hand" – the scale of the individual human body. The sudden

---

35 Andrew Thacker, *Moving through Modernity: Space and Geography in Modernism* (New York; Manchester: Manchester University Press, 2003), 7–8. Meg Brayshaw uses the term "trans-scalar" in relation to *Waterway* and to Dark's ethical vision in "Trans-Scalar Sydney, Narrative Form and Ethics in Eleanor Dark's *Waterway*", *JASAL: Journal of the Association for the Study of Australian Literature* 17, no. 1 (2017): 1–10.

and disorienting leap from the personal scale to a global perspective, described in expressionist terms as being "lifted away from the earth", and seeing "the globe of the world spinning beneath him", registers a shift from a located perspective to "a more detached overview of a wider global space" – a shift which Hegglund associates with a cosmopolitan viewpoint, "in which the viewing subject rises above the place-bound attachments of the nation-state to take the measure of the world as a wider totality".[36] The fast pace of this literary scale jumping, involving a modernist "interplay between totalizing universality and fragmented particularity", reflects the rapidity with which global impulses were brought into proximity with local experience in interwar modernity.[37]

Yet Channon's global view is also mediated by his position from within "a great island continent alone in its south sea", suggesting the interconnection of global and national scales. Gazing from a "vast distance", he views Europe as "the patches where parasitic man had lived longest and most densely", and from which humankind "went out to infect fresh lands". This description of old-world Europe as "parasitic" provides a glimpse of resistant nationalism, reflecting Channon's situated position from one of the "fresh lands" that has suffered the effects of colonisation. The distinction between "fresh lands" and "the patches where ... man had lived longest", disrupts the assumed affiliation between Australian and British imperial interests, suggesting a settler nationalism that strategically invests in the national scale in order to prevent settler culture from being subsumed by the more powerful colonial entity.

Channon is ultimately unable to sustain a "Godlike" perspective in this scene, desiring "nothing but to return" to the local and individual scale. Dark writes that he "came back wearily, as one might return with relief and gratitude to a shabby home, to the consciousness of his own humanity" (122). His return to the location of his own body is expressed in terms of a homecoming to a "shell of humanity", with Dark's frequent use of the term humanity suggesting that she saw the individual as a constituent part of the "communal life" of all humankind (121). But how was this constituent role to be realised in a period when Australia's interests might differ from those of other, more powerful nations? Furthermore, how could the individual human subject be connected to the broader polity at a time when liberal intellectuals sought to protect the former from the latter? Dark raises these questions but does not fully resolve them, instead again turning to the realm of culture as a means of reconciling some of the tensions in the novel.

---

36 Hegglund, *World Views*, 8–9.
37 Hegglund, *World Views*, 14, 20–21. The term "jumping scales" is used by Neil Smith to illuminate the "active social and political connectedness of apparently different scales, their deliberate confusion and abrogation", in "Contours of a Spatialized Politics: Homeless Vehicles and the Production of Geographical Scale", *Social Text*, no. 33 (1992): 66.

"Let's Go and Join the Revolution": Aesthetic Utopianism and Politics

As in *Sun Across the Sky*, *Waterway* frequently turns to culture as the realm wherein social conflicts will be addressed and resolved; however, in *Waterway* Dark's approach to culture is somewhat more materialist and politically engaged. A number of her characters undertake cultural or political work, including the nationalist writing and publishing of Roger, Lesley's freelance journalism, Lois' painting and the humanist writing of Channon. In *Sun Across the Sky*, Dark's conception of art is largely romantic but in *Waterway* she draws attention to some of the uneven material conditions underpinning cultural production. Winifred, for instance, wants to invest money in establishing a publishing house for poetry that has been rejected by "Roberts and Anderson" (an allusion to Angus & Robertson), although she is prevented from doing so by her capitalist husband (20). One of the Sydney "society" figures, Manning-Everett, is a newspaper tycoon: Dark describes him as a man of "mean spirit and a poor nerve", who thought nothing of ordering "a plate of soup for which he would pay, indifferently, the price of two square meals for a hungry man" (259). Roger reflects on the difficulty faced by small-scale publishers when competing with mass forms of media such as Manning-Everett's newspaper, *The Messenger*:

> if Roger Blair doesn't get enough support to carry on his paper – who cares? Who even knows? Culture isn't news … A sordid murder's news, and an American film star's news, and a Paris-trained mannequin … But the fostering of a national consciousness isn't news, a magazine in which the nation can become articulate without having to compete with cheap syndicated trash – that isn't news! (76)

Dark was personally familiar with the difficulties that Stephensen faced in establishing a national publishing house. After she took the risk of publishing *Prelude to Christopher* (1934) with Stephensen's new press, P.R. Stephensen & Co., half the printed copies of the novel were seized when the company went into liquidation, and Dark was forced to purchase these remaining five hundred copies to convince Collins that the English edition would have a market in Australia. Dark's involvement in the FAW, which actively campaigned against censorship from the mid-1930s, may also have increased her awareness of the uneven structures of cultural distribution.

The class basis of Dark's aesthetic utopianism remains with the professional middle classes in *Waterway*, whom she suggests should be involved in serious cultural work rather than in the proliferation of mass forms of culture which feed complacency and reinforce dogma. In Lesley, Dark provides a portrait of a writer who is unsure of how best to use her talents for the public good: Lesley writes for women's periodicals, producing "stories, paragraphs at whose fatuity she scowled or giggled according to her mood, brief articles, household hints, and earnest advice to wives upon how to retain their husbands' waning love" (189). Like Kit in *Sun*

Across the Sky, Lesley's short story writing is framed as "just another example of deft literary architecture" rather than anything of cultural significance (187). Lesley experiences a "conviction that the time and energy which she was using so badly could be used well" and asks herself, "But how?" (189). Her union with Roger provides the answer, suggesting that she will begin using her talents for more worthwhile cultural purposes. If the marriage between a scientist and an artist was Dark's representation of the perfect union in *Sun Across the Sky*, then the pairing of a woman writer with a cultural-nationalist publisher in *Waterway* shows Dark's awareness that new kinds of cultural production, including more politically and nationally engaged writing, may be needed to navigate the changing political landscape of the late 1930s.

Dark makes Lesley and Roger's marriage, like that of Lois and Oliver, symbolic of larger ideological reconciliations. In this way, the romantic plotline of the middlebrow domestic novel is asked to do additional work. Lesley is caught in the love triangle of a romance plot: she wavers over Sim Hegarty, who represents luxury, sophistication and romance, but ultimately chooses the earnest Roger in a decision that symbolises the triumph of "the things of the Spirit" over capitalism and sensuality (68). Winifred Holtby used a similar strategy in *South Riding*, in which she embeds socialist ideas in a quintessentially middlebrow novel by making the romance plot between Sarah Burton and Robert Carne symbolic of a wider struggle between progress and conservativism.[38] Yet while Holtby is able to challenge the romance plot of the middlebrow novel by having Robert die from a heart attack on the eve of the couple's consummation, so that Sarah continues a life devoted to public service without a husband, the romance ending remains important to *Waterway*. Perhaps this is because, as we saw in earlier chapters of this book, Dark had relatively little freedom to deviate from conventional romantic plotlines if she wanted to secure publication for her novels in London and New York.

As in *Sun Across the Sky*, in *Waterway* Dark attempts to extend the class basis of her aesthetic utopianism to the working classes. Roger thinks with contempt of his fellow Australians' enthusiasm for mass forms of culture: "Surfing, horse-racing, cricket! The Holy Trinity! Lying on the sand, doped with ultra-violet rays, or yelling themselves hoarse over a Melbourne Cup, or getting hysterical over a Test Match!" (76). In contrast, Oliver and Lois view this as part of Australia's vital environment. Thinking of his fellow Australians sunbathing on the beach, Oliver reflects, "you couldn't blame them if they preferred the easy and exhilarating joys of the body to the difficult and elusive joys of the mind" (115). These physical joys include sunbaking, "the winning of a Test Match" or "the coming of a Phar Lap" – the very elements of mass consumer culture that Roger denigrates. Sharing Oliver's perspective, Lois views "[a]ll that physical joy and health" as "a foundation" for

---

38 Ewins, "'Revolutionizing'", 255, 262–63.

the development of a rich Australian culture (115). Oliver provides the clearest articulation of this hope:

> He wasn't an artist, but he had felt all the same the invigorating stimulus which came from an environment so abounding in rude physical enjoyment. Before the seed can germinate, he thought, the soil must be prepared, and here was the preparation going on. And a soil of what richness! What exotic and unique and gorgeous blossoming might it not produce – in time. If it got the time. An incoherent and involuntary prayer forced itself sharply up in him that it might be given the time, that it might be spared a further holocaust of precious lives which it could so ill afford to lose. (115–16)

This passage strongly echoes Oliver's claim in *Sun Across the Sky* that "the background of warmth and colour" is "[p]reparing carefully a soil which would some day bring great beauty to a triumphant blossoming".[39] In cultural-nationalist writing, the soil was frequently used as a metaphor for Australia's distinctive cultural environment, into which British culture had been "transplanted".[40] In *The Timeless Land*, Dark ascribes similar imagery to Captain Arthur Phillip, who thinks of the new colony as a "sickly offshoot" that is "struggling for survival in an inhospitable earth" but which will eventually "live to reach maturity".[41] The persistence of this organic, soil-based imagery in Dark's work suggests her ongoing commitment to the category of the nation.

In both *Sun Across the Sky* and *Waterway*, the future of Australia is associated with the development of a humanist national culture, which Dark believed would flourish if Australia "got the time". This culture cannot be aligned easily with elite taste; rather, it would be ushered in by cultured members of the middle classes such as Lois, Oliver, Roger and Lesley, and shared by the general population, for whom the "physical joy and health" of the Australian environment is "building up in them, too, slowly and imperceptibly ... that fierce love of life for the sake of living which is the true environment of all great art" (*Sun Across the Sky*, 29–30). Although the culture that Dark hoped would develop was a distinctively national one, it would also offer a model of democracy to the world. Dark wrote elsewhere about the connection between Australia's laconic attitudes and a robust democracy:

> when polling-day arrives Australia turns up at the booths with its tennis racquet under its arm or its golf clubs slung across its shoulder ... [but] it is a mistake to assume too hastily, as many do, that this casualness means indifference ... we have

39 Eleanor Dark, *Sun Across the Sky* (London: Collins, [1937] 1946), 29–30. All subsequent references are to this edition and appear in parentheses in the text.

40 Dan Tout, "Reframing 'Inky' Stephensen's Place in Australian Cultural History", *Settler Colonial Studies* 7, no. 1 (2017): 73.

41 Eleanor Dark, *The Timeless Land* (London: Collins, [1941] 1946), 238. All subsequent references are to this edition and appear in parentheses in the text.

our own brand of democracy, and the mere fact that we take it for granted does not mean that we would lightly relinquish it.[42]

Here, Australia is framed as having an inherently democratic vernacular culture, which will produce the very liberal values most needed in a period when "the sway of Demos is being bitterly disputed all over the world".[43]

Dark does attempt to provide a more political component to her aesthetic utopianism in *Waterway*, as her professional middle-class characters confront new social and economic injustices. Lesley feels herself a "fraud" when trying to understand and relate to the problem of unemployment, reflecting that if "you've never been hungry or without a bed to sleep in" then you are trying to help "from the outside" (250). The use of the second person suggests that Dark anticipated a middle-class reader who would similarly struggle to connect with the plight of the worker. As with other examples of the political middlebrow, Dark uses the individual experiences of her characters to frame her socialist politics in ways that might be more acceptable to middle-class readers.[44] When Lesley and Roger confront a mass protest of unemployed, disaffected workers in the Domain, they are willing to join in, with Lesley saying, "Let's go and join the revolution" (252). Although this might be stated with some irony, the presence of the protest and ensuing riot in Dark's novel suggests that at this stage, the culturally invested intellectual could no longer avoid politics: in Christina Stead's words, the writer must "enter the political arena" and "take lessons from workmen".[45] Literally swept up in the crowd and unable to turn back, Lesley finds herself "[f]or the first time in her life … included in a look – an expression … which people safely sheltered from a thunderstorm give to people still scurrying for cover" (254). In this moment, Lesley finds herself in solidarity with the worker, and viewed as outside by those who are "sheltered" by economic security. The reader is similarly invited to inhabit Lesley's experience and participate in what Janice Radway describes as difference made understandable.[46]

When Lesley is offered a "kind of escape" by sheltering from the riot in Sim's luxury car, she refuses it in a symbolic gesture (257). Dark focalises the narrative through Lesley as Sim opens the door of the car and gestures for her to enter:

> Here, as always, Sim had that to offer – the easy way, the good things of life not battled for, not striven or sweated for, but just handed to you for nothing. The heat and turmoil about her, the reek of humanity, the ugliness, the endeavour, the fear

---

42 Eleanor Dark, "Australia and the Australians", in *Australia Week-End Book* 3, eds. Sydney Ure Smith and Gwen Morton Spencer (Sydney: Ure Smith, 1944), 17–19.
43 Dark, "Australia", 17.
44 Ewins, "'Revolutionizing'", 274.
45 Stead, "Writers Take Sides", 435.
46 Janice Radway, *A Feeling for Books: The Book-of-the-Month Club, Literary Taste, and Middle-Class Desire* (Chapel Hill: University of North Carolina Press, 1997), 284.

and the hope, the brutality and the lusty humour were all translated into parts of another struggle in which, whether she liked it or not, she was involved. (257)

Dark's depiction of the crowd in this passage shows that she was not completely at ease with the mass protest. As in her early, unpublished novel "Pilgrimage", in which she described the women typists as "the scrapings of the city",[47] here she associates the crowd with "the reek of humanity", "ugliness" and "brutality". Yet in *Waterway* the crowd is also linked with "hope" and "lusty humour", and Dark frames it as part of a struggle in which the cultural intellectual is necessarily involved. Lesley and Roger's choice to remain entangled with the crowd is a show of class solidarity that goes beyond anything in Dark's prior novels. In contrast, the wealthy Arthur Sellman, who also becomes entangled with the rioting crowd against his will, experiences the contact with Otherness as form of threat, sensing "danger ... to all his jealously guarded world", and resists this opportunity for learning, finding refuge in "the well-oiled smoothness of clichés and catchwords", thinking, "That sort of thing's the thin end of the wedge for out and out Communism" (264, 265, 294).

Ethical Encounters and the Face-to-face

The riot in *Waterway* is one of the few times in Dark's work when she is able to scale from the individual human person to collective, political action.[48] She frames the crowd as the aggregate of many discontented individuals, with Jack viewing its "latent, undirected power" as "his own bitterness, his own frustration, his own resentment multiplied a thousand times" (258). Yet it is not the riot that restores social order and reconciles problems in *Waterway*, but the plot development of the ferry crash, which resolves a number of relational conflicts; for instance, by causing the death of Arthur so that Winifred and Ian are freed to marry. Dark's reliance on "[c]oincidence and accident", which so frustrated M. Barnard Eldershaw,[49] reflects the ongoing connection between her writing and the middlebrow novel form.

The collision of the commuter ferry with an international mail steamer breaks into the plot of *Waterway* in a way that signals a dramatic confrontation with the evolutionary teleology of Channon's liberal humanism. The extended scene of the collision also shifts the focus from the political ramifications of the mass protest, to the ethical actions and choices of individual characters. In a scene that appears to operate in slow motion, as "[a] second expands, becomes monstrous ... senses expand, widening their focus like the lens of a camera" (320), Dark zooms in on the actions and thoughts of the various characters, and this modernist experimentation

---

47   Eleanor Dark, "Pilgrimage", Eleanor Dark Collection, Varuna, the National Writers' House, 153.
48   Other examples include the convict riots that feature in *Storm of Time* (1948).
49   M. Barnard Eldershaw, *Essays in Australian Fiction* (Freeport, NY: Books for Libraries Press, [1938] 1970), 188.

with time and narrative perspective allows her to move from the realm of politics to the more familiar ground of ethics.

Dark uses the characters' reactions to the ferry crash to demonstrate the heroic and ethical capabilities of liberal humanism over capitalism. Arthur, who is represented throughout the novel as materialistic and mean-spirited, responds to the ferry crash by becoming "quite insane with fear" (312). To propel himself out of the cabin, he kicks Channon in the stomach – an action that tragically becomes Channon's "last contact with the humanity, to which … he had finally pinned his faith" (313). As Channon drowns, he reflects on Arthur's unethical behaviour, feeling that "it was strange and rather sad that Arthur should have fought so desperately for so warped and trivial a life, abandoned all pity, all generosity, all for a few more years of unprofitable existence" (313). In contrast, Channon, although losing his life, achieves spiritual insight:

> there came to him, slowly this time like the steadily expanding lift of a sunrise, that sense of revelation which he had already found – and lost – so many times … he was possessed by a faith which his clouding brain would have no time to tarnish, a truth which to his dying cells and the slowing rhythm of his life, was Truth at last, complete, unassailable, serene. For what shall it profit a man if he gain the whole world, and lose his own soul…? (313–14)

The "Truth" that Channon reaches in this final moment is conveyed through the Biblical reference to Mark 8:36. Arthur has, in a materialistic sense, gained "the whole world", and yet he has lost "his own soul" through the unethical action of destroying another to save himself. Arthur is left with "an overwhelming, an intolerable solitude", whilst Channon reaches a sense of revelation "like the steadily expanding lift of a sunrise" (315). The overwhelmingly positive imagery reinforces Channon's commitment to a Christian-inspired form of humanism.

While Arthur shows no remorse for causing a fatal injury to Channon, Jack instinctively saves Arthur when he sees him in danger. Dark writes of Jack pulling Arthur to safety:

> He did not consider his action at all … It did not occur to him to free himself, by unclasping his hand, of the burden which he supported. His creed was not unlike the Professor's though he had never consciously formed it, and had never learned that it might apply to moral as well as physical strength. But to abandon the man while there was still an ounce of unused energy in his body would have been to him a denial and a betrayal of himself. (323)

Jack's creed is, according to the narrator, similar to that of Channon: it involves an intuitive recognition of the value of a fellow human life, which would make Jack's abandonment of Arthur "a denial and betrayal of himself" and thus a betrayal of the very human spirit that Dark so values. Jack's act of sacrifice is the counter-point to Arthur's attack on Channon, ultimately reinforcing the Professor's belief that humankind "faces at the end no far and disembodied deity, but the being, such as it may be, whom he has spent his life in fashioning" (295).

The emphasis in these scenes is on the ethical realm of the face-to-face, which offers individuals a moment of ethical encounter between the self and the face of the Other.[50] It is ethical rather than political, as it relies on individual choices and actions which do not easily translate into organised politics. What would the actions of Channon and Jack look like, writ large in terms of a global solution? How is Lesley's rejection of Sim and selection of Roger to be realised on a structural level? Dark's answer seems to be that when many enlightened individuals make ethical choices and actions, the aggregated result will have large-scale effects. Roger states of social reform, "When enough intelligent people begin to examine [a problem] … without bias as an academic problem, it will be solved. Unless the victims get tired of waiting for that" (250). It is a statement that articulates Dark's preference for a cultural and evolutionary solution, while at the same time placing this in tension with the possibility of imminent action and revolution. The fact that these tensions are left unresolved in *Waterway* reflects both Dark's deep-seated suspicion of organised politics and her growing awareness of the need for political engagement.

Aesthetic Utopianism and the Second World War

Although this chapter and the one that precedes it focus on Dark's aesthetic utopianism during the late interwar period, the ideas about art and culture introduced in *Sun Across the Sky* and developed in *Waterway* also appear in the writing she produced during the Second World War. In particular, *The Little Company*, which was published in the last year of the war, reveals Dark's ongoing commitment to aesthetic utopianism, as well as the increasing pressures she faced in reconciling such a stance with materialist political problems. It is worth discussing here as part of a sequence of novels that includes *Sun Across the Sky* and *Waterway*.

The Little Company focuses on a group of intellectuals living in Katoomba in the increasingly hostile political environment of wartime Australia (specifically 1941–42). These figures feel they are being "dragged … nervously, nearer and nearer to the climax, borne down … into catastrophe".[51] The sense of historical and social rupture in this work is even greater than in Dark's 1930s novels, as she depicts

---

50   This term is from Emmanuel Levinas, *Totality and Infinity: An Essay on Exteriority*, trans. Alphonso Lingis (Pittsburgh, PA: Duquesne University Press, 1969).
51   Eleanor Dark, *The Little Company* (Sydney: Collins, 1945), 38. All subsequent references are to this edition and appear in parentheses in the text.

war as severing the continuity of past and present: as the main character, Gilbert Massey, reflects:

> Nothing that happened in this world-storm could convert the mad succession of nights and days into a 'present'. They were suspended in history ... mere whirling events at which human beings, whirling with them, clutched in the hope that they would fall into place some day, somehow, and form a pattern for rational existence. (318)

Gilbert is a novelist, and the sense of historical crisis is embodied in his experience of writer's block, wherein he is literally unable to find continuity between thoughts, ideas and events. *The Little Company* also reveals Dark's growing awareness of some of the material challenges affecting cultural production: plot points include police visits to confiscate banned books and raids on bookstores. Contemporary political events intrude upon the narrative through capitalised news headlines, conveying the saturation of mass forms of communication such as newspapers and radio, and creating a sense that the characters are both paralysed by and "living in history" (38).

Gilbert ultimately overcomes his writer's block, signalling Dark's ongoing investment in aesthetic solutions. He concludes that to see the years as "utterly chaotic ... would be to feel oneself annihilated", and finds value in the "straining, unceasing effort towards comprehension" which involves "toiling laboriously like an ant to add his grain of comprehension to the world's sum" (318). *The Little Company* ends with Gilbert eager to "get on with his task of recording and interpreting even a trivial fragment of this enormous world-story" (319). Whereas *Sun Across the Sky* foregrounds poetry and visual art, in *The Little Company* Dark offers novel writing as the solution to the problem of connecting the past, present and future – a choice that David Carter reads as indicative of the elevation of the novel form in the work of a number of Australian interwar and Second World War writers.[52] It is worth noting, however, that the aesthetic resolution in *The Little Company* remains curiously deferred. The novel concludes with Gilbert dismissing his siblings' argument over the relative merits of the role of the artist-intellectual under capitalism and communism: he thinks of their debate as "metaphysical hair-splitting" and instead chooses to "reach for [his] pen" (319). The story he intends to write – which he has already written in fragmented form – is "the old but always new story of the dynamic of humanity pulling against its inertia, condensed in time, narrowed down in place, expressed in terms of one obscure life, and yet still heroic by virtue of its timeless social implications" (241). Dark's readers never get to access this story, as it begins where her novel ends – a paradox that indicates both her belief in the possibility of an aesthetic solution, and the difficulty of achieving one.

It was not only Dark who, in the 1930s and Second World War period, explored such questions about the capacity of art and literature to provide continuity in

---

52   Carter, *Always Almost*, 193.

a moment of extreme political and social crisis. As Carter notes, the work of M. Barnard Eldershaw similarly invests in aesthetic utopianism and reveals the difficulties of such a position. A number of Barnard Eldershaw's novels from the same period also feature writer characters, including *The Glasshouse* (1936), *Plaque with Laurel* (1937) and the experimental novel *Tomorrow and Tomorrow and Tomorrow* (1947; 1983). The latter work, written during the war years, resonates with Dark's *The Little Company* in that it also elevates novel writing and features a central character who is a writer.[53] *Tomorrow and Tomorrow and Tomorrow* is set four hundred years in the future in a socialist utopia. The central character, Knarf, has written a work of historical fiction using the "antique form of the novel", sections of which he reads aloud to a friend, Ord, an archaeologist.[54] Knarf's novel, "Little World Left Behind", is set in Sydney in the period from the 1920s to the 1940s – a period that encompasses the Depression, the Second World War and ensuing conflicts which, in Barnard Eldershaw's alternative timeline, culminate in the deliberate destruction of Sydney by fire. Whereas Ord's archaeological approach to history represents a scientific and materialist methodology, Knarf's writing suggests the imaginative and humanist possibilities of the novel: novels provide "an attempt to get the chaos of circumstances into some sort of shape, using every method of attack, every ingenuity" (81).

Yet Barnard Eldershaw ultimately trouble Knarf's attempts to achieve cultural continuity through novel writing. As Ian Saunders observes, the acts of writing and reading are always highly contested in this novel.[55] The reader of *Tomorrow and Tomorrow and Tomorrow* only accesses "Little World Left Behind" in a fragmented form, as the twenty-fourth century frame narrative frequently intrudes upon and at times undercuts the action of Knarf's novel. Furthermore, the content of Knarf's book hints at the inadequacy of writing to intervene in and resolve social crises. Looking back on the 1930s – "one of the really tragic periods of history" (135) – Knarf recounts to Ord:

> Never were people so aware, so powerless to act. It was a decade of books. Books poured from the presses, prodigal of information, focussing attention on the

---

53 In a letter to Dark, Marjorie Barnard noted the similarities between *The Little Company* and *Tomorrow and Tomorrow and Tomorrow*: "we were both tearing at the same knot with different fingers, both using that most difficult creation, another writer, as our means, our sounding board". Marjorie Barnard to Eleanor Dark, 25 August 1945, Eleanor Dark Papers, National Library of Australia, MS 4998, Binder 3. For an exploration of the relationship between the work of M. Barnard Eldershaw and Eleanor Dark, see Ian Saunders, "On Appropriation: Two Novels of Dark and Barnard Eldershaw", *Australian Literary Studies* 20, no. 4 (2002): 287–300.

54 M. Barnard Eldershaw, *Tomorrow and Tomorrow and Tomorrow* (London: Virago, [1947] 1983), 79. All subsequent references are to this edition and appear in parentheses in the text. An earlier, partially censored version of this novel was published under the title *Tomorrow and Tomorrow* in 1947.

55 Ian Saunders, "Memory, Community and Writing in *Tomorrow and Tomorrow and Tomorrow*", *Southerly* 64, no. 1 (2004): 111–12.

present. Eye witnesses' accounts. Books of foreign correspondents who had had it straight from the horse's mouth. Men listening. Everything predicted. Hitler writing a book *Mein Kampf* telling the world what he would do, how he would do it. Then doing it … The whole impulse of the decade expending itself in books. (138)

The imagery of an excess of books, contrasted with people's "powerless[ness] to act", calls into question the extent to which Knarf's own book will make an impact on readers. These questions are explored further through the twenty-fourth-century narrative climax of the Votometer, in which Knarf's son, Ren, attempts to engage his fellow citizens in the political process, only to find that the dominant public opinion is one of indifference. The failure of the democratic process, and the fact that Knarf and Ord miss the vote due to Knarf's preoccupation with reading his manuscript aloud, undermines the hope of a more progressive future and raises serious doubts as to the role of the literary intellectual in shaping social change. Nonetheless, *Tomorrow and Tomorrow and Tomorrow* concludes with a tentatively hopeful vision of the future. Knarf affirms his son's commitment to liberalism, telling Ren, "The idea of liberty is very old, it has recurred again and again in man's history. There must be some seeds of it in every one's blood, but overlaid now for a long time" (454). For Knarf, the spirit of liberalism cannot be revived "in a hurry", as demonstrated by the failure of the Votometer; rather, "[i]t will have to be a slow organic growth", achieved through what he describes as "[i]maginative effort" (454). Knarf's own historical novel provides the key example of such imaginative effort, suggesting that, for all its doubts, *Tomorrow and Tomorrow and Tomorrow* remains tentatively invested in the social role of both the writer and the novel form. Taken together, *Tomorrow and Tomorrow and Tomorrow* and *The Little Company* suggest that the particular kind of aesthetic utopianism which Dark first articulated in *Sun Across the Sky* and then developed in *Waterway* reached its pinnacle – and to a large extent exhausted itself – during the ensuing global conflict.

Sydney Harbour and Interwar Modernity: "Haled With Glamour and Romance"

As we have seen throughout this book, Dark's interwar writing provides an ambivalent response to modernity, wherein the mass change and technological innovations of the period are both embraced and resisted. *Waterway* is similarly poised between the allure of international modernity and an increasing awareness of its inherently uneven qualities. Dark brings these contradictory impulses to bear upon the contested site of Sydney Harbour, which she uses both to celebrate the romance of modernity and point to the discriminatory relations that shaped Australia's position as a provincial nation.

As a coastal suburb situated on the southern promontory of Sydney's harbour, Watsons Bay operates as a symbolic and liminal space in the novel: it is connected

Figure 5.1 Unknown photographer. Michael (Mick) Dark, Brien (Bim) O'Reilly and Eleanor Dark on Sydney Harbour near Vaucluse, 1934. Eleanor Dark Collection, Varuna, the National Writers' House. © Jill Dark.

both to the inner harbour of Sydney and the Pacific Ocean of international space. Dark knew South Head well (Fig. 5.1). She lived for a time at "Benison", the waterfront house of her father Dowell O'Reilly and stepmother Mollie in Vaucluse, a suburb neighbouring Watsons Bay.[56] A number of *Waterway*'s characters view the harbour as "haled with glamour and romance", with one describing it as "this long and shining finger of the sea itself" (36, 37). This image of the harbour as a "finger" suggests its constituent relationship within the larger "body" of water that connects Sydney to the wider world via the Pacific Ocean. Frank Dalby Davison also employed aqueous imagery to describe Australia's relationship to Europe, writing of Australia as "a billabong connected with the main river by a channel, rising and falling with the river, but slightly out of time with it".[57] Dark is even more insistent on Australia's imbrication in wider international space, and she envisions its connections as diffuse and multi-directional. Denis Harnet, the harbour pilot's son, associates the harbour with the multiple routes of traffic between Sydney and other places:

> There was always something to watch. There were the great ships that went to America and to England. And the colliers and the coastal steamers that went south

56　Marivic Wyndham, *"A World-Proof Life": Eleanor Dark, A Writer in Her Times 1901–1985* (Sydney: UTS ePress, 2007), 53–54.

57　Frank Dalby Davison, *While Freedom Lives* (Sydney: Tomalin & Wigmore, 1938), 12.

to Melbourne or north to Brisbane and Cairns; there were island ships bringing in copra and coconuts from the Solomon Islands, and ships from Suva and Rabaul, from Sourabaya and Singapore. (97)

Through listing Australia's Pacific neighbours – Suva, Rabaul, Sourabaya and Singapore – Dark links the harbour with the romance of travel. The description positions Sydney as part of a hemispheric Asia–Pacific, as well as connected to the more traditional vectors of America and England, and to other subnational spaces such as Melbourne and Cairns. In this way, *Waterway* contributes to studies of interwar Australian culture that suggest it was outwardly oriented rather than defensive and isolationist.[58] It also anticipates contemporary uses of Sydney Harbour as a point of transnational exchange in novels such as Gail Jones' *Five Bells* (2011) and Michelle de Kretser's *Questions of Travel* (2013).

It is significant that Dark structures *Waterway* around coastal Sydney, given the cultural-nationalist emphasis on pastoral settings during this period. In looking for a source of homegrown, indigenous settler culture that would register resistance to "the incursions of modernity", cultural nationalists frequently advocated "a return to what they believed were the unique values of their national heritage" in the bush-realist tradition of the 1890s.[59] This pastoral vision was largely a reconstruction that had little relevance for modern, urban Australians of the 1930s.[60] *Waterway* acts to reorient the cultural imaginary outwards towards the harbour rather than inwards towards the centre. Ian thinks of the harbour as "the main highway of the city" (36), drawing on the 1930s association of highways with "unimpeded, frictionless flow".[61] Significantly, it is the harbour, "this gleaming waterway", and not "the long, tortuous street which led between high canyon-sides of buildings, along the route where once bullock teams had plodded a bush track" that is depicted as Sydney's "main highway" (36). Harnet's dismissal of the Great Western Highway, with its pioneer history of "bullock teams" and "a bush track", in favour of the harbour, suggests a subtle repudiation of Australia's pastoral tradition.

In her valorisation of the harbour as a site of romance and international traffic, Dark challenges defensive nationalist anxieties about imported culture. As noted in the discussion of *Prelude to Christopher* in Chapter 2, defensive nationalisms were often expressed through the economic metaphors of import and export, which

---

58   See, for example, Victoria Kuttainen, Susann Liebich and Sarah Galletly, *Transported Imagination: Australian Interwar Magazines and the Geographical Imaginaries of Colonial Modernity* (Amherst, NY: Cambria Press, 2018); Elizabeth McMahon, *Islands, Identity and the Literary Imagination* (London; New York: Anthem Press, 2016).

59   Matthews, *Dance Hall*, 11.

60   Robert Dixon, "Australian Fiction and the World Republic of Letters, 1890–1950", in *The Cambridge History of Australian Literature*, ed. Peter Pierce (Cambridge: Cambridge University Press, 2009), 238–39.

61   Edward Dimendberg, "The Will to Motorization: Cinema, Highways and Modernity", *October* 73 (1995): 93–94; Robert Dixon, "Shooting in Occupied Space: Frank Hurley in the Middle East, 1940–46", *History of Photography* 38, no. 1 (2014): 42.

relied on "a simple binary: the good was recognised as indigenous, the bad as foreign".[62] Through combining the metaphors of import and export with the racialised language of hygiene, commentators often suggested that foreign, imported ideas could infect or taint local culture.[63] Stephensen, for instance, wrote with anxiety about Australia's openness to international modernity: "Ships come and go, from Europe, America, Asia, and Africa … All is in flux. Can it be a cultured nation?"[64] In contrast, Dark imbues the traffic of international goods with a sense of glamour, as Ian and Winifred connect romantically over the "odd mixtures" of imported raw materials shipped into the harbour, "*Charcoal, coconuts, coke, copra … salt, sand, sugar, sulphur*" (38).

Dark also associates the harbour with the romance of European explorer history. Lois reflects that, "no matter how soberly you lived on the shores of this harbour, no matter for what dreary purpose you travelled upon its glittering water, your life could never be entirely unaffected by its happy air of adventure and of holiday" (113–14). She thinks of the daily commute of a shopgirl to Manly as a journey "lit with glamours which had also attended the journeys of Marco Polo and Diaz, Vasco de Gama and Magellan, Christopher Columbus and Captain Cook!" (113–14), thus connecting the experiences of the Modern Girl to the "deep time" of European colonial history through the chronotope of the harbour.[65] While some cultural nationalists responded to the heightened mobility of the modern moment by seeking rootedness in place, Dark depicts Sydney as a place of "unsettled settlers, a people whose history was movement".[66] Capturing Lois' perspective, Dark writes of the journey to Manly:

> You had the strange movement of the sea under your feet, and the salty breath of it blowing into your lungs; you saw gulls and heard their wild crying; for a few minutes as you passed the Heads there was nothing between you and the edge of the world but blue ocean. Even when you disembarked you were only on a mere shaving of land; the quiet water of the harbour lapped it on one side, and the vast breakers of the ocean assaulted it on the other, and something of their magic blew over the place like a spell, so that people discarded, not only their clothes, but their haste and their problems too … Men, women and children walked the streets in sunburned semi-nakedness; merry-go-rounds spun madly; in the aquarium vast captive sharks swam endlessly in terrible and sullen longing for the sea … the

---

62   Matthews, *Dance Hall*, 12.
63   Meaghan Morris, "Import Rhetoric: Semiotics in/and Australia", in *The Foreign Bodies Papers*, Local Consumption Series, eds. Peter Botsman, Chris Burns and Peter Hutchings (Sydney: Local Consumption Publications, 1981), 125–26.
64   Stephensen, *Foundations*, 11–12.
65   Wai Chee Dimock, *Through Other Continents: American Literature Across Deep Time* (Princeton, NJ: Princeton University Press, 2006), 3–4. Brigid Rooney uses Bakhtin's theory of the chronotope in relation to Sydney Harbour in *Waterway*, in "Time's Abyss: Australian Literary Modernism and the Scene of the Ferry Wreck", in *Scenes of Reading*, 101–14.
66   Matthews, *Dance Hall*, 9.

whole population succumbed to the nostalgia of an ocean-faring race, and went down to the sea … (114)

This compelling description of visitors existing "on a mere shaving of land", with "nothing between you and the edge of the world but blue ocean", romanticises the transient origins of settler Australia: an "ocean-faring race". It connects more with the picture that Christina Stead paints of a "Sea People" on an "island continent … in a water hemisphere" in the preface of *For Love Alone* (1945), than with the nationalist yearning for a return to the pastoral tradition.[67]

In *Waterway*, Dark uses the harbour to remind readers of the close proximity between colonial and modern temporalities. As Brigid Rooney notes, the celebrations and advertising for Sydney's Sesquicentenary also frequently collapsed the colonial events of 1788 with the modern moment of 1938 through the symbolic site of the harbour.[68] Ian tells his son that the era of Captain Cook "wasn't much more than a hundred and fifty years ago", and Dark conveys this sense of folded time when Oliver looks at the harbour and reflects that it "was as quiet now … as it must have been on the dawn of that day a hundred and fifty years ago" (11, 41). Dark's depiction of the harbour resonates with Mikhail Bakhtin's concept of the chronotope, defined as "the intrinsic connectedness of temporal and spatial relationships that are artistically expressed in literature".[69] In the chronotope, there is a concise convergence of past and future, region and world, within one space.[70] Ian watches a ship arriving on the horizon, and associates it with "an idea of effort and of conquest": the ship appears insubstantial, coming "over the rim of the world, out of infinity like a wraith", fashioned of "pearly insubstantial mist", so that it is at once a modern ship carrying imported goods and a ghostly reminder of the First Fleet's arrival in Sydney Cove (39, 40). Dark's frequent references to material relics of Australia's sea-faring history also remind readers of the proximity between past and present: these include the Watsons Bay memorial to harbourmaster Robert Watson, who arrived in Sydney as quartermaster of the First Fleet vessel HMS *Sirius*; the anchor commemorating the wreck of the *Dunbar* in 1857; and a pilot

---

67 Christina Stead, *For Love Alone* (Bondi Junction: Imprint Classics, [1945] 1991), 1. Meg Brayshaw argues that the "aqueous poetics" and "engagement with contemporary Sydney, the waterway and the possibilities of narrative form" in the works of interwar and Second World War Australian women writers, including Eleanor Dark, Christina Stead, Dymphna Cusack, M. Barnard Eldershaw and Kylie Tennant, reveals a "distinctly Australian, modern urban poetics". Meg Brayshaw, *Sydney and its Waterway in Australian Literary Modernism* (Sydney: Palgrave Macmillan, 2021), 29; "Reflectant Tides: The Aqueous Poetics of Sydney in Women's Fiction, 1934–1947" (PhD thesis, Western Sydney University, 2018).
68 Rooney, "Time's Abyss", 106–07.
69 M.M. Bakhtin, *The Dialogic Imagination: Four Essays*, ed. Michael Holquist, trans. Caryl Emerson and Michael Holquist (Austin: University of Texas Press, 1981), 84. The essay in which Bakhtin introduces the idea of the chronotope, "Forms of Time and of the Chronotope", was written in 1937–38.
70 John David Pizer, *The Idea of World Literature: History and Pedagogical Practice* (Baton Rouge: Louisiana State University Press, 2006), 36.

steamer called *Captain Cook*. This latter ship was a familiar sight to Sydneysiders, and it featured on the cover of both the English and American editions of *Waterway*, based on an illustration drawn by Dark's brother Bim O'Reilly. On the cover, the figurehead looks to the left in front of a silhouette of the modern city skyline (Fig. 5.2), creating a sense of simultaneity between colonial past and modern present. Importantly, the figure appears to be facing away from the city, perhaps signalling that it is headed towards Watsons Bay, or the Pacific Ocean that lies beyond the Heads. This image acts as an interesting inversion of the journey recorded in the archival account that Dark uses as an epigraph at the beginning of *Waterway*, in which David Collins describes Governor Phillip arriving at "*a harbour capable of affording security*". These twin gestures – of looking out and looking in, arriving and departing – capture the flexible commitments of Dark's regional cosmopolitanism.

Australian readers appear to have appreciated the cosmopolitan outlook of *Waterway*. Reviewers mostly agreed that it was a stronger book than *Sun Across the Sky*. One review claimed that *Waterway* "might as easily have happened in Knightsbridge or Manhattan, in Ottawa or Johannesburg as in Australia".[71] The reviewer in the Melbourne *Argus* argued that Dark's novel provided evidence that "Australian novelists … are slowly raising the standard of their writing to a plane which gives them a right to be mentioned on terms of equality with the novelists of that other 'new' country – the United States".[72] The reviewer in the Hobart *Mercury* expressed appreciation for Dark's cosmopolitan approach to Australian literature:

> Miss Dark [*sic*] continues to add to the laurels of Australian literature with every book she writes. By Australian I do not mean books about wattles and gum trees or kangaroos and emus, but the literature that is part of the national feeling and culture, expressing its standard of growth, but choosing, if desired, the world as its subject. Miss Dark has cast her theme in Sydney, but … her tale might as easily be placed in London or any British city … [it will] appeal to readers wherever they are, being human instead of local.[73]

By framing *Waterway* as "human instead of local", the *Mercury* reviewer seems to respond to a perceived desire from the Australian reading public for outwardly oriented books: ones that were able to represent Australian culture but also take "the world as [their] subject". Patrick Buckridge and Eleanor Morecroft argue that, in the mid to late 1930s, there was a growing sense amongst Australians that they "needed to read and think more globally", which formed part of a cultural response to a "growing awareness of instability, threat and uncertainty in the world".[74]

---

71 "Books", *Australian Women's Weekly*, 9 July 1938, from Eleanor Dark's album of newspaper clippings, Dark Papers, MLMSS 4545, Box 24. Other reviews mentioned in this chapter are also from this source, unless otherwise stated.

72 K.A., "Tangled Threads in Sydney", *Argus* (Melbourne), 25 June 1938.

73 "*Waterway*", *Mercury* (Hobart), 2 July 1938.

Figure 5.2 Book cover of the English edition of *Waterway* (London: Collins, 1938). Eleanor Dark Papers. Mitchell Library, State Library of New South Wales. MLMSS 4545, Box 24.

Although Australians frequently turned to books written by overseas writers for such reading, Dark's growing international reputation, and the sophisticated characters and modern narrative techniques featured in her novels, meant that her works also provided a form of "world-mindedness".[75]

"A Menace, a Terror, Death Waiting"

Given its emphasis on movement, currents and urban modernity, it is little wonder that Australian critics responding to the transnational turn in literary studies have focused on *Waterway* as the novel in Dark's oeuvre that is most open to a transnational reading. Susan Carson and Brigid Rooney both explore it in terms of the circulation of 1930s internationalist political and cultural ideas.[76] These

---

74   Patrick Buckridge and Eleanor Morecroft, "Australia's World Literature: Constructing Australia's Global Reading Relations in the Interwar Period", in *Scenes of Reading*, 51.

75   Buckridge and Morecroft, "Australia's World Literature", 51. Reviewers in America similarly recognised that *Waterway* engaged with pressing international issues such as "the dangers inherent in passionate nationalism" and "means for preventing war". See Rex Hunter, "The Book of the Day: An Australian Novel Recalls a Tragedy and Looks Back on the Story of the Continent", *New York Sun*, 8 February 1938.

readings allow us to recognise Dark as a writer who expressed cosmopolitan commitments as well as an investment in the settler nation. Yet, as these scholars acknowledge, Dark did not view the global in completely positive or utopian terms. In *Waterway*, she represents Sydney Harbour not only as a site of cosmopolitanism and glamour, but also as a place where various forms of international traffic converge and even collide. In this way, the novel reflects Dark's growing awareness of the uneven structures that contributed to class inequality and Australia's peripheral status within a world-system.

The traversing of space, Dark suggests, is an inherently class-based phenomenon. She creates a parallel between Jack and the wealthy Sim: united by the "true democracy of childhood", at age twelve "you couldn't see any difference between Jack Saunders, son of Bert Saunders, fisherman and bottle-oh, and Sim Hegarty, whose father had just been knighted" (58). By the time of the novel's setting, however, Jack is keenly aware of the social difference between the two men:

> Hadn't they [Sim and Jack] stood on that jetty not a stone's throw away when they were eleven years old … straining their eyes upward to a speck in the sky, a plane making its ceremonial entrance through the Heads on the first flight from England? Hadn't he said, clutching Sim's arm: "Crikey! When I grow up I'm goin' to fly an aeroplane!" And hadn't Sim's eyes come round to his … and hadn't he cried: "I am, too! …"
>
> Well, the sky was lousy with them now, but he, Jack Saunders, had never been up in one yet … when Sim had done his solo flight he'd been a blasted hero, with his picture in the papers. *"Son of Sir James Hegarty."* And that was the bloody truth – that was the whole show! That was why he got what he wanted. (58–59)

This passage captures the initial promises of modernity associated with the compression of time and space through air travel. Dark then shifts to the present, recognising Jack's unequal access to these promises, as revealed by the fact that Jack "had never been up in [an aeroplane] yet", whereas Sim has already completed a solo flight. As we have seen, Dark associated the arrival of the first flight from England to Australia with the increased proximity of other nations within twentieth-century modernity. Here, however, the same flight is transfigured into a reflection on social inequality, suggesting Dark's growing awareness of class-based struggles.

Dark also frames settler-colonial history in terms of global collisions and conflicts rather than as equal relations between parties. Dark spent considerable time undertaking historical research in order to write an essay on Caroline Chisholm for inclusion in *The Peaceful Army: A Memorial to the Pioneer Women of Australia, 1788–1938* (1938), the Sesquicentenary collection edited by Flora Eldershaw, and in preparation for writing *The Timeless Land*; this research meant

---

76   Carson, "Paris", 229–44; Rooney, "Time's Abyss", 101–14.

she was highly aware of Sydney and its harbour as a contact zone in which people of different nationalities, classes and racial backgrounds came into proximity with one another.[77] The historical extract with which she begins *Waterway* includes the ominous "*shouts of defiance and prohibition*" from people of the Eora nation crying "*Warra warra – Go away, go away*" (10), resonating with the contemporary protests of the Day of Mourning staged by the Aborigines Progressive Association (APA) and the Australian Aborigines League (AAL), timed to coincide with the Sesquicentenary celebrations in January 1938. Dark is critical of some of the destructive effects of colonisation, describing the city as a malignant growth whose "parent cells ... fastened upon the land" with the arrival of its "invaders" (11, 383). She criticises "civilised man" for bringing new diseases to Australia "like spectres in his train" (56–57), an idea that anticipates her portrayal of the disastrous effects of smallpox on Aboriginal communities in *The Timeless Land*.

The harbour is not only figured as a site of historical violence, but also of imminent local and global conflict, further conveying Dark's scepticism of utopian understandings of interwar modernity. Denis is disturbed by the sight of a battleship on the harbour: "It made you feel queer because you could see its beauty, and yet you could feel its evil; your heart didn't know which way to turn – to admire it, to hate it" (98). The presence of the battleship reminds readers of the potential for Australia to be drawn into a second global war. Although this global conflict does not fully arrive by the end of *Waterway*, the harbour does become the site of local tragedy in the ferry wreck. In this moment, "the bright harbour [was] no longer a picture for you to gaze at, but a menace, a terror, death waiting" (311). The collision between a local and international vessel punctures Ian's utopian vision of the frictionless flow of traffic along the "main highway of the city", transforming the harbour into a site of conflict. Although Sydney is depicted as inextricably connected to the broader world in *Waterway*, these connections are not always framed as positive, but also contribute to discriminatory power relations in the past and present.

Throughout her interwar writing, Dark tried to acknowledge the historical injustices committed against First Nations peoples. Yet while her work shows a modernist "openness to cultures" which goes beyond that of many other settler writers of her time,[78] it also frequently reinforces the idea of Indigenous peoples as outside of modernity. In the opening scene of *Waterway*, Oliver imagines Sydney Harbour from the point of view of an Eora man witnessing the arrival of the First Fleet: "You could become a different kind of man, tall and deep-chested, black-skinned and bearded, standing upon some rocky peak with the dawn wind

---

77   See Eleanor Dark, "Caroline Chisholm and Her Times", in *The Peaceful Army: A Memorial to the Pioneer Women of Australia, 1788–1938*, ed. Flora Eldershaw (Sydney: Women's Executive Committee and Advisory Council of Australia's 150th Anniversary Celebrations, 1938), 59–84.

78   Bonnie Kime Scott, "First Drafts for Transnational Women's Writing: A Revisiting of the Modernisms of Woolf, West, Fauset and Dark", *Hecate* 35 (2009): 26.

on your naked body, your shield and spear and throwing-stick in your hands" (11). This transformation of modern settler subject into a precolonial Aboriginal man is achieved "with the aid of dim light, narrowed eyes, and a little imagination" (11). Dark's characteristic use of the second person pronoun creates a slippage between Oliver and the reader, reinforcing the idea that becoming "a different kind of man" not only describes Oliver's imaginative vision, but also suggests the process of reading. In inviting the reader to occupy a radically different perspective, Dark demonstrates both the imaginative possibilities and limitations of middlebrow personalism: this moment functions as an opportunity for connection, identification and empathy, while framing Aboriginal culture as something that can be assumed, appropriated and cast off at will.

After imagining himself as a member of the Eora, Oliver returns to his own middle-class settler identity. He is able to dismiss his imaginings of precolonial Australia and reinvest in the organic community of Watsons Bay:

> You might sigh for lovely places violated and lovely names forgotten; you might grieve for a brave and ancient race fading slowly to extinction, its language scantily recorded, its virtues unremembered, its miseries ignored.
>
> But you must return to your own life ... What you see now, spreading itself over the foreshores, reaching back far out of sight, and still back into the very heart of the land, is something in whose ultimate good you must believe or perish. The red roofs and the quiet grey city become intimate and precious – part of a story of which you yourself are another part, and whose ending neither you nor they will see. (12–13)

We can see from this passage that, for all of its expressed sympathies for Aboriginal culture, the emphasis of *Waterway* is on the "ultimate good" of the local community represented by the "red roofs" of Watsons Bay, on the nation "reaching ... back into the very heart of the land" to which it is connected and on the wider international space into which Sydney Harbour flows. *Waterway*'s climax of the ferry crash displaces Aboriginal dispossession onto a narrative of modern settler tragedy, performing what Brigid Rooney describes as "a mythic back-projection, replacing black bodies with white".[79] As Meg Brayshaw writes, "Dark recognises the fissure of colonial violence in Australian settler modernity, but cannot incorporate restitution or reparation into her ethical model."[80] *Waterway* is therefore both attuned to and shaped by the uneven conditions of 1930s settler-colonial modernity. As we will see in the chapter that follows, these tensions become even more apparent in Dark's more sustained representation of Aboriginal cultures in *The Timeless Land*.

---

79 Rooney, "Time's Abyss", 109.
80 Brayshaw, *Sydney and its Waterway*, 110.

Conclusion

Waterway is striking in the way that it registers tensions between Dark's aesthetic utopianism and her increasing political awareness, and between her cosmopolitan and more regional commitments. Along with *Sun Across the Sky*, it represents some of the difficulties that Dark encountered in adapting her writing to address the increasing pressures of the late interwar period: in moving from an emphasis on the face-to-face to more programmatic and material solutions, in reconciling the local and national scales with the global implications of cosmopolitan humanism and in shifting the evolutionary teleology of liberalism to one capable of responding to the rupture of impending world war.

The conclusion of *Waterway* is generally interpreted as resolving the novel's tensions through providing an image of national belonging. Brigid Rooney argues that the novel "convenes around its scene of ferry wreck a predominantly national – albeit culturally progressive national – community of spectator-survivors", and that this ending "reifies and resolves contradiction".[81] David Carter similarly argues that *Waterway* ends with an "image of harmony", providing "final resolution" through a "sense of Australian history as the story of civilisation in discord and harmony with its environment".[82] Carter's reading focuses particularly on Oliver's concluding reflections about the Australian landscape, in which he expresses the desire to become "shaped to some pattern" by the Australian land – a pattern that will make settler Australians "one with it at last" (384).

And yet this description of settler indigenisation is not the final image of *Waterway*. Rather, Dark ends with the following, more ambivalent description from Oliver's point of view:

> The long waterway … lost itself in a western haze of paling gold, the bridge spanned it like a rainbow, the city skyline sank into a lavender-coloured mist. He turned with a sigh which was the released breath of contentment rather than regret, and looked down at the shadowed sea. A little sailing boat with all her canvas out was racing for the Heads, making for the harbour like a bird homing. (384)

The image of Oliver turning from the westward gaze of the city and harbour to the Pacific Ocean on the other side of South Head is a curious one on which to end the novel. Robert Dixon suggests that, at the beginning of *Waterway*, Oliver's "divided" gaze, both "westward into 'the heart of the land'" and "eastward toward the Pacific", could signify "the conflicting demands of international modernism and cultural nationalism".[83] If this is the case, then it is significant that Oliver

---

81 Rooney, "Time's Abyss", 108–09.
82 Carter, *Always Almost*, 182.
83 Dixon, "Australian Literature, Scale and the Problem of the World".

makes a final turn towards the open sea; that is, towards international modernity. What is the meaning of the "little sailing boat with all her canvas out racing for the Heads" that Oliver observes there? This image could re-enact the historical moment with which the novel began, when the First Fleet entered the Heads of Sydney Cove, connecting modern Sydney to its colonial past in a moment of modernist synchronicity. The description of the boat "making for the harbour like a bird homing" could alternatively be read as an image of return that, like Channon's imaginative voyaging, Winifred's preference for the "brown boronia" of local place or Dark's own sense of relief in returning to Sydney, signals the importance of place-based attachments even for those who are committed to a cosmopolitan and internationalist awareness. The diminutive size of the "little sailing boat" recalls the unequal relations between the commuter ferry and the international mail steamer, with Dark's narrative focus on the smaller vessel suggesting a strategic commitment to the less powerful nation, which is in need of protection from the calamitous collision with oncoming global catastrophe. Another interpretation is that the boat "racing for the Heads" evokes the romance and adventure of a transient "ocean-faring people" who live for the moment of liminality in which, as Lois expresses it, there is "nothing between you and the edge of the world but blue ocean" (114). The ending appears to perform the twin gestures of arrival and departure that I have identified with Dark's regional cosmopolitanism, as Oliver faces outwards towards a boat that is coming inwards. It is tempting to try to make these diverse views cohere; what is more difficult is to accept that they might be held in suspension, to see them in tension, and to view *Waterway* as a modernist novel which acts as "a kind of vast discursive container, filled with … contradictory languages … an arena in which discursive battles inevitably are being waged".[84]

---

84 Karen Jacobs, *The Eye's Mind: Literary Modernism and Visual Culture* (Ithaca, NY: Cornell University Press, 2001), 6.

6

"An Exercise in Imagination": The Limits of Empathy in *The Timeless Land* (1941)

> As an exercise in imagination it will be suggested to the children that they try to place themselves in the dark skins of the natives who saw the arrival of the First Fleet. What would they think of the appearance of the white man? His weapons? His dwellings? His possessions? His customs?
>
> Eleanor Dark, Exercise written for student listeners of the ABC Junior History Broadcasts, 1942.[1]

> Art, like science, belongs not to countries but to the world, and there is no better means of promoting understanding, tolerance and cooperation between nations than by an interchange of cultural ideas. At no time in history has it been more urgently necessary that the various peoples of the earth should understand each other's way of life, so that when the war is ended they may establish an enduring peace, free from prejudice and mutual distrust.
>
> Eleanor Dark, Statement written for the NSW Aid Russia Committee, 1941.[2]

In September of 1941, the American publisher Macmillan released what would become the most celebrated and commercially successful work of Eleanor Dark's oeuvre: the historical novel *The Timeless Land* (1941). Followed by a British edition in October and an Australian one in November, *The Timeless Land* fitted well with both the international trend in historical sagas and a contemporary Australian interest in reassessing the colonial past.[3] It also offered something new: an emphasis on Aboriginal characters' points of view that was relatively unusual for the time,

---

1   Enclosed in Eleanor Dark to B.W. Kirke [ABC], 6 August 1942, Eleanor Dark Papers, Mitchell Library, State Library of New South Wales, MLMSS 4545, Box 30.
2   Enclosed in Eleanor Dark to Secretaries of the NSW Aid Russia Committee, 11 October 1941, Dark Papers, MLMSS 4545, Box 30.

and a unique way of combining aspects of literary modernism with the more traditional narrative elements of realist historical fiction.

The success of *The Timeless Land* brought Dark increased credibility as both a writer and historical expert. In the year following the novel's release, the Australian Broadcasting Commission (ABC) invited her to contribute a talk to the Junior History Broadcasts, which offered an "all-Australian programme" written and delivered by a variety of local teachers, writers and cultural figures, and aimed at middle school students.[4] Of the fifteen segments offered, six were written by women: these included a play about Lachlan Macquarie by Marjorie Barnard, two radio plays set in the nineteenth century by Tasmanian playwright Catherine Shepherd, a talk about Matthew Flinders by Ernestine Hill, author of the historical novel *My Love Must Wait* (1941), and a discussion of Aboriginal encounters with Governor Arthur Phillip written by Dark. The title of Dark's talk was "Governor Phillip and the First Fleeters as seen by Bennilong and other blacks". As the epigraph to this chapter shows, Dark suggested that students undertake a preparatory "exercise in imagination" in which they would "try to place themselves in the dark skins of the natives who saw the arrival of the First Fleet".

This exercise aptly sums up what Dark saw as the larger ethical project of *The Timeless Land*: an invitation to readers to participate in a form of empathetic engagement with the Other – in this case, the imagined Indigenous Other – and thereby to see Western culture in new ways. The idea of seeing through another's eyes is crucial to *The Timeless Land*, as Dark invites readers to view historical events through the points of view of a wide range of characters from various social and cultural groups, including the Gadigal, Wangal, Cammeraygal and Gweagal of the Eora Nation (Dark uses variations of these spellings), the convict classes, free settlers and officers of the First Fleet. Dark makes particular use of non-white and lower-class white characters' perspectives to offer strong critiques of aspects of Western culture, including the rigid class system, the high value placed on the acquisition of property and material wealth and the exploitation of the natural environment. Her invitation to empathetic identification can be viewed as an essentially middlebrow tactic of personalism, whereby the act of reading offers the reader the opportunity to identify emotionally with an alternate self.[5] In appealing to imagined Aboriginal perspectives to recover elements of cultural authenticity that Dark believed settler culture – and, more broadly, mid-century Western modernity – had lost or was yet to achieve, *The Timeless Land* also shares strong resonances with other modernist literary works that drew significantly on ideas of primitivism.

---

3   David Carter, "What America Also Read: Australian Historical Fiction in the American Marketplace, 1927–48", *Antipodes* 29, no. 2 (2015): 384.

4   Draft Programme for Junior History School Broadcasts, enclosed in B.W. Kirke to Eleanor Dark, 5 August 1942, Dark Papers, MLMSS 4545, Box 30.

5   Janice Radway, *A Feeling for Books: The Book-of-the-Month Club, Literary Taste, and Middle-Class Desire* (Chapel Hill: University of North Carolina Press, 1997), 283.

The ideas of historian Dominick LaCapra provide a useful means by which to evaluate Dark's narrative strategies of empathy and identification in *The Timeless Land*. LaCapra proposes the concept of "empathic unsettlement", in which secondary witnesses compose narratives about historical trauma that "neither confuse one's own voice or position with the victim's nor seek facile uplift, harmonization, or closure but allow the unsettlement that they address to affect the narrative's own movement".[6] Crucially, empathic unsettlement seeks to avoid appropriating the experiences and historical specificity of trauma survivors. As LaCapra argues:

> It is dubious to identify with the victim to the point of making oneself a surrogate victim who has a right to the victim's voice or subject-position. The role of empathy and empathic unsettlement in the attentive secondary witness does not entail this identity; it involves a kind of virtual experience through which one puts oneself in the other's position while recognizing the difference of that position and hence not taking the other's place.[7]

At times Dark was able to invoke empathic unsettlement with some degree of nuance; often, however, *The Timeless Land* relies upon a range of strategies to resolve narrative tensions. These include providing premature or "truncated" forms of narrative closure, or the "conflation of subject positions", for instance through equating convict experiences with those of Aboriginal people.[8]

This chapter will examine both the opportunities and limitations of Dark's use of primitivism, empathy and emotion, considering these tactics in light of the particular context of a mid-century, settler-colonial nation, and in terms of her engagement with international markets. It will approach *The Timeless Land* as one of the most powerful and troubling articulations of Dark's liberal humanist vision and middlebrow modernist aesthetics.

"Throw[ing] Open the Windows of Our Imagination": Writing History and Fiction

In a scene that echoes and extends the opening moments of *Waterway* (1938), Dark begins *The Timeless Land* with Bennilong (Woollarawarre Bennelong) and his father Wunbula gazing out from the cliffs of Sydney's South Head, awaiting the arrival of "the boat with wings" which later emerges in the form of the First Fleet.[9]

---

6   Dominick LaCapra, "Trauma, Absence, Loss", *Critical Inquiry* 25, no. 4 (1999): 723.
7   LaCapra, "Trauma, Absence, Loss", 722.
8   Dominick LaCapra, *History and its Limits: Human, Animal, Violence* (Ithaca, NY: Cornell University Press, 2009), 65.
9   Dark uses the spelling "Bennilong", although "Bennelong" is now the accepted version. Eleanor Dark, *The Timeless Land* (London: Collins, [1941] 1946), 20. All subsequent references are to this edition and appear in parentheses in the text.

Dark's choice to begin the novel with a precolonial, Aboriginal point of view was, as historian Tom Griffiths describes it, a "stunning imaginative leap from the ships to shore".[10] Dark told her English publisher, William Collins, "Most books about the early settlement of this country have begun with the coming of the whites – a kind of assumption that this was the beginning of its history."[11] The opening scene of *The Timeless Land* directly challenges this idea. The front matter of the book, which includes a map of the early colony, a Preface by Dark, a "Glossary of Aboriginal Words and Phrases", and a bibliography listing archival sources and anthropological works that she consulted, reassures the reader that the novel will be both educative and accessible.

The Timeless Land is arranged into seven sections. The section covering "1770–1788" acts as a prologue; the proceeding five chapters cover each of the first five years of the early British colony in Sydney (1788 to 1792); and the novel ends with an epilogue set several years later, when Bennilong returns to Australia from England.[12] Aboriginal characters' perspectives feature throughout the novel and are offset against other viewpoints such as those of the convicts and officers. Dark told her publisher that she wanted "to tell a story of the white settlement partly from the black man's point of view".[13]

Although *The Timeless Land* was Dark's first novel set in an historical rather than a contemporary period, her growing interest in Australian history can be seen in her former works, including *Waterway* and the essay on Caroline Chisholm written for the Sesquicentenary collection, *The Peaceful Army* (1938). In writing *The Timeless Land*, Dark spent many hours in the Mitchell Library taking notes from archival sources such as letters and diary entries, and consulting key accounts of the early colony, including David Collins' *Account of the English Colony in New South Wales* (1798) and Watkin Tench's *Narrative of the Expedition to Botany Bay* (1789) and *Complete Account of the Settlement* (1793). In 1940, she and Eric followed the footsteps of the 1789 expedition led by William Dawes from Emu Plains to Mount Hay, and this venture shaped her writing of this scene in the novel.[14]

The Timeless Land reflects a wider resurgence of interest in the colonial past in the works of 1930s and 1940s Australian writers. Events such as the Sydney Sesquicentenary brought questions of national history to the fore: writers were given

---

10 Tom Griffiths, *The Art of Time Travel: Historians and Their Craft* (Carlton, Vic.: Black Inc., 2016), 26.
11 Eleanor Dark to W.A.R. Collins, 23 June 1939, Dark Papers, MLMSS 4545, Box 22.
12 It was William Collins' idea to begin *The Timeless Land* with Dark's description of Bennilong and Wunbula, rather than with the prologue she had written. The omitted prologue explores the Australian continent as it operated in the minds of European explorers prior to 1770. See typed rough draft of intended "Prologue", Dark Papers, MLMSS 4545, Box 5; W.A.R. Collins to Eleanor Dark, 29 November 1940, Dark Papers, MLMSS 4545, Box 22.
13 Eleanor Dark to W.A.R. Collins, 26 March 1939, Dark Papers, MLMSS 4545, Box 22.
14 Barbara Brooks with Judith Clark, *Eleanor Dark: A Writer's Life* (Sydney: Pan Macmillan, 1998), 345.

incentives to reflect on aspects of Australia's national identity by such initiatives as the Commonwealth Sesquicentenary literary competition. Novels with historical settings frequently won the major Australian literary prizes in the interwar period, such as the Australian Literary Society Gold Medal and the *Bulletin* novel competitions. Women contributed significantly to the writing of historical novels, with key works from this period including Henry Handel Richardson's trilogy *The Fortunes of Richard Mahony* (1917–29), G.B. Lancaster's *Pageant* (1933), Dark's *The Timeless Land* trilogy (1941–53), and M. Barnard Eldershaw's *A House is Built* (1929) and *Tomorrow and Tomorrow and Tomorrow* (1947; 1983). A number of the plays written by Australian women playwrights also featured historical settings. Catherine Shepherd's three-act play *Daybreak* (1938) is set in Hobart Town in 1830 and presents a sympathetic attitude towards convicts. *Daybreak* was awarded the National Theatre Prize, performed around the country, adapted for radio, published in written form and, in 1954, performed as part of Hobart's Sesquicentenary celebrations. Dymphna Cusack's *Red Sky at Morning* (1935), set in Parramatta in 1812 and similarly engaged with issues of convictism, was also published, adapted for radio and even turned into a film in 1944. Male writers also produced works of historical fiction: Brian Penton published *Landtakers* (1934) and *Inheritors* (1936), the first two instalments of an unfinished historical trilogy set in Queensland, and Ion L. Idriess and Frank Clune wrote popular fiction that often had historical underpinnings.

Australian writers who dealt with historical themes were often treated as historical experts in the interwar and Second World War periods, in part because there was minimal engagement with national history from professional historians. Tertiary studies in Australian history were still in a very nascent stage, and even when a new group of historians started to emerge in the 1950s and 1960s, such as Max Crawford, A.G.L. Shaw, Douglas Pike, Manning Clark and Russel Ward, these writers gave very little attention to Aboriginal history.[15] Instead it was the creative writers who were engaging with important questions about Australia's national story.[16] The overlap between creative writing and the writing of history can be seen in the way that a number of women novelists also produced non-fiction historical studies: Barnard Eldershaw, in particular, drew on their university training in history to write *Phillip of Australia* (1938), *My Australia* (1939) and *The Life and Times of John Piper* (1939). The 1930s saw the beginning of what Laurie Hergenhan describes as "modern, synthesizing and revaluing studies of Australian history", as a number of important non-fiction studies on Australian history and cultural life were published in this decade, including Keith Hancock's *Australia*

---

15   See Ann Curthoys, "Expulsion, Exodus and Exile in White Australian Historical Mythology", *Journal of Australian Studies* 23, no. 61 (1999): 14–15; Griffiths, *Art of Time Travel*, 27.

16   Susan Sheridan, "Historical Novels Challenging the National Story", *History Australia* 8, no. 2 (2011): 8–9; *Along the Faultlines: Sex, Race and Nation in Australian Women's Writing, 1880s–1930s* (St. Leonards: Allen & Unwin, 1995), 156.

(1930), P.R. Stephensen's *The Foundations of Culture in Australia: An Essay Towards National Self Respect* (1936), Barnard Eldershaw's *Essays in Australian Fiction* (1938) and Vance Palmer's *National Portraits* (1940s).[17] Australian writers were occupied by the same pressing issues that energised authors elsewhere in the English-speaking world: the international rise of fascism and censorship, and failures of capitalism and colonialism and the threats posed to democratic liberalism. Historical fiction and historical studies allowed writers to look back at the past in order to investigate how such issues had taken hold, influenced the present or might be prevented in the future. Writing to her American publisher in 1941, Dark explained her realisation that history could provide a means of investigating some of the roots of contemporary problems: "I did realise that so-called 'modern' problems are not new, but only old problems now reaching culmination point, and that they were already well rooted in the times of which I was writing."[18]

The integrity of Dark's historical research meant that historians at the time valued *The Timeless Land* and approached it as a work of history. Manning Clark wrote to Dark expressing his appreciation for the novel; he visited Varuna in 1946 and invited her to address his students at the University of Melbourne about her research.[19] Years later, Clark sent Dark a copy of the new edition of the first volume of his *History of Australia* (1962), writing, "if there is any value in the work at all this lies in part from the inspiration in reading *The Timeless Land*, and I would like you to accept the book in gratitude for all that I owe to your own work".[20] After completing the second volume (1968), he informed Dark that "some of the inspiration to say something about why we are as we are, and some of the drive to find out, if it ever were possible to find out, what we are, came from reading your work, and talking to you".[21] Clark appreciated Dark's work even though, at this point of his career, his historical studies gave little attention to Aboriginal history – a contradiction that Tom Griffiths reads as evidence of "the power of disciplinary thinking", as professional, academic historians at the time largely neglected Australia's precolonial story or the presence of frontier violence, thereby producing and reinforcing a rupture between "history and prehistory", and "civilisation and 'the primitive'".[22]

The Timeless Land also drew the admiration of contemporary anthropologists. Dark consulted with Phyllis Kaberry while writing the book, and acknowledged

---

17   Laurie Hergenhan, *Unnatural Lives: Studies in Australian Convict Fiction* (St. Lucia: University of Queensland Press, 1993), 109.
18   Eleanor Dark to James Putnam [Macmillan], 8 September 1941, Dark Papers, MLMSS 4545, Box 22.
19   Brooks with Clark, *Eleanor Dark*, 331–32.
20   Manning Clark to Eleanor Dark, 22 August 1963, Eleanor Dark Papers, National Library of Australia, MS 4998, Binder 3.
21   Manning Clark to Eleanor Dark, 2 August 1973, Eleanor Dark Collection, Varuna, the National Writers' House.
22   Griffiths, *Art of Time Travel*, 27.

Kaberry's *Aboriginal Woman* (1939) as a key source for *The Timeless Land*. Kaberry encouraged Dark's efforts, writing to her, "I am interested in the Aborigines as individuals and human beings, and not as specimens, and I think the novel is an excellent medium for presenting them as human beings".[23] Professor of anthropology at the University of Sydney, A.P. Elkin, congratulated Dark on her use of "the Aboriginal material", writing of *The Timeless Land*, "The work is well written and your history and anthropology are good – and they live." [24] British-American anthropologist M.F. Ashley Montagu, who described himself as "a more or less lone, and far removed fighter, for the rights of the aboriginal [*sic*] in Australia", wrote to Dark from the United States, thanking her for *The Timeless Land* and expressing hope that the novel would "have some effect upon the heart and conduct of white Australians in their dealings with and planning for the aboriginals".[25] Ashley Montagu published a review of *The Timeless Land* in *Oceania*, the Australian journal of social and cultural anthropology, which demonstrates how this work of fiction was taken seriously in its time for its treatment of Aboriginal cultural material.[26] Creative writers such as the Jindyworobak poets Ian Mudie and Roland Robinson also responded warmly to Dark's novel, with both men sending Dark copies of poems inspired by *The Timeless Land*.[27]

While Dark's approach to history and culture was evidently taken seriously by figures from a range of disciplines, including history and anthropology, it is worth noting that the relationship between fact and fiction in *The Timeless Land* is never straightforward. Dark is careful to emphasise the historical underpinnings of her novel by including the list of sources; however, in the Preface she also points out that much of *The Timeless Land* derives from her imagination. She claims, "I make no claim to strict historical accuracy either in my dealings with the white men or the black" (9). While many of the characters are based on historical figures (including Bennilong, Captain Arthur Phillip, David Collins, William Dawes and Watkin Tench), others are invented, and it is this interaction between fact and fiction that gives the novel much of its energy. Dark integrates extracts from archival sources into the narrative, creating an interesting interplay between

---

23   Phyllis Kaberry to Eleanor Dark, 15 June 1940, Dark Papers, NLA MS 4998, Binder 1.
24   A.P. Elkin to Eleanor Dark, 29 April 1942, Dark Papers, NLA MS 4998, Binder 2.
25   M.F. Ashley Montagu to Eleanor Dark, 1 December 1941, Dark Papers, NLA MS 4998, Binder 2.
26   In his review, Montagu argues that *The Timeless Land* "give[s] the reader a far truer and fuller understanding of the settlement [of Sydney] than most purely historical works could ever do". He particularly praises Dark for her "sympathy for the native, and her insight into the workings of his mind [which] have succeeded in creating a living picture of him as a human being such as no ethnologist could fail to recognize, approve, and admire". M.F. Ashley Montagu, "Review: *The Timeless Land*", *Oceania* 12, no. 3 (1942): 303.
27   Ian Mudie to Eleanor Dark, "Benarra's Farewell", copy of poem with note to Eleanor Dark, 1942, Dark Papers, NLA MS 4998, Binder 2; Roland Robinson to Eleanor Dark, 24 December 1945, Eleanor Dark Collection, Varuna, the National Writers' House. Robinson wrote to Dark, "I think your '*Timeless Land*' is the best expression of its kind in Australian literature" and enclosed an inscribed copy of his *Beyond the Grass-Tree Spears* (1944), explaining that *The Timeless Land* had "inspired me to write the title verses" of the book.

historical record and fiction, and inviting her readers to reflect on the process of constructing history.

M. Barnard Eldershaw's wartime novel *Tomorrow and Tomorrow and Tomorrow* similarly foregrounds questions about the writing of history, and ultimately champions the creative power of the novelist over the work of professional historians. As a novelist, Knarf sees the past "through the eyes of his imagination", and his historical novel aims to portray the now-extinct Australians as "life in a different key … transposed not lost".[28] In contrast, he believes that his friend Ord, an archaeologist, is only able to see history in a highly forensic and scientific manner: "the trouble with historians," he reflects, is that they tend to provide "a story so fantastic and remote that it was difficult to think of these people as fully human" (11). As if to demonstrate the creative power of fiction, the novel that Knarf narrates is the creative outlet through which he explores his encounter with archaeological evidence of the Hyde Park War Memorial. In "Little World Left Behind", the statue of the "brooding Anzac" is transformed into Harry Munster, the everyman who is swept along by the force of history and operates as the vehicle through which Knarf explores the alienation brought about by capitalism. Both *Tomorrow and Tomorrow and Tomorrow* and *The Timeless Land* suggest the limits of accessing history in an objective or scientific manner, and foreground fiction as the site wherein the past is brought alive in compelling and unsettling ways.

The ideas raised by Dark's novel about the relationship between history and fiction, and the uses of empathy in accessing the past, anticipate the controversies that emerged in response to Kate Grenville's much later novel, *The Secret River* (2005). While Grenville is far more cognisant than Dark of the problems associated with claiming to speak for Aboriginal characters, *The Secret River* is similar to *The Timeless Land* in its efforts to confront the violent legacies of colonialism using the imaginative possibilities of the middlebrow novel form. Grenville's book can be viewed as part of a series of early twenty-first-century Australian novels by settler writers which deal with white and Indigenous relations, often by delving into the nation's history of frontier violence: other works in this sequence include Alex Miller's *Journey to the Stone Country* (2002), Andrew McGahan's *The White Earth* (2004) and Gail Jones' *Sorry* (2007). These novels were written during or just after the so-called history wars – a series of public debates that occurred during John Howard's term of office, in which conservative historians (principally Keith Windschuttle) expressed opposition to what they deemed as the "black-armband" versions of history of leftist intellectuals (of which Henry Reynolds was treated as representative). *The Secret River* became caught up in these debates and was criticised by historians on both sides of the political spectrum.[29]

---

28   M. Barnard Eldershaw, *Tomorrow and Tomorrow and Tomorrow* (London: Virago, [1947] 1983), 11, 13. All subsequent references are to this edition and appear in parentheses in the text.

29   For accounts of the controversy sparked by Kate Grenville's *The Secret River*, see Nicholas Birns, *Contemporary Australian Literature: A World Not Yet Dead* (Sydney: Sydney University Press,

In particular, the controversy over *The Secret River* centred on Grenville's public comments about the role of empathy in enlivening history. In a claim that could have been expressed by Dark in relation to *The Timeless Land*, Grenville spoke in an interview of her novelistic approach to depicting historical events: "The historians are doing their thing, but let me as a novelist come to it in a different way, which is the way of empathising and imaginative understanding of those difficult events."[30] When asked where *The Secret River* stood in relation to the recent history wars, Grenville said it would be "up on a ladder, looking down": historians had "got themselves into these polarised positions", whereas a novelist could "stand up on a stepladder and look down at this, outside the fray, and say there is another way to understand it".[31] This image of a stepladder particularly exercised a number of professional Australian historians. In an essay in the *Australian Financial Review*, Mark McKenna defended the right of the historian to utilise the tool of empathy:

> Grenville claims for her fiction the power of empathy and understanding, leaving the historians at the bottom of the ladder, tearing one another apart as they argue over mere details and facts. Surely it is not only the novelist who can stand outside polarised debates and seek to understand the past, seek to find empathy … Grenville elevates fiction to a position of interpretive power over and above that of history.[32]

McKenna treated Grenville's claims as representative of "the dangers that arise when novelists … claim for fiction, at the expense of history, a superior ability to provide empathy and historical understanding".[33] In her piece for the *Quarterly Essay*, Inga Clendinnen also defended "historians' role as custodians and interpreters of the past" against the challenge which she believed was "now being mounted by Australian novelists".[34] Clendinnen was particularly scathing about Grenville's use of "Applied Empathy: the peculiar talent of the novelist to penetrate other minds through exercising her imagination upon fragmentary, ambiguous, sometimes contradictory evidence".[35] She wrote of the limitations of an empathetic approach:

2015), 133–36; Liliana Zavaglia, *White Apology and Apologia: Australian Novels of Reconciliation* (Amherst, NY: Cambria Press, 2016), 122–26.

30 Kate Grenville, "Books and Writing: Kate Grenville", interview by Ramona Koval, ABC Radio National, 17 July 2005, transcript, https://www.abc.net.au/radionational/programs/archived/booksandwriting/kate-grenville/3629894.

31 Grenville, interview.

32 Mark McKenna, "Writing the Past", *Australian Financial Review*, 16 December 2005, https://www.afr.com/life-and-luxury/arts-and-culture/writing-the-past-20051216-jeipe.

33 McKenna, "Writing the Past".

34 Inga Clendinnen, "The History Question: Who Owns the Past?", *Quarterly Essay*, no. 23 (2006): 15. Kate Grenville maintains that the controversy stemmed from a misapprehension of her original comments. See Kate Grenville, "Facts and Fiction", https://kategrenville.com.au/short-pieces/facts-and-fiction/.

35 Clendinnen, "The History Question", 20.

Historical novelists spend time getting the material setting right, but then, misled by their confidence in their novelist's gift of empathetic imagination, they sometimes project back into that carefully constructed material setting contemporary assumptions and current obsessions.[36]

Clendinnen argued that in contrast to novelists, "historians must keep their emotions bridled by intellect. It is because of that bridling that they have more chance than any novelist of penetrating sensibilities other than their own".[37] Anthropologists, she allowed, drew on similar tools to those used by historians: "long observation, cool thought and the constant awareness that [their] own intuitions could be of no use at all".[38]

The debate sparked by *The Secret River* reveals a division between the disciplines of history and creative writing in early twenty-first-century Australian culture. Such a rift clearly did not exist in Dark's context, allowing for *The Timeless Land* to be appreciated as a form of history and anthropology, even as Dark deliberately complicated the novel's relationship to these disciplines. Perhaps the warm reception of Australian historians and anthropologists to Dark's novel is due to the lack of density in these fields at the time, particularly in relation to studies of Aboriginal cultures and history, which meant that Dark's novel was viewed as a welcome contribution rather than a threat. In recent years, historians such as Tom Griffiths have sought to reconnect the fields of history and literature for a twenty-first-century context, by drawing attention to the literary craft involved in writing history. Griffiths devotes a chapter of his study *The Art of Time Travel: Historians and Their Craft* (2016) to Dark's *The Timeless Land*, arguing that it deserves recognition not only as a great work of literature but also as a "path-breaking" work of history.[39]

Writing the Nation and the World

Although the historical fiction produced by Australian writers in the 1930s and early 1940s focused predominantly on the national past, this does not mean that these works were parochial and nativist in their perspectives. In fact, in the late interwar and Second World War periods there was a new urgency to understand Australian culture in relation to the wider world. As Patrick Buckridge explains of the late 1930s, "Australia's global political environment, particularly its wartime strategic relations with Europe and the United States, was taking on a new importance, the consequences of which certainly included a new sense of the visibility of Australian literature in the wider world, and of the inevitability of

---

36 Clendinnen, "The History Question", 27–28.
37 Clendinnen, "The History Question", 36.
38 Clendinnen, "The History Question", 23.
39 Griffiths, *Art of Time Travel*, 32.

cross-national literary comparisons."[40] *The Timeless Land* provides a strong example of the internationalism of Australian interwar and Second World War writing. It was chosen for the American Book-of-the-Month Club in October 1941 (Fig. 6.1), and this selection boosted the book's sales not only in the United States but also in Australia and England. Once again, American critics noted with apparent surprise the parallels between the Australian colonial story and their own: the reviewer for the *New York Herald Tribune* wrote, "Many Americans, vaguely educated to think our colonial beginnings a unique act of history, know scarcely the first thing of the parallel saga of the great continent, almost as large as the USA, 'down under'. It happens to be a very remarkable story … even more clearly defined than in our own history."[41] The double-page report that appeared in the *Book-of-the-Month Club News*, written by the selection committee member Dorothy Canfield, acknowledged that "Americans are not only ignorant of, but honestly not very much interested in early days in Australia".[42] Canfield countered this by suggesting that *The Timeless Land* offered something universal: it would bring American readers in "contact with greatness" and allow them to understand the colonial situation with new insight, as "[t]his novel about the settling of Australia brings us our first profound, satisfying, emotionally moving interpretation in fiction of what the arrival of white settlers in a new land really meant".[43] In typically middlebrow terms and in a widely quoted report, Canfield distinguished *The Timeless Land* from both "history" and "anthropology", describing it instead as "creative fiction of a high order": "What it does is throw open the windows of our imagination and let in a flood of understanding on the heaped-up piles of facts all too familiar with us in our own pasts."[44]

The international success of *The Timeless Land* can be attributed in part to the fact that the novel built upon a contemporary, transnational trend in historical fiction. The historical romance or family saga was one of the dominant genres of the interwar period, popularised by such British examples as John Galsworthy's *Forsyte Saga* (1906–21) and taken up with great success by Australian writers such as Henry Handel Richardson.[45] As David Carter and Roger Osborne show,

40 Patrick Buckridge, "'Greatness' and Australian Literature in the 1930s and 1940s: Novels by Dark and Barnard Eldershaw", *Australian Literary Studies* 17, no. 1 (1995): 30. See also Patrick Buckridge and Eleanor Morecroft, "Australia's World Literature: Constructing Australia's Global Reading Relations in the Interwar Period", in *Scenes of Reading: Is Australian Literature a World Literature?*, eds. Robert Dixon and Brigid Rooney (North Melbourne: Australian Scholarly, 2013), 47–59.

41 Milton Rugoff, "The Birth of a Nation – Down in Australia", *New York Herald Tribune*, 5 October 1941, from Eleanor Dark's album of newspaper clippings, Dark Papers, MLMSS 4545, Box 24. Other reviews mentioned in this chapter are also from this source, unless otherwise stated.

42 Dorothy Canfield, "*The Timeless Land* by Eleanor Dark", *Book-of-the-Month Club News*, September 1941, 2.

43 Canfield, "*The Timeless Land*", 2.

44 Canfield, "*The Timeless Land*", 2.

45 Carter, "What America Also Read", 384.

Australian writers found that historical fiction travelled well to both English and American book markets: a number of historical novels by Australian writers were released and reviewed in America between the late-1920s and the mid-1940s, and both Richardson's *Ultima Thule* (1929) and *The Timeless Land* were chosen for the Book-of-the-Month Club.[46] The predominance of historical fiction is (perhaps paradoxically) one of the markers of the contemporaneity and transnationalism of Australian literature in this period.[47]

Dark appears to have been aware that *The Timeless Land* would garner popular interest, writing to her London agent at Curtis Brown in 1939 that the book might "appeal more widely than my past ones, as there seems to be rather a fashion for semi-historical stuff at present".[48] Ten years prior to this, Marjorie Barnard had noted that "the period novel is on the crest of a high wave of popularity", relating this to "a time of literary vigour and versatility".[49] Yet as ever, the popularity of Dark's work drew some consternation from her Australian contemporaries: in a somewhat backhanded compliment, Nettie Palmer wrote to Dark of *The Timeless Land*, "It's amazing that such a good book should be so popular: or put it the other way, it's extremely fortunate, and rare, that a popular book should be so good."[50]

Although *The Timeless Land* is often treated as one of the more nationally focused works of Dark's oeuvre, it in fact reveals her growing awareness of international market trends. Noting the similar structure of *Sun Across the Sky* (1937) and *Waterway*, William Collins had suggested she move away from "one-day action books" and write a more substantial work with a chronological structure.[51] Although Dark was always sceptical of reviewers and critics, in writing *The Timeless Land* she seemed more prepared "openly to countenance considerations of market and popular appeal".[52] Owing to this, some critics have tended to read the historical trilogy as a point of rupture in Dark's writing, emphasising its departure from the compressed timescales and psychological introspection of her earlier works. Mid-century critics such as G.A. Wilkes and H.M. Greene approached Dark's shift to historical fiction favourably; Drusilla Modjeska's later reassessment, on the other hand, treated *The Timeless Land* as indicative of a larger and disappointing move away from experimental, modernist writing in Australian literature (a phenomenon

---

46 David Carter and Roger Osborne, *Australian Books and Authors in the American Marketplace 1840s–1940s* (Sydney: Sydney University Press, 2018), 231; Carter, "What America Also Read", 372.

47 Carter, "What America Also Read", 382.

48 Eleanor Dark to John Green, 29 August 1939, Dark Papers, MLMSS 4545, Box 22.

49 M. Barnard Eldershaw, "The Period Novel: An Infinity of Problems", *Sydney Morning Herald*, 23 November 1929, 13. Although published under the collective pseudonym M. Barnard Eldershaw, this article appears to have been written solely by Marjorie Barnard.

50 Letter from Nettie Palmer to Eleanor Dark, 14 October 1942, Dark Papers, NLA MS 4998, Binder 2.

51 W.A.R. Collins to Eleanor Dark, 5 November 1937, Dark Papers, MLMSS 4545, Box 25.

52 Marivic Wyndham, *"A World-Proof Life": Eleanor Dark, a Writer in Her Times 1901–1985* (Sydney: UTS ePress, 2007), 181.

Figure 6.1 Cover of *Book-of-the-Month Club News* announcing selection of *The Timeless Land* for the Book-of-the-Month Club, September 1941. Eleanor Dark Papers. Mitchell Library, State Library of New South Wales. MLMSS 4545, Box 24.

she saw as largely the fault of international publishers and reviewers).[53] Other scholars have suggested ways of reading Dark's work that broach this limiting opposition between cosmopolitan modernism and nationally focused historical fiction. In particular, Susan Carson, Brenton Doecke, Paul Giles and Bonnie Kime Scott show that *The Timeless Land* continued Dark's engagement with aesthetic modernism: it offers an experimental approach to time and reflects a modernist interest in other cultures.[54] Rather than showcasing the difference between modernist fiction and historical realism, *The Timeless Land* points to possible intersections between the two. I have included it as part of this study of Dark's interwar writing, even though the book's publication date sits just outside the temporal scope of the interwar period, in order to counteract the tendency to treat Dark's historical writing as separate from the novels with contemporary settings.

Middlebrow Orientalism

Dark's commitment to a readerly ethics based on empathy and identification can be traced across all of her works, although it is perhaps most evident in *The Timeless Land*. The reader learns of the arrival of a boat carrying white people several years earlier – presumably that of Captain James Cook in 1770 – from the point of view of Bennilong, who knows of the event from the "Corroboree of the Bereewolgal" created by his father, which depicts "mysterious beings with faces pale as bones, who spoke an incomprehensible language, and wore coverings not only all over their bodies, but even upon their heads and feet" (21). By reframing familiar historical events through an alternate perspective, Dark provides a form of empathic unsettlement by inviting white readers to view their own culture as strange.

Dark continues to develop this idea of seeing events through alternate, cross-cultural perspectives. Describing the first encounter between a fictional Eora Elder, Tirrawuul, and Captain Arthur Phillip, she writes:

> They studied each other curiously.
>
> Tirrawuul saw a smallish man, quite incredibly ugly, with a pale face and a very large nose. He was covered from head to foot, and, though his coverings were not as splendid as those of the men with the weapons, Tirrawuul, himself a leader, could recognise in him a confidence and authority which offered no outward trappings.

---

53 See Drusilla Modjeska, "'A Hoodoo on That Book': The Publishing Misfortunes of an Eleanor Dark Novel", *Southerly* 57, no. 2 (1997): 73–96.

54 See Susan Carson, "Making the Modern: The Writing of Eleanor Dark" (PhD thesis, University of Queensland, 1999); Brenton Doecke, "Challenging History Making: Realism, Revolution and Utopia in *The Timeless Land*", *Australian Literary Studies* 17, no. 1 (1995): 49–57; Paul Giles, *Backgazing: Reverse Time in Modernist Culture* (Oxford: Oxford University Press, 2019); Bonnie Kime Scott, "First Drafts for Transnational Women's Writing: A Revisiting of the Modernisms of Woolf, West, Fauset and Dark", *Hecate* 35 (2009): 10–28.

Phillip saw an elderly savage, quite incredibly ugly, with greying, tangled hair, and alert dark eyes. He was stark naked, and strangely ornamented with raised scars across his body and upper arms. But he stood very erect, and wore his air of leadership with unconscious dignity. (48)

The emphasis in this scene is on providing the two characters' impressions of one another ("Tirrawuul saw …", "Phillip saw …"), rather than offering the reader an accurate portrait of either character or an authentic description of history. In attempting to read the other, both Tirrawuul and Phillip initially focus on surface level markers such as hair, facial features and clothing; this causes some misunderstanding (or *misreading*), such as when Phillip dismisses Tirrawuul as an "elderly savage". Dark's use of parallel syntax and paragraph structure to describe Phillip's and Tirrawuul's respective impressions of the other, and the ironic repetition of the phrase "quite incredibly ugly", hints at the similarities between their misreadings: both struggle to see beyond their own cultural expectations. Here, Dark's depiction of the past combines with a modernist scepticism about the ability of ocular knowledge to provide access to reliable information.[55] In the opening Preface, Dark destabilises the idea of accurate historical representation, raising questions as to the reliability of colonial eyewitness accounts:

There are many accounts of these [Aboriginal] people in the journals of those who came to Australia with the First Fleet; but as was inevitable between races unacquainted with each other's languages, and unfitted to appreciate the significance of each other's customs, there were constant misunderstandings … That they recorded faithfully what they saw cannot be questioned; that they placed the correct interpretation upon it is not so certain. (9)

As Brenton Doecke points out, Dark's willingness to contest official versions of history and to depict Australian history as "a field of contestation, rather than pretending to describe things as they really were" was quite radical for the time.[56] As in Dark's 1930s novels, which provide multiple, synchronous perspectives brought into relation by a compressed time frame, *The Timeless Land* suggests that "[w]e can never know the 'facts' except as they have been refracted by certain viewpoints, never have access to events except via different interpretations of them".[57] Dark's writing does not aim for historical authenticity but rather, as Paul Giles asserts, "in typical modernist fashion, [it] acknowledges the inevitable ironies involved in a retrospective appropriation of the past".[58]

---

55   See Martin Jay, "Scopic Regimes of Modernity", in *Vision and Visuality*, ed. Hal Foster (New York: New Press, 1999), 3–27; "The Disenchantment of the Eye: Surrealism and the Crisis of Ocularcentrism", *Visual Anthropology Review* 7, no. 1 (1991): 15–38; Karen Jacobs, *The Eye's Mind: Literary Modernism and Visual Culture* (Ithaca, NY: Cornell University Press, 2001).

56   Doecke, "Challenging History Making", 56.

57   Doecke, "Challenging History Making", 56.

Despite their initial negative judgements of one another in *The Timeless Land*, both Tirrawuul and Phillip develop a more sympathetic understanding in this scene. Each character is able to acknowledge a similar quality of leadership in the other. In this way, Dark models the kind of empathetic and careful looking, feeling and imagining that may allow the reader to move beyond surface impressions and recognise features of commonality rather than only difference in the cultural Other. The scene also reflects Dark's investment in the white liberal discourse in which colonisation is framed as a form of tragic misunderstanding rather than a deliberate act of violent dispossession. Kate Grenville expresses a similar view in *The Secret River*. In describing the historical research she conducted for the novel, Grenville said in an interview, "what I came away with overwhelmingly was the feeling that there had been no particular ill-will on both sides, at least in the beginning, but a complete inability to communicate ... it was a tragic, tragic inability to communicate across a gulf of culture".[59] Given this interpretation of colonisation, it is little wonder that white liberal writers such as Dark and Grenville placed so much emphasis on the empathic possibilities afforded by reading and writing fiction: novels become the site wherein an essential cultural and political skill is developed.

In her report for the *Book-of-the-Month Club News*, Canfield remarked on Dark's unorthodox approach in inviting readers to see through the eyes of not only the colonists but also Australia's First Nations peoples:

> We see the black folk through the eyes of the English men and women – convicts and officers alike – as naked, improvident, dirty, incalculably ignorant, scarcely human. And then, through the magic of a creative imagination, we see the white men as they looked to the blacks.[60]

The Timeless Land would no doubt have appealed to the progressive values of Canfield – one of Jaime Harker's "progressive middlebrow" cultural figures, whose own fiction tackled such issues as racial segregation and anti-Semitism in America.[61] As Harker observes, "middlebrow reading is about sentiment – it causes

---

58   Giles, *Backgazing*, 410.
59   Grenville, interview. Historian John Hirst argued that Grenville's belief that "conflict comes from misunderstanding" reflected a "liberal fantasy". John Hirst, *Sense & Nonsense in Australian History* (Melbourne: Black Inc., 2009), 151–52. See Zavaglia, *White Apology and Apologia*, 123; Birns, *Contemporary Australian Literature*, 133.
60   Canfield, "*The Timeless Land*", 3.
61   See Jaime Harker, *America the Middlebrow: Women's Novels, Progressivism, and Middlebrow Authorship Between the Wars* (Amherst: University of Massachusetts Press, 2007); "Progressive Middlebrow: Dorothy Canfield, Women's Magazines, and Popular Feminism in the Twenties", in *Middlebrow Moderns: Popular American Women Writers of the 1920s*, eds. Lisa Botshon and Meredith Goldsmith (Boston, MA: Northeastern University Press, 2003), 111–34; Janis P. Stout, "Writing Politically: Dorothy Canfield and the 'Wrongness of the World'", *MFS: Modern Fiction Studies* 60, no. 2 (2014): 266–70.

the reader to feel intensely, to identify passionately, to respond personally", and authors of books chosen for the Book-of-the-Month Club often used such emotional appeals to promote humanitarian ideas.[62]

In using empathetic appeals to address issues of cultural and racial difference, *The Timeless Land* resonates with what Christina Klein calls middlebrow orientalism. In her analysis of Cold War American texts, Klein associates middlebrow orientalism with such cultural products as the Rodgers and Hammerstein musical *The King and I* (1951), which allowed American audiences to learn more about South-East Asia in ways that combined fantasy with education, and romance with history, thus contributing to "transforming strangers into friends".[63] Victoria Kuttainen, Sarah Galletly and Susann Liebich apply Klein's concept to the ways in which interwar Australian culture and leisure magazines such as *The Home* "helped their readers become acquainted with Asian and Pacific peoples and cultures, building relationships of asymmetrical friendships and encounter, in real and imagined ways, even as they remained suffused with assumptions about cultural and racial superiority".[64] These accounts acknowledge that, while middlebrow orientalism often relied upon racist tropes, and provided what LaCapra calls facile forms of uplift, it could nonetheless play an important educative role in arousing readers' curiosity about other cultures.

The ethical invitation to the reader to look through the eyes of the Other had significant political implications for Dark in the international context of the Second World War. She started writing *The Timeless Land* in September 1937 during her visit to Canada and on the voyage home to Australia.[65] In the tumultuous years that followed, she questioned the direction in which Australia and the wider world were heading and struggled to complete the novel "in the face of an overwhelming … feeling that novels – particularly about things which happened 150 years ago! – are now supremely unimportant".[66] Yet at the same time she became increasingly committed to the idea that literature could play a crucial, even urgent role at a time of international conflict. Dark's publishers shared her hopes that *The Timeless Land* would bring about greater intercultural understanding in the context of the emerging war in the Pacific. Writing to her in 1941, Collins of London expressed the hope that *The Timeless Land* would "help to bring the two countries, Australia

62   Harker, *America*, 18; "Progressive Middlebrow", 119.

63   Christina Klein, *Cold War Orientalism: Asia in the Middlebrow Imagination, 1945–1961* (Berkeley: University of California Press, 2003), 9, 17.

64   Victoria Kuttainen, Susann Liebich and Sarah Galletly, *Transported Imagination: Australian Interwar Magazines and the Geographical Imaginaries of Colonial Modernity* (Amherst, NY: Cambria Press, 2018), 101.

65   In an article published in the *Boston Post*, Dark is quoted as saying, "I actually began writing my book in Canada and on my way home from the United States in 1937". "Eleanor Dark", *Boston Post*, 19 October 1941. This fact is also indicated by the dates that Dark provides at the conclusion of *The Timeless Land*: "September, 1937 – July, 1940" (she returned from her three-month trip on 23 October 1937).

66   Eleanor Dark to John Green [Curtis Brown], 10 June 1940, Dark Papers, MLMSS 4545, Box 22.

and the States, together, the more they know about each other, especially in these times".[67] *The Timeless Land* certainly circulated much more than any of Dark's former books: it was reviewed widely, and Dark received letters of appreciation from readers across the world. In October 1941, when invited by the NSW Aid Russia Committee to present a paper as part of the Literature and Drama section of their proposed conference, she sent a written statement asserting the importance of art in "promoting understanding, tolerance and cooperation between nations".[68] In particular, Dark drew attention to the urgent necessity that "the various peoples of the earth should understand each other's way of life".[69] In other words, the arts proffered a means of bridging differences between individuals that, when scaled up, provided a model for global neighbourliness. The invitation to white Australian schoolchildren to consider their culture and history from the point of view of an unaccustomed perspective, and to readers of *The Timeless Land* to do the same, therefore represented a significant ethical-political act of cross-cultural understanding for Dark.

Race and Class in *The Timeless Land*

The middlebrow orientalism of *The Timeless Land* is perhaps best described as a form of *middlebrow Aboriginalism*. This phrase employs Bob Hodge and Vijay Mishra's term Aboriginalism, which they use to describe a particular set of representations of Aboriginal culture in settler Australian literature. As in Edward Said's concept of orientalism, Aboriginalism involves both "a fascination with the culture of the colonised along with a suppression of their capacity to speak or truly know it".[70] Hodge and Mishra point to examples of an Aboriginalist tradition in the writings of Mary Gilmore, anthropologist A.P. Elkin, the Jindyworobak school of poetry of the 1930s and 1940s and Dark's *The Timeless Land*.[71] In particular, the concept of the Dreamtime or the Dreaming was important to these settler writers' evocations of Aboriginal culture: this concept was celebrated by such writers as "proving the intricate and mystical incapacity of Aborigines to comprehend linear history in the European mode".[72] Key concepts that underpinned Aboriginalism,

---

67   W.A.R. Collins to Eleanor Dark, 1 October 1941, Dark Papers, MLMSS 4545, Box 22.
68   Eleanor Dark, Statement written for NSW Aid Russia Committee, enclosed in Eleanor Dark to Secretaries of the NSW Aid Russia Committee, 11 October 1941, Dark Papers, MLMSS 4545, Box 30.
69   As one practical strategy, Dark suggested that "Australian writers might submit copies of their books for publication in the USSR, and ask that Russian writers might, similarly, send their work to Australia". Eleanor Dark to Secretaries of the NSW Aid Russia Committee, 11 October 1941, Dark Papers, MLMSS 4545, Box 30.
70   Bob Hodge and Vijay Mishra, *Dark Side of the Dream: Australian Literature and the Postcolonial Mind* (Sydney: Allen & Unwin, 1991), 27.
71   Hodge and Mishra, *Dark Side*, 29–30.
72   Hodge and Mishra, *Dark Side*, 27.

such as that of the Dreamtime and the dying race theory, also had political functions, including the denial of Aboriginal modernity and land rights.

Despite its radical position in the context of representations of Australian history in its time, *The Timeless Land* poses some of the most significant challenges for readers of Dark's work today. The novel both drew on and played a key role in shaping the Aboriginalist tradition in Australian literature. Her romantic idea of the mythic timelessness of the Australian land and its First Nations peoples greatly limited her ability to engage with the material demands being made by Aboriginal people at the time she was writing. As Hodge and Mishra point out, for all her expressed sympathy for Aboriginal perspectives, Dark's concept of timelessness "in effect removes [Aboriginal people] from history".[73] Dark's treatment of Aboriginal characters was contentious in her time because, according to a number of mid-century critics, it was overly sympathetic.[74] Now the novel is jarring in that a white writer seeks to speak with authority on behalf of Aboriginal characters, and with an incomplete knowledge of the complex cultural matters that she tries to tackle. The sources on which Dark drew to learn about Aboriginal culture include works by now discredited ethnographic and anthropological writers, including Baldwin Spencer and F.J. Gillen, A.P. Elkin, Phyllis Kaberry and Daisy Bates – works that, as Michael Griffiths points out, contribute to a burdensome "genealogy of texts by non-Indigenous literary culture-makers [that] weighs heavily on the history of the present".[75] As Griffiths asserts, literary appropriations of Aboriginal culture by settler writers, such as Katharine Susannah Prichard's *Coonardoo* (1928) and Xavier Herbert's *Capricornia* (1938), "are not simply literary works in some splendid aesthetic isolation: they are a means by which many Australians come to know Indigenous culture".[76] This latter point is certainly the case for *The Timeless Land*, which was included on Australian secondary and tertiary curricula in the mid-century period.

The Timeless Land is in some ways quite tentative about the extent to which empathy can bridge racial and cultural differences. Many scenes depict only a partial form of understanding between white and black cultures. Dark's Arthur Phillip is a humanitarian and liberal figure who genuinely tries to understand the Eora people he encounters but finds that "the more one associated with them the less comprehensible they became" (301). The breakdown in communication between black and white Sydney communities reaches a climax when Phillip is speared in what Dark portrays as a lamentable moment of mutual misunderstanding. Despite this, Phillip feels a sense of spiritual "unity" with Bennilong and has an "urgent desire to know that whatever differences of race

73 Hodge and Mishra, *Dark Side*, 30.
74 See, for example, G.A. Wilkes, "The Progress of Eleanor Dark", *Southerly* 12, no. 3 (1951): 139–48; John McKellar, "The Black Man and the White", *Southerly* 9, no. 2 (1948): 92–98.
75 Michael R. Griffiths, *The Distribution of Settlement: Appropriation and Refusal in Australian Literature and Culture* (Crawley, WA: UWA Publishing, 2018), 2.
76 Griffiths, *Distribution of Settlement*, 2.

and custom might hold them apart, there was still a personal confidence between them, a sense of mutual trust" (306). Phillip leaves the colony without having fully achieved the common understanding he seeks, and the tragic tone of the novel's epilogue throws into doubt the wisdom of his patronage of Bennilong.

Dark's hesitation to develop fully the idea of interracial understanding is due perhaps in part to her awareness of the historical reality of frontier violence. Although she depicts Phillip as a man of "indestructible faith in human dignity and worth" (161), she nonetheless points out that his values were those of his times: for example, Phillip orders the forceful capture of Bennilong, Colbee and Arabanoo and then is surprised when they resent his efforts to use them as cultural interpreters and mediators. The tragic mode in which Dark frames white characters' attempts to understand Indigenous people also reflects her investment in the dying race theory: her belief that such efforts ultimately proved fruitless in preventing the large-scale destruction of Aboriginal cultures. In the Preface she writes of Aboriginal Australians: "The race is nearly gone, and with it will go something which the 'civilised' world has scorned too easily" (10). Although at the time of writing, the dying race idea was becoming increasingly unsustainable in the face of visible Aboriginal protest such as the 1938 Day of Mourning, Dark drew on the works of anthropologists who were strong proponents of this theory. *The Timeless Land* reinforces this narrative of tragic loss, in particular through the character of Bennilong, who by the novel's epilogue is reduced to the position of a drunkard rejected by both white and black cultures: in the words of the narrator, "a lonely, comical, tragic and immortal figure" (49).[77]

Dark appears somewhat more hopeful that empathy and imagination can overcome class differences than racial ones. The child Patrick Mannion, free settler and son of Irish gentry, watches the convicts disembarking from the Second Fleet and asks himself, "were they really people?" (250). Although the convicts "certainly had arms and legs and heads", Patrick feels "they were obviously a different *kind* of people" (250). An encounter with Johnny Prentice, child of convict parents, brings Patrick his "own first dim comprehension of human suffering, the first faint crack

---

77 Dark's representation of Bennelong had a significant influence on the way this Wangal elder was perceived in the twentieth century. In 1966, she wrote the entry on him for the *Australian Dictionary of Biography*, and here she continued to promote the idea of a man torn irrevocably between two cultures. Historian Emma Dortins describes Dark as the "modern originator of Bennelong's tragedy", and Tom Griffiths similarly points out that Dark's "tragic biographical mode has endured even against the grain of evidence". The dominant narrative of Bennelong as a tragic figure is being challenged and refuted by early twenty-first-century historians and biographers. Emma Dortins, "The Many Truths of Bennelong's Tragedy", *Aboriginal History* 33 (2010): 53; Griffiths, *Art of Time Travel*, 32. See also Kate Fullagar, "Woollarawarre Bennelong: Rethinking the Tragic Narrative", *Aboriginal History* 33 (2010): 3–6; "Bennelong in Britain", *Aboriginal History* 33 (2010): 31–51; Grace Karskens, *The Colony: A History of Early Sydney* (Sydney: Allen & Unwin, 2009); Keith Vincent Smith, *Bennelong: The Coming in of the Eora, Sydney Cove 1788–1792* (Sydney: Kangaroo Press, 2001); Keith Vincent Smith, "Bennelong Among His People", *Aboriginal History* 33 (2009): 7–30.

in his armour of detachment" (256). By conceiving of Johnny as human and capable of suffering, Patrick is able to recognise the humanity and unjust treatment of all members of the convict class:

> Already, in a few moments, he was beginning to understand … He saw the miserable huts in the Cove … he saw the grey, slow-moving line of convicts setting out for their day's work at the brickfields … He remembered the convict women on the ship, and realised for the first time that they were really women like his mother, and could have little boys of their own like himself. He remembered … an impression of a naked back, and blood, and a sound he had never heard before, a man's voice crying out in pain … (256)

This passage describes the process by which the convicts become human in Patrick's mind. It is significant that the "filament of understanding" between Patrick and Johnny occurs between children who will grow up in the colony (and whose stories are developed in the subsequent instalments of the trilogy), as it reflects Dark's hope that the "moulding process of the land" would eventually produce a more equitable Australia (81).

Not all of Dark's characters embrace this vision of a classless community. Patrick's father, Stephen Mannion, resists any feelings of empathy and commonality between himself and the convicts. This is captured when he walks past a convict being punished in the stocks:

> Its dirty and bony hands hung limply on either side of the leaden-coloured face which protruded grotesquely through the board, and confirmed Mr. Mannion in his conviction that these people were indeed of another clay. The unfortunate wretch, he thought with distaste, looked more like an ape than a man; and, merciful heaven, how he stank! (383)

The negative connotations of "grotesquely", "ape" and "stank" convey Stephen's refusal to acknowledge a common basis of humanity between himself and the convict; it is a similar reaction to that invoked in Arthur Sellman by the rioting crowd of unemployed workers in *Waterway*. In a strategy that Liliana Zavaglia also observes in several early twenty-first-century "novels of reconciliation", including Andrew McGahan's *The White Earth* and Kate Grenville's *The Secret River*, Dark offers a "moral spectrum of whiteness" in which more moderate, liberal positions such as Patrick Mannion's are championed and more extreme forms of racism such as that of his father condemned – an approach that, "through empathetic imagination … bequeaths the modern liberal subject a moral position that avoids complicity with the worst of contact violence".[78]

Dark attempts to link issues of class with those of race by frequently conflating Aboriginal and convict experiences. Johnny's father, Andrew Prentice, develops feelings of compassion towards Aboriginal peoples because he relates their suffering to that of the lower classes in England. As Andrew faces the possibility that his plot of land on the Nepean will be taken by the redcoats who are moving further and further west, he starts to empathise with the plight of local Aboriginal groups who similarly face losing their land to "the great law of Possession ... stretching out greedy hands towards their continent":

> Prentice stood watching them, and as he watched he felt himself invaded by an emotion which had never moved him before – compassion ... His old hatred of "them" – the dominant class of his own race – was now aroused on behalf of that other race, whose blood mixed with his own in the veins of his infant son. "They" [the dominant class] had flung him and his kind out of their own land, but that was not enough. "They" must have this land too, and make of it another hell on earth for the poor as they made their own. (340–41)

Andrew's newly developing feelings of compassion rely upon a parallel between Aboriginal dispossession and the treatment of convicts: two asymmetrical forms of injustice that Dark nonetheless tries to equate at various points throughout the trilogy, in particular to reinforce her critique of Western capitalism. The linking between the two is perhaps intended as a bridge by which Dark's white readers might develop feelings of compassion for the racial Other. Yet as Dominick LaCapra asserts, "Historical trauma is specific and not everyone is subject to it or entitled to the subject-position associated with it."[79] The conflation of subject positions – "the confusion of empathy or compassion with identification"[80] – allows Dark to circumvent the ways in which convicts and their descendants participated in and benefited from acts of colonisation. Zavaglia notes similar attempts to create parallels between the suffering of white convict characters and the experiences of Aboriginal peoples in more recent novels by settler writers. As she states in relation to *The Secret River*, "the attempt to balance the two tales of black and white suffering ... is fraught with complication and unwittingly produces an apologia for whiteness".[81] While hailing from two very different historical periods, we might think of *The Timeless Land* and *The Secret River* as approaching frontier history from a similar position of liberal whiteness that, as Zavaglia argues, involves the "double movement of apology and apologia" and reflects the "conflicted yet intimately connected desires of defence and regret".[82]

Dark does not develop fully the political implications of her critique of the British class system in *The Timeless Land*. Moments of mutual understanding are limited to

---

78 Zavaglia, *White Apology and Apologia*, 131–32. See also Jeanine Leane on this point, in "Tracking Our Country in Settler Literature", *JASAL: Journal of the Association for the Study of Australian Literature* 14, no. 3 (2014): 14.
79 LaCapra, "Trauma, Absence, Loss", 722.
80 LaCapra, *History and Its Limits*, 65.
81 Zavaglia, *White Apology and Apologia*, 130.
82 Zavaglia, *White Apology and Apologia*, 3.

individual encounters between characters, and to the thoughts that Dark ascribes to historical figures such as Phillip, Tench and Dawes. As he is preparing to leave the colony, Phillip expresses the somewhat radical view to David Collins that the want of food is the true source of any crime: "if there had been some means arrived at in our own land whereby hunger should be made unknown, there might have been fewer of these unhappy people to bring to Botany Bay" (414). Yet Dark does not develop what kind of system or "means" this might be – perhaps because the development of this idea sits outside of the historical scope of the narrative. Similarly, in another scene she depicts Tench writing a section of what would become *A Complete Account of the Settlement at Port Jackson*: "*The first step in any community which wishes to preserve honesty, should be to set the people above want*" (330).[83] Dark describes Tench "struggling with a thought whose obvious common sense was, even a century and a half later, to remain unappreciated" (329–30). This moment of narrative intrusion provides a direct reference to Dark's own context – a time by which the kind of humanist socialism envisioned by Tench had still not been achieved. Dark similarly gestures towards such a future moment when writing of the rebellion stirring in the convict population in response to capital punishment:

> All that day, wherever a group of convicts worked … a dark undercurrent of shackled power ran dangerously, gathering the accumulated bitterness of past generations, fortifying it with new resentments, to hand it on, a little fiercer, a little stronger, to the hour when it would become at last omnipotent and destroying.
> That hour was not yet … but hope waited for their children. (108)

The narrator's reference to "the hour" when the convicts' collective struggle would bring about revolutionary change is quite compelling in this passage and reflects Dark's growing sympathy with working-class struggles. As Brenton Doecke points out, the narrator is speaking from a point in time that is neither 1788, nor one hundred and fifty years hence; rather this point "seems to be completely outside any historical perspective that must justifiably be adopted through examining the actual course of Australian history", making it more of "a prediction or hope that such an hour will come".[84]

Although Dark does not offer any concrete ideas as to how this kind of humanist socialism could be achieved, she does link it closely with Aboriginal forms of community. In the Preface, she asserts that Western culture "might have learned much from a people who … had developed that art [of living] to a very high degree", describing Aboriginal culture as one in which the adage of "Life, liberty, and the pursuit of happiness" was "a taken-for-granted condition of their existence" (10). In the scene depicting Tench writing his account of the early colony, Dark goes

---

83 Dark uses italics to indicate that this is an archival extract.
84 Doecke, "Challenging History Making", 55.

so far as to suggest that his "revolutionary sentiment" about freeing the people from material want stemmed from his encounter with Aboriginal culture:

> He found himself thinking of the black people and their system in a land which gave them enough, but only just enough, for survival. Here, they said, was the land, and no man had a stronger claim than his neighbour upon what it offered in the way of subsistence. (330)

This passage is based on speculation, as Dark imagines an interconnection between Tench's socialist ideas and his experience of First Nations peoples. It appears that Aboriginal culture (or at least her conception of it) allowed Dark to imagine a different, more equitable way of organising society – one that she felt had not been achieved at the time of writing *The Timeless Land*.

Dark made a number of efforts to live out her socialist commitments at the time she was writing and publishing *The Timeless Land*. In November 1940 she asked her British agent to donate one-third of any royalties from the English edition of the novel to a fund for London children from the working classes.[85] She spent much of her time during the war years helping to establish a free library for children in Katoomba. The library (part of the Children's Library and Craft Movement established in Australia by the Rivett sisters, Elsie and Mary, in 1922) aimed to provide books and opportunities for painting, music and writing to local children and those who had been evacuated to the Blue Mountains. Dark sought fundraising from her old school, Redlands, and from members of the Fellowship of Australian Writers; she also contributed some of the royalties from the American edition of *The Timeless Land* towards the library and brought friends such as Katharine Susannah Prichard to see it.[86] A photograph shows Eric, Eleanor and a young Michael Dark at the launch of the new library, opened by Clive Evatt, the Minister for Education, in July 1942 (Fig. 6.2). As *The Blue Mountains Advertiser* explained:

> The object of the Children's Library Movement … goes beyond the mere lending of books and teaching of crafts, and aims at providing for children a place which is "theirs" – a place pleasing to the eye, friendly and informal in atmosphere, where they can spend their leisure hours in absorbing and creative occupations.
>
> Those interested in the movement feel that in time of war such a place becomes not less, but more necessary for children, as a psychological counter blast to the atmosphere of strife and destruction which prevails, and which children unconsciously absorb.[87]

---

85   The donation was made anonymously on Dark's behalf to the Civilian War Distress Fund. Wyndham, *"A World-Proof Life"*, 182.
86   See Brooks with Clark, *Eleanor Dark*, 254–55.
87   "Boys' and Girls' Library and Crafts Club Nearing Completion", *The Blue Mountains Advertiser*, 3 July 1942, 2.

Figure 6.2 Unknown photographer. Opening ceremony of the Katoomba Children's Library. At the podium from left: Mary Matheson, Joseph Jackson MLA, Hon. Clive Evatt, Dr Eric Dark, Eleanor Dark, Michael (Mick) Dark on chair, Mayor Freelander, B.J. Milliss. July 1942. Blue Mountains City Library, Local Studies Collection, courtesy of Michael Dark. © Jill Dark.

In the address he gave at the opening, Evatt linked the educative work of the library to the broader desire "to see children grow up into a world that will be characterised by real equality and justice, economically and socially; where there will be no depression and unemployment and social injustice", asserting that "this aim can be helped by education in its broadest sense, by leading people out of darkness into light, out of illiteracy into knowledge".[88] Dark's involvement in the library seems typical of the kind of cultural and political work with which she was most comfortable: it was personal and local; it tackled class issues by providing children from low socio-economic backgrounds with educative opportunities; it was based on a philosophical commitment to the importance of reading and the arts; and to Dark it was made "not less, but more necessary" by the war.

Critiquing Capitalist Modernity

As we saw in the previous two chapters, Dark's interwar writing was increasingly critical of a number of aspects of Western culture, including the legacies of colonialism and capitalism that she saw as culminating in the economic, social and

---

88   Quoted in "Minister for Education Commends Children's Library Movement", *The Blue Mountains Advertiser*, 31 July 1942, 1.

political catastrophes of the 1930s. In the essay she wrote on Caroline Chisholm for the Sesquicentenary collection, Dark identified "three black shadows" on Australia's history: "the treatment of convicts, the treatment of emigrants, and the treatment of the Aborigines".[89] Considering the question of "where we are heading as a nation" ("as we must upon a hundred and fiftieth birthday"), Dark suggested that pursuing the "less spectacular and not unattainable goal" of freeing people from material want would be more advantageous than chasing after "those dreams of 'empire' that were so freely predicted for us" – dreams that, to "many in these troubled times", represent "one of the greatest obstacles to peace".[90] In a subsequent essay published in 1944 titled "Australia and the Australians", Dark described "the blunder of our dealings with the black Australians whose land we stole" as the "darkest of all blunders, heaviest upon our conscience".[91] Dark was remarkably prescient in exploring these questions. Professional historians did not take up the issue of convict history until the 1960s, nor investigate Aboriginal history until the 1980s and 1990s. To some, Dark's criticisms of British imperialism and Australian colonial history appeared out of tune with the wartime context: Australian publisher Sydney Ure Smith, who commissioned "Australia and the Australians", deemed the essay too negative to be published in the American collection for which it was intended. Instead, he published it in *The Australian Week-End Book*, and urged Dark to remove the word "stole" from the essay, arguing that he did not want to encourage either anti-British or anti-Australian sentiment at a time of war: "I dislike the idea of pointing out our own weaknesses at such a time."[92] Dark refused to change the word.

Dark critiques Western imperialism much more fully in *The Timeless Land* than in any of her prior novels. In particular, she draws attention to the brutality of the transportation and penal systems, framing these institutions as fundamental affronts to human liberty. She articulates this mostly in ethical, liberal terms, suggesting that the ill treatment of another class group is not only unjust, but also degrades the humanity of the oppressors. Dark frequently uses the perspective of Aboriginal characters to articulate this idea. In one scene, Bennilong witnesses the first execution of a convict in Sydney Cove (Thomas Barrett in 1788, who was hanged after he was found stealing from the public stores):

> surely and effortlessly, the black man saw to the heart of the problem, knew that while execution may be lawful … humiliation and indignity will recoil upon the

---

89 Eleanor Dark, "Caroline Chisholm and Her Times", in *The Peaceful Army: A Memorial to the Pioneer Women of Australia, 1788–1938*, ed. Flora Eldershaw (Sydney: Women's Executive Committee and Advisory Council of Australia's 150th Anniversary Celebrations, 1938), 62.
90 Dark, "Caroline Chisholm", 84.
91 Eleanor Dark, "Australia and the Australians", in *Australia Week-End Book*, 3rd edn, eds. Sydney Ure Smith and Gwen Morton Spencer (Sydney: Ure Smith, 1944), 10.
92 Sydney Ure Smith to Eleanor Dark, 2 April 1944, Dark Papers, MLMSS 4545, Box 29.

heads of those who inflict them, warping and flawing their image of themselves …
There was a sickness, he thought, uneasily, in the hearts of the white men. (113)

Dark uses Bennilong's reflections to provide a form of empathic unsettlement, inviting the reader to question foundational Western concepts such as property ownership, criminality and punishment. As Tom Griffiths writes, "Bennilong's perspective enabled Dark to examine, and see as strange, the imperial and material foundations of her own Western liberal society."[93] In particular, Dark unsettles the idea that natural resources such as food should be privately owned – a notion that underpinned the concept of stealing that in turn necessitated the transportation system and capital punishment. Notwithstanding the problems of a settler writer claiming to speak from the point of view of an Aboriginal character, this scene demonstrates the potential of empathic unsettlement to "place … in jeopardy fetishized and totalizing narratives that deny the trauma that called them into existence": in other words, to refuse "prematurely (re)turning to the pleasure principle, harmonizing events, and … recuperating the past in terms of uplifting messages or optimistic, self-serving scenarios".[94]

It is at times quite surprising how far Dark takes these critiques of Western culture. It reveals the strength of her belief that, in the late interwar and early Second World War years, Western capitalist modernity was at a point of complete collapse. She wrote to Miles Franklin in 1941 that "no one ever had a more evil magic to contend with than the intellectual torpor and psychological collapse of the white race today".[95] Although she viewed such a collapse as imminent, she saw the roots of this "so-called 'modern' problem" in the colonial context of which she was writing.[96] She continued to believe in a form of socialism underpinned by the belief that "the things the earth produced belonged to everyone in common".[97] Indeed, this conviction strengthened as she witnessed the Depression and the Second World War.

Dark's willingness to offer such a strong leftist critique of white culture supports the point that, even as they turned to the past for inspiration, writers of Australian historical fiction in the late interwar and Second World War periods were often far from nostalgic and sentimental. As David Carter shows, historical fiction of this era contributed to the "major reassessments of the colonial legacy" that were occurring in Australia and more globally in this period, with Australian novels "often exploring the destructive aspects of colonization even where a progressive history of nation building was redeemed from an unlikely past".[98] Susan Sheridan

---

93 Griffiths, Art of Time Travel, 28.
94 LaCapra, "Trauma, Absence, Loss", 723.
95 Eleanor Dark to Miles Franklin, 10 October 1941, quoted in Wyndham, "A World-Proof Life", 184.
96 Eleanor Dark to James Putnam, 8 September 1941, Dark Papers, MLMSS 4545, Box 22.
97 Eleanor Dark, "Political Parties", quoted in Wyndham, "A World-Proof Life", 141.
98 Carter, "What America Also Read", 381.

notes that the writings of authors such as M. Barnard Eldershaw, Eleanor Dark and Brian Penton frequently challenged national myths: these works drew attention to previously obscured aspects of Australian history, such as the presence of frontier violence, racial inequality, and the mistreatment of convicts and women, at a time when professional historians were largely ignoring these issues.[99] Brenton Doecke similarly argues that the historical novels of Dark and her contemporaries offer "a far more complex and powerful critique of Australian society than is usually suggested when they are merely lumped together as the works of old-fashioned realists and nationalists".[100]

Primitivism in *The Timeless Land*

Yet Dark's powerful appraisal of Western culture needs to be considered in light of a key point: namely, that her critique relies upon a form of "primitivism" that facilitates her vision of an indigenised settler community. This future community provides the ultimate source of harmony and facile uplift in the novel. *The Timeless Land* can be read as a prime example of literary primitivism, wherein Western writers attempt to use a reconstructed version of Indigenous cultures to critique capitalist modernity. This phenomenon not only took place in high modernist texts, such as the writings of D.H. Lawrence and T.S. Eliot, and the artworks of Pablo Picasso and Paul Gauguin, but also in more middlebrow and popular works, including Charles Chauvel's Australian film *Uncivilised* (1936), which drew on the Tarzan films. A particularly Australian version of the international phenomenon of primitivism was prevalent at the time that Dark was writing *The Timeless Land* and can be seen in the use of Aboriginal culture by the Jindyworobak poets or by visual artists such as Margaret Preston. Peter Kirkpatrick examines the trademark Aboriginalism – their primitivist construction of Aborigines and Indigenous culture" of Jindyworobak poets Ian Mudie, Rex Ingamells and Roland Robinson.[101] Their Aboriginalism involved turning towards Indigenous culture as a source of renewal and authenticity: as Ingamells expressed it in his treatise *Conditional Culture* (1938), "From Aboriginal art and song we must learn much of our new technique; from Aboriginal legend, sublimated through our thought, we must achieve something of a pristine outlook on life."[102] This desire for a "pristine outlook", and the belief that it could be found and at least partially recovered in the aesthetic representation of a culture that these poets viewed as premodern and largely extinct, was a distinctly modern and metropolitan Western desire. So-called

---

99   Sheridan, "Historical Novels", 7–8.
100 Doecke, "Challenging History Making", 50.
101 Peter Kirkpatrick, "'Fearful Affinity': Jindyworobak Primitivism", in *Adelaide: a Literary City*, ed. Philip Butterss (Adelaide: University of Adelaide Press, 2013), 126.
102 Rex Ingamells, "Conditional Culture" [1938], in *The Writer in Australia: A Collection of Literary Documents 1856–1964*, ed. John Barnes (Melbourne: Oxford University Press, 1969), 264.

primitive cultures offered Western writers a means of accessing those aspects of traditional culture that they believed had been lost by modernity: temporal continuity, cultural authenticity and reconciliation between humankind and the natural environment. As such, for interwar and mid-century Australian writers such as the Jindyworobak poets, "Indigenous culture offered a solution to the wider problem of modernity itself".[103]

Likewise in *The Timeless Land*, pre-invasion Aboriginal culture offers Dark an image of an intact, culturally whole human experience. She writes of Aboriginal people through the voice of the narrator:

> They were the children of the human family, having the gaiety, the monkey-like inquisitiveness, the monkey-like lack of application of the very young ... they were incapable of even guessing at the workings of his [the white man's] mind – the mind which had travelled so far from their primitive wisdom in its search for knowledge that it was already astray in the labyrinths of its own psychological chaos. It was a mind which had gained subtlety and lost simplicity, a mind which explored the universe, but had long, long ago lost sight of itself. (130)

This passage draws on and reinforces a number of highly problematic tropes related to the "primitive": Aboriginal people are depicted as "monkey-like" and infantile, and thus are presented as lower on the evolutionary ladder. Yet, in a manoeuvre that is typical of primitivism, Dark frames "primitive wisdom" in a positive light: it is preferable to the "psychological chaos" of the modern white man which has "long ago lost sight of itself".

Dark uses the first section of *The Timeless Land* to provide a utopian image of so-called primitive life. The young Bennilong lives in harmony with his environment:

> He was conscious of the world, and conscious of himself as a part of it. Fitting into it. Belonging to it. Drawing strength and joy and existence from it, like a bee in the frothing yellow opulence of the wattle. He was conscious of an order which had never failed him, of an environment which had never startled or betrayed him ... (19)

Dark's narrator asserts that for Bennilong's community, "knowing wealth as contentment, as freedom from hunger, as well-being in the tribe, it was a rich land" (24). Dark's Aboriginal characters embrace a communal way of living that involves a more equitable distribution of natural resources: "Food was for the seeking, and seeking it they wandered, needing under the mild sky no roof but a fragile one of bark and boughs, and leaving it lightly, as a bird leaves a twig where it has rested" (25). In particular, Bennilong's father, Wunbula, acts as an important symbol of this

---

103 Kirkpatrick, "'Fearful Affinity'", 137.

Edenic relationship between tribal culture and the Australian natural environment. Wunbula is a maker of songs, corroborees and artworks: Dark's narrator claims he has "that inspired awareness which is the heritage of creatures who live and move to the rhythms of nature" (28). Importantly, Wunbula does not live to see the degradation of his culture, and thereby remains symbolic of a fully realised, vitalist and uncorrupted man. For him, "Eternity was ever-present ... past and future interwoven with his own life by legend and unvarying tradition, so that all time was the frame for his mortality, and contentment his heritage" (25). Dark suggests that change is outside the scope of Wunbula's understanding.

In contrast to Wunbula, Bennilong is drawn into the corrupt values of Western culture and ultimately suffers the "spiritual disunity" of being caught between two conflicting identities (300). Dark writes of Bennilong: "All his life he had been tormented by these two allegiances – to the old tribal life, governed by its ancient Law ... and to some adventurousness of the blood and spirit which ardently sought and welcomed change" (370). Here Dark pits the forces of modernity – change, rupture and exploration – against the idealised image of an "ancient" and unchanging form of tribal life embodied in Wunbula. Dark writes of Bennilong in the novel's epilogue:

> He had lost his awareness of eternity, his fellowship with ages past and ages yet to come. He had lost that close and serene communion with mystery, by which the inner life of his people was nourished and sustained. Once, he thought, life was whole, like the body of a man. Once the past, the present, and the future were intricately woven together, and with them was entwined the life of man, body and spirit, one life. Once there had been no time but the eternal dream-time, not far away, though it stretched back into the ages, not incomprehensible, though it pushed forward into the future, but one with the everlasting present which dwells in the heart of man. Thus life had been whole, like the body of a man. But now something had assailed it. Change had gashed it like a knife, and the spirit flowed out of it like blood. (445–46)

This passage details the elements of human experience that, according to many Western writers and artists at the beginning of the twentieth century, had been destroyed by technological modernity: continuity between past and present, an awareness of mystery – what Dark describes as the "delicate awareness of unreasoning things" (24) – and a sense of wholeness in life and body. Thus this passage acts as a lament not just for a culture that Dark saw as doomed to extinction, but for all that Western modernity had lost.

Asking himself "what was mankind," the conflicted Bennilong thinks instinctively of the figure of Wunbula with which the novel begins: "silhouetted against the sea as it had stood upon that summer day so many years ago" (446). By the novel's conclusion, this image of complete, whole humankind has been sullied: "His outline was blurred, his features defaced" (446). This spiritual deterioration is reinforced by Bennilong's final act of defacing Wunbula's rock painting of the winged boat. Dark communicates this loss in universal terms, asking through the perspective of Bennilong, "what shall a man believe who believes no longer in mankind?" (446).[104] This loss of faith in liberal humanism appears to have haunted Dark in the wartime period: in her subsequent novel *The Little Company* (1945), protagonist Gilbert Massey states that the central question of the age – the issue that has "split the world in two, split nations, split parties, split friendships and families" – is "do you believe in human beings, or don't you?"[105]

If we read Dark's image of Wunbula as one that seeks to reconcile a distinctly modern set of ruptures, then this figure stands as a poignant symbol of all that Western culture desired to recover. It allows us to read *The Timeless Land* in continuity with Dark's novels with contemporary settings, which similarly address these ruptures by offering a variety of images of continuity. In *Sun Across the Sky*, it is art that is able to offer a means of reconnecting what modernity has severed. In *The Little Company*, literature and in particular novel writing offer a tentative means of restoring continuity in the context of the historical catastrophe of wartime. The final novel that Dark published, *Lantana Lane* (1959), looks to the small-scale producers of the Sunshine Coast as emblems of an "anachronistic" way of life that continues to value the "gossamer-threads of primitive belief in man's identity with his place [that] still drift about the world – tenuous, but oddly strong; too frail to be grasped, but obstinately clinging".[106] Such "primitive" values as "treading on earth, getting sweaty, seeing the sun rise, [and] making things grow" are framed as highly precarious in the Cold War context of "exploding H-bombs", "*la pluie atomique*" and urban expansion (64, 204, 252).

Dark's depiction of Aboriginal culture in *The Timeless Land* is therefore much more about what she – and more broadly, Western culture and its articulation in a particular settler context – was yearning for than about Aboriginal culture itself. As Wiradjuri scholar Jeanine Leane suggests, literary texts in which settler authors invoke Aboriginal culture should be read primarily as "examples of settlers' changing consciousnesses of Aboriginal presence, of their own presence here and of their quest to belong", rather than for any historical truth these texts might provide about Aboriginal peoples or cultures.[107] This point is underscored by some of the errors in Dark's representation of Sydney Aboriginal groups, and her willingness to

---

104 Intriguingly, it was Wunbula and not Bennilong that Manning Clark invoked when writing to Dark many years later about the legacy of *The Timeless Land*: "Long live that picture you evoked of Wunbula seeing the winged boat, and all that followed from that memorable day." Clark hoped that his *History of Australia* would "try to tell that story, of what happened here, even if no one could probably do justice to its tragic grandeur" – a comment that underscores how much Clark's view was shaped by the elegiac and tragic mode of Dark's novel. Manning Clark to Eleanor Dark, 2 August 1973, Eleanor Dark Collection, Varuna, the National Writers' House.

105 Eleanor Dark, *The Little Company* (Sydney: Collins, 1945), 128.

106 Eleanor Dark, *Lantana Lane* (London: Collins, 1959), 252. All subsequent references are to this edition and appear in parentheses in the text.

107 Leane, "Tracking our Country", 2.

draw Aboriginal words and customs from a variety of anachronistic sources, even while acknowledging she was doing so. She writes in the Preface:

> where I have wanted to introduce songs, words, legends, customs, for which I have been able to find no record for these particular groups, I have borrowed shamelessly from other tribes, often far distant. The result, from an ethnologist's point of view, must be quite horrible; but I am not really very repentant. These people were all of one race, and it is the quality of the race which I have tried to suggest, without regard to minor tribal differences. The important thing has seemed to me to be that these were the *kind* of songs they sang, the *kind* of legends they loved, the *kind* of customs and beliefs by which they ordered their lives. (9)

This passage reveals some of Dark's erroneous views about Aboriginal culture, including that the differences between groups and nations constituted only "minor tribal differences". It also emphasises that the depiction of Aboriginal cultures provided in *The Timeless Land* is a reconstructed one. Dark was aware of this point, writing, "I must emphatically insist that my portrayal is not intended to be taken too literally" (9). Although she undertook more thorough research than did many of the Jindyworobak poets, Dark's depiction of Aboriginal cultures relies on a similar sense of collage and pastiche. Furthermore, her interest in Aboriginal culture appears to have had little to do with engaging with Aboriginal lives and land rights in the present – suggesting that this interest was, to some extent, like that of the Jindyworobaks, "poetic rather than scientific, a source of inspiration ... rather than a recognition of Aboriginal culture in its own terms".[108]

Primitivism and Settler Belonging

While *The Timeless Land* is invested in a form of primitivism that is similar to that of other modernist texts produced in Western contexts, it also articulates this primitivism in ways that speak to a particular settler experience of modernity. The "pristine outlook" that Rex Ingamells sought in the concept of "Alcheringa" (an Arunta [Arrernte] word that the Jindyworobaks "misleadingly translated as the Dreamtime")[109] represents not only the desires of a Western culture exhausted by capitalism, but also more specifically the hopes of the settler nation for a form of cultural authenticity or indigeneity that would distinguish it from imperial culture.

---

108 John McLaren, *Writing in Hope and Fear: Literature as Politics in Postwar Australia* (Cambridge, UK: Cambridge University Press, 1996), 16. Eleanor Dark did come into contact with the local Aboriginal community in The Gully in Katoomba through Eric's medical work and when the Darks employed a local man to work in their garden; however, she felt that her first real contact with traditional Aboriginal culture was when she travelled to Central Australia in 1948. Brooks with Clark, *Eleanor Dark*, 351.

109 McLaren, *Writing in Hope and Fear*, 16.

Dark's primitivism, as well as her commitment to textual strategies of empathy, identification and education, are implicated in such settler-colonial desires. It is this conjunction of Australian settler nationalism, modernist primitivism and middlebrow personalism that makes *The Timeless Land* such a striking mid-century work.

Dark's ready acceptance of the dying race theory meant that she could not imagine a future wherein Aboriginal culture would recover the form of cultural authenticity she celebrated in the opening section of *The Timeless Land*. Instead, she suggests that settler culture might inherit the spiritual legacies of Aboriginal Australia through undertaking a process of adjustment and acclimatisation brought about by the natural environment. To make this point, Dark creates a strong link between Aboriginal Australians and the Australian land. Interacting with Bennilong's community, Phillip reflects that the Wangal have the same "watchful" and timeless quality as the land itself: both are "watching out of some colossal past in whose arms they had rested so securely for as many ages that no change seemed possible" (280). He muses, "The watchful land, the watchful dark eyes made his hundred years seem the hundredth part of a second. Millions of years lay over the quiet trees; thousands of years dwelt undisturbed in the hearts and minds of these people" (280). By establishing this close link between Aboriginal peoples and the natural environment, Dark is able to suggest that white settler society may, in time, access the timeless qualities of an ancient and mysterious country, even if they lose touch with Aboriginal people themselves. Thus, as in all of Dark's writing, it is white settler culture that receives the inheritance of Aboriginal culture, rather than living members of Aboriginal communities.

Despite its historical setting, the orientation of *The Timeless Land* is towards this future community that exists outside the temporal scope of the narrative. Phillip – a man who "could see visions" – imagines "a city on these shores", envisioning Sydney Cove transformed by "wharves crowded with shipping … wide streets and lofty buildings, and the homes of a free and happy people" (67–68, 80). While in *Waterway* Oliver Denning gazes at the harbour and is able to "annihilate the city" as he imagines a return to a precolonial, Indigenous past (11), in *The Timeless Land* Phillip annihilates the miserable, shanty-like early colony in favour of the possibilities of the modern future. Dark makes it clear that the process by which settler Australians will become "a free and happy people" cannot be accomplished within the relatively short temporal scope of *The Timeless Land*'s historical setting. Rather, this future community will be shaped by the land itself as, over time, the environment will bring about "a wakening of the heart and a new perception of the eyes of the beholder" (416).

Indeed, Dark suggests that a fully indigenised settler community will emerge only when settler culture ceases to exploit the material resources of the natural environment and instead lives in an ecologically sustainable way. Preparing to leave the colony to return to England, Phillip asks, "How long would it be … before people of his race could know it as their own?" and concludes it will take many generations for the land to "accept them only when, with difficulty and humility, they had learned that she was not theirs, but they were hers":

> He saw them, driven by their reckless greed, and by an obscure urge for conquest of so aloof and invulnerable a foe, exhausting her earth, fouling her rivers, despoiling her trees, savagely imposing upon the pattern of her native loveliness traditional forms which meant beauty in other lands. He heard them crying out to her insatiably: "Give! Give!" and was aware of her silent inviolability which would never give until they had ceased to rob. (416)

The kind of future community summoned by *The Timeless Land* will be distinct from British culture: it will reject the "traditional forms which meant beauty in other lands" (416). As Phillip muses, "How did one learn to know a country such as this? Not by building a squalid little England here upon the shores, and clinging to it!" (416). Instead, a distinct environment requires a new form – or rather, one that is so acclimatised to the new environment that it begins to take on aspects of Aboriginal culture. Like the new kind of Australian racial type that P.R. Stephensen believed had developed over time, Dark suggests that the distinctiveness of the Australian people will come from the unique qualities of the Australian environment.[110] Stephensen linked place with ethnicity by suggesting that the physical environment was forming a new kind of white Australian race.[111] Dark's vision of a future community is similarly underpinned by an organicist understanding of Australian settler culture formed in dynamic relationship with the environment.

Crucially, this community has not materialised by the end of *The Timeless Land*; in fact, the health of the colony seems to weaken after Phillip's departure for England, as Governor Hunter struggles to wrest power back from the New South Wales Corps, who Dark refers to as "the colony's first capitalists" (440). Furthermore, the narrator hints that the goal of a non-exploitative, free people living in harmony with the natural environment has not been achieved even in the one hundred and fifty years that follow. Yet Dark offers glimpses of her ideal settler community, suggesting that she was using her writing to call such a community into being. Drawing on images of settler indigenisation that were frequently expressed in interwar and mid-century Australian art and writing, she depicts an "adjusted" settler community as an acclimatised plant, or a tanned male body. In her depiction of the Sydney colony, Dark dwells particularly on the colonists' attempts to cultivate crops in a foreign environment, using these as a metaphor for the fragility of the new white community, the blindness of its leaders to resources other than

---

110　P.R. Stephensen, *The Foundations of Culture in Australia: An Essay Towards National Self Respect* (Gordon, NSW: W.J. Miles, 1936), 11.

111　Ellen Smith, "White Aborigines: Xavier Herbert, P.R. Stephensen and the *Publicist*", *Interventions* 16, no. 1 (2014): 101.

those imported from Britain and the potential of settler culture to adapt to the new surroundings. Watkin Tench reflects that, like the settlers, the crops of wheat, barley, oats and maize planted at Rose Hill (Parramatta) "must struggle to adapt themselves to new conditions" (297). Phillip thinks of the colony as a "sickly offshoot ... struggling for survival in an inhospitable earth" but is optimistic about its future: "He had sown the seed, he had tended and cherished the plant, and he believed with all his heart that it would live to reach maturity. Let him but keep sap running in it, and the seeds which fell from it would fall not on alien, but on native soil" (238). These images pick up on the organicist, nationalist images related to the soil and native plants that are present in Dark's other interwar novels, such as *Return to Coolami* (1936). They also clearly resonated with Jindyworobak poet Ian Mudie who, in the poem he sent to Dark and claimed was "[i]nspired by *The Timeless Land*", wrote (from the perspective of an Aboriginal figure, Benarra): "And so we vanish with the shadows / passing to you the heritage of place / that yet shall breed a new Australian race / welded to its soil as once were we."[112]

Dark also expresses the desire for an indigenised settler community through the image of the acclimatised white male body. She associates this body with Aboriginal culture, thereby demonstrating the unusual conjunction that appeared in a number of mid-century Australian texts, whereby settler writers articulated their desire for cultural authenticity through identifying with Aboriginality.[113] In Xavier Herbert's *Capricornia* (1938) – a novel which Dark read and greatly admired[114] – the mixed-race protagonist Norman Shillingsworth searches for his origins and, in particular, for his white father, Mark. Although the novel is usually read in terms of an Aboriginal child's search for his white father, Ellen Smith argues that it can be read as "a white man's search for an Aboriginal son" – a son who eventually "provides the white man with a retrospective claim to autochthonous belonging".[115] Similarly in *The Timeless Land*, Dark appeals to the figure of the mixed-race child to redeem and legitimise the settler character Andrew Prentice. On arriving at Sydney Cove as a convict, Andrew feels no moral responsibility towards his English wife, Ellen, and their children, and experiences "hatred of this land" (64). Making his escape from the colony, Andrew travels towards the Nepean River where he is cared for by a group of local Aboriginal people, who provide him with a wife, Cunnembeillee. He then establishes a home on the Nepean and later in

---

112 Ian Mudie to Eleanor Dark, "Benarra's Farewell", copy of poem with note to Eleanor Dark, 1942, Dark Papers, NLA MS 4998, Binder 2.

113 See Smith, "White Aborigines", 97–98.

114 Dark's work was pitted against that of Xavier Herbert when *Sun Across the Sky* and *Waterway* vied with *Capricornia* for the Commonwealth Sesquicentennial Award. Herbert's novel won. Dark wrote to Herbert expressing her admiration for his novel; Herbert subsequently wrote to Dark in glowing terms about *Waterway*: "Your *Waterway* is exquisite, dear Eleanor, in every line. Your technique – your marvelous unique execution – is as faultless – as Sydney Harbour in the dawn." Xavier Herbert to Eleanor Dark, 23 March 1939, Dark Papers, NLA MS 4998, Binder 1.

115 Smith, "White Aborigines", 109.

the Blue Mountains. Cunnembeillee gives birth to Billalong, a child whose physical features suggest the indigenisation of the settler figure:

> Billalong's wavy hair was dark, but not so dark as Cunnembeillee's, and his skin, though tanned by exposure, was still much fairer than hers … It was in the shape of the child's features, he [Andrew] decided, that his own blood showed. The nose was small and straight, and its nostrils not so spreading as those of the black people. The eyes were not so deeply sunk, and the brows not so jutting … (322)

Billalong's mixed-race body is fetishised here in a way that conveys the "quiet, unhurried process of envelopment and absorption" by which "the strange land, the *terra incognita*" is able to take "[w]hat had been thrust upon it as shame and degradation and hypocrisy" – in this case, Andrew's convictism – and transform it into "merely human life" (164). As in *Capricornia*, the mixed-race son is invoked to "confer Aboriginality back onto the father".[116] With a son who represents the fusion of white and black culture, and a wife who is able to "walk with confidence" in the bush surroundings, Andrew attains a sense of belonging in his new environment: "The land had taken him, used him, fashioned new life from him; his blood and his breath were now, even when he died, a part of it for ever" (324).

Andrew's ultimate moral transformation is portrayed when he chooses to sacrifice his own life for those of Cunnembeillee and Billalong, redeeming his former acts of indifference towards Ellen and their white children. Andrew observes Cunnembeillee and Billalong drowning in floodwater and struggles between an "instinct for self-preservation" and a morally awakening self (406). Risking recapture by the watching colonists, Andrew's ultimate decision to rescue his wife and child brings "a kind of delirious triumph … an indescribable sense of conquest, a fierce and reckless joy":

> Now let them see, he thought, and let them shoot! Not until I chose did they find me and not their cleverness discovered me, but my own free action! They have done me a great wrong in the past, but this final wrong they shall not do to me – that for them I should lie in hiding while my woman and my child drown before my eyes! (408)

Andrew literally exchanges place with Cunnembeillee and Billalong in this scene, allowing them to use his body as a foothold to reach safety. Although this choice results in his death, it is framed as a heroic, Christ-like sacrifice that redeems a lifetime of self-interest and affirms the liberal values of individual choice and human freedom. Significantly, the narrative focus is on Andrew's moral redemption and the continuity of his bloodline through Billalong, rather than on the survival of Cunnembeillee – a point that reinforces Smith's argument that while "[r]econciling

---

116 Smith, "White Aborigines", 111.

white paternity and Aboriginal progeny provides a legitimating narrative for the nation", this form of nationalism is an "intensely patriarchal" one, so that "it is perhaps the figure of the Aboriginal woman who bears the brunt of this attempt to hold together the fantasy of white Australian ethnicity and belonging".[117]

Dark also uses Andrew's white son Johnny as a figure of settler indigenisation. As a child who remembers little of his life in England, Johnny is representative of the kind of native-born settler child that Dark goes on to explore in the latter parts of the trilogy: he is unafraid of the Australian environment and shows a keen respect for Aboriginal culture. Johnny also runs away from the colony and, in a bizarre plot twist at the end of *The Timeless Land*, is accepted by Cunnembeillee and Billalong as the reincarnated form of the drowned Andrew. The symbolic replacement of the father by the son provides a form of generational indigenisation that occurs through the patrilineal relationship between father and son: Andrew becomes Johnny who in turn becomes "Dyon-ee" (an indigenised version of his English name). The novel ends with Johnny living with his half-brother Billalong and other Aboriginal friends in a secluded home in the Blue Mountains: "His life was a native's life; he was one of them, speaking their language fluently by now" (436). Like Billalong, Johnny's physical features showcase his integration into the natural environment: "His bright, dark eyes had acquired the restless alertness of the natives' eyes and the eyes of the shy kangaroos and wallabies which lived in the hills about him, but his thatch of flaming hair still proclaimed him alien" (435). It is significant that the individuals who are most able to achieve this kind of "absorption" are the children of the colonists, for as Governor Hunter reflects at the conclusion of the novel, it is "in them … that the future lay" (164, 440). Johnny becomes a central figure in the two latter instalments of the trilogy, taking the form of an Aryan Aborigine who is eventually "re-civilised" through acquiring a white wife. The characterisation of Johnny/Dyon-ee provides another instance in *The Timeless Land* when Dark attempts to make a white character stand in for an Aboriginal subject position. In LaCapra's terms, such conflation indicates that empathy has crossed over to appropriation.

The images of the indigenised settler subject in *The Timeless Land* offer narrative solutions to a problem that is intrinsically part of the settler condition: "how to become indigenous, without becoming, or being able to become, Indigenous".[118] In other words, they represent attempts by settler culture to attain the authenticity of the "whole" Aboriginal man embodied in Dark's portrait of Wunbula. Such an attempt is always partial and incomplete, due to the fact that Dark represents the Aboriginal past as essentially lost, and projects the formation of a fully acclimatised settler society as always out of reach of the novel's temporal scope. The recovery of the premodern self and the formation of the fully indigenised settler subject

---

117 Smith, "White Aborigines", 113–14.
118 Dan Tout, "Reframing 'Inky' Stephensen's Place in Australian Cultural History", *Settler Colonial Studies* 7, no. 1 (2017): 76.

are only possible in the temporal continuity of the "timeless land", wherein past and present are collapsed or merged, and in the moments of readerly empathy when the settler reader is invited to become one with an Aboriginal character. The future on which *The Timeless Land* is concentrated is therefore endlessly deferred, both due to the unique challenges confronted by a settler society in attempting to achieve a sense of cultural authenticity and, more broadly, by the inherent paradox of the primitivist project: "an undertaking to become primitive in a world where, it seemed, such a possibility had been voided".[119] This paradox made primitivism both a highly useful and ultimately conflicted strategy for mid-century settler writers. Although primitivism is often viewed as nostalgic and backward-looking – it is, after all, a hankering after a premodern past – it is also future-oriented in that it seeks to reinvigorate something through the aesthetic mode. Ben Etherington makes this point in his important reassessment of literary primitivism, arguing that primitivism is inherently speculative and utopian in nature: it "seeks out the remnants of the extinguished primitive, but its orientation is to the undeclared future. Such are primitivism's contradictions and vectors of force".[120] Etherington points out that, while primitivism is not associated with any one political position, "[a]cross primitivist works ... there is a common desire for a determinate negation of the world order that culminated in imperialist capitalism".[121] *The Timeless Land* shares in this desire to imagine a different world order and, like other examples of literary primitivism, it "holds an important place in the utopian memory of attempts to negate the social logic of globalizing capital",[122] even while it contributes to a problematic legacy of settler literature's appropriations of Indigeneity.

Future Directions of *The Timeless Land*

The Timeless Land changed Dark's status as a writer, raising her profile in Australia and bringing her international visibility. The novel was translated into multiple languages, including Japanese, Swedish and German. In the years following its release, Dark received numerous invitations to speak about the book, as well as requests to have it turned into a film.[123] She published the latter two instalments of the trilogy in 1948 and 1953, respectively; however, these never captured the popular imagination in the same way as *The Timeless Land*. Macmillan rejected the second instalment, *Storm of Time*, and it was published in America by McGraw-Hill's Whittlesey House. The latter publisher then rejected the final

---

119 Ben Etherington, *Literary Primitivism* (Stanford, CA: Stanford University Press, 2018), xi.
120 Etherington, *Literary Primitivism*, xv.
121 Etherington, *Literary Primitivism*, xvi. Etherington refers to this as "primitivism's *decolonial horizon*", which he distinguishes from historical decolonisation.
122 Etherington, *Literary Primitivism*, xiii.
123 *The Timeless Land* was not filmed until much later. The ABC miniseries providing a condensed version of the trilogy, was released in 1980.

instalment, *No Barrier*. As David Carter and Roger Osborne note, the international demand for historical fiction and family sagas that provided the conditions for Australian writers to be published in America in the interwar and Second World War years had largely passed by the late 1940s.[124]

Today, many scholars show a preference for Dark's more obviously experimental and modernist works, such as *Prelude to Christopher* (1934) and *Waterway*; however, other academics in the wake of the transnational turn and the concurrent development of the new modernist studies have explored the links between Dark's 1930s novels and historical fiction. How will *The Timeless Land* fare in the future? One key way in which the novel intersects with current scholarly approaches is in terms of its conservationist and ecological commitments, which may well speak to an eco-critical approach. From *Return to Coolami* onwards, Dark's novels draw attention to the destruction of the natural environment that operated as part of Western capitalist modernity. Provisional work has already been undertaken on this in relation to *The Timeless Land*: Bonnie Kime Scott notes that the novel's "attention to environmental depredation offers ... a forward look, to eco-feminist studies".[125] Tony Hughes-d'Aeth points out the importance of environmental themes in Australian novels of the 1930s and early 1940s, citing *The Timeless Land* and Herbert's *Capricornia* as key examples.[126] Susan Carson argues that Dark's writing, and in particular the *Timeless Land* trilogy, "fulfilled an important, but undervalued, role in the development of a national conservation consciousness".[127] As Carson points out, Dark tried to live out her ideal of a non-exploitative settler relationship with the land, through her bushwalking, gardening and participation in rock climbing expeditions with Eric. At the time of writing *The Timeless Land*, she made frequent visits to a cave in Katoomba which the Dark family adopted as a retreat from 1937 onwards. They referred to the cave as Jerrekellimi – a term that evokes Aboriginal forms of naming but was in fact comprised of the family's initials. The best studies of Dark's ecological commitments seek not simply to recuperate her views but acknowledge that her works' ecological considerations are inextricably intertwined with settler-colonial desires.

The role of women is another aspect of *The Timeless Land* that deserves further attention. This novel is less invested in women characters than any of Dark's earlier works. This, along with the relative lack of focus on women (and at times the

---

124 Carter and Osborne, *American Marketplace*, 270.

125 Scott, "First Drafts", 21.

126 Tony Hughes-d'Aeth, "A Critique of Eco-Criticism", in *Reading Down Under*, eds. Amit Sarwal and Reema Sarwal (New Delhi: SSS Publications, 2009), 118; "Australian Writing, Deep Ecology and Julia Leigh's *The Hunter*", *JASAL: Journal of the Association for the Study of Australian Literature* 1 (2002): 20.

127 Susan Carson, "Conversations with the Land: Environmental Questions and Eleanor Dark", in *Land and Identity: Proceedings of the 1997 Conference University of New England Armidale New South Wales 27–30 September 1997*, eds. Michael Deves and Jennifer A. McDonnell (Association for the Study of Australian Literature, 1998), 191.

anti-women stance) of contemporaneous novels such as M. Barnard Eldershaw's *Tomorrow and Tomorrow and Tomorrow*, led Drusilla Modjeska to conclude that feminist issues took a backseat to anti-fascist concerns in Australian women's writing of the late interwar and Second World War periods.[128] Yet there are glimpses of Dark's continued interest in the role of women in *The Timeless Land*. She makes Bennilong's sister Carangarang a creator of songs, even while pointing out that it was not the traditional role of Aboriginal women to create such songs (33). His younger sister Warraweer also composes songs and exercises a subversive power that challenges the authority of men, while Bennilong's wife, Barangaroo, has "a gleam in her eyes which was anything but meek" and is able to perceive the danger posed by the white invaders much more readily than does Bennilong (39). Dark also contests Lieutenant Clark's view of women convicts as "damned whores" by pointing out that convict women such as Ellen Prentice used their sexuality as a means of assuaging poverty and providing food for their children (106). In the latter two parts of the trilogy, Dark explores much more fully the role of settler women in the new colony, in particular through the characterisation of Conor, who becomes the wife of Stephen Mannion.

As this chapter has shown, the internationalism of *The Timeless Land* is another important and under-investigated aspect of the novel. The fact that Dark started writing it towards the end of her visit to North America is rarely acknowledged in critical studies of her work. It could be argued that the idea of seeing Australia from a geographically different perspective – from the outside rather than the inside – is essential to *The Timeless Land*. In addition to the startling reversal of perspective that opens the narrative, it ends with another striking inversion, as in the epilogue Bennilong returns from his voyage to England and looks at Sydney Cove from the perspective of a conflicted stranger: he is now the one arriving in a "boat with wings" and finding the land strange. In the novel's tragic ending, this experience of being outside his natural environment renders Bennilong unable to belong in his homeland and brings about a sense of cultural alienation that curiously mirrors that of Phillip returning to England from Australia. Dark was clearly reflecting on what it meant to be inside or outside of local and national communities, even as she was writing a novel that would bring her work increased mobility in international markets and secure her place as an author dedicated to Australian national culture.

In the years following the publication of *The Timeless Land*, Dark continued to articulate the need for a kind of international neighbourliness. In an essay entitled "This Land of Ours", published in 1949, Dark reinforced the sentiments she expressed in *Waterway* through Professor Channon, warning Australians: "Our closely-knit national individuality might, unless we are watchful, degenerate into xenophobia. Love for our country remains natural and right, but is no longer enough; we must learn, like the rest of humanity, that 'the world is our village'".[129]

---

128 See Drusilla Modjeska, *Exiles at Home: Australian Women Writers 1925–1945* (Sydney: Sirius Books, 1981).

Although committed to the distinctive settler culture she saw emerging in Australia, Dark also cautioned that the "indigenous culture we are developing can find its full usefulness only if we see it as a contribution to world culture, revealing to us our neighbours, and if we accept in return the other national cultures which reveal our neighbours to us".[130]

Conclusion

One of the questions this chapter raises is of the radical nature of Dark's middlebrow orientalism. *The Timeless Land* offered Dark's white readers an accessible and engaging narrative that invited them to imagine Australian history in strikingly new ways; as such, it may well have contributed to readers opening up to notions of cultural difference. This is certainly how Dark's historical fiction has been framed by many appreciative critics: as an important if flawed part of a chronology of a more progressive and liberal Australia. In her introduction to the HarperCollins 2013 release of *Storm of Time*, for example, Dark's biographer Barbara Brooks concludes that:

> writers like Eleanor Dark helped to open the minds of a generation of readers to another point of view. She would say understanding comes through conflicting ideas; it is by looking at a question from different points of view that you find an answer.[131]

Yet such a claim can obscure the particular historical conjunction that occurred in the works of many settler Australian writers in the period of the "White Australia" policy, in which "a deep identification with Aboriginality and with the political struggle for Aboriginal rights became the core of a set of fantasies about white Australian ethnicity and the great Australian novel".[132] As Ellen Smith shows in her examination of P.R. Stephensen's writings in the right-wing nationalist magazine the *Publicist* and Xavier Herbert's novel *Capricornia*, a seemingly sympathetic attitude towards Aboriginal Australians could and did coincide with settler nationalist desires and racist attitudes. Dark's so-called celebration of Aboriginal culture in *The Timeless Land* similarly facilitates settler-colonial fantasies of belonging. In particular, the novel is underpinned by the idea that more enlightened white characters will, through the process of "envelopment and absorption", come to belong to the land in a legitimate and indigenous way (164) –

129 Eleanor Dark, "This Land of Ours", in *This Land of Ours: Australia*, eds. George Farwell and Frank H. Johnston (London: Angus & Robertson, 1949), 15.
130 Dark, "This Land of Ours", 15.
131 Barbara Brooks, "Introduction", in Eleanor Dark, *Storm of Time* (Sydney: HarperCollins, [1948] 2013), n.p.
132 Smith, "White Aborigines", 97–98.

a projected harmonious future that operates as a form of facile uplift that detracts from the novel's efforts at empathic unsettlement. While mourning the destruction of Aboriginal culture at the hands of white invaders, *The Timeless Land* points towards a settler future that, Dark hopes, will be informed by Aboriginal culture even as it usurps its position.

However exceptional Dark's inclusion of Aboriginal perspectives might appear for its time, *The Timeless Land* is therefore part of a tradition of settler writing produced in the interwar and mid-century periods that provided seemingly "liberal humanist expressions of white affect toward Aboriginal people" that relied upon the fetishisation and appropriation of Aboriginal culture to assert settler claims of belonging.[133] Although Dark supported a leftist political agenda rather than the proto-fascist one of *The Publicist*, she nonetheless contributed towards an Aboriginalist discourse that represented Aboriginal culture with a combination of fascination and appropriation. Michael Griffiths suggests that the kind of empathetic understanding purportedly shown towards Aboriginal culture by such interwar and mid-century settler writers should not be read as a tribute but as appropriation:

> By imagining appropriation as a tribute to Aboriginality, the melancholic and nostalgic character of this particular form of settler common sense makes fetishism a psychic alibi for theft. Australian settler colonialism, with its literary and cultural nationalisms, is structured around appropriation, exoneration, and replacement. As Jeanine Leane remarks, "[c]ultural appropriation is not empathy. It is stealing someone else's story, someone else's voice."[134]

Griffiths uses the term "settler melancholia" to characterise texts in which "Indigenous disappearance ... is [treated as] a tragedy, but one that renders possible the appropriation of Indigeneity for settler subjects".[135] The key point here is that empathy and lament sit alongside – and in fact *enable* – ideas of replacement and settler indigenisation in these works by settler writers. This point has significant implications for the concept of middlebrow orientalism, which offers a kind of reading that relies upon a liberal form of empathy for and interest in the cultural Other. Proponents of the concept of middlebrow orientalism (and of the historical middlebrow in general) tend to offer positive reappraisals of this form of reading, suggesting that, however flawed in their approach, these texts stimulated mid-century readers' curiosity about and understanding of the non-white Other. On the other hand, critics influenced by settler-colonial studies suggest that the tactics of empathy used by settler writers *only* reinforced and reified the logics of

133 Griffiths, *Distribution of Settlement*, 4.
134 Griffiths, *Distribution of Settlement*, 9.
135 Griffiths, *Distribution of Settlement*, 4.

settler colonialism – a point which some Australian literary critics have rejected as too deterministic.[136]

Often, Dark's modernist aesthetics and middlebrow Aboriginalism did help to reinforce settler desires for cultural legitimacy, as when her experimental approach to time facilitated the depiction of Aboriginal people as outside of time and thus supported ideas of primitivism and the denial of Aboriginal land rights in the present. At other times, however, this aesthetics allowed Dark to challenge some of the ideas that underpinned the modern settler nation, and achieve a form of empathic unsettlement, even if only in brief and provisional ways. In an extraordinary passage in the second instalment of the historical trilogy, *Storm of Time*, Governor King imagines the first decades of British presence in Australia put into reverse. For a moment, he envisions:

> a whole, frightening sequence of logic which set the events of seventeen years into reverse, dissolved towns and houses and roads and cultivated fields into mist, and erased the white man like a figure from a slate. It showed him for one mad moment the flood running backward, sucking the invaders into this little cove again, and on to a fleet of ghostly ships that silently, with no wind behind them, receded down the shining harbour, out the Heads, beyond the horizon, leaving this ancient and inscrutable land ...[137]

This passage demonstrates what Paul Giles terms as Dark's "recursive style" – an aesthetics that frequently depicts the passage of time running from present to past – which Giles counts as one of several instances of such reversals in modernist culture.[138] King's vision of time in reverse works here to suggest the contingency and precarity of the settler-colonial project. Similarly in *The Timeless Land*, the sense of arrested time in Australia makes Phillip question the reality of Western achievement and even his own existence:

> This ship upon which one stood, its achievement, its workmanship, the many ingenious devices by which the ocean had been conquered – why did they suddenly seem less than nothing, so that for a nightmarish second one wondered if one had dreamed them – if one had dreamed oneself – if there were, indeed, any such place as England, any such man as Arthur Phillip, any such creed and code as those by which one had lived faithfully for nearly fifty years? (54)

In this example, Dark's experimental approach towards temporality provides a striking image of the subjective nature of Western notions of modern progress.

---

136 See Tim Rowse, "Indigenous Heterogeneity", *Australian Historical Studies* 45, no. 3 (2014): 297–310.
137 Eleanor Dark, *Storm of Time* (Sydney: Collins, 1948), 342–43.
138 See the chapter on Eleanor Dark in Giles, *Backgazing*, 199–232.

In this study of Dark's interwar fiction, I have generally tried to champion Dark's middlebrow commitments due to a desire to move away from the privileging of aesthetic difficulty and modernist novelty that frequently operates within literary studies, towards a more inclusive approach that values the contributions of women who were often linked with the middlebrow, and to take seriously the pleasure that readers continue to find in middlebrow texts. As an educator, I share some of Dark's ethical commitments to education, accessibility and affect. Perhaps this is why I find myself drawn to the argument that middlebrow forms of readerly empathy – however limited and implicated in settler-colonial desires – might constitute a meaningful form of intercultural understanding. Yet I am also challenged by the idea that celebrating Dark's attempts at empathic unsettlement as forms of tribute to Indigenous culture – even very flawed forms of tribute – risks perpetuating the very ideas of liberal whiteness in which *The Timeless Land* at times unquestioningly participates. Furthermore, it fails to recognise the historical conjunction between settler melancholia, primitivism and tactics of elimination that existed within settler-colonial texts at this time, as well as the ongoing legacy of white liberalism that continues to shape twenty-first-century settler writing. Empathy is not enough to navigate out of settler colonialism, especially when that empathy is expressed through cultural appropriation and other forms of facile uplift. Equally, modernist experimentation, while enabling new ways of depicting subjectivity, culture and history, also frequently worked to reinforce settler colonialism. Dark herself wrote, through the imagined perspective of Bennilong: "a man, looking into the eyes of another man, sees himself therein" (113). In my case, *The Timeless Land* reflects back to me my own, often unconscious investment in ideas of liberal whiteness and education, and invites me to ask difficult questions about the limitations of both empathy and literary modernism in settler writing.

Conclusion: News from Australia

In 1946, the recent winner of the Pulitzer Prize for Poetry and the newly appointed Poet Laureate, Karl Shapiro, sent Eleanor Dark a copy of a poem titled "News to Australia", which was subsequently published in America's *The New Republic* and Australia's *Meanjin*.[1] The poem was dedicated to Eleanor and Eric Dark, whom Shapiro had met in 1942 when he visited their home while serving at an army hospital in the Blue Mountains. The three formed a firm friendship and continued to correspond when Shapiro was stationed at a mobile field hospital in New Guinea. In "News to Australia", Shapiro writes from America, "I do not wish you were here", as "Australia may be better, / The farther the better".[2] In a backhanded compliment, the final stanza of the poem praises Australia's cultural isolation at a time of international crisis:

> I pray that Australia remain at the periphery
> Of the Western Problem, learn to diminish pace,
> Receive our events through bad communications,
> Misunderstand us, learn from us less.
> Where the signs of heaven and earth are reversed
> And the seasons opposite to English literature,
> Different from the mouthings of many poets,
> The fauna the property of another era,
> The natives with the longest memory of time;
> May distance forbid the tourist, the salesman,
> The screaming comedian, the book of the week,
> The shine of accessories that rusts the man ...
> Befriend your insularity, be far,
> Hug the antipodes, survive.[3]

---

1   Karl Shapiro to Eleanor Dark, 24 May 1946, Eleanor Dark Papers, National Library of Australia, MS 4998, Binder 3.
2   Karl Shapiro, "News to Australia", *The New Republic*, 3 June 1946, 808.

Shapiro provides a striking example of what Paul Giles refers to as "the trope of inversion": an image of the global South as a world in reverse, used by a number of American writers to represent Australia.[4] Shapiro frames Australia's "distance" and "insularity" as strategic virtues, expressing hope that this will protect it from what he sees as the symbols of invasive American cultural mediocrity: the tourist, the salesman, the comedian and "the book of the week".

Despite the fact that Shapiro's poem reinforces a diffusionist paradigm of modernity – a set of spatial and temporal relations that place Australia at the world's periphery and Europe and America at its centre – "News to Australia" is in fact the product of a profound moment of multi-directional cultural exchange. Shapiro's description of Australia as a place where the "natives" have "the longest memory of time" is surely a reference to Eleanor Dark's *The Timeless Land* (1941), which he read and praised in the letters that he wrote to the Darks from New Guinea, describing it to Eric as "my favourite Australian book", and telling Eleanor that it "had left a wonderful flavor with me".[5] By the time "News to Australia" was published, *The Timeless Land* had already been selected for the Book-of-the-Month Club in America, an institution which significantly shaped mainstream, middlebrow book culture in America in the mid-century period, and which brought Dark the highest sales of her career. Australia was far from a peripheral influence on Shapiro's work, either. One of his wartime poetry collections was published in Melbourne, and he recalled assembling another in the living room of Varuna, the Darks' home in Katoomba.[6] His Pulitzer-winning collection, *V-Letter and Other Poems* (1944), contained titles such as "Hill at Parramatta", "Sydney Bridge" and "Christmas Eve: Australia".[7] This cultural influence worked in the other direction as well: in *The Little Company* (1945), Dark included a dashing American G.I. character that was probably based on Shapiro.[8]

As these instances of mutual influence suggest, the cultural exchange between Dark and Shapiro operated in both directions: his "News to Australia" was therefore also constituted by news *from* Australia, mediated through the traffic of letters to and from Australia and the Asia-Pacific at a time when Australia's prime minister, John Curtin, famously declared Australia's new connection to America and its freedom from "any pangs as to our traditional links or kinship with the United

---

3   Shapiro, "News", 809.
4   Paul Giles, *Antipodean America: Australasia and the Constitution of U.S. Literature* (New York: Oxford University Press, 2014), 26. For Giles' examination of Karl Shapiro's Australian connection, and its effect on his engagement with American culture, see Chapter 5, "Pacific Theaters: The Poetry of Violence, from World War II to Vietnam", 366–409.
5   Karl Shapiro to Eric Dark, 15 November 1943; Karl Shapiro to Eleanor Dark, 7 June 1943. These letters are from the Eleanor Dark Collection, Varuna, the National Writers' House.
6   Karl Shapiro to Eleanor Dark, 1 August 1944, Eleanor Dark Collection, Varuna, the National Writers' House. *The Place of Love* was published in Melbourne in 1942.
7   See Karl Shapiro, *V-Letter and Other Poems* (New York: Reynal & Hitchcock, 1944).
8   Barbara Brooks with Judith Clark, *Eleanor Dark: A Writer's Life* (Sydney: Pan Macmillan, 1998), 257.

Kingdom".[9] America and Australia were "bound together in ... circuitous geographic ways", not only in the mid-century period but long before, so that Shapiro's poem demonstrates how antipodal images of Australia as upside down and a step behind functioned as "an imaginary rather than a historical conception, one dependent more upon a mystique of the land than on any social realities associated with it".[10] Once we look at Dark's cultural output from the point of view of a transnational paradigm, we see that it was not constituted, after all, by Shapiro's terms of "distance", "insularity" and "periphery", but by forms of contact, mobility and exchange. Some of these mobilities were caused by necessity rather than choice, such as the fact that Australian writers had to rely on overseas publishers for local visibility. Yet they also often acted as enabling rather than *only* constraining factors, connecting Dark and other Australian writers to wider reading markets. Dark's interwar fiction thus participated in the multi-directional transmission of modernist aesthetics, liberal humanist ideas and middlebrow modes of reading and writing, as they circulated around Australia and the world.

As this study has shown, in her interwar fiction Dark engaged with great confidence with both national and international forms of culture. Her belief in the strength of Australian writers and artists is demonstrated in *Waterway* (1938), in which she satirises a Eurocentric perspective of Australia as always behind or far away from the modern centre. In a humorous scene in the Art Gallery of New South Wales, the artist Lois Denning is confronted by an ingratiating local critic who expresses the belief that Australia does not provide the right cultural environment for great art:

"But here ..." she had swept a hand, incredibly disdainful, round the room "... in this *small* community, so *far* from the influences which worked together to create, for instance, Van Gogh, Picasso ... so *far* ..."

Lois interrupted crossly:

"That's silly. There are influences everywhere."

The young woman had pounced.

"Ah! That is just it, that is *exactly* it! You have put your finger on the heart of the trouble ... it is that influence which is ruining art ... I speak widely to include all the arts ... in this country! One cannot ... one *cannot* ... escape the influence of one's environment!"

Lois had asked, with a flicker of interest:

"Why should one?"

"Why ...? But, my dear Mrs Marshall, an environment that stifles ..."

Lois said, hiding a yawn:

"Well, Van Gogh had an environment, too, I suppose. He seemed to survive it."

---

9   John Curtin, "The Task Ahead", *The Herald* (Melbourne), 27 December 1941, 10.

10   Giles, *Antipodean*, 6, 24.

"Ah, but what a *different* environment! … [Australia] is lacking in all those graces and traditions which belong to culture … it is … inimical to art."

Lois, who used up all her patience on her work, had said wearily but distinctly: "Oh, bosh!"

The young woman baulked, offended; then, clutching at some impression that to be offended was bourgeois, un-Bohemian and inartistic, she had mustered an unconvincing laugh, and asked:

"Can you account, then, for the *small* amount of first-class artistic work we have produced? Can you tell me why, as a nation, we are artistically negligible? Can you explain why this country is culturally a desert? …"

Lois, her natural politeness totally exhausted, had suggested:

"Could it be, do you think, because there are too many people like you in it?"[11]

The parallel made here, between Lois' painting, produced in Watsons Bay, and the work of Pablo Picasso and Vincent Van Gogh, produced in the literary capital of Paris (what Pascale Casanova describes as the "Greenwich Meridian" of world literary space), is a bold one for the period.[12] It asserts Dark's confidence in the ability of Australian artists to produce works of genius equal to and contemporaneous with the avant-garde styles produced in more metropolitan contexts like Paris, London and New York. In contrast to the view that Australia has an "environment that stifles" and is "so *far*" from the influences that shaped Van Gogh and Picasso, Dark suggests that Australia had precisely the kind of vitality that would produce, over time, "the true environment of all great art".[13] In this way, Dark appears to anticipate a polycentric model of cultural production, such as that of Susan Stanford Friedman, wherein "[m]ultiple modernities" produce "multiple modernisms", from all directions.[14]

Furthermore, Dark's hopes for a vibrant, productive and modern Australian culture capable of rivalling that of Paris and London are framed in this scene in middlebrow terms. In contrast to the critic who accosts Lois, speaking in an affected manner and hoping to express a progressive attitude, Lois hides behind the large hat that she wears to the art gallery, and speaks in common sense terms that are dismissive of highbrow aesthetic pretension. Lois' interlocutor expresses a form of cultural cringe; Dark was highly impatient with the view, articulated by such figures as G.H. Cowling, that Australia lacked tradition and culture, instead asserting that "Australia is as interesting, no more and no less, as any other country to write about".[15] Dark also positions herself here against "ultra-modernism": the

---

11   Eleanor Dark, *Waterway* (North Ryde, NSW: Angus & Robertson, [1938] 1990), 276–78. All subsequent references are to this edition and appear in parentheses in the text.
12   Pascale Casanova, *The World Republic of Letters*, trans. M.B. DeBevoise (Cambridge, MA; London: Harvard University Press, 2004), 109.
13   Eleanor Dark, *Sun Across the Sky* (London: Collins, [1937] 1946), 29–30.
14   Susan Stanford Friedman, "Periodizing Modernism: Postcolonial Modernities and the Space/Time Borders of Modernist Studies", *Modernism/modernity* 13, no. 3 (2006): 427.

fashionable "Bohemian" values of the woman speaking to Lois. This ultra-modernism was in many ways a bogeyman that functioned to allow Dark (and other commentators of the day) to position her own views as those of a sensible middle ground. Dark wanted her vision of a liberal Australian artistic culture to be generalist and inclusive, rather than specialist and highbrow, and she sought to mediate between mass commercial culture on the one hand, and the elitism of both ultra-modernism and anglophile cultural conservatism on the other. She believed that "[g]enius … does not need circles or self-conscious intelligentsia" but rather "asks only to feel the thrusting urge of growth about it – a clamour and a flood of life" (116). If this was the case, then Australia was well equipped to provide exactly the right climate for artistic greatness.

Yet despite the confidence that Dark expressed in her interwar writing, a tension also appears between her enthusiastic embrace of international modernity, and a leftist and place-based awareness of the inherent unevenness of the modern world. The beginnings of this ambivalence can be seen in Dark's 1920s periodical writing, in which she expressed enthusiasm about some aspects of technological modernity and gender reform, while moderating other elements of these social changes. Although she celebrated the new role of the technical expert in *Slow Dawning* (1932), in *Prelude to Christopher* (1934) Dark explored the threats posed to individual freedom by the values of scientific efficiency and instrumentalism. In *Return to Coolami* (1936), she drew significantly on elements of commercial culture such as popular cinema and motor travel; however, in *Sun Across the Sky* (1937) and *Waterway* Dark warned against some of the dangers of mass culture. Dark's experience as a woman also made her sensitive to the ways in which mid-century modernity involved destructive elements that she associated with masculinity, including mass war and damage inflicted on the natural environment. Her anti-imperialist settler nationalism meant that she was aware of Australia's close but asymmetrical relationships to both Britain and America – an awareness that was confirmed by her dealings with overseas literary agents and publishers. Dark's distinctive style of middlebrow modernism can therefore be read as an aesthetic expression of settler-colonial modernity's relational but also asymmetrical involvement in international literary space, as it involved a negotiation with various forms of power, authority and opportunity.

This push and pull in Dark's work, between the allure of international modernity and an awareness of its uneven structures and temporalities, seems to anticipate contemporary theoretical debates between the optimism of a transnational paradigm, which emphasises circulation, diffusion and multi-directional forms of cultural contact, and the world-systems theories of such critics as Immanuel Wallerstein and Franco Moretti, which suggest that cultural production involves a profoundly unequal and discriminatory set of relations.[16]

---

15   Eleanor Dark, quoted in Jean Devanny, *Bird of Paradise* (Sydney: Frank Johnson, 1945), 251.

While a circulation model captures some elements of Dark's engagement with modernity, such as the travel of material products and cultural ideas along international routes of exchange, it does not fit well with the constraints that she faced in producing a middlebrow modernist style that would satisfy publishers and critics in Australia, London and New York. Nor does it completely fit with the suspicions of international modernity that Dark came to express by the end of the interwar period. Again, a middle position somewhere between these two paradigms, rather than an either/or approach, seems most apt for a writer who strongly resisted dualisms.

Dark offered her own, localised metaphors which capture the complex interplay of the relational and uneven qualities of mid-century modernity, including those of the Great Western Highway and Sydney Harbour. In *Return to Coolami* and *Waterway*, the highway and the harbour are invested with chronotopic significance, as Dark fuses the temporal scales of precolonial, colonial and contemporary history in important sites of Australian modernity. Reflecting the enthusiasm for frictionless forms of speed and mobility in the interwar years, Dark describes both the harbour and the highway as linked with "glamour and romance" (*Waterway*, 37).[17] Yet both of these sites are transformed into places of conflict and friction, as a near-fatal car accident punctures the enthusiasm for speed in the earlier novel, and a catastrophic collision between a local and an international vessel transforms the harbour from a benign playground to "a menace, a terror, death waiting" by the end of *Waterway*, registering fears about Australia's vulnerability at a time of impending global crisis (311).

The ferry crash in *Waterway* marks a transition in Dark's writing, from a more optimistic and utopian vision of interwar modernity to a growing awareness of its uneven structures and political crises. Dark extended her critique of Western capitalist modernity in the fiction she published during the Second World War. In *The Timeless Land* (1941) she pits the values of late eighteenth-century Western culture – "the law of personal power and personal possessions" – against the communal ones of her version of Aboriginal culture.[18] In this novel the harbour operates as the site of significant colonial violence against Aboriginal peoples and convicts. In *The Little Company*, Dark went on to depict Sydney Harbour as witness to ominous contemporary global conflicts in the form of the historic Japanese submarine attack. In this novel, Dark critiques both reactionary nationalism and left-wing programmatic politics, including communism, although she continues to identify with a socialist form of humanism. As discussed in Chapter 5, *The Little Company* also reveals Dark's ongoing investment in aesthetic solutions, although it

16 See Immanuel Wallerstein, *The Modern World-System* (New York: Academic Press, 1974); Franco Moretti, *Modern Epic: The World-System from Goethe to García Márquez* (London; New York: Verso, 1996).

17 Eleanor Dark, *Return to Coolami* (London: Collins, 1936), 205.

18 Eleanor Dark, *The Timeless Land* (London: Collins, [1941] 1946), 299. All subsequent references are to this edition and appear in parentheses in the text.

registers the increasing pressures of the Second World War period on the figure of the artist.

Dark's fears about Western modernity would only deepen in the postwar period, so that her novels of the late 1940s and 1950s represent a sustained questioning of mid-century narratives of progress. In the second and third instalments of the *Timeless Land* trilogy, released in 1948 and 1953 respectively, Sydney Harbour features as an increasingly ambivalent site: while it connects the early colony to liberating democratic ideas from Europe, it also transports international goods such as rum, which are exploited by the capitalist classes. *Storm of Time* is biting in its criticisms of the ruling classes' "lust for wealth and power".[19] Nonetheless, the novel affirms the hope, articulated by Conor Mannion, that "in so new and large a land there should surely be decent subsistence for all, and even ... freedom for all" (259). The characters quote from Thomas Paine's *Common Sense* (1775–76) and *The Rights of Man* (1791), hoping for an Australia that will *"receive the fugitive, and prepare in time an asylum for mankind"* (405). In the final instalment of the trilogy, *No Barrier*, the highway over the Blue Mountains that figured as such a positive symbol of speed and progress in *Return to Coolami* is used to represent the corrupt values of the ruling classes. By the novel's conclusion, a small group of outsiders seeks their freedom in an alternate community that will, they hope, fulfil Paine's vision of an "asylum" capable of welcoming the "fugitive".[20] The increasingly critical tone of these two novels reflects Dark's growing belief that the progressive, humanist community she had envisioned during the interwar years had failed to materialise in the postwar years.[21]

In *Lantana Lane* (1959), Dark moves away from the site of Sydney altogether, writing about a small-scale farming community modelled on the town of Montville in South East Queensland's Sunshine Coast hinterland, where she and Eric lived between 1951 and 1957. Whereas in *Return to Coolami*, speed and mobility are treated with some enthusiasm, in *Lantana Lane* the small-scale farmers associate it with a lack of neighbourliness. The Lane-dwellers fear that the proposed building of a highway through their rural farming community will make the Lane "so wide, so smoothly surfaced, that in our own comings and goings we shall be travelling too fast to call a greeting, or even wave a hand".[22] *Lantana Lane* suggests that peripheral locations are in danger of being amalgamated into the larger whole in an "era of expansion", in which "[c]ommerce and industry extend their operations,

---

19 Eleanor Dark, *Storm of Time* (Sydney: Collins, 1948), 590. All subsequent references are to this edition and appear in parentheses in the text.
20 Eleanor Dark, *No Barrier* (London: Collins, 1953), 383.
21 Dark's left-leaning politics came under scrutiny at this time. She was denounced as a supporter of the Communist Party in Parliament in 1947, despite the fact that she had never belonged to any political party. See Susan Carson, "Surveillance and Slander: Eleanor Dark in the 1940s and 1950s", *Hecate* 27, no. 1 (2001): 32–43.
22 Eleanor Dark, *Lantana Lane* (London: Collins, 1959), 253. All subsequent references are to this edition and appear in parentheses in the text.

organisations multiply, and science reaches into outer space" (140). The novel is particularly concerned about the fate of "little nations" that struggle to emerge from the "benevolent shelter" of "the big nations" (81).

Although Shapiro's terms of "periphery", "isolation" and "distance" do not capture the truly international quality of Dark's interwar writing, then, they do anticipate her postwar, strategic hopes that the small-scale and the peripheral – including the ethical realm of the face-to-face, the "little company" of freedom-seekers and a "little nation" such as Australia – might be shielded and allowed to survive in an era threatened by global catastrophe. Increasingly, as the interwar period turned into the postwar era, Dark's writing attempted to carve out a space for those elements of modernity that she saw as being endangered by aggressive modernity: the less powerful nation, the local, the small-scale community, the individual and a style of reading that enables one to empathise with an alternative self. In a similar way, this study has aimed to carve out a space for the elements that have often been framed as outside of the purview of modernism and modernity, including regionalism, the middlebrow, popular culture, the settler-colonial nation and liberal humanism. In a twenty-first-century academic context, in which theoretical approaches such as the new modernist and world literature studies frame their effect as one of "expansion",[23] it is important that these distinctive engagements with modernity are not subsumed into the larger categories of either avant-garde modernism or the global scale. Dark's work can play an important role in illuminating these elements and revealing the diversity of cultural responses to mid-century modernity.

In particular, this study has sought to emphasise the middlebrow elements of Dark's interwar modernism. The new modernist studies might suggest that Dark's middlebrow modernism is simply part of her "engagement with the historical conditions of modernity in a particular location", and hence should be called simply modernism.[24] Yet this kind of expansion can impede us from recognising different and distinctive responses to modernity by obscuring the category of the middlebrow altogether. As Nicola Humble observes, the recent "preoccupation" with modernism in literary studies can have a "distorting effect", minimising "all sorts of interesting aesthetic experiments going on in these [middlebrow] texts, and not necessarily in the way they trespass on modernist territory".[25] While Dark's modernism is important, "a multiplicity of cultural agendas" existed in the first half of the twentieth century, "not all of which positioned artists and intellectuals comfortably in allegiance with difficulty, highbrow culture, and the academy".[26] Just

---

23 Douglas Mao and Rebecca L. Walkowitz use this term to capture the impact of the new modernist studies, in "The New Modernist Studies", *PMLA* 123, no. 3 (2008): 737.
24 Friedman, "Periodizing Modernism", 432.
25 Humble in Elke D'hoker and Nicola Humble, "Theorizing the Middlebrow: An Interview with Nicola Humble", *Interférences littéraires/Literaire interferenties* 7 (2011): 262–63.
26 Ann L. Ardis, "The Dialogics of Modernism(s) in the *New Age*", *Modernism/modernity* 14, no. 3 (2007): 427.

as we need to retain a focus on the category of the nation, even as we examine its imbrication in international space, it is important to recognise the ways in which mid-century writers had to negotiate a highly stratified cultural field which was divided – often in unstable and changing ways – into lowbrow, middlebrow and elite forms of culture.

I have argued that Dark's interwar fiction provides an important case for Australian literary studies, but also for the broader, more powerful disciplinary fields of global modernist and world literature studies. In the Australian context, it troubles the distinction between nationalist realism and experimental modernism and adds to the growing body of work that suggests the entanglements between these modes. It also shifts attention to the realm of the middlebrow as a crucial site where Australian literary modernism emerged in the years between the wars. In Dark's work, the modernist was not always elite, masculine and cosmopolitan, but often accessible, feminine and entangled with national commitments; at the same time, cultural nationalism was not always realist but often converged with modernist styles. It is tempting to view Dark's aesthetic of middlebrow modernism as a completely distinct category between, on the one hand, the cosmopolitan, high modernism of Christina Stead and Patrick White and, on the other, the nationalism and realism of Miles Franklin, Katharine Susannah Prichard and Vance Palmer; yet to do so would risk reifying the very distinctions and categorisations that Dark's work calls into question. Instead, the position of her work betwixt and between these styles and commitments offers not so much a new and distinct category, but rather points to the porousness and connections between the modernist, middlebrow and nationalist in the Australian situation. In this way, it helps us to think outside of the categories that have traditionally structured accounts of twentieth-century Australian literature, and to notice the interconnections between them.

More broadly, Dark's regional cosmopolitanism suggests that writers who engaged with cosmopolitan, world issues could also show deep commitments to the national and local scales. In these ways, her writing challenges binary approaches which pit local attachments against worldly ones, instead suggesting a more flexible and dialectical form of cosmopolitanism: a regional cosmopolitanism. At the same time, however, Dark's work draws attention to the difficulty of translating modernist regional cosmopolitanism into a practical politics. Critics who advocate a form of cosmopolitanism based on modernist textual practices, such as Rebecca Walkowitz, may be too quick to assume that an aesthetic and ethical position can materialise into a political one – a tendency that reflects the larger aspiration of literary criticism of the late twentieth century and early twenty-first centuries to conflate aesthetic representation with political representation.[27] As the title of her

---

27   Rebecca L. Walkowitz, *Cosmopolitan Style: Modernism Beyond the Nation* (New York: Columbia University Press, 2006). On this tendency, see John Guillory, *Cultural Capital: The Problem of Literary Canon Formation* (Chicago: University of Chicago Press, 2013), 3–82.

study suggests, Walkowitz assumes in *Cosmopolitan Style: Modernism Beyond the Nation* (2006) that a dialectical and critical form of cosmopolitanism will entail a move away from the nation – a point that may be true for Joseph Conrad, James Joyce and Virginia Woolf, the British modernist writers she examines, but appears less applicable to the settler modernisms produced in semi-peripheral locations such as Australia. In this sense, the concepts produced in the metropolitan centres of literary studies, such as regional cosmopolitanism, can be modified and made more nuanced by coming into contact with the complexities of a settler-colonial situation.

One of the questions that this study has raised is the extent to which aesthetic interventions – whether modernist or middlebrow – can offer political solutions. As the 1930s progressed, Dark increasingly embraced aesthetic utopianism: instead of structural solutions, she offered (in characteristically modernist style) the figure of the artist, and an aesthetics based on experimentation, playfulness and spatial and temporal complexity – styles and ideas that she mediated for middlebrow tastes. Her interwar middlebrow modernist writing certainly had ethical implications: it offered invitations to the reader to inhabit alternative selves and develop empathy for the marginalised Other; it provided complex ways of thinking about the relationships between the local, national and global scales; and it brought the precolonial and colonial layers of the past to the surface of the modern present. And yet because Dark's interwar writing not only lacked a coherent political basis that could move her critique beyond liberal individualism, but also rejected the need for one, it struggled to bridge the gap between ethics and politics, and to address the racial and class-based inequalities that structure settler society. Of the works discussed in this study, *The Timeless Land* perhaps comes closest to acknowledging that Western capitalist modernity needed to be replaced by an entirely different system – as Dark's Arthur Phillip puts it, by "some means ... whereby hunger should be made unknown" (414). Although Dark is wary of extrapolating the full nature of such a system, she links it with Aboriginal culture in terms of a respect for "the land" and a belief that "no man had a stronger claim than his neighbour upon what it offered in the way of subsistence" (330). Paradoxically, in linking the future of settler culture to an Indigenous past that she frames as irrevocably lost, Dark's novel suggests both the desire of settler culture to claim a form of Indigeneity, and the impossibility of doing so.

The difficulty of using aesthetic means to resolve social and political issues is one that we would do well to acknowledge in our own context. The new area of modernist studies frequently emphasises the political implications of modernist textual interventions: according to two of the key proponents of this field, Douglas Mao and Walkowitz, the aesthetic and formal complexity of modernist textual practices offers important antidotes to twenty-first-century neo-conservatism, giving modernism a "special allure" in a period of crisis when "the future of thinking seems uncertain ... anti-intellectualism seems ascendant ... [and there is] resistance to all but the simplest positions and solutions".[28] Marxist critics such as Max Brzezinski, however, argue that in their attempts to connect the aesthetic to the political, new modernist critics frequently rely upon the "fuzzy advocacy of the freedom found in humanism, internationalism, cosmopolitanism, antistatism, and doctrinaire antinationalism", so that their work can be linked to neoliberalism and free market economics, even as they try to position themselves against such forces.[29] Brzezinski cautions that, in "these new imperial times, dominated by corporate-led globalization and transnational warfare, the simple satisfactions of individual freedom of thought, no matter how modernist the style, are dramatically insufficient, both theoretically and politically".[30] As John Guillory notes, literary criticism is located within the academy – the product of "the institutional forms of syllabus and curriculum" – and as such is itself embedded in and determined by the very state forces that it often tries to repudiate through textual analysis.[31] There is a significant connection, then, between Dark's aesthetic utopianism and that of contemporary literary studies: both are underpinned by the belief that individual cultural expressions play an important role in a period of crisis, emphasising "personal mode[s] of protest against modernization".[32] In recuperating Dark's middlebrow modernist writing, it is important that we not overstate the political implications of her aesthetic utopianism, but rather recognise her struggle to relate the individual and the aesthetic to the social and the political – a struggle that we must continue to wrestle with in and for our own times and institutional locations.

The intersections that Dark's writing reveals – between regionalism and cosmopolitanism, nationalism and modernism, modernity and settler colonialism, commercial and high expressions of culture, and liberal humanism and experimental aesthetics – are not unique to her work or exclusive to settler contexts. Instead, these examples of modernity's constitutive relations can be observed to varying degrees in other instances, such as the modernist liberal humanist novels of E.M. Forster, or the high middlebrow writing of Rebecca West. Yet because of Dark's staunch commitment to the middlebrow tactics of negotiating, calibrating and balancing between extremes, and her geographical and cultural position in a semi-peripheral location, these relationships are revealed quite clearly in her work – perhaps more so than in other metropolitan examples. My examination of Dark's interwar writing therefore demonstrates how Australian literary studies can have a "provincialising" or "disciplining" effect on studies of European or metropolitan modernisms, by hinting at relationships that are more obscured in these locales.[33] For instance, the ways in which this study brings settler colonialism to the forefront

---

28   Douglas Mao and Rebecca L. Walkowitz, "Introduction: Modernisms Bad and New", in *Bad Modernisms*, eds. Douglas Mao and Rebecca L. Walkowitz (Durham, NC: Duke University Press, 2006), 16.

29   Max Brzezinski, "The New Modernist Studies: What's Left of Political Formalism?", *The Minnesota Review*, no. 76 (2011): 123.

30   Brzezinski, "New Modernist", 124.

31   Guillory, *Cultural Capital*, vii.

32   Brzezinski, "New Modernist", 122.

of Dark's engagement with both modernism and the middlebrow can help to point to the significance of settler colonialism in the American situation, where, as Paul Giles argues, it has often been overlooked because "colonialism's dystopian emphasis on embedded power relations tends to run counter to a utopian rhetoric of agency and renewal that has traditionally driven the cognate fields of American literature and American studies".[34] The Australian situation, then, with its *perceived* sense of isolation and distance from metropolitan contexts, can provide critical distance from the terms of reference often used to understand concepts such as modernism and modernity. The distance that Dark's work provides is that of the middle distance of the settler Australian situation: positioned ambiguously between the coloniser and the colonised; connected to imperial and transpacific routes of exchange and yet occupying an unequal position within them; interested in global views yet unable and unwilling to abandon the pull of more localised sites of belonging; constrained by and contributing to the discriminatory power relations of a world system; promiscuously borrowing from low, middlebrow and high expressions of culture; and threaded into an international modernity that is both surprisingly relational and profoundly uneven.

---

33 Robert Dixon and Brigid Rooney, "Introduction: Australian Literature, Globalisation and the Literary Province", in *Scenes of Reading: Is Australian Literature a World Literature?*, eds. Robert Dixon and Brigid Rooney (North Melbourne: Australian Scholarly, 2013), xxii–xxiii.
34 Giles, *Antipodean*, 11.

Works Cited

This study refers to a wide range of book reviews and articles published in Australian, English and American newspapers and magazines. Most of these have been sourced from the albums of press clippings in the Eleanor Dark Papers, held at the Mitchell Library, State Library of New South Wales. Individual articles and reviews have not been listed in the bibliography, although details can be found in the main text and notes. Similarly, individual letters to and from Eleanor Dark have not been listed, although details of these can also be found in the main text and notes. Letters to and from Dark have been drawn from the Eleanor Dark Papers at the Mitchell Library; the Eleanor Dark Collection at Varuna, the National Writers' House; and the Eleanor Dark Papers at the National Library of Australia.

The individual short stories written by Dark and cited in this study are listed in the works cited. For consistency, these have been listed under the name of Eleanor Dark, with the pseudonym under which they were published provided in brackets (where applicable). For full lists of Dark's published works, see the appendices in the biographies written by Barbara Brooks with Judith Clark, and Marivic Wyndham, respectively.

Aborigines Progressive Association, J. T. Patten and W. Ferguson. "Aborigines Claim Citizen Rights!: A Statement of the Case for the Aborigines Progressive Association." *Publicist*, 1938. https://trove.nla.gov.au/work/26332375.

Ailwood, Sarah. "Anxious Beginnings: Mental Illness, Reproduction and Nation Building in 'Prelude' and *Prelude to Christopher*." *Katherine Mansfield Studies* 2 (2010): 20–38.

Alexander, Neal, and James Moran. "Introduction: Regional Modernisms." In *Regional Modernisms*, 1–21. Edinburgh: Edinburgh University Press, 2013.

Allison, Mark. "Utopian Socialism, Women's Emancipation, and the Origins of *Middlemarch*." *ELH* 78, no. 3 (2011): 715–39.

Anderson, Amanda. "Liberal Aesthetic." In *Theory after "Theory,"* edited by Jane Elliott and Derek Attridge, 249–62. New York: Routledge, 2011.

Anderson, Benedict. *Imagined Communities: Reflections on the Origin and Spread of Nationalism*. Rev. edn. London; New York: Verso, 1991.

Anderson, Francis. "Liberalism and Socialism." Address as President of Section G of the Australian Association for the Advancement of Science, 1922, 1–10. https://trove.nla.gov.au/work/16455397?q&versionId=19314545.

Appiah, Kwame Anthony. *Cosmopolitanism: Ethics in a World of Strangers*. New York: W.W. Norton, 2006.

–––. "Cosmopolitan Patriots." *Critical Inquiry* 23, no. 3 (1997): 617–39.

Apter, Emily. "Saidian Humanism." *Boundary 2* 31, no. 2 (2004): 35–53.

Ardis, Ann L. *Modernism and Cultural Conflict, 1880–1922* (Cambridge, UK; New York: Cambridge University Press, 2002).

–––. "The Dialogics of Modernism(s) in the *New Age*." *Modernism/modernity* 14, no. 3 (2007): 407–34.

Ardis, Ann L., and Patrick Collier. *Transatlantic Print Culture, 1880–1940: Emerging Media, Emerging Modernisms*. New York; Basingstoke: Palgrave Macmillan, 2008.

Armstrong, Paul B. "Two Cheers for Tolerance: E.M. Forster's Ironic Liberalism." *Modernism/modernity* 16, no. 2 (2009): 281–99.

Arnold, Matthew. *Matthew Arnold, Prose Writings: The Critical Heritage*, edited by Carl Dawson and John Pfordresher. London; Boston: Routledge, 1979.

Arthur, Jason. *Violet America: Regional Cosmopolitanism in U.S. Fiction Since the Great Depression*. Iowa City: University of Iowa Press, 2003.

Ashley Montagu, M.F. "Review: *The Timeless Land*." *Oceania* 12, no. 3 (1942): 303–04.

Bakhtin, M.M. *The Dialogic Imagination: Four Essays*, edited by Michael Holquist. Translated by Caryl Emerson and Michael Holquist. Austin: University of Texas Press, 1981.

Barnard, Marjorie. "How *Tomorrow and Tomorrow* Came to be Written." *Meanjin* 29, no. 3 (1970): 328–30.

–––. *The Persimmon Tree and Other Stories*. Sydney: Clarendon Publishing Co., 1943.

Barnard Eldershaw, M. *Essays in Australian Fiction*. Freeport, NY: Books for Libraries Press, [1938] 1970.

–––. *My Australia*. London: Jarrolds Publishers, 1939.

–––. *Tomorrow and Tomorrow and Tomorrow*. London: Virago, [1947] 1983.

Beilharz, Peter. "The Young Evatt – Labor's New Liberal." *Australian Journal of Politics and History* 39, no. 2 (1993): 160–70.

Bell, Pamela. "Art That Never Was: Representations of the Artist in Twentieth-Century Australian Fiction." PhD thesis, University of Sydney, 2003.

Bergson, Henri. *Creative Evolution*. Translated by Arthur Mitchell. New York: H. Holt and Company, [1907] 1911.

–––. *Time and Free Will: An Essay on the Immediate Data of Consciousness*. New York: Dover Publications, [1889] 2012.

Berman, Jessica. "Ethical Folds: Ethics, Aesthetics, Woolf." *MFS: Modern Fiction Studies* 50, no. 1 (2004): 151–72.

–––. "Toward a Regional Cosmopolitanism: The Case of Mulk Raj Anand." *MFS: Modern Fiction Studies* 55, no. 1 (2009): 142–62.

Birns, Nicolas. *Contemporary Australian Literature: A World Not Yet Dead*. Sydney: Sydney University Press, 2015.

Black, Prudence, and Stephen Muecke. "Antipodean Modernisms: Australia and New Zealand." In *The Oxford Handbook of Modernisms*, edited by Peter Brooker, Andrzej Gąsiorek, Deborah Longworth and Andrew Thacker, 961–75. New York: Oxford University Press, 2010.

Bongiorno, Frank. "'Every Woman a Mother': Radical Intellectuals, Sex Reform and the 'Woman Question' in Australia, 1890–1918." *Hecate* 27, no. 1 (2001): 44–64.

Bostock, John, and L.J.J. Nye, *Whither Away: A Study of Race Psychology and the Factors Leading to Australia's National Decline*. Sydney: Angus & Robertson, 1936.

Botshon, Lisa, and Meredith Goldsmith. "Introduction." In *Middlebrow Moderns: Popular American Women Writers of the 1920s*, edited by Lisa Botshon and Meredith Goldsmith, 3–24. Boston, MA: Northeastern University Press, 2003.

Brayshaw, Meg. "Reflectant Tides: The Aqueous Poetics of Sydney in Women's Fiction, 1934–1947." PhD thesis, Western Sydney University, 2018.

———. *Sydney and its Waterway in Australian Literary Modernism*. Sydney: Palgrave Macmillan, 2021.

———. "Trans-Scalar Sydney, Narrative Form and Ethics in Eleanor Dark's *Waterway*." *JASAL: Journal of the Association for the Study of Australian Literature* 17, no. 1 (2017): 1–10.

Brocco, Rosa Maria. *Merchants of Hope: British Middlebrow Writers and the First World War, 1919–1939*. Providence, RI: Berg, 1993.

Brooker, Peter, and Andrew Thacker. "Introduction: Locating the Modern." In *Geographies of Modernism: Literatures, Cultures, Spaces*, edited by Peter Brooker and Andrew Thacker, 1–5. London; New York: Routledge, 2005.

Brooks, Barbara. "Introduction." In Eleanor Dark, *Storm of Time*, n.p. Sydney, NSW: HarperCollins, [1948] 2013.

———. "Rereading *Prelude to Christopher*." In Eleanor Dark, *Prelude to Christopher*, 185–89. Rushcutters Bay, NSW: Halstead Press, [1934] 1999.

———. "*Waterway*: The Multilayered City; History, Economics and Dream." *Hecate* 27, no. 1 (2001): 11–18.

Brooks, Barbara, with Judith Clark. *Eleanor Dark: A Writer's Life*. Sydney: Pan Macmillan, 1998.

Brooks, David. *The Sons of Clovis: Ern Malley, Adoré Floupette and a Secret History of Australian Poetry*. St. Lucia: University of Queensland Press, 2011.

Bruno, Guiliana. *Atlas of Emotion: Journeys in Art, Architecture, and Film*. London; New York: Verso, 2002.

Brzezinski, Max. "The New Modernist Studies: What's Left of Political Formalism?" *The Minnesota Review*, no. 76 (2011): 109–25.

Buckley, Jerome Hamilton. *Season of Youth: The Bildungsroman from Dickens to Golding*. Cambridge, MA: Harvard University Press, 1974.

Buckley, Vincent. *Essays in Poetry, Mainly Australian*. Carlton, Vic: Melbourne University Press, 1957.

———. "Utopianism and Vitalism in Australian Literature." *Quadrant* 3, no. 2 (1959): 39–51.

Buckridge, Patrick. "'Greatness' and Australian Literature in the 1930s and 1940s: Novels by Dark and Barnard Eldershaw." *Australian Literary Studies* 17, no. 1 (1995): 29–37.

Buckridge, Patrick, and Eleanor Morecroft. "Australia's World Literature: Constructing Australia's Global Reading Relations in the Interwar Period." In *Scenes of Reading: Is Australian Literature a World Literature?*, edited by Robert Dixon and Brigid Rooney, 47–59. North Melbourne: Australian Scholarly, 2013.

Burke, Joanna. *Dismembering the Male: Men's Bodies, Britain and the Great War*. Chicago: University of Chicago Press, 1996.

Caputo, John D. "Adieu – sans Dieu: Derrida and Levinas." In *The Face of the Other and the Trace of God: Essays on the Philosophy of Emmanuel Levinas*, edited by Jeffrey Bloechl, 276–311. New York: Fordham University Press, 2000.

Carey, Jane. "'Not Only a White Race, but a Race of the Best Whites': The Women's Movement, White Australia and Eugenics between the Wars." In *Historicising Whiteness: Transnational Perspectives on the Construction of an Identity*, edited by Leigh Boucher, Jane Carey and Katherine Ellinghaus, 162–170. Melbourne: RMIT Publishing in association with the School of Historical Studies, University of Melbourne, 2007.

Carson, Susan. "A Girl's Guide to Modernism's Grammar: Language Politics in Experimental Women's Fiction." *Hecate* 30, no. 1 (2004): 176–83.

. "Conversations with the Land: Environmental Questions and Eleanor Dark." In *Land and Identity: Proceedings of the 1997 Conference University of New England Armidale New South Wales 27-30 September 1997*, edited by Michael Deves and Jennifer A. McDonnell, 191-96. Association for the Study of Australian Literature, 1998.

---. "Finding Hy-Brazil: Eugenics and Modernism in the Pacific." *Hecate* 35, no. 1-2 (2009): 124-133.

---. "From Sydney and Shanghai: Australian and Chinese Women Writing Modernism." In *Pacific Rim Modernisms*, edited by Mary Ann Gillies, Helen Sword and Steven Yao, 173-98. Toronto: University of Toronto Press, 2009.

---. "Making the Modern: The Writing of Eleanor Dark." PhD thesis, University of Queensland, 1999.

---. "Paris and beyond: The Transnational/National in the Writing of Christina Stead and Eleanor Dark." In *Transnational Ties: Australian Lives in the World*, edited by Desley Deacon, Penny Russell and Angela Woollacott, 229-44. Acton, ACT: Australian National University E Press, 2008.

---. "Pathology and Modernity: Medical Discourses and its Fictions." Paper presented to North Eastern Modern Language Association Conference. Boston, USA, February 2009. https://eprints.qut.edu.au/50249/2/50249.pdf.

---. "Seeing a Hard Country: Lawrence's Australian Landscape." Paper based on a presentation to the D.H. Lawrence Society of North America 12th International Conference. Sydney, Australia, 29 June-3 July 2011.

---. "Surveillance and Slander: Eleanor Dark in the 1940s and 1950s." *Hecate* 27, no. 1 (2001): 32-43.

Carter, David. *Always Almost Modern: Australian Print Cultures and Modernity*. North Melbourne: Australian Scholarly, 2013.

---. "Critics, Writers, Intellectuals: Australian Literature and its Criticism." In *The Cambridge Companion to Australian Literature*, edited by Elizabeth Webby, 269-71. Cambridge; Melbourne: Cambridge University Press, 2000.

---. "Literary, but Not Too Literary; Joyous, but Not Jazzy: *Triad* Magazine, Antipodean Modernity and the Middlebrow." *Modernism/modernity* 25, no. 2 (2018): 245-67.

---. "Modernising Anglocentrism: *Desiderata* and Literary Time." In *Republics of Letters: Literary Communities in Australia*, edited by Peter Kirkpatrick and Robert Dixon, 85-98. Sydney: Sydney University Press, 2012.

---. "Modernity and the Gendering of Middlebrow Book Culture in Australia." In *The Masculine Middlebrow, 1880-1950: What Mr. Miniver Read*, edited by Kate Macdonald, 135-49. New York: Palgrave Macmillan, 2011.

---. "'Some Means of Learning of the Best New Books': *All About Books* and the Modern Reader." *Australian Literary Studies* 22, no. 3 (2006): 329-41.

---. "The Mystery of the Missing Middlebrow or The C(o)urse of Good Taste." In *Imagining Australia: Literature and Culture in the New New World*, edited by Judith Ryan and Chris Wallace-Crabbe, 173-201. Cambridge, MA; London: Harvard University Press, 2004.

Carter, David, and Roger Osborne. *Australian Books and Authors in the American Marketplace 1840s-1940s*. Sydney: Sydney University Press, 2018.

Casanova, Pascale. *The World Republic of Letters*. Translated by M.B. DeBevoise. Cambridge, MA; London: Harvard University Press, [1999] 2004.

Chanin, Eileen, Steven Miller and Judith Pugh. *Degenerates and Perverts: The 1939 Herald Exhibition of French and British Contemporary Art*. Carlton, Vic: Miegunyah Press, 2005.

Chowrimootoo, Christopher. *Middlebrow Modernism: Britten's Operas and the Great Divide*. Berkeley, CA: University of California Press, 2018.

Clark, Axel. *Christopher Brennan, A Critical Biography*. Carlton, Vic: Melbourne University Press, 1980.

Cleary, Joe. "Realism after Modernism and the Literary World-System." *Modern Language Quarterly* 73, no. 3 (2012): 255–68.

Clendinnen, Inga. "The History Question: Who Owns the Past?" *Quarterly Essay*, no. 23 (2006): 1–72.

Clifford, James. "Mixed Feelings." In *Cosmopolitics: Thinking and Feeling Beyond the Nation*, edited by Pheng Cheah and Bruce Robbins, 362–70. Minneapolis: University of Minnesota Press, 1998.

———. *Routes: Travel and Translation in the Late Twentieth Century*. Cambridge, MA: Harvard University Press, 1997.

Cockburn, Jon. "Olivetti and the Missing Third: Fashion, Working Women and Images of the Mechanical-flâneuse in the 1920s and 1930s." *Fashion Theory* 19, no. 5 (2015): 637–86.

Cohen, Keith. *Film and Fiction: The Dynamics of Exchange*. New Haven, CT: Yale University Press, 1979.

Connolly, Olga Asal. "The Early Work of Eleanor Dark." PhD thesis, Florida State University, 1995.

Conor, Liz. *The Spectacular Modern Woman: Feminine Visibility in the 1920s*. Bloomington: Indiana University Press, 2004.

Cooper, Melinda J. "'A Masterpiece of Camouflage': Modernism and Interwar Australia." *Modernist Cultures* 15, no. 3 (2020): 316–40.

———. "'Adjusted' Vision: Interwar Settler Modernism in Eleanor Dark's *Return to Coolami*." *Australian Literary Studies* 33, no. 2 (2018): 1–28.

———. "'Being Made into a Machine': An Extract from Eleanor Dark's Unpublished Novel 'Pilgrimage'." *Hecate* 43, no. 1–2 (2017): 95–104.

———. "News from Australia: Global Modernism Studies and the Case of Australian Modernism." In *The Routledge Companion to Australian Literature*, edited by Jessica Gildersleeve, 181–92. New York: Routledge, 2021.

———. "'[W]hen the Highway Catches Up with Us': Negotiating Late Modernity in Eleanor Dark's *Lantana Lane*." *Queensland Review* 23, no. 2 (2016): 207–23.

Cowling, G.H. "The Future of Australian Literature." *Age* (Melbourne), 16 February 1935, 6.

Crombie, Isobel. *Body Culture: Max Dupain, Photography and Australian Culture, 1919–1939*. Melbourne: Images Publishing Group in association with National Gallery of Victoria, 2004.

Curthoys, Ann. "Eugenics, Feminism, and Birth Control: The Case of Marion Piddington." *Hecate* 15, no. 1 (1989): 73–89.

———. "Expulsion, Exodus and Exile in White Australian Historical Mythology." *Journal of Australian Studies* 23, no. 61 (1999): 1–19.

Curtin, John. "The Task Ahead." *The Herald* (Melbourne), 27 December 1941, 10.

Dale, Leigh. *The English Men: Professing Literature in Australian Universities*. Canberra: Association for the Study of Australian Literature, 1997.

Dalziell, Tanya. *Settler Romances and the Australian Girl*. Crawley, WA: University of Western Australia Press, 2004.

Damrosch, David. *What is World Literature?* Princeton, NJ: Princeton University Press, 2003.

Dangerfield, George. *The Strange Death of Liberal England*. New York: Capricorn Books, [1935] 1961.

Darby, Robert. "'An Instinct For Freedom': Political Undercurrents in the Short Fiction of Marjorie Barnard." *Literature and History* 26, no. 1 (2017): 56–73.

Dark, Eleanor. "Australia and the Australians." In *Australia Week-End Book*, 3rd edn, edited by Sydney Ure Smith and Gwen Morton Spencer, 9–19. Sydney: Ure Smith, 1944.

———. [Patricia O'Rane] "Benevolence: The Story of a Hypocrite." *Triad*, 1 July 1926, 4–6.

———. "Caroline Chisholm and Her Times." In *The Peaceful Army: A Memorial to the Pioneer Women of Australia, 1788–1938*, edited by Flora Eldershaw, 59–84. Sydney: Women's Executive Committee and Advisory Council of Australia's 150th Anniversary Celebrations, 1938.

———. Diary, 1936–1939. Eleanor Dark Papers. Mitchell Library, State Library of New South Wales. MLMSS 4545, Box 21.

——— [Patricia O'Rane] "How Uncle Aubrey Went to London." *Bulletin*, 30 May 1928, 57.

---. *Lantana Lane*. London: Collins, 1959.
---. "Murder on the Ninth Green." *Bulletin*, 12 December 1934, 28–30.
---. *No Barrier*. London: Collins, 1953.
---. "Pilgrimage." Unpublished manuscript. Eleanor Dark Collection. Varuna, the National Writers' House.
---. *Prelude to Christopher*. Rushcutters Bay, NSW: Halstead Press, [1934] 1999.
---. *Return to Coolami*. London: Collins, 1936.
---. *Slow Dawning*. London: John Long, 1932.
---. *Storm of Time*. Sydney: Collins, 1948.
---. *Sun Across the Sky*. London: Collins, [1937] 1946.
---. [Patricia O'Rane] "The Book, the Bishop and the Ban." *Bulletin*, 2 July 1925, 47–48.
---. ["Henry Head"] "The Desire of the Moth." *Art in Australia*, no. 10, December 1924, n.p.
---. *The Little Company*. Sydney: Collins, 1945.
---. *The Timeless Land*. London: Collins, [1941] 1946.
---. "This Land of Ours." In *This Land of Ours: Australia*, edited by George Farwell and Frank H. Johnston, 11–15. London: Angus & Robertson, 1949.
---. *Waterway*. Sydney: Angus & Robertson, [1938] 1990.
---. [Patricia O'Rane] "Wheels." *Bulletin*, 12 December 1925, 44.
---. [Patricia O'Rane] "Wind." *Bulletin*, 21 January 1926, 47–48.
Dark, Eric Payten. *Diathermy in General Practice*. Sydney: Angus & Robertson, 1930.
---. *Medicine and the Social Order*. Sydney: E.P. Dark, 1942.
Davidson, Kathleen. "Landscapes and Mindscapes: The Confluence of Modernism and Ecopoetics in Eleanor Dark's *Return to Coolami*." *Philament: A Journal of Literature, Arts, and Culture* 24, no. 2 (2018): 1–31.
Davison, Frank Dalby. *While Freedom Lives*. Sydney: Tomalin & Wigmore, 1938.
Day, A. Grove. *Eleanor Dark*. Boston: Twayne, 1976.
Delaney, Paul. *Literature, Money and the Market: From Trollope to Amis*. Basingstoke: Palgrave, 2002.
Devanny, Jean. *Bird of Paradise*. Sydney: Frank Johnson, 1945.
Dever, Maryanne. "'No Time is Inopportune for a Protest': Aspects of the Political Activities of Marjorie Barnard and Flora Eldershaw." *Hecate* 17, no. 2 (1991): 9–21.
D'hoker, Elke, and Nicola Humble. "Theorizing the Middlebrow: An Interview with Nicola Humble." *Interférences Littéraires/Literaire Interferenties* 7 (2011): 259–64.
Dijkstra, Bram. *Idols of Perversity: Fantasies of Feminine Evil in Fin-De-Siècle Culture*. New York: Oxford University Press, 1986.
Dimendberg, Edward. "The Will to Motorization: Cinema, Highways and Modernity." *October* 73 (1995): 90–137.
Dimock, Wai Chee. *Through Other Continents: American Literature Across Deep Time*. Princeton, NJ: Princeton University Press, 2006.
Dixon, Robert. *Alex Miller: The Ruin of Time*. Sydney: Sydney University Press, 2014.
---. "Australian Fiction and the World Republic of Letters, 1890–1950." In *The Cambridge History of Australian Literature*, edited by Peter Pierce, 223–54. Port Melbourne: Cambridge University Press, 2009.
---. "Australian Literature, Scale and the Problem of the World". Unpublished manuscript, 2018. Microsoft Word file.
---. "Australian Literature, Scale, and the Problem of the World." In *Text, Translation, Transnationalism: World Literature in Twenty-First Century Australia*, edited by Peter Morgan, 173–95. Melbourne: Australian Scholarly, 2016.
---. "Home or Away? The Trope of Place in Australian Literary Criticism and Literary History." *Westerly* 54, no. 1 (2009): 12–17.

---. "Introduction." In *Authority and Influence: Australian Literary Criticism 1950–2000*, edited by Delys Bird, Robert Dixon and Christopher Lee, xiii–xxxviii. St. Lucia: University of Queensland Press, 2001.

---. "National Literatures, Scale and the Problem of the World." *JASAL: Journal of the Association for the Study of Australian Literature* 15, no. 3 (2015): 1–10.

---. *Photography, Early Cinema and Colonial Modernity: Frank Hurley's Synchronized Lecture Entertainments*. London: Anthem, 2013.

---. "Returning to the Scene of the Crime: On Re-reading *The Transit of Venus*." In *Shirley Hazzard: New Critical Essays*, edited by Brigitta Olubas, 79–93. Sydney: Sydney University Press, 2014.

---. "Shooting in Occupied Space: Frank Hurley in the Middle East, 1940–46." *History of Photography* 38, no. 1 (2014): 40–55.

---. *Writing the Colonial Adventure: Race, Gender, and Nation in Anglo-Australian Popular Fiction, 1875–1914*. Cambridge: Cambridge University Press, 1995.

Dixon, Robert, and Brigid Rooney. "Introduction: Australian Literature, Globalisation and the Literary Province." In *Scenes of Reading: Is Australian Literature a World Literature?*, edited by Robert Dixon and Brigid Rooney, ix–xxxvi. North Melbourne: Australian Scholarly, 2013.

Dixon, Robert, and Veronica Kelly. "Australian Vernacular Modernities: People, Sites and Practices." In *Impact of the Modern: Vernacular Modernities in Australia 1870s–1960s*, edited by Robert Dixon and Veronica Kelly, xiii–xxiv. Sydney: Sydney University Press, 2008.

Docker, John. *In a Critical Condition: Reading Australian Literature*. Ringwood, Vic: Penguin, 1984.

Doecke, Brenton. "Challenging History Making: Realism, Revolution and Utopia in *The Timeless Land*." *Australian Literary Studies* 17, no. 1 (1995): 49–57.

Dortins, Emma. "The Many Truths of Bennelong's Tragedy." *Aboriginal History* 33 (2010): 53–75.

Doyle, Laura. "Modernist Studies and Inter-Imperiality in the *Longue Durée*." In *The Oxford Handbook of Global Modernisms*, edited by Mark Wollaeger with Matt Eatough, 669–96. New York: Oxford University Press, 2012.

Doyle, Laura, and Laura Winkiel. "Introduction: The Global Horizons of Modernism." In *Geomodernisms: Race, Modernism, Modernity*, edited by Laura Doyle and Laura Winkiel, 1–14. Bloomington: Indiana University Press, 2005.

Driscoll, Beth. *The New Literary Middlebrow: Tastemakers and Reading in the Twenty-First Century*. Sydney: Palgrave Macmillan, 2014.

Duffy, Enda. *The Speed Handbook: Velocity, Pleasure, Modernism*. Durham, NC: Duke University Press, 2009.

Edquist, Harriet. "Ghosts of the Past: Mapping the Colonial in Eleanor Dark's Fiction." In *Mapping Different Geographies*, edited by Karel Kriz, William Cartwright and Lorenz Hurni, 247–55. Berlin; Heidelberg: Springer, 2010.

Ehland, Christoph, and Cornelia Wächter, "Introduction: '... All Granite, Fog and Female Fiction.'" In *Middlebrow and Gender, 1890–1945*, edited by Christoph Ehland and Cornelia Wächter, 1–17. Leiden; Boston: Brill Rodopi, 2016.

Eliot, George. *Middlemarch: A Study of Provincial Life*, edited by Rosemary Ashton. New York: Penguin, [1871–1872] 1994.

Ennis, Helen. *Photography and Australia*. London: Reaktion Books, 2007.

Esty, Jed. *A Shrinking Island: Modernism and National Culture in England*. Princeton, NJ: Princeton University Press, 2004.

Etherington, Ben. *Literary Primitivism*. Stanford, CA: Stanford University Press, 2018.

Evatt, H.V. *Liberalism in Australia: An Historical Sketch of Australian Politics Down to the Year 1915*. Sydney: The Law Book Co. of Australasia, 1918.

Ewins, Kristin. "'Revolutionizing a Mode of Life': Leftist Middlebrow Fiction by Women in the 1930s." *ELH* 82, no. 1 (2015): 251–79.

Fabian, Johannes. *Time and the Other: How Anthropology Makes its Object*. New York: Columbia University Press, 2014.

Feigel, Lara. *Literature, Cinema and Politics, 1930–1945: Reading Between the Frames*. Edinburgh: Edinburgh University Press, 2010.

Ferens, Dominika. "Winnifred Eaton's 'Japanese' Novels as a Field Experiment." In *Middlebrow Moderns: Popular American Women Writers of the 1920s*, edited by Lisa Botshon and Meredith Goldsmith, 65–86. Boston, MA: Northeastern University Press, 2003.

Ferrier, Carole. *As Good as a Yarn with You: Letters Between Miles Franklin, Katharine Susannah Prichard, Jean Devanny, Marjorie Barnard, Flora Eldershaw and Eleanor Dark*. Cambridge, UK; Oakleigh, Vic: Cambridge University Press, 1992.

Flesch, Juliet. *From Australia with Love: A History of Modern Australian Popular Romance Novels*. Fremantle, WA: Fremantle Arts Centre, 2004.

Forster, E.M. *Abinger Harvest*. London: Edward Arnold & Co., 1936.

———. *Howards End*. London: Penguin, [1910] 1989.

Franklin, Miles. *Laughter, Not for a Cage: Notes on Australian Writing, with Biographical Emphasis on the Struggles, Function, and Achievements of the Novel in Three Half-Centuries*. Sydney: Angus & Robertson, 1956.

Friedman, Susan Stanford. "Periodizing Modernism: Postcolonial Modernities and the Space/Time Borders of Modernist Studies." *Modernism/modernity* 13, no. 33 (2006): 425–43.

———. "Planetarity: Musing Modernist Studies." *Modernism/modernity* 17, no. 3 (2010): 471–99.

———. *Planetary Modernisms: Provocations on Modernity Across Time*. New York: Columbia University Press, 2015.

———. "World Modernisms, World Literature, and Comparativity." In *The Oxford Handbook of Global Modernisms*, edited by Mark Wollaeger with Matt Eatough, 499–525. New York: Oxford University Press, 2012.

Fullagar, Kate. "Bennelong in Britain." *Aboriginal History* 33 (2010): 31–51.

———. "Woollarawarre Bennelong: Rethinking the Tragic Narrative." *Aboriginal History* 33 (2010): 3–6.

Galletly, Sarah. "The Spectacular Traveling Woman: Australian and Canadian Visions of Women, Modernity, and Mobility between the Wars." *Transfers: Interdisciplinary Journal of Mobility Studies* 7, no. 1 (2017): 70–87.

Garman, Emma. "Feminize Your Canon: Eleanor Dark." *Paris Review*, 9 January 2019. https://www.theparisreview.org/blog/2019/01/09/feminize-your-canon-eleanor-dark/.

Garton, Stephen. "Eugenics in Australia and New Zealand: Laboratories of Racial Science." In *The Oxford Handbook of the History of Eugenics*, edited by Alison Bashford and Philippa Levine, 243–57. New York: Oxford University Press, 2010.

Gilbert, Sandra M., and Susan Gubar, *The Madwoman in the Attic: The Woman Writer and the Nineteenth-Century Literary Imagination*. New Haven, CT: Yale University Press, 1979.

Gildersleeve, Jessica. "Traumatic Cosmopolitanism: Eleanor Dark and the World at War." *Hecate* 41, no. 1–2 (2016): 7–17.

Gildfind, Helen. "The Difficult Business of Writing: The Story of *Return to Coolami*'s Publication." *Antipodes* 27, no. 2 (2013): 157–60.

Giles, Fiona. "Romance: An Embarrassing Subject." In *The Penguin New Literary History of Australia*, edited by Laurie Hergenhan, 223–237. Ringwood, Vic: Penguin Books, 1988.

Giles, Paul. *Antipodean America: Australasia and the Constitution of U.S. Literature*. New York: Oxford University Press, 2014.

———. *Backgazing: Reverse Time in Modernist Culture*. Oxford: Oxford University Press, 2019.

Giuffre, Giulia. "Eric Dark for Eleanor Dark." In *A Writing Life: Interviews with Australian Women Writers*, 102–15. Sydney; Boston: Allen & Unwin, 1990.

Grattan, C. Hartley. "On Australian Literature, 1788–1938." *The Australian Quarterly* 10, no. 2 (1938): 19–33.

Greaves, Robyn. "A 'Grim and Fascinating' Land of Opportunity: The *Walkabout* Women and Australia." *JASAL: Journal of the Association for the Study of Australian Literature* 14, no. 5 (2014): 1–12.

Green, H.M. *A History of Australian Literature, Pure and Applied: A Critical Review of all Forms of Literature Produced in Australia from the First Books Published After the Arrival of the First Fleet Until 1950, with Short Accounts of Later Publications Up to 1960*. Sydney: Angus & Robertson, 1961.

Greif, Mark. *The Age of the Crisis of Man: Thought and Fiction in America, 1933–1973*. Princeton, NJ: Princeton University Press, 2003.

Grenville, Kate. "Books and Writing: Kate Grenville." Interview by Ramona Koval. ABC Radio National, 17 July 2005. Transcript. https://www.abc.net.au/radionational/programs/archived/booksandwriting/kate-grenville/3629894.

---. "Facts and Fiction." https://kategrenville.com.au/short-pieces/facts-and-fiction/.

Griffiths, Michael R. *The Distribution of Settlement: Appropriation and Refusal in Australian Literature and Culture*. Crawley, WA: University of Western Australia Publishing, 2018.

Griffiths, Tom. *The Art of Time Travel: Historians and Their Craft*. Carlton, Vic: Black Inc., 2016.

Guillory, John. *Cultural Capital: The Problem of Literary Canon Formation*. Chicago: University of Chicago Press, 2013.

Haese, Richard. *Rebels and Precursors: The Revolutionary Years of Australian Art*. Ringwood, Vic: Allen Lane, 1981.

Halliwell, Martin, and Andrew Mousley. *Critical Humanisms: Humanist/Anti-Humanist Dialogues*. Edinburgh: Edinburgh University Press, 2003.

Hammill, Faye. *Women, Celebrity and Literary Culture Between the Wars*. Austin: University of Texas Press, 2007.

Hammill, Faye, and Michelle Smith. *Magazines, Travel, and Middlebrow Culture: Canadian Periodicals in English and French, 1925–1960*. Liverpool: Liverpool University Press, 2015.

Hanna, Clifford. "Recollections Through English Spectacles." *Australian Literary Studies* 9, no. 2 (1979): 236–42.

Hansen, Miriam Bratu. "The Mass Production of the Senses: Classical Cinema as Vernacular Modernism." *Modernism/modernity* 6, no. 2 (1999): 59–77.

Harker, Jaime. *America the Middlebrow: Women's Novels, Progressivism, and Middlebrow Authorship Between the Wars*. Amherst: University of Massachusetts Press, 2007.

---. "Progressive Middlebrow: Dorothy Canfield, Women's Magazines, and Popular Feminism in the Twenties." In *Middlebrow Moderns: Popular American Women Writers of the 1920s*, edited by Lisa Botshon and Meredith Goldsmith, 111–34. Boston, MA: Northeastern University Press, 2003.

Harris, Alexandra. *Romantic Moderns: English Writers, Artists and the Imagination from Virginia Woolf to John Piper*. London: Thames & Hudson, 2010.

Hegglund, Jon. *World Views: Metageographies of Modernist Fiction*. Oxford: Oxford University Press, 2012.

Hergenhan, Laurie. *Unnatural Lives: Studies in Australian Convict Fiction*. St. Lucia: University of Queensland Press, 1993.

Herring, Scott. "Regional Modernism: A Reintroduction." *MFS: Modern Fiction Studies* 55, no. 1 (2009): 1–10.

Heseltine, H.P. "'Cyrus Brown of Sidney Town': Christopher Brennan and Dowell O'Reilly." In *Bards, Bohemians, and Bookmen: Essays in Australian Literature*, edited by Leon Cantrell, 136–52. St. Lucia: University of Queensland Press, 1976.

Heyward, Michael. *The Ern Malley Affair*. St. Lucia: University of Queensland Press, 1993.

Hirst, John. *Sense & Nonsense in Australian History*. Melbourne: Black Inc., 2009.

Ho, Janice. "The Crisis of Liberalism and the Politics of Modernism." *Literature Compass* 8, no. 1 (2011): 47–65.

Hodge, Bob, and Vijay Mishra. *Dark Side of the Dream: Australian Literature and the Postcolonial Mind*. Sydney: Allen & Unwin, 1992.

Honey, Maureen. "Feminist New Woman Fiction in Periodicals of the 1920s." In *Middlebrow Moderns: Popular American Women Writers of the 1920s*, edited by Lisa Botshon and Meredith Goldsmith, 87–110. Boston, MA: Northeastern University Press, 2003.

Hughes-d'Aeth, Tony. "A Critique of Eco-Criticism." In *Reading Down Under*, edited by Amit Sarwal and Reema Sarwal, 114–25. New Delhi: SSS Publications, 2009.

———. "Australian Writing, Deep Ecology and Julia Leigh's *The Hunter*." *JASAL: Journal of the Association for the Study of Australian Literature* 1 (2002): 19–31.

Humble, Nicola. "Sitting Forward or Sitting Back: Highbrow v. Middlebrow Reading." *Modernist Cultures* 6, no. 1 (2011): 41–59.

———. *The Feminine Middlebrow Novel, 1920s to 1950s: Class, Domesticity, and Bohemianism*. Oxford: Oxford University Press, 2001.

Huxley, Aldous. *Music at Night and Other Essays*. New York: Doubleday, Doran & Co., 1931.

Huyssen, Andreas. *After the Great Divide: Modernism, Mass Culture, Postmodernism*. Bloomington: Indiana University Press, 1986.

———. "Geographies of Modernism in a Globalizing World." In *Geographies of Modernism: Literatures, Cultures, Spaces*, edited by Peter Brooker and Andrew Thacker, 6–18. Abingdon, Oxon; New York: Routledge, 2005.

Ingamells, Rex. "Conditional Culture" [1938]. In *The Writer in Australia: A Collection of Literary Documents 1856–1964*, edited by John Barnes, 245–65. Melbourne: Oxford University Press, 1969.

Jacobs, Karen. *The Eye's Mind: Literary Modernism and Visual Culture*. Ithaca, NY: Cornell University Press, 2001.

James, David. "Localising Late Modernism: Interwar Regionalism and the Genesis of the 'Micro Novel.'" *Journal of Modern Literature* 32, no. 4 (2009): 43–64.

Jameson, Fredric. *A Singular Modernity: Essay on the Ontology of the Present*. London: Verso, 2002.

Jay, Martin. *Downcast Eyes: The Denigration of Vision in Twentieth-Century French Thought*. Berkeley: University of California Press, 1993.

———. "Scopic Regimes of Modernity." In *Vision and Visuality*, edited by Hal Foster, 3–27. New York: New Press, 1999.

———. "The Disenchantment of the Eye: Surrealism and the Crisis of Ocularcentrism." *Visual Anthropology Review* 7, no. 1 (1991): 15–38.

Johnston, Anna. "Becoming 'Pacific-Minded': Australian Middlebrow Writers in the 1940s and the Mobility of Texts." *Transfers: Interdisciplinary Journal of Mobility Studies* 7, no. 1 (2017): 88–107.

———. "1943: Ernestine Hill's *The Great Australian Loneliness* is Packed into U.S. Armed Service Kitbags." In *Telling Stories: Australian Literary Cultures 1935–2010*, edited by Tanya Dalziell and Paul Genoni, 84–90. Melbourne: Monash University Press, 2013.

Johnston, Anna, and Mitchell Rolls. *Travelling Home, Walkabout Magazine and Mid-Twentieth-Century Australia*. London; New York: Anthem Press, 2016.

Jordan, Deborah. "'Written to Tickle the Ears of the Groundings in Garden Cities:' The Aesthetic of Modernity: Vance and Nettie Palmer and the *New Age*." In *Impact of the Modern: Vernacular Modernities in Australia 1870s–1960s*, edited by Robert Dixon and Veronica Kelly, 91–108. Sydney: Sydney University Press, 2008.

Joy, Eileen A., and Christine M. Neufeld. "A Confession of Faith: Notes toward a New Humanism." *Journal of Narrative Theory* 37, no. 2 (2007): 161–90.

Karskens, Grace. *The Colony: A History of Early Sydney*. Sydney: Allen & Unwin, 2009.

Kern, Stephen. *The Culture of Time and Space 1880–1918*. Cambridge, MA: Harvard University Press, 1983.

Kirkpatrick, Peter. "'Fearful Affinity': Jindyworobak Primitivism." In *Adelaide: A Literary City*, edited by Philip Butterss, 125–46. Adelaide: University of Adelaide Press, 2013.

———. "Hellbound for Snowy River." *Meanjin* 73, no. 2 (2014): 32–41.

---. "Jindy Modernist: The Jindyworobaks as Avant-Garde." In *Republics of Letters: Literary Communities in Australia*, edited by Peter Kirkpatrick and Robert Dixon, 99–112. Sydney: Sydney University Press, 2012.

---. "'New Words Come Tripping Slowly': Poetry, Popular Culture and Modernity, 1890–1950." In *The Cambridge History of Australian Literature*, edited by Peter Pierce, 199–222. Cambridge: Cambridge University Press, 2009.

---. "Slessor's Darlinghurst Nights: Troping the Light Fantastic." In *ASAL Annual Conference Proceedings, 3–8 July 1994*, 7–13. Association for the Study of Association Literature, 1994.

---. "When Skyscrapers Burst into Lilac." In *Kenneth Slessor: Critical Readings*, edited by Philip Mead, 176–97. St. Lucia: University of Queensland Press, 1997.

Klein, Christina. *Cold War Orientalism: Asia in the Middlebrow Imagination, 1945–1961*. Berkeley: University of California Press, 2003.

Knott, John William. "The 'Conquering Car': Technology, Symbolism and the Motorisation of Australia before World War II." *Australian Historical Studies* 31, no. 114 (2000): 1–26.

Kuttainen, Victoria. "Illustrating Mobility: Networks of Visual Print Culture and the Periodical Contexts of Modern Australian Writing." *JASAL: Journal of the Association for the Study of Australian Literature* 17, no. 2 (2017): 1–16.

---. "Trafficking Literature: Travel, Modernity, and the Middle Ground of Canadian and Australian Middlebrow Print Cultures." *International Journal of Canadian Studies* 48 (2014): 85–103.

Kuttainen, Victoria, and Sarah Galletly. "Making Friends of the Nations: Australian Interwar Magazines and Middlebrow Orientalism in the Pacific." *Journeys: The International Journal of Travel and Travel Writing* 17, no. 2 (2016): 23–48.

Kuttainen, Victoria, and Susann Liebich. "Worldly Tastes: Mobility and the Geographical Imaginaries of Interwar Australian Magazines." *Transfers: Interdisciplinary Journal of Mobility Studies* 7, no. 1 (2017): 52–69.

Kuttainen, Victoria, Susann Liebich and Sarah Galletly. *Transported Imagination: Australian Interwar Magazines and the Geographical Imaginaries of Colonial Modernity*. Amherst, NY: Cambria Press, 2018.

Labovitz, Esther. *The Myth of the Heroine: The Female Bildungsroman in the Twentieth Century: Dorothy Richardson, Simone de Beauvoir, Doris Lessing, Christa Wolf*. New York: P. Lang, 1986.

LaCapra, Dominick. *History and its Limits: Human, Animal, Violence*. Ithaca: Cornell University Press, 2009.

---. "Trauma, Absence, Loss." *Critical Inquiry* 25, no. 4 (1999): 696–727.

Lake, Marilyn, and Henry Reynolds. *Drawing the Global Colour Line: White Men's Countries and the Question of Racial Equality*. Carlton, Vic: Melbourne University Publishing, 2008.

Lassner, Phyllis, Ann Rea and Genevieve Brassard. "Reading Sideways: Middlebrow into Modernism." *The Space Between* 9, no. 1 (2013): 7–10.

Lawrence, D.H. *Kangaroo*, edited by Bruce Steele. Cambridge: Cambridge University Press, [1923] 1994.

Lawrence, D.H., and Edward D. McDonald. *Phoenix: The Posthumous Papers of D.H. Lawrence*. New York: The Viking Press, 1936.

Leane, Jeanine. "Tracking our Country in Settler Literature." *JASAL: Journal of the Association for the Study of Australian Literature* 14, no. 3 (2014): 1–17.

Leavis, F.R. *Education and the University: A Sketch for an "English School."* London: Chatto & Windus, 1948.

---. *For Continuity*. Essay Index Reprint Series. Freeport, NY: Books for Libraries Press, [1933] 1968.

---. *Mass Civilisation and Minority Culture*. Cambridge: Minority Press, 1930.

Leavis, F.R., and Denys Thompson. *Culture and Environment*. London: Chatto & Windus, 1933.

Leavis, Q.D. *Fiction and the Reading Public*. London: Chatto & Windus, 1932.

Lever, Susan. *Real Relations: The Feminist Politics of Form in Australian Fiction*. Rushcutters Bay, NSW: Halstead Press, 2000.

Levinas, Emmanuel. *Totality and Infinity: An Essay on Exteriority*. Translated by Alphonso Lingis. Pittsburgh, Pennsylvania: Duquesne University Press, 1969.

Limbrick, Peter. *Making Settler Cinemas: Film and Colonial Encounters in the United States, Australia, and New Zealand*. New York: Palgrave Macmillan, 2010.

———. "The Australian Western, Or a Settler Colonial Cinema Par Excellence." *Cinema Journal* 46, no. 4 (2007): 68–95.

Lippmann, Jilly, and Victoria Kuttainen. "The Troublesome Modern Girl: *Jungfrau*, National Literature, and the Vexations of Transnational Modernity." *The Space Between* 15 (2019): 1.

Macdonald, Kate. "Introduction: Identifying the Middlebrow, the Masculine and Mr Miniver." In *The Masculine Middlebrow, 1880–1950: What Mr. Miniver Read*, edited by Kate Macdonald, 1–23. New York: Palgrave Macmillan, 2011.

———. "Gender, Disability, Wartime: The Woman's Body and the Disabled Ex-Serviceman in the First World War." In *Middlebrow and Gender, 1890–1945*, edited by Christoph Ehland and Cornelia Wächter, 60–78. Leiden; Boston: Brill Rodopi, 2016.

McGregor, Russell. *Imagined Destinies: Aboriginal Australians and the Doomed Race Theory, 1880–1939*. Carlton, Vic: Melbourne University Press, 1997.

McKellar, John. "The Black Man and the White." *Southerly* 9, no. 2 (1948): 92–98.

Mann, Cecil. "Australia Remains a Joke." *Bulletin*, 21 May 1930, 2, 5.

———. "Coonardoo." *Bulletin*, 14 August 1929, 2.

Mao, Douglas, and Rebecca L. Walkowitz. "Introduction: Modernisms Bad and New." In *Bad Modernisms*, edited by Douglas Mao and Rebecca L. Walkowitz, 1–18. Durham, NC: Duke University Press, 2006.

———. "The New Modernist Studies." *PMLA* 123, no. 3 (2008): 737–48.

Markus, Andrew. *Australian Race Relations, 1788–1993*. St. Leonards, NSW: Allen & Unwin, 1994.

Marshik, Celia. *At the Mercy of Their Clothes: Modernism, the Middlebrow, and British Garment Culture*. New York: Columbia University Press, 2016.

Matthews, Jill Julius. *Dance Hall and Picture Palace: Sydney's Romance with Modernity*. Sydney: Currency Press, 2005.

Maxwell, Anne. "Biopolitics and Eleanor Dark's *Prelude to Christopher*." *Australian Literary Studies* 26, no. 2 (2011): 76–90.

———. "Education, Literature and the Emotions: A Salute to Eleanor Dark's *Prelude to Christopher*." *JASAL: Journal of the Association for the Study of Australian Literature* 12, no. 1 (2012): 1–11.

May, Bernice [Zora Cross]. "Patricia O'Rane." *The Australian Woman's Mirror* 4, no. 44 (25 September 1928), 8, 54.

May, Brian. *The Modernist as Pragmatist: E.M. Forster and the Fate of Liberalism*. Columbia: University of Missouri Press, 1997.

McKay, Belinda. "The Art of Living: Vance Palmer and Eleanor Dark on the Sunshine Coast." *Queensland Review* 24, no. 2 (2017): 202–14.

McKenna, Mark. "Writing the Past." *Australian Financial Review*. 16 December 2005. https://www.afr.com/life-and-luxury/arts-and-culture/writing-the-past-20051216–jeipe.

McLaren, John. *Writing in Hope and Fear: Literature as Politics in Postwar Australia*. Cambridge, UK: Cambridge University Press, 1996.

McLean, Ian. *White Aborigines: Identity Politics in Australian Art*. Melbourne: Cambridge University Press, 1998.

McMahon, Elizabeth. *Islands, Identity and the Literary Imagination*. London; New York: Anthem Press, 2016.

McQueen, Humphrey. "Eleanor Dark – Disturbing the Status Quo." Talk given at the Katoomba Section of the Sydney Writers' Festival, 17 May 2011. Canberra: Australian Society for the Study of Labour History. https://bit.ly/3qUbqZf.

———. "Place, Colour and Sedition: D.H. Lawrence's *Kangaroo*: A Study in Environmental Values." *Politics and Culture* 3 (2006): n.p.

———. *The Black Swan of Trespass: The Emergence of Modernist Painting in Australia to 1944*. Sydney: Alternative Publishing, 1979.

Mead, Philip. *Networked Language: Culture & History in Australian Poetry*. North Melbourne: Australian Scholarly, 2008.

Medalie, David. *E.M. Forster's Modernism*. London: Palgrave Macmillan, 2003.

Miller, J. Hillis. *Reading for Our Time: "Adam Bede" and "Middlemarch" Revisited*. Edinburgh: Edinburgh University Press, 2012.

Modjeska, Drusilla. "'A Hoodoo on That Book': The Publishing Misfortunes of an Eleanor Dark Novel." *Southerly* 57, no. 2 (1997): 73–96.

———. *Exiles at Home: Australian Women Writers 1925–1945*. Sydney: Sirius Books, 1981.

Moore, Nicole. *The Censor's Library: Uncovering the Lost History of Australia's Banned Books*. St. Lucia: University of Queensland Press, 2012.

———. "The Rational Natural: Conflicts of the Modern in Eleanor Dark." *Hecate* 27, no. 1 (2001): 19–31.

Moore, Tod. "Saving Private Hegel: Australian Liberalism and the 1914–1918 War." *Australian Journal of Politics & History* 61, no. 4 (2015): 501–14.

Moretti, Franco. "Conjectures on World Literature." *New Left Review* 1, no. 1 (2000): 54–67.

———. *Modern Epic: The World-System from Goethe to García Márquez*. London; New York: Verso, 1996.

———. "World-Systems Analysis, Evolutionary Theory, *Weltliteratur*." *Review* 28, no. 3 (2005): 217–28.

Morris, Meaghan. "Import Rhetoric: Semiotics in/and Australia." In *The Foreign Bodies Papers*, edited by Peter Botsman, Chris Burns and Peter Hutchings, 122–39. Sydney: Local Consumption Publications, 1981.

Morrison, Fiona. *Christina Stead and the Matter of America*. Sydney: Sydney University Press, 2019.

Mousley, Andy. *Re-humanising Shakespeare*. Edinburgh: Edinburgh University Press, 2007.

Muecke, Stephen. *Textual Spaces: Aboriginality and Cultural Studies*. Sydney: New South Wales University Press, 1992.

Mulhern, Francis. *The Moment of "Scrutiny."* London: NLB, 1979.

Munro, Craig. *Inky Stephensen: Wild Man of Letters*. St. Lucia: University of Queensland Press, 1992.

National Gallery of Australia. Notes on Max Dupain's "Advertisement for Hoover." https://cs.nga.gov.au/Detail.cfm?IRN=86635

National Inquiry into the Separation of Aboriginal and Torres Strait Islander Children from Their Families (Australia). *Bringing Them Home: Report of the National Inquiry into the Separation of Aboriginal and Torres Strait Islander Children from Their Families*. Sydney: Human Rights and Equal Opportunity Commission, 1997.

Nile, Richard. "Literary Democracy and the Politics of Reputation." In *The Oxford Literary History of Australia*, edited by Bruce Bennett, Jennifer Strauss and Chris Wallace-Crabbe, 130–46. Melbourne: Oxford University Press, 1998.

———. *The Making of the Australian Literary Imagination*. St. Lucia: University of Queensland Press, 2002.

Nile, Richard, and David Walker. "The 'Paternoster Row Machine' and the Australian Book Trade, 1890–1945." In *History of the Book in Australia, 1891–1945: A National Culture in a Colonised Market*, edited by John Arnold and Martyn Lyons, 3–18. St. Lucia: University of Queensland Press, 2001.

Nussbaum, Martha C. *Not for Profit: Why Democracy Needs the Humanities*. Princeton, NJ: Princeton University Press, 2010.

O'Reilly, Dowell. *Dowell O'Reilly: From His Letters*, edited by Marie O'Reilly. London: Simpkin, Marshall, Hamilton, Kent & Co., 1927.

———. "The 'Ta Ta!' Woman." *Bulletin*, 18 November 1915, 51–52.

O'Reilly, Helen. "The Poet in Her Past: Eleanor Dark and Christopher Brennan." *Southerly* 75, no. 2 (2015): 217–23.

---. "Time and Memory in the Novels of Eleanor Dark." PhD thesis, University of New South Wales, 2009.

Olubas, Brigitta. *Shirley Hazzard: Literary Expatriate and Cosmopolitan Humanist.* Amherst, NY: Cambria Press, 2012.

Outka, Elizabeth. *Consuming Traditions: Modernity, Modernism, and the Commodified Authentic.* Oxford: Oxford University Press, 2009.

Palmer, Nettie. *Modern Australian Literature, 1900–1923.* Melbourne: Lothian Book Publishing Company, 1924.

---. *Nettie Palmer: Her Private Journal "Fourteen Years," Poems, Reviews and Literary Essays*, edited by Vivian Smith. St. Lucia: University of Queensland Press, 1988.

Palmer, Vance. "Battle." *Meanjin Papers* 1, no. 8 (1942): 5–6.

---. "Pacific Nights." *BP Magazine*, June 1931, 29.

Palumbo-Liu, David, Bruce Robbins and Nirvana Tanoukhi. "Introduction: The Most Important Thing Happening." In *Immanuel Wallerstein and the Problem of the World: System, Scale, Culture*, edited by David Palumbo-Liu, Bruce Robbins and Nirvana Tanoukhi, 1–23. Durham, NC: Duke University Press, 2011.

Pearce, Sharyn. *Shameless Scribblers: Australian Women's Journalism 1880–1995.* Rockhampton: Central Queensland University Press, 1998.

Pearse, A.E. "Modernist Poetry: The Case Contra." *Australian Mercury* 1 (1935): 76–77.

Peppis, Paul. "Rewriting Sex: Mina Loy, Marie Stopes, and Sexology." *Modernism/modernity* 9, no. 4 (2002): 561–79.

Perera, Suvendrini. *Australia and the Insular Imagination: Beaches, Borders, Boats, and Bodies.* New York: Palgrave Macmillan, 2009.

Perkins, Maureen. "Timeless Cultures: The 'Dreamtime' as Colonial Discourse." *Time & Society* 7, no. 2 (1998): 335–51.

Pizer, John David. *The Idea of World Literature: History and Pedagogical Practice.* Baton Rouge: Louisiana State University Press, 2006.

Prichard, Katharine Susannah. *Coonardoo.* Sydney: HarperCollins, [1929] 2013.

Priestley. J.B. *The Balconinny and Other Essays.* London: Methuen, 1929.

Radway, Janice. *A Feeling for Books: The Book-of-the-Month Club, Literary Taste, and Middle-Class Desire.* Chapel Hill: University of North Carolina Press, 1997.

---. "The Utopian Impulse in Popular Literature: Gothic Romances and 'Feminist' Protest." *American Quarterly* 33, no. 2 (1981): 140–62.

Rainey, Lawrence. *Institutions of Modernism: Literary Elites and Public Culture.* New Haven, CT; London: Yale University Press, 1999.

Rea, Ann. "'Ordinary' Sexuality, the 'Dirty Little Secret' and the Indecent Highbrow Modernist: Sexuality in *Married Love* and *Lady Chatterley's Lover*." In *Middlebrow and Gender, 1890–1945*, edited by Christoph Ehland and Cornelia Wächter, 248–70. Leiden; Boston: Brill Rodopi, 2016.

Rees, Anne. "Reading Australian Modernity: Unsettled Settlers and Cultures of Mobility." *History Compass* 15, no. 11 (2017): 1–13.

---. "Stepping Through the Silver Screen: Australian Women Encounter America, 1930s–1950s." *Journeys: The International Journal of Travel and Travel Writing* 17, no. 2 (2016): 49–73.

---. "'The Quality and Not Only the Quantity of Australia's People': Ruby Rich and the Racial Hygiene Association of NSW." *Australian Feminist Studies* 27, no. 71 (2012): 71–92.

Reiger, Kerreen M. *The Disenchantment of the Home: Modernizing the Australian Family, 1880–1940.* Melbourne: Oxford University Press, 1985.

Robbins, Ben. "Inscrutable Images and Cultural Migrations: Wartime Noir and the Compson Appendix." *Faulkner Journal* 28, no. 1 (2014): 55–77.

Roe, Michael. *Nine Australian Progressives: Vitalism in Bourgeois Social Thought, 1890–1960.* St. Lucia: University of Queensland Press, 1984.

Rooney, Brigid. "Time's Abyss: Australian Literary Modernism and the Scene of the Ferry Wreck." In *Scenes of Reading: Is Australian Literature a World Literature?*, edited by Robert Dixon and Brigid Rooney, 101–14. North Melbourne: Australian Scholarly, 2013.

Rowley, Hazel. *Christina Stead: A Biography*. Carlton, Vic: Miegunyah Press, 2007.

Rowse, Tim. *Australian Liberalism and National Character*. Melbourne: Kibble Books, 1978.

———. "Indigenous Heterogeneity." *Australian Historical Studies* 45, no. 3 (2014): 297–310.

Rubin, Joan Shelley. *The Making of Middlebrow Culture*. Chapel Hill: University of North Carolina Press, 1992.

Ryan, Simon. *The Cartographic Eye: How Explorers Saw Australia*. Cambridge; Melbourne: Cambridge University Press, 1996.

Sanchez, Rebecca. *Deafening Modernism: Embodied Language and Visual Poetics in American Literature*. New York: New York University Press, 2015.

Saunders, Ian. "Memory, Community and Writing in *Tomorrow and Tomorrow and Tomorrow*." *Southerly* 64, no. 1 (2004): 101–14.

———. "On Appropriation: Two Novels of Dark and Barnard Eldershaw." *Australian Literary Studies* 20, no. 4 (2002): 287–300.

Sawer, Marian. *The Ethical State? Social Liberalism in Australia*. Carlton, Vic: Melbourne University Press, 2003.

Scott, Bonnie Kime. "First Drafts for Transnational Women's Writing: A Revisiting of the Modernisms of Woolf, West, Fauset and Dark." *Hecate* 35 (2009): 10–28.

Seed, David. "British Modernists Encounter the Cinema." In *Literature and the Visual Media*, edited by David Seed, 48–73. Suffolk; New York: D.S. Brewer, 2005.

Shapiro, Karl. "News to Australia." *The New Republic*, 3 June 1946, 808–09.

———. *V-Letter and Other Poems*. New York: Reynal & Hitchcock, 1944.

Sheridan, Susan. *Along the Faultlines: Sex, Race and Nation in Australian Women's Writing, 1880s–1930s*. St. Leonards, NSW: Allen & Unwin, 1995.

———. "Historical Novels Challenging the National Story." *History Australia* 8, no. 2 (2011): 7–20.

———. "'Opposing All the Things They Stand For': Women Writers and the Women's Magazines." In *Republics of Letters: Literary Communities in Australia*, edited by Peter Kirkpatrick and Robert Dixon, 195–204. Sydney: Sydney University Press, 2012.

———. "'Temper Romantic; Bias Offensively Feminine': Australian Women Writers and Literary Nationalism." *Kunapipi* 7, no. 2–3 (1985): 49–58.

———. "Thea Astley: A Woman Among the Satirists of Post-War Modernity." *Australian Feminist Studies* 18, no. 42, (2003): 261–71.

Slaughter, Joseph R. "Enabling Fictions and Novel Subjects: The 'Bildungsroman' and International Human Rights Law." *PMLA* 121, no. 5 (October 2006): 1405–23.

Slemon, Stephen. "Unsettling the Empire: Resistance Theory for the Second World." *World Literature Written in English* 30, no. 2 (1990): 30–41.

Slessor, Kenneth. *Selected Poems of Kenneth Slessor*. Sydney: HarperCollins, 2014.

Smith, Andrew. "Vampirism, Masculinity and Degeneracy: D.H. Lawrence's Modernist Gothic." In *Gothic Modernisms*, edited by Andrew Smith and Jeff Wallace, 150–66. New York: Palgrave, 2001.

Smith, Andrew, and Jeff Wallace. "Introduction: Gothic Modernisms: History, Culture and Aesthetics." In *Gothic Modernisms*, edited by Andrew Smith and Jeff Wallace, 1–10. New York: Palgrave, 2001.

Smith, Ellen. "Local Moderns: The Jindyworobak Movement and Australian Modernism." *Australian Literary Studies* 27, no. 1 (2012): 1–17.

———. "White Aborigines: Xavier Herbert, P.R. Stephensen and the *Publicist*." *Interventions* 16, no. 1 (2014): 97–116.

Smith, Neil. "Contours of a Spatialized Politics: Homeless Vehicles and the Production of Geographical Scale." *Social Text*, no. 33 (1992): 54–81.

Smith, Terry. "Modernism, Modernity and Otherness." *Australian Journal of Art* 13, no. 1 (1996): 144–66.

–––. "Visual Regimes of Colonisation: European and Aboriginal Seeing in Australia." In *Empires of Vision: A Reader*, edited by Martin Jay and Sumathi Ramaswamy, 267–82. Durham, NC: Duke University Press, 2014.

Spivak, Gayatri Chakravorty. "Three Women's Texts and a Critique of Imperialism." *Critical Inquiry* 12, no. 1 (1985): 243–61.

Stead, Christina. *For Love Alone*. Bondi Junction: Imprint Classics, [1945] 1991.

–––. "The Writers Take Sides." *Left Review* 1, no. 2 (July 1935): 435–63, 469–75.

Stephen, Ann, Andrew McNamara and Philip Goad. "Introduction." In *Modernism & Australia: Documents on Art, Design and Architecture 1917–1967*, edited by Ann Stephen, Andrew McNamara and Philip Goad, 1–27. Carlton, Vic: Miegunyah Press, 2006.

–––. *Modern Times: The Untold Story of Modernism in Australia*. Carlton, Vic: Miegunyah Press, 2008.

Stephensen, P.R. *The Foundations of Culture in Australia: An Essay Towards National Self Respect*. Gordon, NSW: W.J. Miles, 1936.

Stetz, Margaret D. "Sideways Feminism: Rebecca West and the *Saturday Evening Post*, 1928." *The Space Between* 9, no. 1 (2013): 61–75.

Stout, Janis P. "Writing Politically: Dorothy Canfield and the 'Wrongness of the World.'" *MFS: Modern Fiction Studies* 60, no. 2 (2014): 251–75.

Strain, Ellen. *Public Places, Private Journeys: Ethnography, Entertainment, and the Tourist Gaze*. New Brunswick: Rutgers University Press, 2003.

Su, John J. "The Beloved Republic: Nostalgia and the Political Aesthetic of E.M. Forster." In *Modernism and Nostalgia: Bodies, Locations, Aesthetics*, edited by Tammy Clewell, 198–215. London: Palgrave Macmillan, 2013.

Sullivan, Melissa, and Sophie Blanch. "Introduction: The Middlebrow – Within or Without Modernism." *Modernist Cultures* 6, no. 1 (2011): 1–17.

Thacker, Andrew. *Moving Through Modernity: Space and Geography in Modernism*. New York; Manchester: Manchester University Press, 2003.

The Teaching of Sex Hygiene: Report of a Conference Organised by the Workers' Education Association of New South Wales, Union Hall, Sydney University, 23–25 November 1916. Sydney: Burrows & Co., 1918.

Torgovnik, Marianna. *Gone Primitive: Savage Intellects, Modern Lives*. Chicago: University of Chicago Press, 1990.

Tout, Dan. "Neither Nationalists nor Universalists: Rex Ingamells and the Jindyworobaks." *Australian Humanities Review* 61 (2017): 1–26.

–––. "Reframing 'Inky' Stephensen's Place in Australian Cultural History." *Settler Colonial Studies* 7, no. 1 (2017): 72–93.

Tracy, Daniel. "From Vernacular Humor to Middlebrow Modernism: *Gentlemen Prefer Blondes* and the Creation of Literary Value." *Arizona Quarterly: A Journal of American Literature, Culture, and Theory* 66, no. 1 (2010): 115–43.

Tregenza, Ian. "Are We 'All Socialists Now'? New Liberalism, State Socialism and the Australian Settlement." *Labour History* 102 (2012): 87–98.

Tromly, Lucas. "'Lady Tiger in a Tea Gown': Decadence, Kitsch, and Faulkner's *Femme Fatale*." *Mississippi Quarterly* 62, no. 3–4 (2011): 457–77.

Trotter, David. *Cinema and Modernism*. Malden, MA: Blackwell Publishers, 2007.

–––. *The Literature of Connection: Signal, Medium, Interface, 1850–1950*. Oxford: Oxford University Press, 2020.

–––. "Virginia Woolf and Cinema." *Film Studies*, no. 6 (2005): 13–26.

Turim, Maureen C. *Flashbacks in Film: Memory and History*. New York: Routledge, 1989.

–––. "The Trauma of History: Flashbacks upon Flashbacks." *Screen* 42, no. 2 (2001): 205–10.

Vaninskaya, Anna. "The Political Middlebrow from Chesterton to Orwell." In *The Masculine Middlebrow, 1880–1950: What Mr. Miniver Read*, edited by Kate Macdonald, 162–76. New York: Palgrave Macmillan, 2011.

Veracini, Lorenzo. "Introducing: Settler Colonial Studies." *Settler Colonial Studies* 1, no. 1 (2011): 1–12.

———. *Settler Colonialism: A Theoretical Overview*. Basingstoke: Palgrave Macmillan, 2010.

———. *The Settler Colonial Present*. London: Palgrave Macmillan, 2015.

Vickers, Adrian. "Kipling Goes South." *Australian Cultural History* 9 (1990): 66–78.

Vincent Smith, Keith. "Bennelong Among His People." *Aboriginal History* 33 (2009): 7–30.

———. *Bennelong: The Coming in of the Eora, Sydney Cove 1788–1792*. Sydney: Kangaroo Press, 2001.

Walker, David. *Anxious Nation: Australia and the Rise of Asia, 1850–1939*. St. Lucia: University of Queensland Press, 1999.

———. *Dream and Disillusion: A Search for Australian Cultural Identity*. Canberra: Australian National University Press, 1976.

———. "Race Building and the Disciplining of White Australia." In *Legacies of White Australia: Race, Culture and Nation*, edited by Laksiri Jayasuriya, David Walker and Jan Gothard, 33–50. Crawley, WA: University of Western Australia Press, 2003.

Walkowitz, Rebecca L. *Cosmopolitan Style: Modernism Beyond the Nation*. New York: Columbia University Press, 2006.

Wallerstein, Immanuel. *The Modern World-System*. New York: Academic Press, 1974.

Warne, Ellen. "Sex Education Debates and the Modest Mother in Australia, 1890s to the 1930s." *Women's History Review* 8, no. 2 (1999): 311–27.

White, Patrick. "The Prodigal Son." In *Patrick White: Selected Writings*, edited by Alan Lawson, 268–71. St. Lucia: University of Queensland Press, 1994.

———. *Voss*. North Sydney: Random House Australia, [1957] 2012.

Wienbaum, Alys Eve, and Modern Girl Around the World Research Group. *The Modern Girl Around the World: Consumption, Modernity, and Globalization*. Durham, NC: Duke University Press, 2008.

Wilkes, G.A. *New Perspectives on Brennan's Poetry*. Sydney: Halstead Press, 1953.

———. "The Progress of Eleanor Dark." *Southerly* 12, no. 3 (1951): 139–48.

Williams, John F. *The Quarantined Culture: Australian Reactions to Modernism, 1913–1939*. New York: Cambridge University Press, 1995.

Williams, Raymond. *Culture and Society 1780–1950*. London: Chatto & Windus, 1958.

Wolfe, Patrick. "Settler Colonialism and the Elimination of the Native." *Journal of Genocide Research* 8, no. 4 (2006): 387–409.

———. *Settler Colonialism and the Transformation of Anthropology: The Politics and Poetics of an Ethnographic Event*. London; New York: Cassell, 1999.

Wollaeger, Mark. "Introduction." In *The Oxford Handbook of Global Modernisms*, edited by Mark Wollaeger with Matt Eatough, 3–22. New York: Oxford University Press, 2012.

Wood, Alice. "Modernism and the Middlebrow in British Women's Magazines." In *Middlebrow and Gender, 1890–1945*, edited by Christoph Ehland and Cornelia Wächter, 39–59. Leiden; Boston: Brill Rodopi, 2016.

Woolf, Virginia. *Collected Essays*. Vol. 2. London: Hogarth Press, 1942.

———. *The Essays of Virginia Woolf*. Vol. 6, edited by Stuart N. Clarke. London: Hogarth Press, 2011.

Woollacott, Angela. *To Try Her Fortune in London: Australian Women, Colonialism, and Modernity*. New York: Oxford University Press, 2001.

Wyndham, Diana H. "Striving for National Fitness: Eugenics in Australia 1910s to 1930s". PhD thesis, University of Sydney, 1996.

Wyndham, Marivic. *"A World-Proof Life": Eleanor Dark, A Writer in Her Times 1901–1985*. Sydney: UTS ePress, 2007.

Yiannitsaros, Christopher. "'I'm Scared to Death She'll Kill Me': Devoted Ladies, Feminine Monstrosity, and the (Lesbian) Gothic Romance." *The Irish Journal of Gothic and Horror Studies* 8 (2010): 41–52.

York, Lorraine. *Literary Celebrity in Canada*. Toronto: University of Toronto Press, 2016.

Young, Paul. "Peripheralizing Modernity: Global Modernism and Uneven Development." *Literature Compass* 9 (2012): 611–16.

Zavaglia, Liliana. *White Apology and Apologia: Australian Novels of Reconciliation*. Amherst, NY: Cambria Press, 2016.

Index

www.ingramcontent.com/pod-product-compliance
Lightning Source LLC
Chambersburg PA
CBHW081331090726
47907CB00011B/2450